16th International Workshop on Treebanks and Linguistic Theories 2018 (TLT16)

Prague, Czech Republic
23-24 January 2018

Editor:

Jan Hajic

ISBN: 978-1-5108-8134-1

TLT16
January 2018

Proceedings of the 16th International Workshop on
Treebanks and Linguistic Theories

January 23–24, 2018
Prague, Czech Republic

Edited by Jan Hajič.

These proceedings with papers presented at the 16th International Workshop on Treebanks and Linguistic Theories are included in the ACL Anthology, supported by the Association for Computational Linguistics (ACL) at http://aclweb.org/anthology; both individual papers as well as the full proceedings book are available.

TLT16 takes place in Prague, Czech Republic on January 23–24, 2018.

Preface

The Sixteenth International Workshop on Treebanks and Linguistic Theories (TLT16) is being held at
Charles University, Czech Republic, 23–24 January 2018, for the second time in Prague, which hosted
TLT already in 2006. This year, TLT16 is co-located with the Workshop on Data Provenance and Annotation in Computational Linguistics 2018 (January 22, 2018, at the same place and venue) and immediately
followed by the 2nd Workshop on Corpus-based Research in the Humanities, held in Vienna, Austria.

This year, TLT16 received 32 submissions of which 15 have been selected to be presented as oral
presentations, and additional seven have been asked to present as posters. We were happy that our in-
vitation to give a plenary talk has been accepted by both Lilja Øvrelid of University of Oslo in Norway
(with a talk "Downstream use of syntactic analysis: does representation matter?") and Marie Candito,
of University of Paris Diderot, France ("Annotating and parsing to semantic frames: feedback from the
French FrameNet project"). We have also included a panel discussion on the very topic of Treebanks and
Linguistic Theories – to discuss opinions of the future of the field and the workshop with the participants.

We are grateful to the members of the program committee, who worked hard to review the submissions
and provided authors with valuable feedback. We would also like to thank various sponsors, mainly the
Faculty of Mathematics and Physics of Charles University, providing local and logistical and accounting
and financial support, and the Centre for Advanced Study (CAS) at the Norwegian Academy of Science
and Letters for supporting one of the invited speakers.

Last but not least, we would like to thank all authors for submitting interesting and relevant papers,
and we wish all participants a fruitful workshop.

December 2017

Jan Hajič (also in the name of local organizers), Charles University, Prague, Czech Republic
Sandra Kuebler, Indiana University, Bloomington, Indiana, USA
Stephan Oepen, University of Oslo, Norway, and CAS, Norwegian Academy of Science and Letters, Oslo
Markus Dickinson, Indiana University, Bloomington, Indiana, USA

Program Committee Co-chairs

Program Chairs

Jan Hajič   Charles University, Prague
Sandra Kübler   Indiana University Bloomington
Stephan Oepen   Universitetet i Oslo
Markus Dickinson   Indiana University Bloomington

Reviewers

Patricia Amaral   Indiana University Bloomington
Emily M. Bender   University of Washington
Eckhard Bick   University of Southern Denmark
Ann Bies   Linguistic Data Consortium, University of Pennsylvania
Gosse Bouma   Rijksuniversiteit Groningen
Miriam Butt   Konstanz
Silvie Cinková   Charles University, Prague
Marie-Catherine de Marneffe   The Ohio State University
Koenraad De Smedt   University of Bergen
Tomaž Erjavec   Dept. of Knowledge Technologies, Jožef Stefan Institute
Filip Ginter   University of Turku
Memduh Gokirmak   Istanbul Technical University
Eva Hajicova   Charles University, Prague
Dag Haug   University of Oslo
Barbora Hladka   Charles University, Prague
Lori Levin   Carnegie Mellon University
Teresa Lynn   Dublin City University
Adam Meyers   New York University
Jiří Mírovský   Charles University, Prague
Kaili Müürisep   University of Tartu
Joakim Nivre   Uppsala University
Petya Osenova   Sofia University and IICT-BAS
Agnieszka Patejuk   Institute of Computer Science, Polish Academy of Sciences
Tatjana Scheffler   Universität Potsdam
Olga Scrivner   Indiana University Bloomington
Djamé Seddah   Alpage/Université Paris la Sorbonne
Michael White   The Ohio State University
Nianwen Xue   Brandeis University
Daniel Zeman   Charles University, Prague
Heike Zinsmeister   University of Hamburg

Local Organizing Committee

Jan Hajič (chair)   Charles University, Prague
Kateřina Bryanová   Charles University, Prague
Zdeňka Urešová   Charles University, Prague
Eduard Bejček (publication chair)   Charles University, Prague

Table of Contents

Annotating and parsing to semantic frames:
feedback from the French FrameNet project
Invited talk

Marie Candito
Université Paris Diderot, France
`marie.candito@gmail.com`

Abstract

Building systems able to provide a semantic representation of texts has long been an objective, both in linguistics and in applied NLP. Although advances in machine learning sometimes seem to diminish the need to use as input sophisticated structured representations of sentences, the enthusiasm for interpreting trained neural networks somewhat seems to reaffirm that need.

Because they represent schematic situations, semantic frames (Fillmore, 1982), as intantiated into FrameNet (Baker, Fillmore and Petruck, 1983) are an appealing level of generalization over the eventualities described in texts.

In this talk, I will present some feedback from the development of a French FrameNet, including analysis of the main difficulties we faced during annotation. I will describe how linking generalizations can be extracted from the frame-annotated data, using deep syntactic annotations. I will then investigate what kind of input is most effective for FrameNet parsing, from no syntax at all to deep syntactic representations.

The work I'll present is a joint work with:
- Marianne Djemaa, Philippe Muller, Laure Vieu, G. de Chalendar,
  B. Sagot, P. Amsili (French FrameNet),
- C. Ribeyre, D. Seddah, G. Perrier, B. Guillaume (deep syntax),
- Olivier Michalon, Alexis Nasr (semantic parsing).

Downstream use of syntactic analysis: does representation matter?
Invited talk

Lilja Øvrelid
University of Oslo, Norway
liljao@ifi.uio.no

Abstract

Research in syntactic parsing is largely driven by progress in intrinsic evaluation and there have been impressive developments in recent years in terms of evaluation measures, such as F-score or labeled accuracy. At the same time, a range of different syntactic representations have been put to use in treebank annotation projects and there have been studies measuring various aspects of the "learnability" of these representations and their suitability for automatic parsing, mostly also evaluated in terms of intrinsic measures.

In this talk I will provide a different perspective on these developments and give an overview of research that examines the usefulness of syntactic analysis in downstream applications. The talk will discuss both constituency-based and dependency-based representations, with a focus on various flavours of dependency-based representations, ranging from purely syntactic representations to more semantically oriented representations. The recently completed shared task on Extrinsic Parser Evaluation was aimed at assessing the utility of different types of dependency representations for downstream applications and I will discuss some of our findings based on the results from this task as well as follow-up experiments and analysis.

Distributional regularities of verbs and verbal adjectives:
Treebank evidence and broader implications

Daniël de Kok and **Patricia Fischer** and **Corina Dima** and **Erhard Hinrichs**
Department of General and Computational Linguistics, University of Tübingen
{daniel.de-kok, patricia.fischer, corina.dima, erhard.hinrichs}
@uni-tuebingen.de

Abstract

Word formation processes such as derivation and compounding yield realizations of lexical roots in different parts of speech and in different syntactic environments. Using verbal adjectives as a case study and treebanks of Dutch and German as data sources, similarities and divergences in syntactic distributions across different realizations of lexical roots are examined and the implications for computational modeling and for treebank construction are discussed.

1 Introduction

Due to processes of word formation such as derivation and compounding, lexical roots can be realized in different parts of speech and in different syntactic environments. For example, the derivational suffix *-able* can turn the verbal root *derive* in English into the adjective *derivable*, and the derivational suffix *-ity* can turn *derivable* into the noun *derivability*. A direct corollary of this polycategorial property of lexical roots and their morphological derivatives is their participation in different syntactic constructions and contexts, each of which comes with their construction-specific frequency distributions of collocations, syntactic arguments, modifiers, and specifiers.

In structuralist theories of language, the characterization of linguistic categories and structures in terms of their distributional behavior provides the key insight underlying distributional accounts of phonology, morphology, and syntax, most famously articulated by Harris (1951) and of semantics, as proposed by Firth (1957). The correct modeling of the interface of derivational morphology and syntactic derivations was also one of the central issues in the early days of generative grammar, with proponents of Generative Semantics (Lees, 1960) arguing for a transformational, syntactic account of word formation and Chomsky (1970) arguing for a non-transformational, interpretative account. In non-derivational, lexicalist theories of grammar such as Head-Driven Phrase Structure Grammar, the sharing of argument structure for lexical roots realized in different word classes is modeled by the non-transformational mechanism of lexical rules and sharing of valence information (see Gerdemann (1994) for such an account for nominalizations in German). Most recently, distributional theories of natural language have also served as an inspiration for distributional modeling of words as word embeddings in computational linguistics (Mikolov et al., 2013; Pennington et al., 2014).

Linguistically annotated corpora, so-called *treebanks*, offer excellent empirical resources for the study of the realization of lexical roots in different morpho-syntactic categories and constructions, provided that their annotations are rich enough to capture relevant information about derivational morphology and lemmatization.

2 Case Study

The purpose of the present paper is to systematically study similarities and divergences in syntactic distributions across different realizations of lexical roots. In particular, we are interested in finding out if the syntactic distribution of a particular realization of a lexical root can serve as an additional information source in modeling the meaning of other, possibly less frequent realizations of the same lexical root.

1

Proceedings of the 16th International Workshop on Treebanks and Linguistic Theories (TLT16), pages 1–9,
Prague, Czech Republic, January 23–24, 2018. Distributed under a CC-BY 4.0 licence. 2017.

Keywords: treebank, annotations, verb, adjective, comparison, Dutch, German, PP, preposition

The paper focuses on a case study of the morpho-syntactic category of adjectives, and within that category on verbal adjectives such as *gegeten* 'eaten' in Dutch and *verloren* 'lost' in German, which are derived from the verbal roots *eten* 'to-eat' and *verlieren* 'to-loose', respectively. Verbal adjectives are of primary interest here since their syntactic distribution is that of an adjective, yet at the same time resembles the syntactic distribution of the verbs from which they are derived. As other adjectives, verbal adjectives occur in three syntactic environments: in attributive, pre-nominal position, in predicative position and in adverbial position, as exemplified in (1a), (1b), and (1c) respectively.

(1) a. [Die [**gewählten** / **wählenden**] / Weitere [**gewählte** / **wählende**]] Mitglieder stimmten zu .
   [the [elected   / voting   ] / more   [elected   / voting   ]] members agreed   .

  b. Die Mitglieder sind **gewählt** .
   The members   are   elected .

  c. Sie   gaben **frustriert** auf .
   They gave frustrated in .

Such adjectives are identical in form to the past participles of the verbs they are derived from. Their adjectival nature is underscored by the fact that they exhibit the same strong/weak inflectional alternation characteristic of adjectives in attributive position, as shown in (1a). Such inflectional variation does not occur in predicative and adverbial position so that the distinction between past participle verbs and verbal adjectives cannot be established in terms of linguistic form, but only in terms of syntactic environment. Moreover, present participles occur as predicative adjectives only in lexicalized cases (Lenz, 1993).

At the same time, verbal adjectives share the same type of arguments and modifiers with the verbs that they derive from. This includes in particular prepositional arguments and modifiers. Since the correct attachment of prepositional phrases is notoriously difficult for rule-based and statistical parsers alike, the present study focuses on the distributions of prepositions that are governed by verbs and verbal adjectives. We focus on prepositions in PP modifiers, as well as prepositional complements (PC) of verbs, as illustrated in (2).

(2) Die im Deutschland **gekauften** Fahrräder sind gegen Diebstahl **versichert** .
  The in Germany   bought   bikes   are against theft   insured   .

As discussed in more detail in Section 4, our goal is to predict the distribution of prepositions governed by verbal adjectives from the distributions of the corresponding verbs. When dealing with ambiguous PP attachments to verbal adjectives, the information gained from the distribution of the corresponding verbs can be instrumental in choosing the correct attachment, especially in the case of predicative adjectives.

The current study uses data from two treebanks: the Lassy Large treebank (Van Noord et al., 2013) of written Dutch and the TüBa-D/DP treebank of written German (taz/Wikipedia sections).

3 Delineating the Domain of Verbal Adjectives

Since verbal adjectives combine properties of verbs and adjectives, it is to be expected that there are certain cases where the boundaries between verbal adjectives and verbs/adjectives are not as clear. In this section, we discuss these boundaries and their ramifications for our study.

3.1 Distinguishing Verbal Adjectives from Verbal Participles

An ongoing topic of debate is the word category of past participles that are governed by verbs which can either be auxiliary or copular. Consider (3), where the Dutch past participle form *gewaarborgd* 'guaranteed' can be analyzed as a verb participle that forms the verb cluster governed by the auxiliary verb *zijn* 'are' or a verbal adjective that is the predicative complement to the copular verb *zijn*.

(3) De obligaties [zijn / worden   ] **gewaarborgd** door het Vlaams Gewest .
  The bonds   [are / are-being] guaranteed   by   the Flemish region .

In Dutch, such ambiguities occur with several verbs that can have auxiliary and copular readings, most prominently *zijn* 'to-be', *worden* 'to-become', and *blijven* 'to-remain'.[1] In German only past participles

---

[1]The ambiguity does not occur in all word orders (Zwart, 2011).

governed by the verb *sein* 'to-be' (the so-called Zustandspassiv) are considered ambiguous. For the present work, we simply treat such participles as ambiguous and evaluate them as a separate set, as described in Section 4.[2]

3.2 Deverbal Adjectives

Although verbal adjectives can be derived productively, they can undergo various degrees of lexicalization, which can result in changes in argument structure or semantics as consequences. We will refer to such adjectives as *deverbal adjectives*, and we use the term *verb-derived adjective* throughout this paper as a cover term for verbal and deverbal adjectives. Deverbal adjectives pose two interesting challenges for the present study: First, they can give rise to new senses of a surface form, along with corresponding shifts in distributions of prepositions. For example, the German adjective *geschlossen* in *geschlossene Gesellschaft* 'closed society' has diverged in meaning from the participle of the verb *schließen* (*geschlossen*). However, it is also possible to use *geschlossen* in its verbal sense such as in *geschlossene Tür* 'closed door'. These two senses are combined with different prepositions. For example, *die durch Klaus geschlossene Tür* 'the by Klaus closed door' is a plausible PP-modification, while *die durch Klaus geschlossene Gesellschaft* is not. Unfortunately, this problem cannot be solved without word sense disambiguation, which (paradoxically) relies on co-occurrence statistics. Consequently, in such cases we model the preposition distribution of all senses together.

Secondly, some forms have transformed morphologically and syntactically into full adjectives, while retaining co-occurrence preferences. For example, the Dutch adjective *onomkeerbare* 'irreversible' in (4a) derives from the verb *omkeren* 'to reverse'. The adjective *onomkeerbaar* still accepts the same PP modifier *wegens klimaatverandering* 'by climate-change' as the past participle *omgekeerd* 'reversed' (4b). As discussed in Section 4, we include such adjectives in our German data set tracing them back to their original verb lemma where possible.

(4) a. . . . het wegens   klimaatverandering **onomkeerbare** process van zeespiegelstijging . . .
         . . . the because-of climate-change   irreversible   process of sea-level-rise   . . .

     b. Het process van zeespiegelstijging kan wegens   klimaatverandering niet **omgekeerd** worden .
         The process of sea-level-rise   can because-of climate-change   not reversed   become .

4 Empirical Basis

To study the distribution of prepositions governed by verbs and verbal adjectives, we extract co-occurrences between (i) prepositions; and (ii) verbs and verbal adjectives from the treebanks for the two languages. As discussed in Section 2, we consider both prepositions in PP modifications as well as preposition complements of verbs. We investigate to what extent the preferences for particular prepositions are shared between a verb and a verbal adjective by using the preposition distribution of the verbal adjective as the reference distribution and the preposition distribution of the verb as a predictor. The particulars of this evaluation will be discussed in more detail in Section 5.

In order to obtain reliable probability distributions from co-occurrence counts, a large number of examples for each verb and verbal adjective is needed. Consequently, this study is conducted using large, machine-annotated treebanks. Such automatic annotations, of course, contain parsing errors, and PP attachment is one of the most frequent attachment errors (Kummerfeld et al., 2012; Mirroshandel et al., 2012; de Kok et al., 2017). However, it should be pointed out that there is far less ambiguity in the attachment of prepositions to verbal adjectives since there is usually no ambiguity in the case of PP modification of prenominal verbal adjective modifiers (see the PP attachment in (2)). For example, the parser of de Kok and Hinrichs (2016) attaches 84.47% of the prepositions that have an attributive adjective as their head correctly. Since verbal adjectives form the reference distribution in our experiments, we are evaluating against a set with fewer attachment errors than the average number of preposition attachment

---

[2]A more extensive discussion of this type of ambiguity in German can be found in Maienborn (2007). Zwart (2011) provides a more thorough discussion for the phenomenon in Dutch, and we refer to Bresnan (1980) and Levin and Rappaport (1986) for the analysis of adjectival passives in English.

errors. In the remainder of this section, we describe in more detail the Dutch and German data that is used in our study.

Dutch For our study of PP-modification of verbal adjectives in Dutch we use the Lassy Large treebank of written Dutch (Van Noord et al., 2013). Lassy Large consists of approximately 700 million words across various text genres, including newspaper, medical, encyclopedic, and political texts. Each sentence in Lassy Large is syntactically annotated using the Alpino dependency parser (Van Noord, 2006).

The Alpino lexicon encodes adjectives that are derived from past and present participles using lexical tags that indicate their verbal origin. This information percolates to the feature structures and is available in the final XML serialization of the dependency structure. Consequently, verbal adjectives can be extracted using simple attribute-based queries over the Lassy treebank. The extraction is further accommodated by the fact that the Lassy treebank uses the verb infinitive as the lemma for a verbal adjective, as specified by the D-COI annotation guidelines (Van Eynde, 2005) that Lassy uses for tagging and lemmatization. Consequently, there is a one-to-one mapping of verbal adjectives to their corresponding verbs. Since infinitive modifications are considered to be verbs in Alpino, we do not include them in the present study.

We extract verbs and verbal adjectives and the prepositions that they govern with one of the following three dependency relations: (i) prepositional phrase modification (*pp/mod*); (ii) preposition complements (*pp/pc*); and (iii) locative/directional complements (*pp/ld*). For prenominal modifiers, we include modifications using both the categories *ap* and *ppart*. In the extraction, we also consider prepositions that are multi-word units (such as *ten aanzien van* 'with regards to'), multi-headed prepositions, and reentrancies in the dependency structure.

German For our study of PP-modification in German, we extract the relevant data from two sections of the TüBa-D/DP treebank. The first section consists of articles from the German newspaper taz from the period 1986 to 2009 (393.7 million tokens and 28.9 million sentences). The second is based on the German Wikipedia dump of January 1, 2017 (747.7 million tokens and 40.2 million sentences). Both treebanks were annotated using the parser of de Kok and Hinrichs (2016) and then lemmatized using the SepVerb lemmatizer (de Kok, 2014).

In our study, we consider prepositions in (i) prepositional phrase modifications (*PP*) and (ii) prepositional complements *(OBJP)*, along with their respective verb or verbal adjective governor. In contrast to the Dutch treebank where lexical tags indicate an adjective's verbal origin, such information was not available for the German adjectives. In the German treebank, verbal adjectives are lemmatized to their adjective lemmas. For example, *beschrifteter* 'labeled' is lemmatized to *beschriftet* 'labeled'. Therefore, all adjectives are analyzed by the SMOR morphological analyzer (Schmid et al., 2004) in order to detect verbal components in the adjectives. When the SMOR analysis of an adjective reveals components that imply a verbal reading, the forms are labeled as *verb-derived* in the treebank. In addition, the corresponding base verb lemma is reconstructed from the analysis.

In contrast to the Dutch data, the availability of a wide-coverage morphological analyzer has also made it possible to include many adjectives that have transitioned from verbal adjectives to full adjectives in the data set. For instance, the adjective *unbegrenzbar* 'illimitable' is recognized as a verb-derived adjective and lemmatized to the corresponding verb base form *begrenzen* 'to limit'.

Set partitioning As discussed in Section 3, there is an ambiguity between the verbal and adjectival analyses of participles when the participle is governed by a verb form that can both be auxiliary and copular. For this reason, we create three different co-occurrence sets for both Dutch and German: (i) the confusion set of verbs and verbal adjectives that are in such ambiguous positions; (ii) the set of verbs that are not in such ambiguous positions; and (iii) the set of verbal adjectives that are not in such ambiguous positions.

5   Experiments

The goal of our experiments is to test our thesis that there are distributional regularities between verbal adjectives and their corresponding verbs. As motivated in Section 2, we will look at co-occurrences with prepositions in particular. In our experiments, we will use *relative entropy* (Kullback-Leibler divergence) to determine how much a distribution Q diverges from a reference distribution P (Equation 1).

$$D(P \parallel Q) = \sum_i P(i) \lg \frac{P(i)}{Q(i)} \tag{1}$$

The relative entropy estimates the expected number of additional bits that is required when a sample of P is encoded using a code optimized for Q rather than P. The divergence is zero when the two distributions are identical.

For each subset (Section 4) of our dataset, we estimate a probability distribution $P^*(p|v)$ using maximum likelihood estimation, where p is the preposition, v the verb lemma, and $count(v, p)$ the number of times v governs p with a prepositional phrase or prepositional complement relation in the data set (Equation 2).[3]

$$P^*(p|v) = \frac{\text{count}(v, p)}{\sum_{p\#} \text{count}(v, p\#)} \tag{2}$$

The relative entropy for a conditional distribution is the (possibly weighted) average of relative entropies of verbs (Equation 3). However, the average relative entropy obscures the differences in relative entropy between frequent and infrequent lemmas. Instead, we sort verbal lemmas by their frequency in the set from which P derives. We then plot the moving average of maximally 500 lemmas in frequency order.[4] The resulting graph shows the change in relative entropy as the lemmas become more rare.

$$D(P \parallel Q) = \sum_v P(v) \sum_p P(p|v) \lg \frac{P(p|v)}{Q(p|v)} \tag{3}$$

We perform four experiments in total, computing the divergences in Table 1. In each experiment, the verbal adjective set is used as the reference distribution P. This is motivated by the fact that verbal adjectives have fewer PP attachment ambiguities and thus serve as a better reference distribution. Furthermore, since verbs are often far more frequent than verbal adjectives, one would typically want to predict the co-occurrences of a verbal adjective.

Set for P	Set for Q
Verbal adjectives (Dutch)	Verbs (Dutch)
Verbal adjectives (German)	Verbs (German)
Ambiguous verbal adjectives/participles (Dutch)	Verbs (Dutch)
Ambiguous verbal adjectives/participles (German)	Verbs (German)

Table 1: The four different pairs of distributions that are evaluated.

We only consider lemmas which occur at least 50 times in each of the paired sets of Table 1. Work on word embeddings has shown that a reasonable number of occurrences is required to get a reliable sample of the contexts in which a word occurs. Consequently, low-frequency words are typically discarded (Collobert et al., 2011; Pennington et al., 2014).

As mentioned before in Section 4 the set of prepositions we consider includes, besides the simplex prepositions in each language, also multi-word units, multi-headed prepositions, etc. The resulting sets of prepositions over which the distributions are computed is relatively large: 1060 prepositions for Dutch and 10,665 prepositions for German. The large proliferation of prepositions has two causes: (i) different spelling variations of prepositions (e.g. *voor* 'for' is sometimes emphasized as *vóór*); and (ii) errors

---

[3]Note that including verbs that do not govern a preposition in the denominator would result in an improper probability distribution, since then $\sum_p P^*(p|v) \neq 1$. However, the observation made by one reviewer - that they may need to be counted - leads to an interesting question: Do some verbs have a stronger tendency to be modified by prepositional phrases than others, and are these tendencies shared by verbs and their corresponding verb-derived adjectives?

[4]The use of the raw data points results in very uneven graphs.

caused by the automatic annotation. However, since the large majority of prepositions are in the long tail, they have virtually no bearing on the evaluation.[5]

Unconditional model We compare the verb-based distributions with a baseline model that computes unconditional preposition probabilities over a verb set $Q_u(p)$ (Equation 4).

$$Q_u(p) = \frac{\sum_{v\#} \text{count}(v^\#, p)}{\sum_{v\#, p\#} \text{count}(v^\#, p^\#)} \tag{4}$$

Mixture model Since the adjective sets contain deverbal adjectives, we expect the verb models to overestimate the probabilities of prepositions that co-occur with the verbal reading of the adjective. For example, consider the adjective *geschlossen* 'closed' that is discussed in Section 3.2. Because the verb set only contains the verbal reading of *geschlossen*, it will underestimate the probabilities of prepositions that co-occur with the deverbal reading of *geschlossen*. To smoothen the distribution of the verb model, we also introduce a mixture model $Q_m(p|v)$ that combines the verb and unconditional models (Equation 5).

$$Q_m(p|v) = \frac{Q(p|v) + Q_u(p)}{2} \tag{5}$$

In the following section, we report and discuss the results for the experiments described in this section.

6 Main Results and Implications for Computational Modeling

The main result of our experiments is that verbs and verbal adjectives share significant distributional regularities. This permits the distribution of prepositions for verbal adjectives to be reliably predicted using the preposition distributions of their corresponding verbal lemmas. Figure 1a shows, on the Y-axis, the relative entropy of the three different variants of verb-based distributions (introduced in Section 5) and the reference verbal adjective distribution for Dutch. Aside from a small subset of highly frequent verbal adjectives, the verb distribution (red) turns out to be the best predictor of the verbal adjective distribution. For the more infrequent lemmas, however, the performance of the verb model converges towards the performance of the more general mixture model (blue).

Figure 1b presents the same analysis using the German data. The general trend is the same for both Dutch and German: the verb distribution is the best for modeling frequent verbal adjectives (the first 800-900 lemmas).[6] The mixture distribution provides a surprisingly stable approximation, even as the frequency of the verbal adjectives decreases. In both languages the verb and mixture models outperform the unconditional model baseline (black).

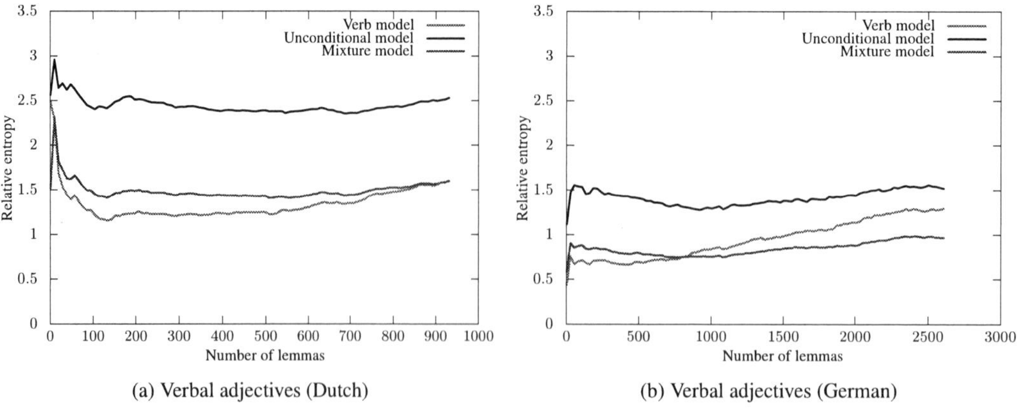

(a) Verbal adjectives (Dutch)　　　　　　(b) Verbal adjectives (German)

Figure 1: Prediction of prepositions attached to verbal adjectives.

---

[5]Only 347 of the Dutch prepositions and 690 of the German prepositions occur at least 50 times in our datasets.

[6]The large difference in the number of verbal adjectives in Dutch and German is cause by the fact that for German we also consider verb-derived adjectives like *unbegrenzbar* 'illimitable', see Section 4. These are not considered for Dutch.

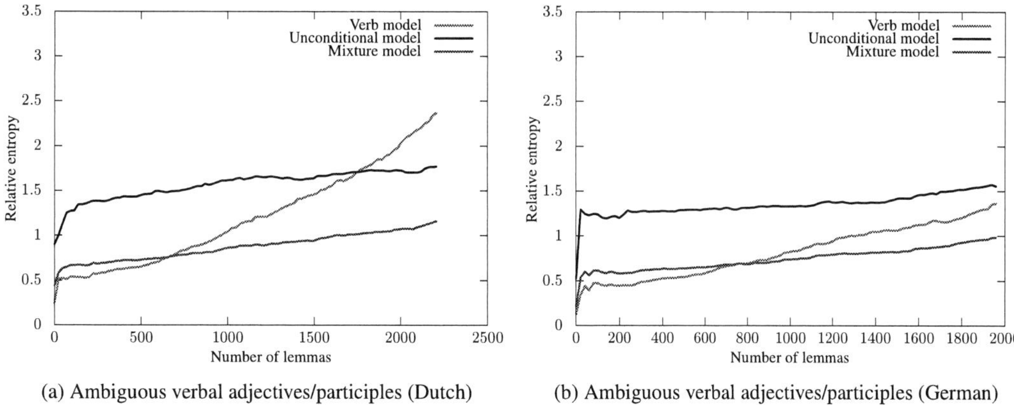

(a) Ambiguous verbal adjectives/participles (Dutch)   (b) Ambiguous verbal adjectives/participles (German)

Figure 2: Prediction of prepositions attached to ambiguous verbal adjectives/participles.

Figures 2a and 2b display the relative entropy values obtained by the verb, mixture and unconditional models with respect to the distribution of ambiguous verbal adjectives/participles. The graphs show similar trends as in the unambiguous verbal adjectives case.[7]

To conclude, the case study has shown that there is a significant overlap in the syntagmatic distribution of different morphosyntactic realizations of a verb lemma. To be able to exploit this overlap in distributional and computational modeling, it is crucial that different morphosyntactic realizations of a lexical root are linked to the same lemma. The utility of incorporating sub-word information in distributional modeling has already been recognized and led to the development of character-based representations. However, these representations have been largely constructed on the basis of small supervised training sets. Such small training sets only contain a limited vocabulary, giving representation learners little opportunity to learn the similarities that exist between different morphological realizations of a verbal lemma. As shown by our study, reliable distributions require a reasonably large sample of co-occurrences, which is not provided by such small data sets. The performance of the verb model deteriorates as the number of available samples decreases. In preliminary work, we have seen that a fairly large sample is needed to faithfully model the underlying distribution.

7 Implications for Treebanking

Our study of distributional regularities of verbs and verbal adjectives has shown that treebanks have the potential to contribute to models with good generalization behavior. However, discovering such regularities is greatly helped by providing the necessary annotations in the treebank. In this section, we give a brief overview of which annotations are particularly relevant to the analysis of verbs and verbal adjectives.

To estimate co-occurrence distributions of verb lemmas and words that enter a dependency relation with them, the verbal and adjectival occurrences of each verb should be annotated with the verbal lemma in a treebank. Even though many treebanks annotate tokens with their lemmas, verbal adjectives are typically lemmatized to their adjectival lemma and not their verbal lemma (see Section 4). In addition, it would be useful if treebanks annotated forms that have fully transitioned into adjectives with their original verb lemma as well.

Another annotation that would have been useful to our study, would be a lexical attribute that indicates whether a verb-derived adjective has a verbal or a deverbal reading. This is particularly useful in cases where verbal and deverbal readings have the same surface form, such as the adjective *geschlossen* that was discussed in Section 3.2. Separation of the verbal readings from the deverbal readings would make it possible to only rely on the verb distribution for predicting the co-occurrences of verbal adjectives.

---

[7]For the Dutch dataset, the ambiguous verbal adjectives/participles make up 17.05% of the dataset, compared to only 3.49% ambiguous cases for German. The reason is that Dutch has several verbs that have both auxiliary and copular readings, while in German only *sein* 'to-be' can be ambiguous (see Section 3.1).

7

Finally, the extraction of verb and preposition co-occurrences for German was hampered by the annotation of prepositional phrase conjunctions and verb conjunctions. The dependency annotation guidelines (Foth, 2006) use shallow analyses of conjunctions, including PP conjunctions, such the one in (5a). A deeper structure needs to be constructed to infer that the second occurrence of the preposition *über* 'about' is also governed by *ärgert* 'agitates'. Conversely, a prepositional phrase can be governed by more than one verb or verbal adjective, as shown in (5b). However, such annotations are not possible in the German treebank that we used, since the annotation guidelines adhere to the single-headedness principle. Deeper annotations, such as those provided in the Lassy Large treebank - which was automatically annotated using the Alpino parser for Dutch (Van Noord, 2006) - help tremendously in exhaustive co-occurrence extraction.

(5)   a.   Staffelt   ärgert   sich   über   den   Lärm   und   auch   über   Senator   Haase
        Staffelt   agitates   himself   about   the   noise   and   also   about   senator   Haase

      b.   Vertaald   ,   ingeleid   en   van   toelichtingen   voorzien   door   H.   Savenije
        Translated   ,   prefaced   and   of   comments   supplied   by   H.   Savenije

Acknowledgments

Financial support for the research reported in this paper was provided by the German Research Foundation (DFG) as part of the Collaborative Research Center "The Construction of Meaning" (SFB 833), project A3.

References

Joan Wanda Bresnan. 1980. *The passive in lexical theory*. Massachusetts Institute of Technology, Center for Cognitive Science.

Noam Chomsky. 1970. Remarks on Nominalization. In Roderick A. Jacobs and Peter S. Rosenbaum, editors, *Readings in English Transformational Grammar*. Ginn, Boston, pages 184–221.

Ronan Collobert, Jason Weston, Léon Bottou, Michael Karlen, Koray Kavukcuoglu, and Pavel Kuksa. 2011. Natural Language Processing (almost) From Scratch. *Journal of Machine Learning Research* 12(Aug):2493–2537.

Daniël de Kok. 2014. TüBa-D/W: a large dependency treebank for German. In *Proceedings of the 13th International Workshop on Treebanks and Linguistic Theories*. Tübingen, Germany, pages 271–278.

Daniël de Kok and Erhard Hinrichs. 2016. Transition-based dependency parsing with topological fields. In *Proceedings of the 54th Annual Meeting of the Association for Computational Linguistics (Volume 2: Short Papers)*. Association for Computational Linguistics, Berlin, Germany, pages 1–7. http://anthology.aclweb.org/P16-2001.

Daniël de Kok, Jianqiang Ma, Corina Dima, and Erhard Hinrichs. 2017. PP Attachment: Where do We Stand? In *Proceedings of the 15th Conference of the European Chapter of the Association for Computational Linguistics (EACL): Volume 2, Short Papers*. Valencia, Spain, pages 311–317. http://www.aclweb.org/anthology/E17-2050.

John Rupert Firth. 1957. A synopsis of linguistic theory 1930-1955. In *Studies in Linguistic Analysis (special volume of the Philological Society)*. The Philological Society, Oxford, pages 1–32.

Kilian A. Foth. 2006. Eine Umfassende Constraint-Dependenz-Grammatik Des Deutschen .

Dale Gerdemann. 1994. Complement Inheritance as Subcategorization Inheritance. In John Nerbonne, Carl Pollard, and Klaus Netter, editors, *German in Head-Driven Phrase Structure Grammar*. Center for Study of Language and Information: Stanford University, CSLI Lecture Notes, pages 341–363.

Zelig Harris. 1951. *Methods in Structural Linguistics*. University of Chicago Press: Chicago.

Jonathan K. Kummerfeld, David Hall, James R. Curran, and Dan Klein. 2012. Parser showdown at the Wall Street corral: An empirical investigation of error types in parser output. In *Proceedings of the 2012 Joint Conference on Empirical Methods in Natural Language Processing and Computational Natural Language Learning*. Association for Computational Linguistics, Jeju Island, Korea, pages 1048–1059. http://www.aclweb.org/anthology/D12-1096.

Robert B. Lees. 1960. The Grammar of English Nominalizations. *International Journal of American Linguistics* 26(3). Part II.

Barbara Lenz. 1993. Probleme Der Kategorisierung Deutscher Partizipien. *Zeitschrift für Sprachwissenschaft* 12(1):39–76.

Beth Levin and Malka Rappaport. 1986. The Formation of Adjectival Passives. *Linguistic inquiry* 17(4):623–661.

Claudia Maienborn. 2007. Das Zustandspassiv. Grammatische Einordnung–Bildungsbeschränkung–Interpretationsspielraum. *Zeitschrift für germanistische Linguistik* 35(1-2):83–114.

Tomas Mikolov, Ilya Sutskever, Kai Chen, Greg S. Corrado, and Jeff Dean. 2013. Distributed representations of words and phrases and their compositionality. In *Advances in Neural Information Processing Systems (NIPS)*. Lake Tahoe, Nevada, United States, pages 3111–3119.

Seyed Abolghasem Mirroshandel, Alexis Nasr, and Joseph Le Roux. 2012. Semi-supervised Dependency Parsing using Lexical Affinities. In *Proceedings of the 50th Annual Meeting of the Association for Computational Linguistics (Volume 1: Long Papers)*. Association for Computational Linguistics, Jeju Island, Korea, pages 777–785. http://www.aclweb.org/anthology/P12-1082.

Jeffrey Pennington, Richard Socher, and Christopher Manning. 2014. GloVe: Global vectors for word representation. In *Proceedings of the 2014 Conference on Empirical Methods in Natural Language Processing (EMNLP)*. Doha, Qatar, pages 1532–1543.

Helmut Schmid, Arne Fitschen, and Ulrich Heid. 2004. SMOR: A German computational morphology covering derivation, composition, and inflection. In *Proceedings of the IVth International Conference on Language Resources and Evaluation (LREC 2004)*. Lisbon, Portugal, pages 1263–1266.

Frank Van Eynde. 2005. Part of Speech Tagging En Lemmatisering Van Het D-Coi Corpus. *Intermediate, project internal version* .

Gertjan Van Noord. 2006. At last parsing is now operational. In *TALN06. Verbum Ex Machina. Actes de la 13e conference sur le traitement automatique des langues naturelles*. Leuven, Belgium, pages 20–42.

Gertjan Van Noord, Gosse Bouma, Frank Van Eynde, Daniël De Kok, Jelmer Van der Linde, Ineke Schuurman, Erik Tjong Kim Sang, and Vincent Vandeghinste. 2013. Large scale syntactic annotation of written Dutch: Lassy. In *Essential Speech and Language Technology for Dutch*, Springer, pages 147–164.

Jan-Wouter Zwart. 2011. *The syntax of Dutch*. Cambridge Syntax Guides. Cambridge University Press.

UD Annotatrix: An annotation tool for Universal Dependencies

Francis M. Tyers
School of Linguistics
НИУ ВШЭ
Moscow
`ftyers@hse.ru`

Mariya Sheyanova
School of Linguistics
НИУ ВШЭ
Moscow
`masha.shejanova@gmail.com`

Jonathan North Washington
Linguistics Department
Swarthmore College
Swarthmore, PA
`jonathan.washington@swarthmore.edu`

Abstract

In this paper we introduce the UD ANNOTATRIX annotation tool for manual annotation of Universal Dependencies. This tool has been designed with the aim that it should be tailored to the needs of the Universal Dependencies (UD) community, including that it should operate in fully-offline mode, and is freely-available under the GNU GPL licence.[1] In this paper, we provide some background to the tool, an overview of its development, and background on how it works. We compare it with some other widely-used tools which are used for Universal Dependencies annotation, describe some features unique to UD ANNOTATRIX, and finally outline some avenues for future work and provide a few concluding remarks.

1   Introduction

Once available for only a handful of languages, treebanks are becoming much more widespread. In many respects this is thanks to the activities of the Universal Dependencies (or UD, Nivre et al., 2016) community, which is an inclusive cross-linguistic consistently-annotated collection of treebanks. The collection today includes over 100 treebanks for over 54 languages, making it among the most diverse collections of freely-available openly-licensed language data.

A large proportion of the treebanks currently available through Universal Dependencies are conversions from previous annotation schemes. However, recently treebanks are being released which have been annotated from scratch, leading to the need for annotation interfaces. There are a number of existing interfaces in use for annotating UD treebanks from scratch, from the web-based such as BRAT (Stenetorp et al., 2012) and *Arborator* (Gerdes, 2013) to offline tools like *TrEd*[2] and the *TDT Editor* of the Turku Dependency Treebank (Haverinen et al., 2014).[3]

One of the things that these tools have in common is that they are not designed specifically for Universal Dependencies and so do not provide a convenient way of treating issues such as the two-level segmentation scheme (where a single surface token may be split into several syntactic words, e.g. Spanish *dímelo* 'say it to me' → dí|me|lo) and generally cannot take advantage of the annotation guidelines to provide validation feedback to the user (for example punctuation nodes may not have any dependents).

In addition, they are either based on web technologies that require some kind of server component (BRAT, *Arborator*) or are offline tools that require a number of dependencies (*TrEd* and the *TDT Editor*).

In this paper we describe UD ANNOTATRIX, a tool which can be used both online and offline, based on web technologies that is multiplatform and provides a simple interface to edit treebanks in the the CoNLL-U format[4] of Universal Dependencies.

---

[1] `http://www.github.com/jonorthwash/ud-annotatrix`
[2] `https://ufal.mff.cuni.cz/tred/`
[3] `https://github.com/TurkuNLP/TDT_editor`
[4] `http://universaldependencies.org/format.html`

Proceedings of the 16th International Workshop on Treebanks and Linguistic Theories (TLT16), pages 10–17,
Prague, Czech Republic, January 23–24, 2018. Distributed under a CC-BY 4.0 licence. 2017.

Keywords: annotation, interface, Universal Dependencies

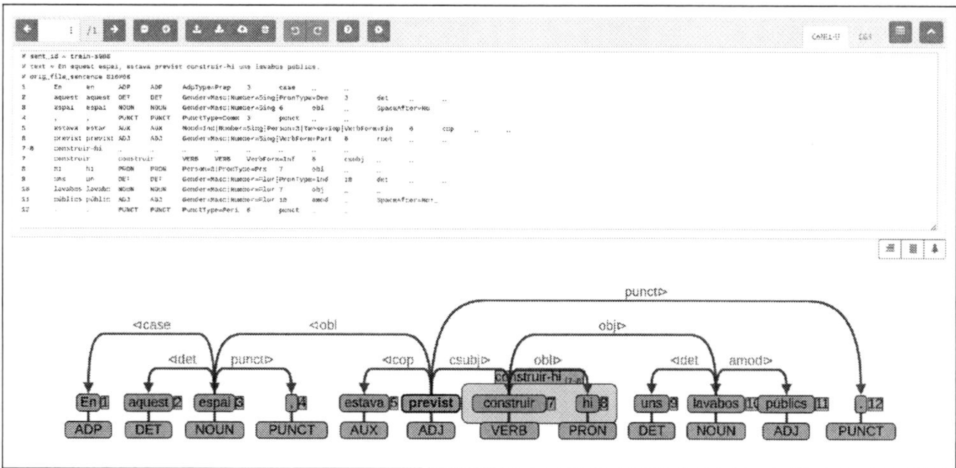

Figure 1: Main interface in horizontal alignment mode (see 2.4). The CoNLL-U code appears in an edit box and can be edited directly and can be hidden. The tree appears below the edit box. In addition a *table view* is supported which allows the user to view and edit the CoNLL-U data in a convenient HTML table format, with an option to toggle the visibility of individual columns.

The remainder of the paper is laid out as follows: Section 2 describes the layout and main features of the interface, Section 3 describes how it was implemented, Section 4 describes related work and how the software fits in with the general tool landscape, Section 5 describes several avenues for future work and finally Section 6 gives some concluding remarks.

2   Features

ANNOTATRIX is a tool primarily aimed at the annotation in UD of files containing up to 10,000 dependency trees. The main design principles that we have taken into account when designing ANNOTATRIX are: that the interface should display a single tree per page; the code should be stored in CoNLL-U format and able to be edited directly; the interface should as far as possible help the user by highlighting errors and proposing solutions; the tool should be zero-install and usable offline (for example for annotation sessions on flights without WiFi); and finally the features should be guided by the UD developer and user community. In taking these principles into account we have tried to prioritise the most useful functionality first with the aim of making a usable tool that can be extended based on user feedback.

2.1   Graphical editing functionality

When opening ANNOTATRIX, the user is presented with a textbox and a toolbar. The user can then either input code in a number of formats (see §2.2) into the textbox, or elect to upload a file.

Once a file is uploaded or some text is inserted, a tree appears below. The user can then click on a node, and click on another node in order to create a dependency link from parent to child. The link appears in grey, and the user can click on a direction arrow to specify a dependency relation, which can be autocompleted. There are a number of heuristics to speed up this process; for example, if the dependent is punctuation, then the `punct` relation is specified by default. It is also possible to remove dependency links by selecting them with a right click and then pressing either the DELETE or BACKSPACE key.

If different tokenisation is required, nodes can be split by right clicking and indicating where the split should be in a text box. Token indices are automatically renumbered. Nodes may also be merged, either as single tokens or as multi-word tokens. For example, given the input *verlo* 'to see it' in Spanish, the single token *verlo* would be split into *ver lo* and then joined into a single token span of *verlo* with two syntactic words.

Every action made in graphical mode can be reverted and made again. A detailed description of graphical editing functionality can be found on the help-page of the application.

2.2 Input formats

At the moment, Annotatrix supports five input formats (see descriptions below). They can be pasted into the text box or uploaded as a file. Code pasted into the window goes through a format detection and cleaning process. For example, if CoNLL-U format is detected but there are no tabs, a sequence of more than one space is considered a column separator. Here is a list of supported formats:

CoNLL-U: This is the standard format used in Universal Dependencies. Multilevel tokenisation and comments are supported. Null nodes and editing enhanced dependencies are currently unsupported, but support for them is planned.

CG: The input/output format used by the VISL CG3 system (Bick and Didriksen, 2015) is the native format of the Kazakh (Tyers and Washington, 2015; Makazhanov et al., 2015) and Kurdish Kurmanji (Gökırmak and Tyers, 2017) treebanks.

Stanford Dependency: A common format for specifying dependency trees in *Annodoc*[5] and the Universal Dependencies documentation. Trees can be visualised in SDParse but for editting they should be converted to CoNLL-U.

Bracket notation: Traditional bracket notation can be used for labelled dependency trees. Used in the Russian constructicon.[6] As with SDParse, visualisation is supported, but not editing.

Plain text: Plain text can be converted to CoNLL-U by a naïve spaces-and-punctuation tokenisation algorithm implemented as a regular expression.

Examples of each format can be found in Appendix A. The native format for editing is CoNLL-U, all other formats can be used for visualisation, but in order to edit the trees, they must be converted to CoNLL-U.

2.3 Text and table view

There are two ways of viewing the columns of the CoNLL-U file: CoNLL-U-formatted dependencies can be viewed in a simple HTML textarea, which allows the user to edit the file directly, as well as in a *table view* where the user is presented with a table with columns that can be shown and hidden. The table view allows better use of the available space to be made by hiding columns that might not be relevant (for example the XPOSTAG, DEPS and MISC columns) and also by aligning the contents of the columns. An example of table view can be seen in Figure 3.

2.4 Types of visual alignment

For very long sentences, ANNOTATRIX offers an experimental *vertical* alignment, where the tree can be viewed from top-to-bottom instead of from left-to-right. This can make better use of the available screen space by allowing more nodes to fit on the screen (the height is fixed where as the width depends on the length of the token).

In addition, we offer rudimentary support for languages with right-to-left writing systems (e.g. Hebrew, Uyghur and Arabic) to make annotating them more comfortable.[7] The full range of bidirectional (BiDi) support is not available, but we plan to add it in the future. An example of right-to-left layout with Sorani Kurdish can be found in Figure 2. ANNOTATRIX also has full Unicode support, including combining diacritics in abugida scripts.

2.5 Saving corpora

Rudimentary support for a server mode has been implemented. This mode provides support for saving user corpora on server and then accessing the saved corpora via a unique URL. This option allows the user to share their corpora with other users and makes ANNOTATRIX a simple collaboration tool.

---

[5] http://spyysalo.github.io/annodoc/
[6] https://spraakbanken.gu.se/eng/resource/konstruktikon-rus
[7] To our knowledge ANNOTATRIX is the only dependency-tree editting program to do this.

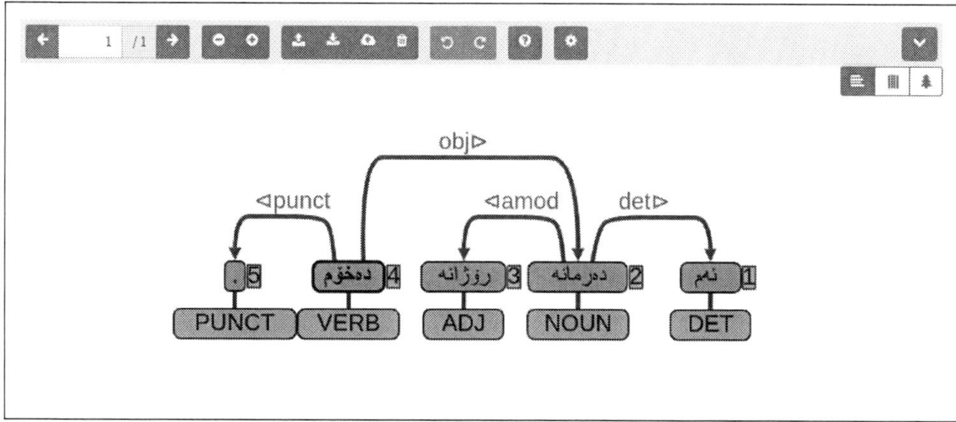

Figure 2: Support for right-to-left writing systems. Example in Sorani Kurdish reads "I take this daily medicine". This also demonstrates how the input box can be hidden to maximise space for the dependency tree.

Currently the versions of ANNOTATRIX deployed online are not linked to the server backend, but one can clone the project code and deploy it on their own web-server to use its functionality. Also, functionality is currently very limited, but more functionality is planned for the future. For example, it can be improved by adding support for tracking the editing history or by enabling the users to register and view the saved corpora on their personal page. For implementation details, see Section 3.1.

In addition to server-side saving, the entire corpus being annotated using the interface is exportable in CoNLL-U format.

2.6 Validation

ANNOTATRIX contains a number of features which help the user to annotate correctly. It offers feedback on both dependency relations and on part-of-speech tags. In the case of dependency relations, if a relation is entered which is not a universal relation (or language-specific subrelation) then the arc in the graph turns red and in table view a warning icon is displayed next to the relation with a tooltip indicating that the relation is not valid. For part-of-speech tags, the feedback is only given in table view. See Figure 3 for a demonstration of how this works.

In addition, for punctuation two rules are implemented: if punctuation is added as the head of another node or if punctuation is attached non-projectively, it is detected and the arc is turned red.

3 Implementation

3.1 Stand-alone vs. server versions

ANNOTATATRIX consists of two modules: stand-alone and server. The stand-alone part of the project supports all the functionality described in section 2, apart from saving corpora on server, whereas the server module provides additional functionality.

The stand-alone module is written in JavaScript, using jQuery and a number of dependencies described below. All the dependencies are stored locally, allowing for the offline usage of the interface. The stand-alone version stores the imported corpora in localStorage and allows for editing CoNLL-U files of up to 10,000 tokens.

The server module is written in Python 3, using the Flask web-framework. The data is passed between client and server using AJAX. As mentioned in 2.5, the server module currently has only a limited amount of functionality.

3.2 Visualisation and graphical editing

For visualising the dependency trees, we use the Cytoscape.js library (Franz et al., 2016). Cytoscape.js is an open-source JavaScript graph library primarily developed for biologists, but available to use for different purposes. It is easy-to-use and specifically designed for visualising graphs.

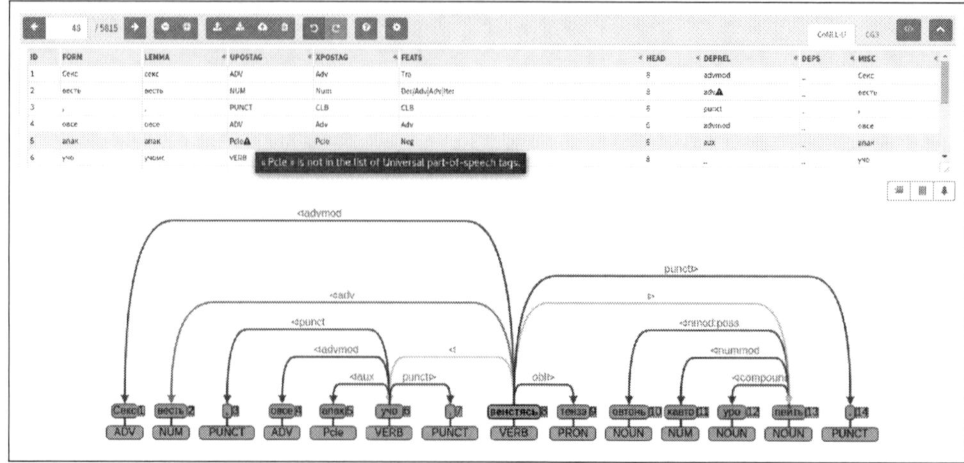

Figure 3: Screenshot showing validation features. In the table view an icon appears next to invalid values and provides a tooltip explaining the problem. In the graph view, arcs which are not labelled are first shown in grey, and then in black if they have a valid label. Arcs with an invalid label or those which are otherwise invalid (for example dependents of punctuation) are shown in red.

As dependency trees typically have much fewer nodes than biological networks and have specific layout requirements, we implemented custom functions for node and arc layout which modify the standard layouts provided by Cytoscape.js. The node layout is built based on the standard grid layout. The custom node layout allows saving horizontal space by making the cell width dependent on the token length. For the dependency links representation, the unbundled-bezier edge form was used. To avoid intersections, the height of an edge was made dependent on the distance between the nodes.

3.3 Format parsing and conversion

The main format which serves the visualisation is CoNLL-U. It is chosen as the most universal and widespread way of coding the dependency trees. For the format parsing, we used the `conllu.js` library[8] written by Magdalena Parks.

All of the other supported formats (i.e. CG, SDParse, bracket notation and plain text) are first converted to CoNLL-U, and then visualised. For unambiguous sentences in the CG format, UD ANNOTATRIX supports visualisation and graphical editing without converting the full corpus to CoNLL-U. Each unambiguous sentence in the CG format is automatically converted to CoNLL-U for visualisation and editing support, and after the changes made in the graphical mode converted back to CG and synchronised with the graph. If the sentence is ambiguous, i.e. at least one token has several analyses, the sentence cannot be converted to CoNLL-U without loosing information. In this case, the tree is not visualised.

The format converters are tested using the the QUnit library.

3.4 Additional libraries

Large open-source libraries which ANNOTATRIX relies on include (in the versions currently used) jQuery 3.2.1,[9] Boostrap 4.0,[10] and Font Awesome 4.7.0.[11] Additionally, preliminary support for localisation has recently been added using Mozilla's l20n 5.0.0,[12] and undo/redo history is implemented using a recent version of Javascript Undo Manager.[13]

---

[8] `https://github.com/FrancessFractal/conllu`

[9] `http://jquery.com`

[10] `http://getbootstrap.com`

[11] `http://fontawesome.io`

[12] `https://github.com/l20n/l20n.js`

[13] `https://github.com/ArthurClemens/Javascript-Undo-Manager`

4   Related work

Currently, the two tools providing the closest functionality to ANNOTATRIX are BRAT (Stenetorp et al., 2012) and *Arborator* (Gerdes, 2013). They are both web-based tools (though they require server installation). They are also both capable of processing CoNLL-U files (natively in the case of *Arborator* and with format conversion in the case of BRAT). A major difference between these two tools and ANNOTATRIX is that they both have more advanced project-management features, with users being able to curate different files and in the case of *Arborator* many useful features for classroom use of the tool (it was originally designed for classroom annotation). The current design of ANNOTATRIX has been optimised for single-file editing by a single user.

Another difference is that both BRAT and *Arborator* are annotation-scheme neutral, they offer validation support but do not offer out-of-the-box support for Universal Dependencies.

5   Future work

One of the main features that has been requested but as yet has not been implemented is the incorporation of search functionality. We envisage two modes of operation, the first could provide simple search-by-label or search-by-token/relation/etc. functionality for offline use on small treebanks. The second would be to incorporate `dep_search` (Luotolahti et al., 2017), which is an extremely powerful query language for searching in dependency parse banks.

An additional feature that we would like to integrate into ANNOTATRIX is the work of de Marneffe et al. (2017) on error finding in UD treebanks. Their current tool allows errors to be flagged, but it should be possible for trees to be fixed as well—i.e., instead of just reporting errors, a patch which fixes the error could be generated.

At the moment, the validation features of ANNOTATRIX are quite limited. It should be possible to write much more intricate rules to validate the trees; code in UD's `validate.py` and in UDapy (Popel et al., 2017) could be used as a basis for this, with priority going to format validation.

There is also a wide range of interface and usability improvements that are being actively worked on. These are all documented as issues in the main GitHub repository. In addition ANNOTATRIX is being actively used in annotation projects such as the Marathi (Ravishankar, 2018) and Bambara (Aplonova and Tyers, 2018) treebanks and we expect that this use will provide useful feedback in terms of bugs and feature requests.

6   Concluding remarks

This paper has presented UD ANNOTATRIX, a free/open-source tool for annotating Universal Dependencies.[14] UD ANNOTATRIX is developed for and by the community of Universal Dependencies users. The current set of features has been described, along with details on implementation, related work, and our plans going forward. It is our hope that ANNOTATRIX will streamline the workflows of many UD annotators, thereby enabling the creation of UD-annotated corpora that are larger and in a wider range of languages, and that the tool will grow and improve as more users notice bugs and request new features.

Acknowledgements

We would like to thank the Google Summer of Code and the Apertium project for supporting the development of ANNOTATRIX. In addition we would like to thank Filip Ginter and Alexandre Rademaker for extremely helpful discussions and suggestions. Tai Warner, Sushain Cherivirala and Kevin Unhammer have also contributed code. And finally, we would like to thank our users, in particular Jack Rueter and Katya Aplonova, for their helpful bug reports and encouragement.

---

[14]All of the source code is available online at `https://github.com/jonorthwash/ud-annotatrix`.

References

Aplonova, E. and Tyers, F. M. (2018). Towards a dependency-annotated treebank for Bambara. In *Proceedings of the 16th International Workshop on Treebanks and Linguistic Theories*, page *this volume*.

Bick, E. and Didriksen, T. (2015). Cg-3 – beyond classical constraint grammar. In *Proceedings of the 20th Nordic Conference of Computational Linguistics, NODALIDA*, pages 31–39. Linköping University Electronic Press, Linköpings universitet.

de Marneffe, M.-C., Grioni, M., Kanerva, J., and Ginter, F. (2017). Assessing the annotation consistency of the universal dependencies corpora. In *Proceedings of the Fourth International Conference on Dependency Linguistics (Depling 2017)*, pages 108–115.

Franz, M., Lopes, C. T., Huck, G., Dong, Y., Sumer, O., and Bader, G. D. (2016). Cytoscape.js: a graph theory library for visualisation and analysis. 32(2):309–311.

Gerdes, K. (2013). Collaborative dependency annotation. In *Proceedings of DepLing 2013*, pages 88–97.

Gökırmak, M. and Tyers, F. M. (2017). A dependency treebank for kurmanji kurdish. In *Proceedings of the Fourth International Conference on Dependency Linguistics (DepLing, 2017)*, pages 64–73.

Haverinen, K., Nyblom, J., Viljanen, T., Laippala, V., Kohonen, S., Missilä, A., Ojala, S., Salakoski, T., and Ginter, F. (2014). Building the essential resources for Finnish: the Turku Dependency Treebank. *Language Resources and Evaluation*, 48(3):493–531.

Luotolahti, J., Kanerva, J., and Ginter, F. (2017). dep_search: Efficient search tool for large dependency parsebanks. In *Proceedings of the 21st Nordic Conference on Computational Linguistics (NoDaLiDa)*.

Makazhanov, A., Sultangazina, A., Makhambetov, O., and Yessenbayev, Z. (2015). Syntactic annotation of Kazakh: Following the Universal Dependencies guidelines. a report. In *3rd International Conference on Turkic Languages Processing, (TurkLang 2015)*, pages 338–350.

Nivre, J., de Marneffe, M.-C., Ginter, F., Goldberg, Y., Hajič, J., Manning, C., McDonald, R., Petrov, S., Pyysalo, S., Silveira, N., Tsarfaty, R., and Zeman, D. (2016). Universal Dependencies v1: A Multilingual Treebank Collection. In *Proceedings of Language Resources and Evaluation Conference (LREC'16)*.

Popel, M., Žabokrtský, Z., and Vojtek, M. (2017). Udapi: Universal api for Universal Dependencies. In *Proceedings of the NoDaLiDa 2017 Workshop on Universal Dependencies (UDW 2017)*, pages 96–101.

Ravishankar, V. (2018). A Universal Dependencies Treebank for Marathi. In *Proceedings of the 16th International Workshop on Treebanks and Linguistic Theories*, page *this volume*.

Stenetorp, P., Pyysalo, S., Topić, G., Ohta, T., Ananiadou, S., and Tsujii, J. (2012). BRAT: a web-based tool for NLP-assisted text annotation. In *EACL '12 Proceedings of the Demonstrations at the 13th Conference of the European Chapter of the Association for Computational Linguistics*, pages 102–107.

Tyers, F. M. and Washington, J. N. (2015). Towards a free/open-source Universal-dependency treebank for Kazakh. In *3rd International Conference on Turkic Languages Processing, (TurkLang 2015)*, pages 276–289.

A   Demonstration of dependency annotation formats

The following sentence is rendered below in several dependency annotation formats.

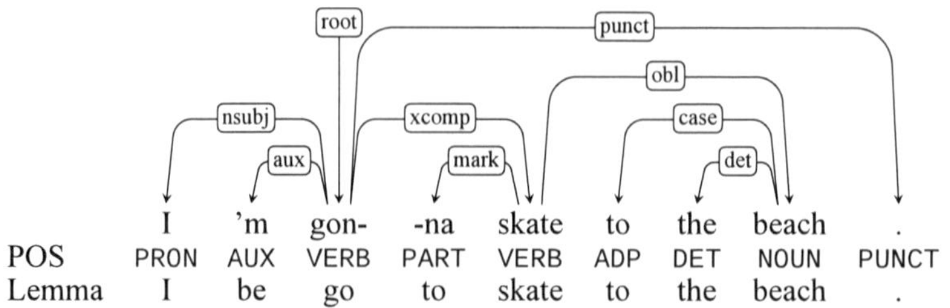

A.1 CoNLL-U

```
1      I        I       PRON    _    _    3    nsubj    _    SpaceAfter=No
2      'm       be      AUX     _    _    3    aux      _    _
3-4    gonna    _       _       _    _    _    _        _    _
3      gon      go      VERB    _    _    _    0        root _
4      na       to      PART    _    _    5    mark     _    _
5      skate    skate   VERB    _    _    3    xcomp    _    _
6      to       to      ADP     _    _    8    case     _    _
7      the      the     DET     _    _    8    det      _    _
8      beach    beach   NOUN    _    _    5    obl      _    SpaceAfter=No
9      .        .       PUNCT   _    _    3    punct    _    _
```

A.2 CG3

```
"<I>"
        "I" PRON @nsubj #1->3
"<'m>"
        "be" AUX @aux #2->3
"<gonna>"
        "go" VERB @root #3->0
                "to" PART @mark #4->5
"<skate>"
        "skate" VERB @xcomp #5->3
"<to>"
        "to" ADP @case #6->8
"<the>"
        "the" DET @det #7->8
"<beach>"
        "beach" NOUN @obl #8->5
"<.>"
        "." PUNCT @punct #9->3
```

A.3 SDParse

```
I 'm gonna skate to the beach .
nsubj(gonna, I)
aux(gonna, 'm)
xcomp(gonna, skate)
obl(skate, beach)
det(beach, the)
case(beach, to)
punct(gonna, .)
```

A.4 Bracket notation

```
[root [nsubj I] [aux 'm]  gonna [xcomp skate [obl [case to] [det the] beach]]]
```

The Treebanked Conspiracy. Actors and Actions in *Bellum Catilinae*

Marco Passarotti
CIRCSE Research Centre
Università Cattolica del Sacro Cuore
Largo Gemelli, 1 - 20123 Milan, Italy
marco.passarotti@unicatt.it

Berta González Saavedra
Dep. de Filología Griega y Lingüística Indoeuropea
Universidad Complutense de Madrid
Pl. M. Pelayo - 28040 Madrid, Spain
bergonza@ucm.es

Abstract

In the context of the *Index Thomisticus* Treebank project, we have recently enhanced the entire text of *Bellum Catilinae* by Sallust with a layer of semantic annotation. By exploiting the results of semantic role labeling, ellipsis resolution and coreference analysis, this paper presents a study of the main Actors and Actions (and their relations) in *Bellum Catilinae*.

1 Introduction

The large majority of the currently available treebanks includes data taken from contemporary books, magazines, journals and, mostly, newspapers. Such data are used for different purposes in both theoretical and computational linguistics, the most widespread being supporting and evaluating theoretical assumptions with empirical evidence and providing data for various tasks in stochastic NLP, like inducing grammars and training/testing tools.

Across the last decade, a small, but ever growing, bunch of dependency treebanks for ancient languages was built. In this respect, the main treebanks now available are those for Latin and Ancient Greek, with The Ancient Greek and Latin Dependency Treebank (AGLDT) (Bamman and Crane, 2011), the *Index Thomisticus* Treebank (IT-TB) (Passarotti, 2011) and the PROIEL corpus (Haug and Jøhndal, 2008).

Treebanks for ancient languages tend to include literary, historical, philosophical and/or documentary texts. This makes the very use of such resources different from that of treebanks for modern languages. Indeed, instead of exploiting data to draw linguistic generalizations, users of such treebanks are more interested in the linguistic features of the texts themselves available in the corpus. For instance, there is more interest and scientific motivation in exploiting the treebanked texts of Sophocles to study their specific syntactic characteristics than in using the evidence provided by such texts as sufficiently representative of Ancient Greek, which they are not.

Not only the use of data is different, but also users are. Indeed, it is quite uncommon that scholars from literature, philosophy or history make use of linguistic resources like treebanks for modern languages in their research work. Instead, they represent some of the typical users of treebanks for ancient languages as well as of diachronic treebanks. Such resources become even more useful for this kind of users from the Humanities when they are enhanced also with a semantic layer of annotation, on top of the syntactic one. This is due to the large interest of such scholars in semantic interpretation of texts through syntax.

In this area, the *Index Thomisticus* Treebank project has recently enhanced a selection of texts taken from the IT-TB and the AGLDT with semantic annotation. This paper describes the dependency-based annotation style applied on these data and presents a use case of exploitation of them for literary analysis purposes. In particular, the analysis focuses on the main Actors and Actions in Sallust's *Bellum Catilinae*.[1] The work is performed by using the results of semantic role labeling, coreference analysis and ellipsis resolution applied on the source data.

---

[1] Written probably between 43 and 40 BCE, *Bellum Catilinae* tells the story of the so called second Catilinarian conspiracy (63 BCE), a plot, devised by Catiline and a group of aristocrats and veterans, to overthrow the Roman Republic. The text of *Bellum Catilinae* available from the AGLDT is the one edited by Ahlberg (1919). It includes 10,936 words and 701 sentences. In this paper, English translations of *Bellum Catilinae* are taken from Ramsey (2014).

Proceedings of the 16th International Workshop on Treebanks and Linguistic Theories (TLT16), pages 18–26,
Prague, Czech Republic, January 23–24, 2018. Distributed under a CC-BY 4.0 licence. 2017.

Keywords: semantic role labeling, ellipsis resolution, coreference, hierarchical clustering

2 Data

In the context of the *Index Thomisticus* Treebank project hosted at the CIRCSE research centre of the Università Cattolica del Sacro Cuore in Milan, Italy (http://itreebank.marginalia.it/), we have added a new layer of semantic annotation on top of a selection of syntactically annotated data taken from the IT-TB and the Latin portion of the AGLDT (González Saavedra and Passarotti, 2014).

In particular, around 2,000 sentences (approx. 27,000 words) were annotated out of *Summa contra Gentiles* of Thomas Aquinas (IT-TB). The entire *Bellum Catilinae* of Sallust (BC) and small excerpts of 100 sentences each from texts of Caesar and Cicero were annotated from the AGLDT.

2.1 Annotation Style

The style of the semantic layer of annotation used in the IT-TB project is based on Functional Generative Description (FGD) (Sgall et al., 1986), a dependency-based theoretical framework developed in Prague and intensively applied and tested while building the Prague Dependency Treebank of Czech (PDT) (Hajič et al., 2000).

The PDT is a dependency-based treebank with a three-layer structure. The (so ordered) layers are a "morphological layer" (morphological tagging and lemmatization), an "analytical" layer (annotation of surface syntax) and a "tectogrammatical" layer (annotation of underlying syntax). Both the analytical and the tectogrammatical layers describe the sentence structure with dependency tree-graphs, respectively named analytical tree structures (ATSs) and tectogrammatical tree structures (TGTSs).

In ATSs every word and punctuation mark of the sentence is represented by a node of a rooted dependency tree. The edges of the tree correspond to dependency relations that are labelled with (surface) syntactic functions called "analytical functions" (like Subject, Object etc.).

TGTSs describe the underlying structure of the sentence, conceived as the semantically relevant counterpart of the grammatical means of expression (described by ATSs). The nodes of TGTSs include autosemantic words only (represented by "tectogrammatical lemmas": "t-lemmas"), while function words and punctuation marks collapse into the nodes for autosemantic words. Semantic role labeling is performed by assigning to nodes semantic role tags called "functors". These are divided into two classes according to valency: (a) arguments, called "inner participants", i.e. obligatory complementations of verbs, nouns, adjectives and adverbs: Actor,[2] Patient, Addressee, Effect and Origin; (b) adjuncts, called "free modifications": different kinds of adverbials, like Place, Time, Manner etc.

Also coreference analysis and ellipsis resolution are performed at the tectogrammatical layer and are represented in TGTSs through arrows (coreference) and newly added nodes (ellipsis). In particular, there are two kinds of coreference: (a) "grammatical coreference", in which it is possible to pinpoint the coreferred expression on the basis of grammatical rules (mostly with relative pronouns) and (b) "textual coreference", realized not only by grammatical means, but also via context (mostly with personal pronouns).

2.2 From ATSs to TGTSs

The workflow for tectogrammatical annotation in the IT-TB is based on TGTSs automatically converted from ATSs.[3] The TGTSs that result from the conversion are then checked and refined manually by two annotators. The conversion is performed by adapting to Latin a number of ATS-to-TGTS conversion modules provided by the NLP framework *Treex* (Žabokrtský, 2011).[4]

For instance, Figure 1 shows the ATS for the sentence "cum [with] eo [him] se [himself] consulem [consul] initium [beginning] agundi [of acting] facturum [would have made]" (BC 21.4) ("[Catiline promised that] as consul with him, he would launch his undertaking"), which presents a case of predicate

---

[2]The definition of Actor in the PDT is semantically quite underspecified, as it refers to "the human or non-human originator of the event, the bearer of the event or a quality/property, the experiencer or possessor" (Mikulová et al., 2006, page 461).

[3]The guidelines for analytical annotation of the IT-TB (as well as of the Latin portion of the AGLDT) are those of Bamman et al. (2007). The guidelines for tectogrammatical annotation are those of the PDT (Mikulová et al., 2006), with a few modifications for representing Latin-specific constructions.

[4]See González Saavedra and Passarotti (2014) for details on ATS-to-TGTS conversion in the IT-TB and, especially, for an evaluation of the accuracy of the conversion process.

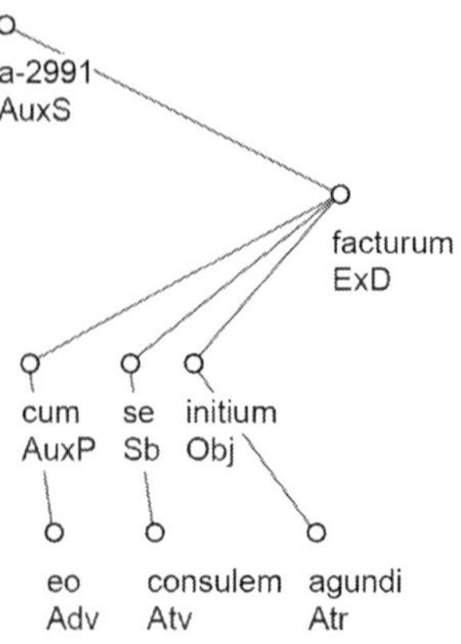

Figure 1: ATS of BC 21.4.

ellipsis. The sentence is an objective subordinate clause lacking the predicate of its governing clause ("[Catiline promised that]"). In ATSs, this is represented by assigning the analytical function ExD (External Dependency) to the main predicate of the sentence. In the ATS of Figure 1, the node for *facturum* is assigned ExD, because here *facturum* depends on a node that is missing and, thus, it is "external" to the current tree.

Figure 2 shows the TGTS for this sentence. The TGTS in Figure 2 resolves the ellipsis of the main clause. Three sentences before this one in the text, Sallust writes "Catiline polliceri" ("Catiline promised [to men]"). The sentence in BC 21.4 still depends on this clause. Once resolved the ellipsis of *polliceor*, the TGTS must represent its arguments. Among these, both the Actor and the Addresse result from ellipsis resolution: Catiline is the Actor and the men (*homo*) are the Addresse. The Patient of *polliceor*, instead, is represented by the entire objective subordinate clause of BC 21.4. In this clause, the Actor is again Catiline, as it is represented by the textual coreference of the node depending on *facio* which is assigned t-lemma #PersPron:[5] this node is not newly added because it is textually represented by the reflexive pronoun *se*. The Patient of *facio* is *initium*, which is specified by a restrictor (RSTR; the verb *ago*) governing a newly added node for a generic Actor (#Gen). Such Actor is assigned when its denotation cannot be retrieved contextually, which mostly happens when impersonal clauses are concerned, like in this case (literaly: "the beginning of acting").

The prepositional phrase "cum eo" ("with him") is represented in the TGTS of Figure 2 by the node for *is* (form *eo*), while that for the preposition *cum* collapses. The personal pronoun *is* is linked with a previous occurrence of the proper name *Antonius* via a textual coreference and it is assigned functor ACMP, which is used for the adjuncts that express manner by specifying a circumstance (an object, person, event) that accompanies (or fails to accompany) the event or entity modified by the adjunct.

In TGTSs, predicative complements (functor: COMPL) are adjuncts with a dual semantic dependency relation. They simultaneously modify a noun and a verb. The dependency on the verb is represented by means of an edge. In Figure 2, this is the edge that connects *facio* with *consul*. The dependency on the noun is represented by means of a specific complement reference, which is graphically represented by a green arrow (going from *consul* to #PersPron in Figure 2).

3   Results and Discussion

One of the added values of tectogrammatical annotation is that it provides information that, although it is accessible to readers, is missing in texts. Looking at the example sentence discussed in the previous section, we see that there is no explicit occurrence of Catiline playing the role of Actor of a verb. Instead, if we exploit tectogrammatical annotation, we can retrieve that actually that sentence says that Catiline performs two different Actions (namely, *polliceor* and *facio*).

---

[5] #PersPron is the t-lemma assigned to nodes representing possessive and personal pronouns (including reflexives).

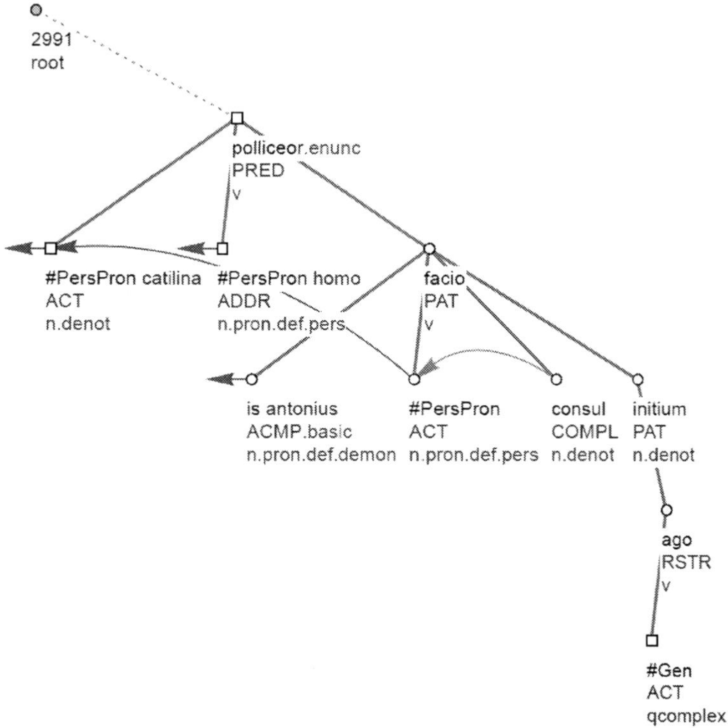

Figure 2: TGTS of BC 21.4.

Tectogrammatical annotation puts us in the condition to answer the basic research question of the work described in this paper: "who does what in *Bellum Catilinae*?". In other words, what we look for are all the couples Actor-Action in BC regardless of the fact that they do explicitly occur in the text.[6]

3.1 Querying the Data

All data can be freely downloaded from the website of the IT-TB project. The treebanks can be queried through an implementation of the PML-TQ search engine (Prague Markup Language Tree Query) (Štěpánek and Pajas, 2010). We ran a bunch of queries in order to retrieve all the couples Actor-Action in BC. The basic query just searches for all the Actors of a verb:

```
t-node $n0 := [ gram/sempos = `v',
echild t-node $n1 := [ functor = `ACT' ] ];
```

This query searches for all the nodes of a TGTS (t-node, named $n0) that are assigned PoS verb (gram/sempos = `v') and govern either directly or indirectly (echild) a node ($n1) with functor ACT (functor = `ACT').[7] The query does not limit the output to nodes with an explicit textual correspondence, but includes also those newly added in TGTSs, as result of ellipsis resolution.

The output resulting from the query above needs further refinement, as it features several cases of both relative and personal pronouns whose denotation is resolved in TGTSs by coreference analysis. For instance, three Actor-Action couples result from the TGTS of Figure 2: #PersPron-*polliceor*, #PersPron-*facio* and #Gen-*ago*. While #Gen is a generic argument whose denotation cannot be retrieved contextually, both the #PersPron nodes are assigned a textual coreference in the TGTS, thus enabling to replace them with the t-lemma they are coreferent with.

---

[6]In this work, we consider Actions as represented by verbs only. Deverbal nominalizations are thus excluded.

[7]Direct or indirect government is set in order to retrieve Actors occurring in coordinated constructions (headed by the coordinating element).

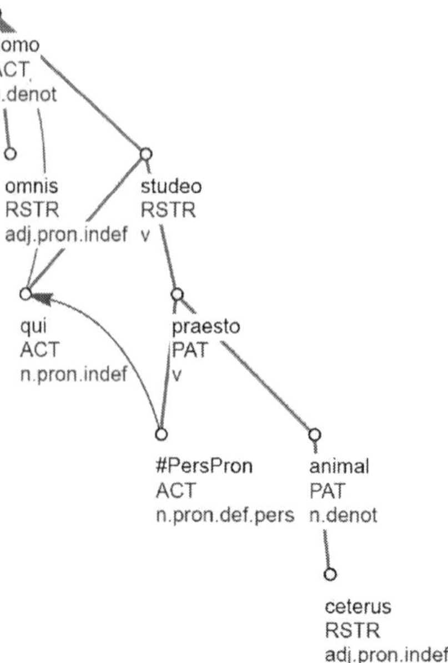

Figure 3: TGTS of BC 1.4 (part).

We ran a number of queries to replace in the output of the basic query all coreferred #PersPron t-lemmas with those of the nodes they are linked with via textual coreference. Then we did the same for all coreferred t-lemmas of relative pronouns, which are linked to their antecedent via grammatical coreference.

Not only such queries must consider both direct and indirect linking, as well as textual and grammatical coreference, but they also have to address mixed indirect coreferences. For instance, this is the case of the first noun phrase in the first sentence of BC: "Omnis [all] homines [men], qui [who] sese [themselves] student [be eager] praestare [to stand out] ceteris [others] animalibus [animals] [...]" (BC 1.1) ("All humans who are keen to surpass other animals [...]"). Figure 3 shows the portion of the TGTS for the first sentence of BC concerning this phrase.

From Figure 3, one can see that the denotation (*homo*) of the #PersPron node playing the role of Actor of *praesto* is retrieved (a) indirectly, by passing through the node for *qui*, and (b) in mixed fashion, i.e. via a textual coreference (from #PersPron to *qui*) plus a grammatical coreference (from *qui* to *homo*).

A model of such kind of complex queries is the following:

```
t-node $n0 := [ functor = 'ACT',
    eparent t-node $n2 := [ gram/sempos = 'v' ],
coref_text.rf t-node $n1 := [ coref_gram.rf t-node $n3 := [ ] ] ];
```

The t-node named $n0 is an Actor that depends either directly, or indirectly (eparent) on t-node $n2, which is a verb. $n0 has a textual coreference with $n1, which in turn has a grammatical coreference with $n3.[8]

3.2 Actors and Actions

Tables 1 and 2 report respectively the main Actions and the main Actors in BC. These are defined as the Actions performed by the highest number of different Actors and, conversely, as the Actors that perform the highest number of different Actions.[9]

---

[8]The longest coreference chain we found in BC includes 5 textual coreferences.

[9]The absence of verbs like *possum* ("can") and *volo, velle* ("to want") in Table 1 is due to the treatment of modal predicates in TGTS (see Mikulová et al., 2006, pages 318-320). Not coreferred Actors are excluded from Table 2. These are the generic Actor (#Gen) and those pronouns that do not undergo coreference analysis in TGTSs, i.e. indefinite and interrogative pronouns (like *alius* and *quis*), as well as both explicit and generated personal pronouns of first and second person.

Action	Actors	Occ.	Generated
sum	179	268	38
habeo	43	84	10
facio	39	87	4
convenio	20	8	2
dico	18	41	9
do	18	22	3
hortor	16	11	2
venio	14	11	0
coepio	13	18	7
puto	13	10	0
peto	13	12	0
cognosco	13	20	0

Table 1: Main Actions.

Action	Actors	Occ.	Generated
catilina	133	61	6
cicero	33	18	0
homo	32	40	3
res	24	147	4
petreius	20	3	0
lentulus	20	27	6
consul	20	32	0
caesar	20	13	0
populus	19	18	0
curius	19	5	0
vulturcius	18	10	0
vir	18	16	0
animus	18	59	2

Table 2: Main Actors.

Beside Actions and the number of their different Actors, Table 1 reports also the total number of occurrences of each Action and, among these, the number of generated occurrences (resulting from ellipsis resolution). The case of *convenio* ("to come together") is worth noting, as it turns out that it has 20 different Actors for just 8 occurrences (2 of which are generated). This happens because in some of its occurrences *convenio* has more than one Actor, like for instance in the sentence "eo [there] convenere [to come together] senatorii [senatorial] ordinis [order] P. Lentulus Sura , P. Autronius , L. Cassius Longinus , C. Cethegus , P. et Ser . Sullae Ser. filii , L. Vargunteius , Q. Annius , M. Porcius Laeca , L. Bestia , Q. Curius" (BC 17.3) ("There were present from the senatorial order...").

Not surprisingly, Catiline is the star of BC, being the Actor of 133 different Actions (i.e. verbs) in 61 occurrences (6 out of which are generated). Traditionally, together with Catiline, the three other main characters of BC are considered to be Caesar, Cato and Cicero, who give the main speeches reported in the text. If we look at the Actions each of them performs and focus on those that Catiline only performs (i.e. those not shared with the others), we can see which Actions are peculiar of Catiline. These are represented by the verbs *dimitto* ("to send out") and *paro* ("to prepare").

Interestingly enough, *dimitto* and *paro* not only correspond to the Actions performed by Catiline only (and not also by Caesar, Cato or Cicero), but they are also those Actions that Catiline most frequently performs (6 times), just after *facio* ("to make") (10) and *habeo* ("to have") (7), and more than *sum* ("to be") (5) and *video* ("to see") (5). If for *dimitto* this result is biased by a case of ellipsis resolution applied on a multiple coordination in one sentence (BC 27.1), *paro* offers a wider range of occurrences. By exploiting semantic role labeling, we can know what Catiline prepares in BC. The most frequent Patients of the occurrences of *paro* in BC with Catiline as Actor are the following: *arma* ("implements of war", "weapons"), *incendium* ("burning"), *insidiae* ("trap") and *interficio* ("to destroy"). Indeed, Catiline is a bad guy in BC.

Given that Catiline plays the role of Actor in BC more than three times more than Cicero, one can expect that most of the Actions performed by Cicero are common with Catiline and that these Actions are more frequently performed by Catiline than Cicero. Actually, there are some deviations from such trend. The most clear example is the verb *refero* ("to bear back", "to report"), whose Actor is Cicero in two occurrences while Catiline does never perform it. Moreover, there are three verbs that feature Cicero as Actor more than once and more than Catiline. These are *cognosco* ("to know") and *praecipio* ("to take in advance", "to warn"). Both these verbs have Cicero as Actor twice and Catiline once. Finally, the Action most frequently performed by Cicero (3) is represented by the verb *iubeo* ("to give an order", "to command"). Also Catiline is Actor of *iubeo*, but only in two occurrences.

In order to understand if the Actors reported in Table 2 can be properly organized into homogeneous groups defined by the Actions of them, we performed a clustering analysis of the results.

3.3 Clustering the Actors

Clustering is the process of organizing objects ("observations") into groups ("clusters") whose members are similar in some way. One of trickiest issues in clustering is to define what 'similarity' means and to find a clustering algorithm that computes efficiently the degree of similarity between two objects that are being compared.

Hierarchical clustering is a specific method of cluster analysis that seeks to build a hierarchy of clusters. Hierarchical clustering can be performed by following two main strategies: (a) agglomerative (bottom-up): each observation starts in its own cluster, and pairs of clusters are merged as one moves up the hierarchy; (b) divisive (top-down): all observations start in one cluster, and splits are performed recursively as one moves down the hierarchy.

In this work, we apply hierarchical agglomerative clustering to compute the degree of similarity/dissimilarity between the Actors reported in Table 2. Such degree is obtained by comparing Actors by the Actions they perform. First, we compute the amount of shared and non-shared Actions between the members of all the possible couples of Actors. Then, we compare the distribution of shared and not shared Actions by their relative frequency.[10] As for the distance measure, the analysis is run on document-term matrices by using the cosine distance[11]

$$d(i;\, i') = 1 - \cos\{(x_{i1}, x_{i2}, ..., x_{ik}), (x_{i'1}, x_{i'2}, ..., x_{i'k})\}\,.$$

The arguments of the *cosine* function in the preceding relationship are two rows, i and i', in a document-term matrix; x_{ij} and $x_{i'j}$ provide the number of occurrences of verb j ($j = 1$, ..., k) in the two sets of Actions corresponding to rows i and i' ("profiles"). Zero distance between two sets (cosine = 1) holds when two sets with the same profile are concerned (i.e. they have the same relative conditional distributions of terms). In the opposite case, if two sets do not share any word, the corresponding profiles have maximum distance (cosine = 0).

As for clustering, we run a "complete" linkage agglomeration method. While building clusters by agglomeration, at each stage the distance (similarity) between clusters is determined by the distance (similarity) between the two elements, one from each cluster, that are most distant. Thus, complete linkage ensures that all items in a cluster are within some maximum distance (or minimum similarity) to each other.

Roughly speaking, according to our clustering method, Actors that share a high number of Actions with similar distribution are considered to have a high degree of similarity and, thus, fall into the same or related clusters. Figure 4 plots the results and includes three main clusters.

Moving from top to bottom, the first cluster includes the two most similar Actors according to the Actions they perform. These are *cicero* and *consul* ("consul"). This happens although BC includes several occurrences of *consul* that are not referred to Cicero. Actually, Marcus Tullius Cicero is the consul par excellence in Roman political history and he was the only consul among the Actors considered here, as Caesar would become consul for the first time in 59 BCE, four years after the facts told in BC. The second most similar couple of Actors is the one including *catilina* and *lentulus* (similar at height 0.76). Catiline was the one who devised the conspiracy narrated in BC. Publius Cornelius Lentulus was one of the main conspirators. In particular, he took the place of Catiline as chief of the conspirators in Rome, when Catiline had to leave the city after the famous second speech of Cicero *In Catilinam*. The two characters are, thus, strictly related. In the same larger cluster are *curius* and *populus* ("people"). Quintus Curius was another conspirator, although his role was actually ambivalent. Being a friend of Catiline, he took part in the conspiracy, but at the same time it was because of him that it was foiled. According to Sallust, Curius, to boast with his mistress Fulvia, told her the details of the conspiracy, which she informed Cicero about. Moreover, Curius accused Caesar of being a conspirator. Such an undefined role is played also by "the people". In those passages where Sallust talks about "the Roman people" ("populus romanus"), these are mostly positively depicted. Conversely, there are also places in

---

[10]All the experiments were performed with the R statistical software (R Development Core Team, 2012). More details on the clustering method used here are in Passarotti and Cantaluppi (2016).

[11]A document-term matrix is a mathematical matrix that holds frequencies of distinct terms for each document. In a document-term matrix, rows correspond to documents in the collection and columns correspond to terms.

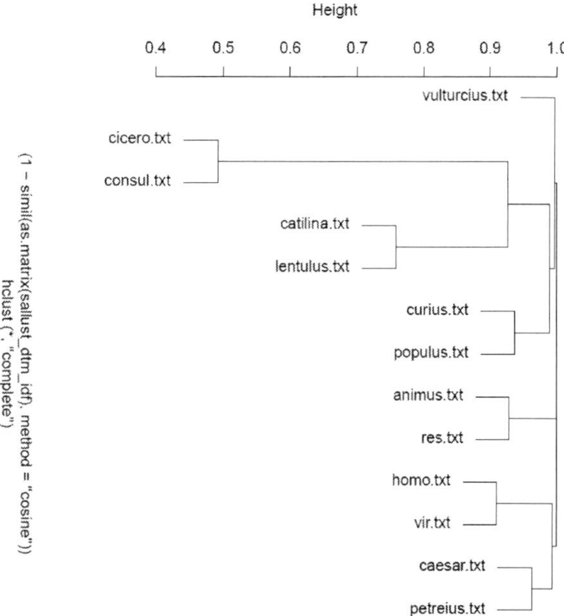

Figure 4: Clustering the Actors.

BC where the people act badly. Finally, Titus Vulturcius, a conspirator playing a subordinate role in the plot, falls into the same cluster, standing quite apart from the others.

The second cluster includes just two lemmas: *animus* ("soul") and *res* ("thing"). These are the only not human Actors, among the ones considered here.

The third cluster features two couples of Actors. The first includes lemmas *homo* ("human being", "man") and *vir* ("adult male", "man"), which are semantically strictly related, standing in hypernym/hyponym relation. The second couple is formed by *petreius* and *caesar*. Marcus Petreius plays a positive role in BC, having led the senatorial forces in the victory over Catiline in Pistoia. It is worth noting that such a positive character in the plot gets clustered together with Caesar. The future dictator Gaius Iulius Caesar hoped for the success of the second conspiracy of Catiline, just like he did for the first. However, Sallust's intent is to lift Caesar of any suspicion of a possible link with Catiline. He emphasizes the Caesar's concern for legality, depicting him (together with Cato) as the faithful guardian of "mos maiorum", the core, unwritten code of Roman traditionalism. Putting Caesar under such a positive light is strictly connected to the fact that, while BC was being written, Caesar was deified by decree of the Roman Senate (on 1st January 42 BCE), after his assassin on the Ides of March 44 BCE.

4   Conclusion

The work described in this paper represents a case study showing how much useful a treebank enhanced with semantic annotation can be for literary studies. In this respect, there is still much to do. On one side, still too few literary texts provided with such annotation layer are currently available. On the other, the use of linguistic resources like treebanks remains dramatically confined in the area of computational and theoretical linguistics, not impacting other communities which might largely benefit from such resources.

To overcome the former, one desideratum is building NLP tools able to provide good accuracy rates of semantic annotation across different domains. As for the latter, developers of treebanks based on literary data and/or texts written in ancient languages must more and more get in touch with different kinds of domain experts from the Humanities, like philologists, historical linguists, philosophers, historians and scholars in literature. Indeed, across the last few years, this looks like a growing trend, with several events and special issues of scientific journals dedicated to different topics in computational linguistics and the Humanities. We hope that this is just the beginning of a fruitful joint work.

References

Axel W. Ahlberg. 1919. *C. Sallusti Crispi. Catiline, Iugurtha, Orationes Et Epistulae Excerptae De Historiis.* Teubner, Leipzig.

David Bamman and Gregory Crane. 2011. The Ancient Greek and Latin dependency treebanks. In *Language Technology for Cultural Heritage*. Springer, pages 79–98.

David Bamman, Marco Passarotti, Gregory Crane, and Savina Raynaud. 2007. *Guidelines for the Syntactic Annotation of Latin Treebanks.* Tufts University Digital Library, Boston, MA.

Berta González Saavedra and Marco Passarotti. 2014. Challenges in enhancing the Index Thomisticus treebank with semantic and pragmatic annotation. In *Proceedings of the Thirteenth International Workshop on Treebanks and Linguistic Theories (TLT-13)*. Department of Linguistics, University of Tübingen, pages 265–270.

Jan Hajič, Alena Böhmová, Eva Hajičová, and Barbora Vidová Hladká. 2000. The Prague dependency treebank: A three-level annotation scenario. In *Treebanks: Building and Using Parsed Corpora*. Kluwer, pages 103–127.

Dag Haug and Marius Jøhndal. 2008. Creating a parallel treebank of the old Indo-European Bible translations. In *Proceedings of the Language Technology for Cultural Heritage Data Workshop (LaTeCH 2008)*. ELRA, pages 27–34.

Marie Mikulová et al. 2006. *Annotation on the Tectogrammatical Layer in the Prague Dependency Treebank.* Institute of Formal and Applied Linguistics, Prague, Czech Republic.

Marco Passarotti. 2011. Language resources. The state of the art of Latin and the Index Thomisticus treebank project. In *Corpus anciens et Bases de donnes,*. Presses universitaires de Nancy, pages 301–320.

Marco Passarotti and Gabriele Cantaluppi. 2016. A statistical investigation into the corpus of Seneca. In *Latinitatis Rationes. Descriptive and Historical Accounts for the Latin Language*. De Gruyter, pages 684–706.

R Development Core Team. 2012. *R: A language and environment for statistical computing.* Foundation for Statistical Computing, Vienna, Austria.

John T. Ramsey. 2014. *Sallust. The war with Catiline. The war with Jugurtha.* Harvard University Press, The Loeb Classical Library 116, Cambridge, MA.

Petr Sgall, Eva Hajičová, and Jarmila Panevová. 1986. *The Meaning of the Sentence in its Semantic and Pragmatic Aspects*. D. Reidel, Dordrecht, NL.

Jan Štěpánek and Petr Pajas. 2010. Querying diverse treebanks in a uniform way. In *Proceedings of the Seventh conference on International Language Resources and Evaluation (LREC 2010)*. ELRA, pages 1828–1835.

Zdeněk Žabokrtský. 2011. Treex – an open-source framework for natural language processing. In *Information Technologies Applications and Theory*. Univerzita Pavla Jozefa Šafárika v Košiciach, pages 7–14.

Universal Dependencies-based syntactic features in detecting human translation varieties

Maria Kunilovskaya
Institute for the Humanities and Social Sciences
University of Tyumen
Tyumen, Russia
m.a.kunilovskaya@utmn.ru

Andrey Kutuzov
Department of Informatics
University of Oslo
Oslo, Norway
andreku@ifi.uio.no

Abstract

In this paper, syntactic annotation is used to reveal linguistic properties of translations. We employ the Universal Dependencies framework to represent learner and professional translations of English mass-media texts into Russian (along with non-translated Russian texts of the same genre) with the aim to discover and describe syntactic specificity of translations produced at different levels of competence. The search for differences between varieties of translation and the native texts is augmented with the results obtained from a series of machine learning classifications experiments. We show that syntactic structures have considerable predictive power in translationese detection, on par with the known low-level lexical features.

1 Introduction

This research aims to detect distinctive syntactic properties of learner and professional translations from English into Russian when compared to the originally authored texts in Russian. The contrasts between them can provide insights into translation quality and be informative in translator education as well as machine translation design.

It is known from previous studies that translations differ from non-translations at all levels of language hierarchy. These linguistic differences are usually referred to as *translationese* (Gellerstam, 1986), and text production processes behind them are explained within the theory of translation universals (Baker, 1993). Quantitative specificity of translated texts is used in translationese detection and classification. It has been shown that learning systems can achieve high performance on shallow data representations (Baroni and Bernardini, 2006), and character n-grams work best (Popescu, 2011).

However, features useful for machine learning algorithms are often difficult to interpret linguistically. At the same time, it is important to know what gives translations their peculiar foreign sound. This knowledge will promote our ability to counteract it, if we want to produce more natural texts in the target language, as well as our awareness of typical linguistic behavior in the situations of language contact.

The concept of translation quality is inherently connected to the idea of translationese. In the most common case of informational texts, we expect translations to blend well with the rest of genre-comparable texts in that language. *Fluency*, the property of translation to read as natural as a non-translation, is one of the three major criteria of translation evaluation, along with *adequacy* and *fidelity* (Secară, 2005). It means that we can use proximity to the reference non-translations as a measure for this component of translation quality. The question remains whether all machine detected differences between translations and non-translations reflect a reduction in fluency and readability. Therefore, it is useful to test the findings on the basis of some external labels or markers of quality. In our research setup we represent translation quality classes by professional and learner translations assuming that translations produced at different levels of competence differ in terms of quality.

In this work we explore the use of syntactic features as possible indicators of translationese for modeling a classifier able to distinguish between novice and professional translators (or between translations and non-translations). Machine classification is used here as an exploratory technique: after we establish the appropriateness of syntactic representations for the purposes of text classification, we identify the most

27

Proceedings of the 16th International Workshop on Treebanks and Linguistic Theories (TLT16), pages 27–36,
Prague, Czech Republic, January 23–24, 2018. Distributed under a CC-BY 4.0 licence. 2017.

Keywords: human translation varieties, translation classification, syntactic features, UD

informative features and test their validity in contrastive and comparative linguistic analysis of our data. This is one of the reasons why we don't use modern neural methods (like LSTMs, for example) working directly on sequences of words or characters: we need interpretable features in this setup. Thus, we rely on more old-fashioned classifiers like SVM.

We use Universal Dependencies (UD) framework (Nivre et al., 2016) in our syntactic analysis. It is a linguistically-motivated initiative aimed to facilitate multilingual research by offering a universal approach to represent and compare sentence structures. Besides, UD provides a better account for free word order languages such as Russian (Jurafsky and Martin, 2014), and gives direct access to annotated treebanks. Unlike previous work in the field of translationese detection and classification, we make use of truly syntactic properties of sentences as defined in Dependency Grammar, not their PoS n-gram emulations or similar quasi-syntactic approaches.

2   Research questions

We are designing a learning system as a heuristic approach to establish syntactic specificity of translations with the view of using their most distinctive syntactic properties as tools in translation quality assessment. Our research questions can be put as follows:

1. Can translated texts be distinguished from non-translations based on syntactic features, given their UD-based representation described below?

2. Are there machine-learnable syntactic differences between translations produced by learner translators and by professionals?

3. If yes to any of the above questions, which features are most correlated with the text class?

4. How can these features be explained by contrastive analysis and translation universals theory?

We resort to comparative and contrastive analyses to offer linguistic explanation for the experimental findings. To this end, we analyze the distributions of features in the sentences, compare them with the respective source segments and typify the results. In this part we are guided by findings within corpus-based translation studies and contrastive knowledge for the given language pair.

3   Related work

Previous work on translation quality assessment (TQA), translational expertise, translationese detection, translation universals and parsing is abundant. There is research that establishes links between the areas of study above. For example, Aharoni (2015) demonstrates that accuracy of translationese detection depends on the quality of machine translation.

One particularly relevant study on machine classification of translations produced at different levels of expertise is Rubino et al. (2016). To solve the task of distinguishing student and professional translations from each other and from originally authored texts, the authors use four distinct feature sets: traditional surface characteristics of sentences (words with mixed-case characters, sentence length, number of punctuation marks) and three sets inspired by information density theory and machine quality estimation. The research is focused on evaluating feature importance and returns mixed results as to what can be used to predict translation experience. In the binary classification (learners vs professionals) their approach achieves the average F1 score of 58.5%.

The assumption that levels of competence (defined extra-linguistically) and practices used in the process influence the quality of the product are corroborated in Carl and Buch-Kromann (2010), who also show that the differences between learners and professionals lie mostly in text fluency. Lapshinova-Koltunski (2017) finds that differences between translational varieties (represented in the author's research as human and machine translations) with regard to the degree and types of cohesion are smaller than between translations and originally authored texts.

Research in translationese detection increasingly relies on utilizing linguistically reasonable (interpretable) features of text as opposed to 'unreasonably effective' character n-grams (Volansky et al.,

2015). Research of this kind uses delexicalized syntactic features to solve the tasks related to translationese detection (Laippala et al., 2015) and classification (Rubino et al., 2016; Rabinovich et al., 2017). One of the feature sets in Laippala et al. (2015) consists of PoS bigrams and trigrams enriched not only with morphological features, but also with syntactic relations extracted from dependency grammar based syntactic trees. This feature set, however, performs slightly worse than PoS with morphological features.

4 Data, features and experimental setup

4.1 Corpus resources and parsing

Our experiments are based on two aligned parallel corpora that contain learner and professional English-to-Russian translations of mass-media texts in a variety of topical domains and a genre-comparable collection of non-translated data.

1. Learner component was sourced from the *Russian Learner Translator Corpus*[1] (Kutuzov and Kunilovskaya, 2014) via filtering by genre.

2. Professional translations were collected from a range of well-established digital mass media such as *Nezavisimaya Gazeta* and *InoSMI.RU* or Russian editions of global mass media such as *Forbes*. All professional translations either have the translator's name or are endorsed by the editing board. Originals for both translational collections come from roughly the same pool of English and American editions (*The Guardian, the New York Times, the Economist, Popular Mechanics*, etc) and were published between 2001 and 2016.

3. The reference corpus consists of the texts from the *Russian National Corpus*[2] (further RNC) belonging to the '*article intended for large adult non-specialist readership*' type; all texts are written after 2003 and are marked as style-neutral.

The Russian texts were tagged and parsed with the *UDPipe 1.2* model (Straka and Straková, 2017) which we trained on the *SynTagRus* treebank from the Universal Dependencies 2.1 release (Dyachenko P.V., 2015; Droganova and Zeman, 2016). The model achieves UAS 89.96 and LAS 87.42 on the corresponding UD2.1 test set. Sentences shorter than 3 words, with disconnected dependency trees, or containing '*root*' relations only, were filtered out, as well as punctuation and null nodes (in case of ellipsis).

Table 1 presents the statistics of the corpora used. With regard to the average sentence length, the translational corpora are significantly different from the RNC at 0.05 level of confidence, while there is no such difference between learner and professional translations.

	Learners translators		Professional translators		RNC
	sources	targets	sources	targets	
Size (tokens)	222 911	204 787	345 843	320 198	3 215 242
No. of sentences	10 345	9 899	14 595	14 427	153 691
Sentence length (averaged over texts)	23.56	22.41	24.15	22.67	21.29
No. of texts	200		200		1 562

Table 1: Basic corpora statistics (after preprocessing and parsing)

4.2 Methodology

We represent texts as feature vectors, produced by averaging the feature vectors of individual sentences in the text. The majority of our features are the UD syntactic relations. Values for syntactic relations are represented as their sentence-level probabilities, i.e. the ratio of the number of occurrences of a given

[1]https://www.rus-ltc.org/
[2]http://www.ruscorpora.ru/en

relation in the sentence to the number of occurrences of all other relations in the same sentence, averaged over all sentences in each text in a corpus. Given this approach to normalizing the data, the *root* relation actually contains only the information on the sentence length: there is only one *root* in each sentence and its probability is contingent on the number of other relations in the sentence, which in its turn equals the number of words in this sentence. As our aim is to detect purely syntactic relations useful for translation classification, we excluded *root* from the feature set. Additional features included basic graph statistics for dependency trees.

Here we present the full list of our 45 features:

- 34 UD dependencies

    - normalized to represent sentence-level probabilities of each particular relation;

- 7 features characterizing abstract structural properties of the dependency graph:

    - average out-degree, maximal out-degree, number of communities in the graph (by the Newman's leading eigenvector method), average community size (in nodes), average path length, density and diameter of the graph;

- 4 other tree complexity measures, calculated from the parsed data:

    - mean hierarchical distance (MHD), suggested in Jing and Liu (2015);
    - mean dependency distance (MDD), defined as 'distance between words and their parents, measured in terms of intervening words' (Hudson, 1995);
    - probability of non-projective arcs;
    - average number of non-projective sentences.

Machine learning classifiers were trained to separate non-translations from translated texts as a single class and to distinguish different translation varieties from each other and from non-translations. We attempt classification into learner and professional translations to see whether we can find a way to predict professional expertise based on the features suggested.

After a series of development experiments we chose the SVM multinomial classification algorithm with balanced class weights. It was shown to score high in various NLP tasks, including translationese detection, in a number of publications, starting with the ground-breaking Baroni and Bernardini (2006). Before training, the feature values were standardized to have zero mean and unit variance of 1.

For comparison, we also report results of a simple baseline system similar to syntactic component in Pastor et al. (2008). It uses bags of part-of-speech trigrams (*'SCONJ PROPN VERB'*, *'NOUN NOUN ADJ'*, etc) as feature vectors for each document, with the values of features being the frequencies of particular trigrams in a given document. Pastor et al. (2008) refer to Nerbonne and Wiersma (2006) motivating their choice of n-gram size. These values were standardized in the same way as the syntactic ones and then fed to the same SVM classifier. Note that this approach produces thousands of features, and thus is considerably more computationally expensive than the one with the syntax features.

5   Results

We calculated macro-F1 score for each classification task using stratified 10-fold cross-validation. The results are presented in Table 2.

The classifiers based on syntactic features perform better (and are trained about 70 times faster) than the PoS-trigrams baseline in all scenarios except when discriminating learner translations from professional ones. In the case of 3-class classification with the full set of features, the two approaches are on par, with the syntactic feature set still outperforming the baseline when only 10 best features are used. Thus, English-to-Russian translations are indeed different from non-translated Russian in their syntactic structures. However, translations produced at different skill levels in addition demonstrate differences in the tier of surface word type sequences. Note also that all our results are considerably higher than those

	Binary classification				**3-class**
	translations/RNC	*learners/RNC*	*prof/RNC*	*learners/prof*	
10 best features					
PoS trigrams baseline	0.735	0.738	0.658	**0.791**	0.603
Syntactic features	**0.818**	**0.796**	**0.740**	0.721	**0.635**
all features					
PoS trigrams baseline	0.820	0.820	0.797	**0.806**	0.707
Syntactic features	**0.866**	**0.841**	**0.871**	0.703	0.707

Table 2: Macro-F1 scores for the classifiers on different feature sets

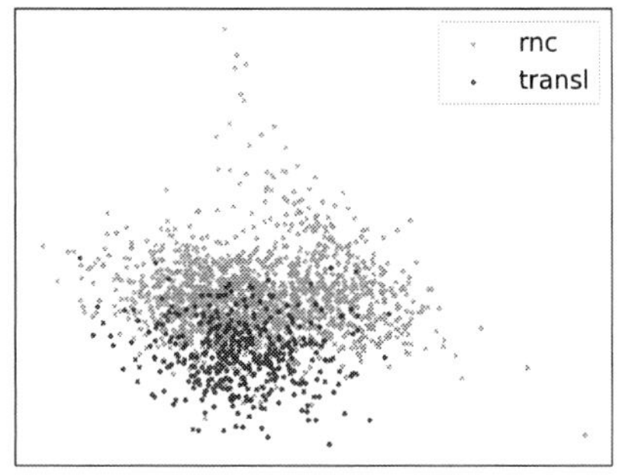

Figure 1: Non-translations (RNC) and translations, syntactic feature space

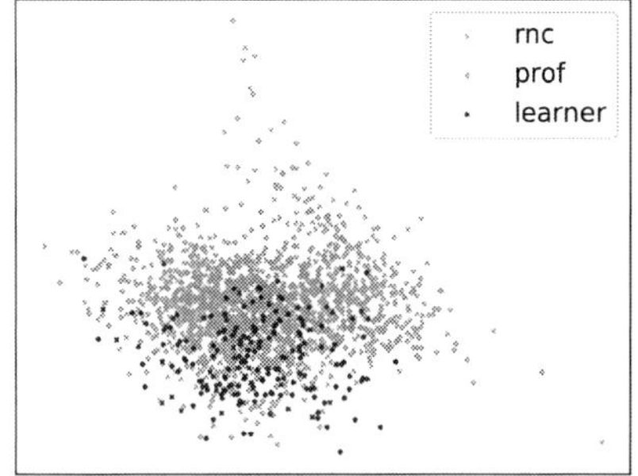

Figure 2: Non-translations (RNC), professional and learner translations, syntactic feature space

reported in Rubino et al. (2016) with a rich set of diverse features including complexity and perplexity in the language models (but with no 'deep' syntactic features)[3].

Figures 1 and 2 visualize the documents in our training data projected from the initial 45-dimensional syntactic feature space into 2 dimensions with PCA (Tipping and Bishop, 1999). For comparison, figures 3 and 4 present similar projections from the PoS-trigrams 2704-dimensional feature space. It can be seen that the texts represented with PoS are much less discernible with regard to our classes: all documents are densely grouped together, with little difference between instances of different types. At the same time, with the syntactic features the documents are distinct from each other and the instances are distributed across the feature space much more uniformly. One can observe a clear tendency for translations to be 'shifted' to a region where non-translations are very rare, and vice versa.

5.1 Best features

The three classifiers that compare translations with the Russian reference corpus rely on the same set of features. The most useful features (in terms of their ANOVA F-value against the class of the text) are listed in Table 3 along with the ratio of their probabilities for each pair of corpora, which indicate the direction and size of discrepancies (all of them are statistically significant).

The set of features that were identified as most useful reflects various aspects of more complex syntax typical for translated sentences (for example, higher probability of clauses). Only three of the features highly correlated with 'translation/non-translation' classes appeared useful in the more difficult task of classifying translational varieties (*'nsubj:pass'*, *'xcomp'* and *'acl:relcl'*).

---

[3]Of course, their results are not directly comparable to ours, as they worked with English-to-German translations.

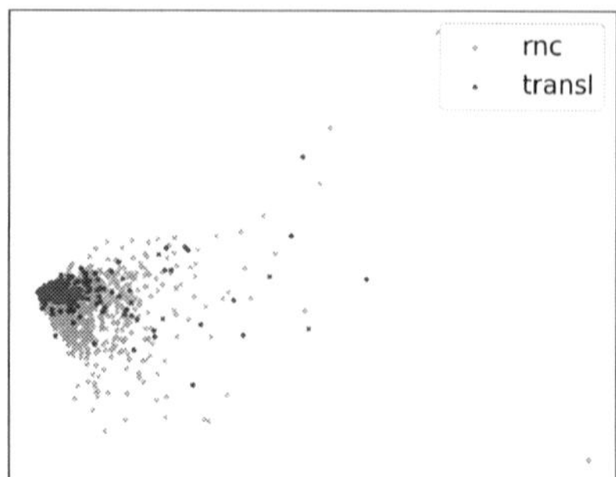

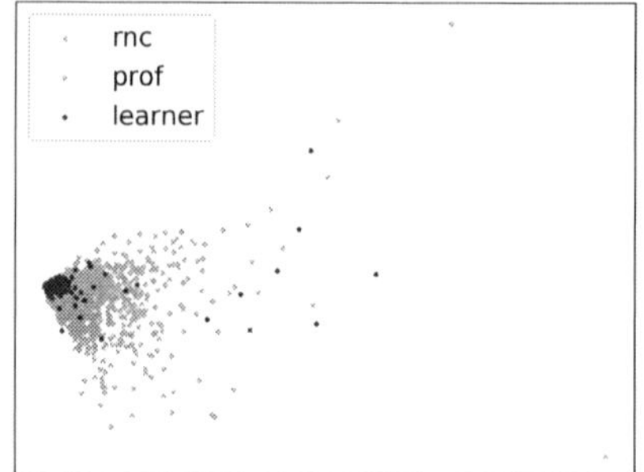

Figure 3: Non-translations (RNC) and translations, PoS feature space

Figure 4: Non-translations (RNC), professional and learner translations, PoS feature space

feature	learners/RNC	prof/RNC
mark	1.86	1.85
ccomp	2.09	2.28
acl:relcl	1.92	1.68
advcl	1.73	1.68
nsubj	1.29	1.34
parataxis	0.66	0.74
aux	2.08	2.29
xcomp	1.44	1.60
obj	1.29	1.33
nsubj:pass	0.62	0.46

feature	learners/prof
nmod	1.11
aux:pass	1.63
nsubj:pass	1.35
iobj	0.82
flat:foreign	0.60
parataxis	0.89
fixed	1.16
acl:relcl	1.14
cc	0.93
xcomp	0.90

Table 3: Most useful features and the ratio of their probabilities in the data

6 Case studies

6.1 Syntactic complication: more fully expressed subordinate clauses

The most useful features in translations vs originally authored texts classifications (including 3-way classification) have to do with the higher probability of dependent clauses (*mark, ccomp, advcl, acl:relcl*). The strong correlation between *mark, nsubj* and relative and adverbial clauses suggests that translators tend to produce complex sentences more often than in naturally occurring Russian texts. They reproduce explicit pronominal subjects in the subordinate clauses, though in Russian they can often be left out. Five lexical items that head the frequency list of *nsubj* dependents (который ('which/that'), это ('this/it'), он ('he/it'), они ('they'), вы ('you')) are 2 to 3 times more frequent in translations that in non-translations. Example 1 gives a typical student translation that transfers the English structural pattern.

(1) ...человек на улице не думает о   ЕС когда он входит в торговый центр
    ...the man in street not think   about EU *when he* enters in shopping   center
    Source: '... the man on the street is not thinking about EU *as he* enters a shopping centre.'

Besides, the clauses are more often joined with explicit subordinating conjunctions to the detriment to other options such as punctuation. This finding corroborates the explicitation hypothesis in translational behavior (Blum-Kulka, 1986) and aligns well with extensive research on cohesive explicitation in translation (Kamenická, 2007; Cartoni and Zufferey, 2011; Becher, 2011).

6.2 *xcomp*: transfer of compound verbal predicates, particularly modal ones

The probability of open clausal complement (*xcomp*) in translations with regard to all other relations in the corpus is on average 1.5 times higher than in the reference corpus. This dependency describes relations between a verb and its adjectival or non-verbal complement. For English it captures complex object constructions and strings with catenative verbs as heads (including verbs with modal semantics such as *need to, have to, be going to, be able to*, but excluding modal auxiliaries) (Huddleston and Pullum, 2002). In Russian, it includes relations with the modal verb мочь ('can') and combinations with aspect and causative catenatives among others (начать учить петь ('to start to teach to sing'). The parser routinely assigns this relation to a verb and a deverbal noun (хоронить погибших ('to bury the deceased'). Despite these discrepancies in the parsing strategies, the cross-linguistic comparison shows that English uses this dependency 1.4 times as often as Russian (1.5% and 1.1% respectively, with the average probability of this relation for the translational corpora being 1.7%).

To find out which constructions drive up the probability of *xcomp* in translations, we looked at the semantic types of the top 25 head verbs in this relation. These cases account for 83% of all occurrences of this dependency in the learner corpus, for 77% in professional translations and for 73% in the RNC. English head nodes in this dependency are much more varied and lexically unrestricted than in Russian. The same 25 head nodes make up 59% of all occurrences of this relation. The structure of the frequency lists for translational corpora is a clear indication of the translational simplification in the form of higher lexical repetitiveness. Translations manage to cover more text with a smaller and less varied set of items.

We found that in translations, notably in learner translations, modal auxiliaries make up 55% of this top of the list in the learners corpus, with мочь ('can') alone covering 45% of all *xcomp*, while in professional translations it is 37% and in non-translated Russian text it is 32%. Another explanation for the increase of *xcomp* relations is the tendency to reproduce English non-finite constructions, especially with causative and aspect verbs as in example 2 from student translations:

(2) Многие десятилетия терроризм продолжал ассоциироваться...
Many   decades   terrorism   *continued   to-be-associated...*
Source: 'Terrorism *continued* for many decades *to be associated* primarily with the assassination of political leaders and heads of state.'

6.3 Passives: more analytical structures

In both translational corpora there are fewer dependencies marked *nsubj:pass* than in the non-translated reference corpus. Learner translations are 1.6 times short of this relation, while professional translations have 2.2 times less of it. This feature is among the 10 most well-correlated with the predicted class in two binary classifications (professionals/RNC and learner/professionals), as well as in the 3-way classification.

It makes sense to consider the values for *aux:pass* together with the above feature. This relation is more probable in student translations than in the output of professionals. The translational varieties appear to be at different sides from the reference corpus, with learners slightly overusing passive auxiliaries (1.4 times more of this dependency) and professionals underusing them (1.2 times less). This discrepancy between two translation varieties makes it one of the most useful features for predicting expertise.

In Russian, the choice of passive constructions is dependent on morphological properties of verbs, particularly on their aspect. The relations between semantic subject and object are mostly realized either by verb forms with the special formant -ся/-сь (imperfective verbs) or by passive participle in the short form with or without the analytical verb быть (*to be*) (perfective verbs). This gives a translator a variety of choices to render the single English grammatical meaning of passive, if she decides that this meaning needs to be rendered. For example, '*The house was built*' has options 'Дом построен' ('*the house is built*'), 'Дом был построен ('*the house was built*'), 'Дом строился' ('*the house was being built*').

To untangle the reasons behind the discrepancies in the distribution of passive auxiliaries and subjects, we looked at the proportions of analytical and the two morphological passives in translated and originally authored Russian. Contrastive analysis showed that English mass-media texts have less passive verbs than comparable Russian discourse. In our data, passive occurred in 15.9% of English sentences, while original Russian texts had 18.6% of passive sentences on average. Analytical passives were used only in every forth passive construction.

In translational data, however, the proportion of passives dropped to 15% and 11% to the number of sentences in the corpus for learner and professional translations respectively. Both groups of translators use more analytical passives, driving up their ratio to all passives from 25% in the RNC to 38% and 35% in learners' and professional data. With that, professionals, when choosing between passive forms, tend to use more forms with -ся/-сь than short past participles. In this corpus, their ratio to other passives is 3% higher than in the learners' output.

7   Discussion

We showed that syntactic representation of translational data is a useful way to approach automatic classification, and the features useful for the classifiers lend themselves to linguistic interpretation. One major finding yielded by this research is the tendency to increase the number of clauses (particularly relative clauses) typical for translated Russian. With that, these clauses tend to express all structural components, particularly conjunctions and subjects, explicitly.

Cross-linguistic comparisons confirm that strings of non-finite verbs joined with two consecutive *xcomp* arcs in the sentence tree (*'Krugman added cartoons to try to make opponents look silly'*) are more common in English than in Russian. In English-to-Russian translations this type of syntactic relation tends to be overrepresented (the average sentence-level probabilities of this relation are 1.7% and 1.1% for translations and Russian non-translations respectively), indicating a possible translationese-prone area. It is particularly true for sentences with the compound modal or aspect predicate.

The specificity of verbal elements in translations included a distinctive distribution of passive forms in translated Russian. We revealed higher proportion of analytical passives in professional, and especially in learner translations. Both translation varieties had less passives than the comparable Russian non-translations, with professional translations being further away from them and having 1.6 times less passive constructions. This trend may reflect the translational norm to avoid passives whenever possible or to rely more on syntactic rather than analytical forms. Educational and normative guidelines on English-to-Russian translation often warn against the overuse of passives (Moiseenko, 2012).

8   Conclusion

This research used syntactic annotation in the task of translation classification with the view to reveal syntactic specificity of translation varieties represented by learner and professional translations. We have compared our results with the PoS-trigrams baseline and have shown that syntactic representations are a fruitful way forward. We focused our attention on predicting translation expertise which is a fairly new area of research, exemplified by (Rubino et al., 2016) only.

The few cases tackled in this study just scratched the top of possibilities offered by the approach. We plan to continue research on syntactic properties of translations in several ways. First, it seems reasonable to use more refined morphosyntactic features as suggested in (Lapshinova-Koltunski, 2017) to provide algorithms with better learning material. Second, the UD framework makes it possible to take into account the linear order of heads and dependents in a relation and the order of relations in the sentence, which looks promising. Another possible extension is studying the role of disconnected parse trees in telling translations from non-translations. Finally, we would like to employ parallel nature of our corpora in a more meaningful way and describe translationese-prone areas in English-Russian translation based on cross-linguistic analysis of the aligned data.

Acknowledgements

This work was supported in part by a grant (Reference No. 17-06-00107) from the *Russian Foundation for Basic Research* (RFBR).

References

Roee Aharoni. 2015. *Automatic Detection of Machine Translated Text and Translation Quality Estimation*. Ph.D. thesis.

Mona Baker. 1993. Corpus Linguistics and Translation Studies: Implications and Applications. In *Text and Technology: In honour of John Sinclair*, J. Benjamins, Amsterdam, pages 232–250.

Marco Baroni and Silvia Bernardini. 2006. A new approach to the study of translationese: Machine-learning the difference between original and translated text. *Literary and Linguistic Computing* 21(3):259–274.

Viktor Becher. 2011. *Explicitation and implicitation in translation. A corpus-based study of English-German and German-English translations of business texts*. Ph.D. thesis.

Shoshana Blum-Kulka. 1986. Shifts of cohesion and coherence in translation. *Interlingual and intercultural communication: Discourse and cognition in translation and second language acquisition studies* pages 17–35.

Michael Carl and Matthias Buch-Kromann. 2010. Correlating translation product and translation process data of professional and student translators. *14 Annual Conference of the European Association for Machine Translation, Saint-Raphaël, France* (May).

Bruno Cartoni and S Zufferey. 2011. How comparable are parallel corpora? Measuring the distribution of general vocabulary and connectives. *Proceedings of the 4th Workshop on Building and Using Comparable Corpora: Comparable Corpora and the Web* (June):78–86.

Kira Droganova and Daniel Zeman. 2016. Conversion of SynTagRus (the Russian dependency treebank) to Universal Dependencies. Technical report, Institute of Formal and Applied Linguistics (ÚFAL MFF UK) Faculty of Mathematics and Physics, Charles University.

Iomdin L.L. Lazursky A.V. Dyachenko P.V. 2015. A deeply annotated corpus of Russian texts (SynTagRus): contemporary state of affairs. *Trudy Instituta Russkogo Yazyka im. V. V. Vinogradova* pages 272–299.

Martin Gellerstam. 1986. Translationese in Swedish novels translated from English. *Translation studies in Scandinavia* .

Rodney Huddleston and Geoffrey Pullum. 2002. *The Cambridge Grammar of the English Language*. Cambridge University Press.

Richard Hudson. 1995. Measuring syntactic difficulty. *Manuscript, University College, London* .

Yingqi Jing and Haitao Liu. 2015. Mean Hierarchical Distance Augmenting Mean Dependency Distance. In *Proceedings of the Third International Conference on Dependency Linguistics (Depling 2015)*. pages 161–170.

Dan Jurafsky and H. James Martin. 2014. *Speech and Language Processing*. Pearson London.

Renata Kamenická. 2007. Defining explicitation in translation. *Sborník prací Filozofické fakulty Brněnské univerzity, Řada anglistická: Brno Studies in English* 33:45–57.

Andrey Kutuzov and Maria Kunilovskaya. 2014. Russian learner translator corpus: Design, research potential and applications. In Petr Sojka, Aleš Horák, Ivan Kopeček, and Karel Pala, editors, *Lecture Notes in Computer Science (including subseries Lecture Notes in Artificial Intelligence and Lecture Notes in Bioinformatics)*. Springer, Springer, volume 8655, pages 315–323.

Veronika Laippala, Jenna Kanerva, Anna Missilä, Sampo Pyysalo, Tapio Salakoski, and Filip Ginter. 2015. Towards the classification of the Finnish Internet Parsebank: Detecting translations and informality. In *Proceedings of the 20th Nordic Conference of Computational Linguistics (NODALIDA 2015)*. Linköping University Electronic Press, Sweden, pages 107–116.

Ekaterina Lapshinova-Koltunski. 2017. Cohesion and translation variation: Corpus-based analysis of translation varieties. *New perspectives on cohesion and coherence* .

Georgiy Moiseenko. 2012. *Translator and Editor Guide*.

John Nerbonne and Wybo Wiersma. 2006. A measure of aggregate syntactic distance. *Proceedings of the Workshop on Linguistic Distances* pages 82–90.

Joakim Nivre, Marie-Catherine de Marneffe, Filip Ginter, Yoav Goldberg, Jan Hajic, et al. 2016. Universal dependencies v1: A multilingual treebank collection. In *Proceedings of LREC-2016*.

Gloria Corpas Pastor, Ruslan Mitkov, Naveed Afzal, and Viktor Pekar. 2008. Translation universals: do they exist? A corpus-based NLP study of convergence and simplification. In *Proceedings of the 8th Conference of the Association for Machine Translation in the Americas (AMTA'08)*. October, pages 21–25.

Marius Popescu. 2011. Studying Translationese at the Character Level. *Proceedings of the International Conference Recent Advances in Natural Language Processing 2011* (September):634–639.

Ella Rabinovich, Noam Ordan, and Shuly Wintner. 2017. Found in translation: Reconstructing phylogenetic language trees from translations. In *Proceedings of the 55th Annual Meeting of the Association for Computational Linguistics (Volume 1: Long Papers)*. Association for Computational Linguistics, pages 530–540.

Raphael Rubino, Ekaterina Lapshinova-Koltunski, and Josef Van Genabith. 2016. Information Density and Quality Estimation Features as Translationese Indicators for Human Translation Classification. In *HLT-NAACL*. pages 960–970.

Alina Secară. 2005. Translation evaluation – a state of the art survey. In *Proceedings of the eCoLoRe/MeLLANGE Workshop, Leeds*. pages 39–44.

Milan Straka and Jana Straková. 2017. Tokenizing, POS Tagging, Lemmatizing and Parsing UD 2.0 with UDPipe. In *Proceedings of the CoNLL 2017 Shared Task: Multilingual Parsing from Raw Text to Universal Dependencies*. pages 88–99.

Michael E Tipping and Christopher M Bishop. 1999. Probabilistic principal component analysis. *Journal of the Royal Statistical Society: Series B (Statistical Methodology)* 61(3):611–622.

Vered Volansky, Noam Ordan, and Shuly Wintner. 2015. On the features of translationese. *Digital Scholarship in the Humanities* 30(1):98–118.

Graph Convolutional Networks for Named Entity Recognition

Cetoli, Alberto   Bragaglia, Stefano   O'Harney, Andrew Daniel   Sloan, Marc
Context Scout
`{alberto, stefano, andy, marc}@contextscout.com`

Abstract

In this paper we investigate the role of the dependency tree in a named entity recognizer upon using a set of Graph Convolutional Networks (GCNs). We perform a comparison among different Named Entity Recognition (NER) architectures and show that the grammar of a sentence positively influences the results. Experiments on the *OntoNotes 5.0* dataset demonstrate consistent performance improvements, without requiring heavy feature engineering nor additional language-specific knowledge.[1]

1   Introduction and Motivations

The recent article by Marcheggiani and Titov (Marcheggiani and Titov, 2017) opened the way for a novel method in Natural Language Processing (NLP). In their work, they adopt a GCN (Kipf and Welling, 2016) approach to perform semantic role labeling, improving upon previous architectures. While their article is specific to recognizing the predicate-argument structure of a sentence, their method can be applied to other areas of NLP. One example is NER.

High performing statistical approaches have been used in the past for entity recognition, notably *Markov* models (McCallum et al., 2000), Conditional Random Fields (CRFs) (Lafferty et al., 2001), and Support Vector Machines (SVMs) (Takeuchi and Collier, 2002). More recently, the use of neural networks has become common in NER.

The method proposed by Collobert et al. (Collobert et al., 2011) suggests that a simple feed--forward network can produce competitive results with respect to other approaches. Shortly thereafter, Chiu and Nichols (Chiu and Nichols, 2015) employed Recurrent Neural Networks (RNNs) to address the problem of entity recognition, thus achieving state-of-the-art results. Their key improvements were twofold: using a bi-directional Long Short-Term Memory (LSTM) in place of a feed-forward network and concatenating morphological information to the input vectors.

Subsequently, various improvements appeared: using a CRF as a last layer (Huang et al., 2015) in place of a `softmax` function, a gated approach to concatenating morphology (Cao and Rei, 2016) and predicting nearby words (Rei, 2017). All such methods, however, understand text as a one dimensional collection of input vectors; any syntactic information – namely the parse tree of the sentence – is ignored.

We believe that dependency trees and other linguistic features play a key role on the accuracy of NER and that GCNs can grant the flexibility and convenience of use that we desire. In this paper our contribution is twofold: on one hand, we introduce a methodology for tackling entity recognition with GCNs; on the other hand we measure the impact of using dependency trees for entity classification upon comparing the results with prior solutions. At this stage our goal is not to beat the state-of-the-art but rather to quantify the effect of our novel architecture.

---

[1]A version of this system can be found at `https://github.com/contextscout/gcn_ner`.

37

Proceedings of the 16th International Workshop on Treebanks and Linguistic Theories (TLT16), pages 37–45,
Prague, Czech Republic, January 23–24, 2018. Distributed under a CC-BY 4.0 licence. 2017.

Keywords: NER, dependency tree, graph, convolution

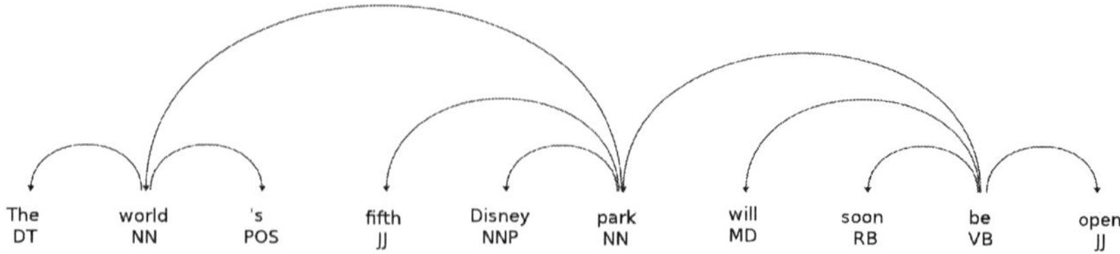

Figure 1: An example sentence along with its dependency graph. GCNs propagate the information of a node to its nearest neighbours.

As a final note, we notice that treebanks offer more information than a one dimensional sequence of words. This information is not used in conventional RNNs systems. Our paper opens the way for exploiting the syntax and dependency structures available in a treebank.

The remainder of the article is organized as follows: in Section 2 we introduce the theoretical framework for our methodology, then the features considered in our model and eventually the training details. Section 3 describes the experiments and presents the results. We discuss relevant works in Section 4 and draw the conclusions in Section 5.

2 Methods and Materials

2.1 Theoretical Aspects

Graph Convolutional Networks (Kipf and Welling, 2016) operate on graphs by convolving the features of neighbouring nodes. A GCN layer propagates the information of a node onto its nearest neighbours. By stacking together N layers, the network can propagate the features of nodes that are at most N hops away.

While the original formulation did not include directed graphs, they were further extended in Marcheggiani and Titov to be used on directed syntactic/dependency trees. In the following we rely on their work to assemble our network.

Each GCN layer creates new node embeddings by using neighbouring nodes and these layers can be stacked upon each other. In the undirected graph case, the information at the k^{st} layer is propagated to the next one according to the equation

$$h_v^{k+1} = \text{ReLU}\left(\sum_{u \in \mathcal{N}(v)} \left(W^k h_u^k + b^k \right) \right), \tag{1}$$

where u and v are nodes in the graph. $\mathcal{N}$ is the set of nearest neighbours of node v, plus the node v itself. The vector h_u^k represents node u's embeddings at the k^{st} layer, while W and b are a weight matrix and a bias – learned during training – that map the embeddings of node u onto the adjacent nodes in the graph; h_u belongs to $\mathbb{R}^m$, $W \in \mathbb{R}^{m \times m}$ and $b \in \mathbb{R}^m$.

Following the example in Marcheggiani and Titov, we prefer to exploit the directness of the graph in our system. Our inspiration comes from the bi-directional architecture of stacked RNNs, where two different neural networks operate forward and backward respectively. Eventually the output of the RNNs is concatenated and passed to further layers.

In our architecture we employ two stacked GCNs: One that only considers the incoming edges for each node

$$\overleftarrow{h}_v^{k+1} = \text{ReLU}\left(\sum_{u \in \overleftarrow{N}(v)} \left(\overleftarrow{W}^k h_u^k + \overleftarrow{b}^k \right) \right), \tag{2}$$

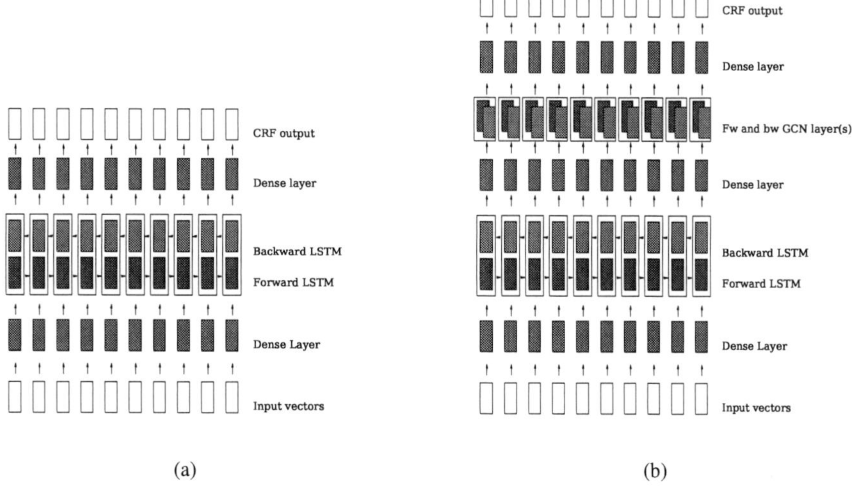

(a)   (b)

Figure 2: bi-directional architectures: (a) LSTM; and, (b) GCN layers.

and one that considers only the outgoing edges from each node

$$\vec{h}_v^{k+1} = \mathrm{ReLU}\left(\sum_{u \in \vec{N}(v)} \left(\vec{W}^k h_u^k + \vec{b}^k \right) \right). \tag{3}$$

After N layers the final output of the two GCNs is the concatenation of the two separated layers

$$h_v^N = \vec{h}_v^N \oplus \overleftarrow{h}_v^N. \tag{4}$$

In the following, we refer to the architecture expressed by Equation 4 as a ***bi-directional GCN***.

2.2 Implementations Details

2.2.1 Using the dataset

We employ the *OntoNotes 5.0* dataset (Weischedel, 2013) for training and testing. This dataset annotates various genres of text for the purpose of entity recognition and co-reference resolution. The annotated sentences are provided with Part-of-Speech (PoS) tags and syntactic information. While we include the PoS tags in our tests, the Phrase Structure Grammar (PSG) structures in the *OntoNotes 5.0* are not used. The dependency graphs that are fed to the graph convolutional network are instead computed by an external parser, *Spacy v1.8.2* (Honnibal and Johnson, 2015).

In principle we could have translated the syntactic trees in the dataset to dependency graphs using - for example - the CCGBank manual (Hockenmaier and Steedman, 2007). We will investigate this approach in future works, while this paper lays down the technique for boosting entity recognition using GCNs.

2.2.2 Models

Our architecture is inspired by the work of Chiu and Nichols (Chiu and Nichols, 2015), Huang et al. (Huang et al., 2015), and Marcheggiani and Titov (Marcheggiani and Titov, 2017). We aim to combine a Bi-directional Long Short-Term Memory (Bi-LSTM) model with GCNs, using CRF as the last layer in place of a `softmax` function.

We employ seven different configurations by selecting from two sets of PoS tags and two sets of word embedding vectors. All the models share a bi-directional LSTM which acts as the foundation upon which we apply our GCN. The different combinations are built using the following elements:

Bi-LSTM   We use a bi-directional LSTM structured as in Figure 2(a). The output is mediated by two fully connected layers ending in a CRF (Huang et al., 2015), modelled as a Viterbi sequence. The best results in the *dev set* of *OntoNotes 5.0* were obtained upon staking two LSTM layers, both for the forward and backward configuration. This is the number of layers we keep in the rest of our work. This configuration – when used alone – is a consistency test with respect to the previous works. As seen in Table 1, our findings are compatible with the results in (Chiu and Nichols, 2015).

Bi-GCN   In this model, we use the architecture created in (Marcheggiani and Titov, 2017) where a GCN is applied on top of a Bi-LSTM. This system is shown in Figure 2(b) (right side). The best results in the *dev set* were obtained upon using only one GCN layer, and we use this configuration through our models. We employ two different embedding vectors for this configuration: one in which only word embeddings are fed as an input, the other one where PoS tag embeddings are concatenated to the word vectors.

Input vectors   We use three sets of input vectors. First, we simply employ the word embeddings found in the *Glove* vectors (Pennington et al., 2014):

$$x_{\text{input}} = x_{\text{glove}}. \tag{5}$$

In the following, we employ the 300 dimensional vector from two different distributions: one with 1M words and another one with 2.2M words. Whenever a word is not present in the *Glove* vocabulary we use the vector corresponding to the word "entity" instead.

The second type of vector embeddings concatenates the *Glove* word vectors with PoS tags embeddings. We use randomly initialized Part-of-Speech embeddings that are allowed to fine-tune during training:

$$x_{\text{input}} = x_{\text{glove}} \oplus x_{\text{PoS}}. \tag{6}$$

The final quality of our results correlates to the quality of our Part-of-Speech tagging. In one batch we use the manually curated PoS tags included in the *OntoNotes 5.0* dataset (Weischedel, 2013) (*PoS (gold)*). These tags have the highest quality.

In another batch, we use the PoS tagging inferred from the parser (*PoS (inferred)*) instead of using the manually tagged ones. These PoS tags are of lower quality. An external tagger might provide a different number of tokens compared to the ones present in the training and evaluation datasets. This presents a challenge. We skip these sentences during training (1602 sentences out of 112300), while considering the entities in such sentences as incorrectly tagged during evaluation.

Finally, we add the morphological information to the feature vector for the third type of word embeddings. The reason – explained in (Cao and Rei, 2016) – is that out-of-vocabulary words are handled badly whilst using only word embeddings:

$$x_{\text{input}} = x_{\text{glove}} \oplus x_{\text{PoS}} \oplus x_{\text{morphology}}. \tag{7}$$

We employ a bi-directional RNN to encode character information. The end nodes of the RNN are concatenated and passed to a dense layer, which is integrated to the feature vector along with the embeddings and PoS information. In order to speed up the computation, we truncate the words by keeping only the first 12 characters. This operation is only done when computing the morphology vector, the word embeddings still refer to the full word. Truncation is not commonly done, as it hinders the network's performance; we leave further analysis to following works.

Dropout   In order to tackle over-fitting, we apply dropout to all the layers on top of the LSTM. The probability to drop a node is set at 20% for all the configurations. The layers that are used as input to the LSTM do not use dropout.

Network output   At inference time, the output of the network is a 19-dimensional vector for each input word. This dimensionality comes from the 18 tags used in *OntoNotes 5.0*, with an additional dimension which expresses the absence of a named entity. No Begin, Inside, Outside, End, Single (BIOES) markings are applied; at evaluation time we simply consider a *name chunk* as a contiguous sequence of words belonging to the same category.

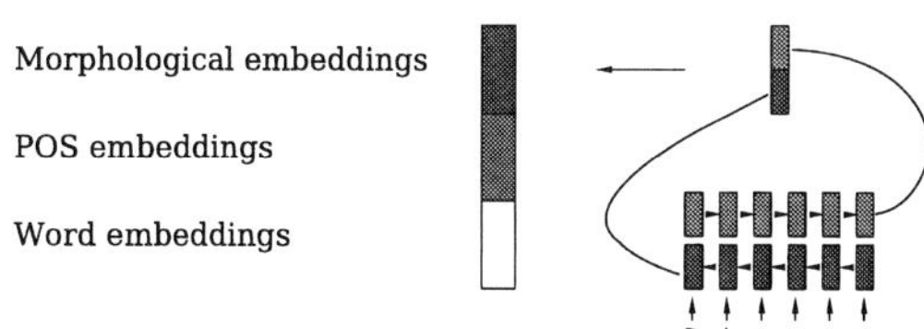

Figure 3: Feature vector components. Our input vectors have up to three components: the word embeddings, the PoS embeddings, and a morphological embedding obtained through feeding each word to a Bi-LSTM and then concatenating the first and last hidden state.

2.2.3 Training

We use *TensorFlow* (Abadi et al., 2015) to implement our neural network. Training and inference is done at the sentence level. The weights are initialized randomly from the uniform distribution and the initial state of the LSTMs are set to zero. The system uses the configuration in Appendix A.

The training function is the CRF loss function as explained in (Huang et al., 2015). Following their notation, we define $[f]_{i,t}$ as the matrix that represents the score of the network for the tth word to have the ith tag. We also introduce A_{ij} as the transition matrix which stores the probability of going from tag i to tag j. The transition matrix is usually trained along with the other network weights. In our work we preferred instead to set it as constant and equal to the transition frequencies as found in the training dataset.

The function f is an argument of the network's parameters θ and the input sentence $[x]_1^T$ (the list of embeddings with length T). Let the list of T training labels be written as $[i]_1^T$, then our loss function is written as

$$\mathcal{S}\big([x]_1^T,[i]_1^T,\theta,A_{ij}\big) - \sum_{[j]_1^T}\exp\big([x]_1^T,[j]_1^T,\theta,A_{ij}+[f]_{[i]_t,t}\big), \tag{8}$$

where

$$\mathcal{S}\big([x]_1^T,[i]_1^T,\theta,A_{ij}\big) = \sum_1^T\big(A_{[i]_{t-1},[i]_t}+f(\theta,A_{ij})\big). \tag{9}$$

At inference time, we rely on the Viterbi algorithm to find the sequence of tokens that maximizes $\mathcal{S}\big([x]_1^T,[i]_1^T,\theta,A_{ij}\big)$. We apply mini-batch stochastic gradient descent with the *Adam* optimiser (Kingma and Ba, 2014), using a learning rate fixed to 10^{-4}.

3 Experimental Results

In this section, we compare the different methods applied and discuss the results. The scores in Table 1[2] are presented as an average of 6 runs with the error being the standard deviation; we keep only the first significant digit of the errors, approximating to the nearest number.

The results show an improvement of $2.2 \pm 0.5\%$ upon using a GCN, compared to the baseline result of a bi-directional LSTM alone (1st row). When concatenating the gold PoS tag embedding in the input vectors, this improvement raises to $4.6\pm0.6\%$. However, the gold tags in the *OntoNotes 5.0* only refer to the sentences within the dataset. Therefore, the performance of the system on new sentences must rely on inferred PoS tags.

The F_1 score improvement for the system while using inferred tags (from the parser) is lower: $3.2\pm0.6\%$.

---

[2] The results from Ratinov and Roth and Finkel and Manning are taken from Chiu and Nichols.

Description	DEV			TEST		
	prec	**rec**	F_1	**prec**	**rec**	F_1
Bi-LSTM + 1M *Glove* + CRF	80.9	78.2	79.5±0.3	79.1	75.9	77.5±0.4
Bi-LSTM + 1M *Glove* + CRF + GCN	82.2	79.5	80.8±0.3	82.0	77.5	79.7±0.3
Bi-LSTM + 1M *Glove* + CRF + GCN + PoS (gold)	82.1	83.7	82.9±0.3	82.4	81.8	82.1±0.4
Bi-LSTM + 2.2M *Glove* + CRF + GCN + PoS (gold)	83.3	84.1	83.7±0.4	83.6	82.1	82.8±0.3
Bi-LSTM + 2.2M *Glove* + CRF + GCN + PoS (inferred)	83.8	82.9	83.4±0.4	82.2	80.5	81.4±0.3
Bi-LSTM + 2.2M *Glove* + CRF + GCN + PoS (gold) + Morphology	86.6	82.7	84.6±0.4	86.7	80.7	83.6±0.4
Bi-LSTM + 2.2M *Glove* + CRF + GCN + PoS (inferred) + Morphology	85.3	82.3	83.8±0.4	84.3	80.1	82.0±0.4
Chiu and Nichols			**84.6**±0.3	86.0	86.5	**86.3**±0.3
Ratinov and Roth				82.0	84.9	83.4
Finkel and Manning				84.0	80.9	82.4
Durrett and Klein				85.2	82.9	84.0

Table 1: Results of our architecture compared to previous findings.

For comparison, increasing the size of the *Glove* vector from 1M to 2.2M gave an improvement of $0.7 \pm 0.5\%$. Adding the morphological information of the words, albeit truncated at 12 characters, improves the F_1 score by $2.2\pm0.5\%$.

Our results strongly suggest that syntactic information is relevant in capturing the role of a word in a sentence, and understanding sentences as one-dimensional lists of words appears as a partial approach. Sentences embed meaning through internal graph structures: the graph convolutional method approach – used in conjunction with a parser (or a *treebank*) – seems to provide a lightweight architecture that incorporates grammar while extracting named entities.

Our results – while competitive – fall short of achieving the state-of-the-art. We believe this to be the result of a few factors: we do not employ BIOES annotations for our tags, lexicon and capitalisation features are ignored, and we truncate words when encoding the morphological vectors.

Another improvement could come from converting the manually parsed trees in the *OntoNotes 5.0* dataset into dependency graphs. Using these graphs during training would eliminate any possible erroneous contributions coming from the external parser.

Our main claim is nonetheless clear: grammatical information positively boosts the performance of recognizing entities, leaving further improvements to be explored.

4   Related Works

There is a large corpus of work on named entity recognition, with few studies using explicitly non-local information for the task. One early work by Finkel et al. (Finkel et al., 2005) uses Gibbs sampling to capture long distance structures that are common in language use. Another article by the same authors uses a joint representation for constituency parsing and NER, improving both techniques. In addition, dependency structures have also been used to boost the recognition of bio-medical events (McClosky et al., 2011) and for automatic content extraction (Li et al., 2013).

Recently, there has been a significant effort to improve the accuracy of classifiers by going beyond vector representation for sentences. Notably the work of Peng et al. (Peng et al., 2017) introduces *graph LSTMs* to encode the meaning of a sentence by using dependency graphs. Similarly Dhingra et al. (Dhingra et al., 2017) employ *Gated Recurrent Units (GRUs)* that encode the information of acyclic graphs to achieve state-of-the-art results in co-reference resolution.

5   Concluding Remarks

We showed that dependency trees play a positive role for entity recognition by using a GCN to boost the results of a bidirectional LSTM. In addition, we modified the standard convolutional network architecture and introduced a bidirectional mechanism for convolving directed graphs. This model is able to improve upon the LSTM baseline: Our best result yielded an improvement of $4.6 \pm 0.6\%$ in the F_1 score, using a combination of both GCN and PoS tag embeddings.

Finally, we prove that GCNs can be used in conjunction with different techniques. We have shown that morphological information in the input vectors does not conflict with graph convolutions. Additional techniques, such as the gating of the components of input vectors (Rei et al., 2016) or neighbouring word prediction (Rei, 2017) should be tested together with GCNs. We will investigate those results in future works.

References

Martín Abadi, Ashish Agarwal, Paul Barham, Eugene Brevdo, Zhifeng Chen, Craig Citro, Greg S. Corrado, Andy Davis, Jeffrey Dean, Matthieu Devin, Sanjay Ghemawat, Ian Goodfellow, Andrew Harp, Geoffrey Irving, Michael Isard, Yangqing Jia, Rafal Jozefowicz, Lukasz Kaiser, Manjunath Kudlur, Josh Levenberg, Dan Mané, Rajat Monga, Sherry Moore, Derek Murray, Chris Olah, Mike Schuster, Jonathon Shlens, Benoit Steiner, Ilya Sutskever, Kunal Talwar, Paul Tucker, Vincent Vanhoucke, Vijay Vasudevan, Fernanda Viégas, Oriol Vinyals, Pete Warden, Martin Wattenberg, Martin Wicke, Yuan Yu, and Xiaoqiang Zheng. 2015. TensorFlow: Large-scale machine learning on heterogeneous systems. Software available from tensorflow.org. http://tensorflow.org/.

Kris Cao and Marek Rei. 2016. A joint model for word embedding and word morphology. *CoRR* abs/1606.02601. http://arxiv.org/abs/1606.02601.

Jason P. C. Chiu and Eric Nichols. 2015. Named entity recognition with bidirectional LSTM-CNNs. *CoRR* abs/1511.08308. http://arxiv.org/abs/1511.08308.

Ronan Collobert, Jason Weston, Léon Bottou, Michael Karlen, Koray Kavukcuoglu, and Pavel Kuksa. 2011. Natural language processing (almost) from scratch. *Journal of Machine Learning Research* 12(Aug):2493–2537.

Bhuwan Dhingra, Zhilin Yang, William W. Cohen, and Ruslan Salakhutdinov. 2017. Linguistic knowledge as memory for recurrent neural networks. *CoRR* abs/1703.02620. http://arxiv.org/abs/1703.02620.

Greg Durrett and Dan Klein. 2015. Neural CRF parsing. *CoRR* abs/1507.03641. http://arxiv.org/abs/1507.03641.

Jenny Rose Finkel, Trond Grenager, and Christopher Manning. 2005. Incorporating non-local information into information extraction systems by Gibbs Sampling. In *Proceedings of the 43rd Annual Meeting on Association for Computational Linguistics*. Association for Computational Linguistics, Stroudsburg, PA, USA, ACL '05, pages 363–370. https://doi.org/10.3115/1219840.1219885.

Jenny Rose Finkel and Christopher D. Manning. 2009. Joint parsing and named entity recognition. In *Proceedings of Human Language Technologies: The 2009 Annual Conference of the North American Chapter of the Association for Computational Linguistics*. Association for Computational Linguistics, Stroudsburg, PA, USA, NAACL '09, pages 326–334. http://dl.acm.org/citation.cfm?id=1620754.1620802.

Julia Hockenmaier and Mark Steedman. 2007. CCGBank: A corpus of CCG derivations and dependency structures. *Comput. Linguist.* 33(3):355–396. https://doi.org/10.1162/coli.2007.33.3.355.

Matthew Honnibal and Mark Johnson. 2015. An improved non-monotonic transition system for dependency parsing. In *Proceedings of the 2015 Conference on Empirical Methods in Natural Language Processing*. Association for Computational Linguistics, Lisbon, Portugal, pages 1373–1378. https://aclweb.org/anthology/D/D15/D15-1162.

Zhiheng Huang, Wei Xu, and Kai Yu. 2015. Bidirectional LSTM-CRF models for sequence tagging. *CoRR* abs/1508.01991. http://arxiv.org/abs/1508.01991.

Diederik P. Kingma and Jimmy Ba. 2014. Adam: A method for stochastic optimization. *CoRR* abs/1412.6980. http://arxiv.org/abs/1412.6980.

Thomas N. Kipf and Max Welling. 2016. Semi-supervised classification with Graph Convolutional Networks. *CoRR* abs/1609.02907. http://arxiv.org/abs/1609.02907.

John D. Lafferty, Andrew McCallum, and Fernando C. N. Pereira. 2001. Conditional random fields: Probabilistic models for segmenting and labeling sequence data. In *Proceedings of the Eighteenth International Conference on Machine Learning*. Morgan Kaufmann Publishers Inc., San Francisco, CA, USA, ICML '01, pages 282–289. http://dl.acm.org/citation.cfm?id=645530.655813.

Qi Li, Heng Ji, and Liang Huang. 2013. Joint event extraction via structured prediction with global features. In *Proceedings of the 51st Annual Meeting of the Association for Computational Linguistics (Volume 1: Long Papers)*. Association for Computational Linguistics, pages 73–82. http://aclanthology.coli.uni-saarland.de/pdf/P/P13/P13-1008.pdf.

Diego Marcheggiani and Ivan Titov. 2017. Encoding sentences with GCN for semantic role labeling. *CoRR* abs/1703.04826. http://arxiv.org/abs/1703.04826.

Andrew McCallum, Dayne Freitag, and Fernando C. N. Pereira. 2000. Maximum entropy Markov models for information extraction and segmentation. In *Proceedings of the Seventeenth International Conference on Machine Learning*. Morgan Kaufmann Publishers Inc., San Francisco, CA, USA, ICML '00, pages 591–598. http://dl.acm.org/citation.cfm?id=645529.658277.

David McClosky, Mihai Surdeanu, and Christopher D. Manning. 2011. Event extraction as dependency parsing. In *Proceedings of the 49th Annual Meeting of the Association for Computational Linguistics: Human Language Technologies - Volume 1*. Association for Computational Linguistics, Stroudsburg, PA, USA, HLT '11, pages 1626–1635. http://dl.acm.org/citation.cfm?id=2002472.2002667.

Nanyun Peng, Hoifung Poon, Chris Quirk, Kristina Toutanova, and Wen-tau Yih. 2017. Cross-sentence N-ary relation extraction with Graph LSTMs. *Transactions of the Association of Computational Linguistics* 5:101–115. http://aclanthology.coli.uni-saarland.de/pdf/Q/Q17/Q17-1008.pdf.

Jeffrey Pennington, Richard Socher, and Christopher D. Manning. 2014. Glove: Global vectors for word representation. In *Empirical Methods in Natural Language Processing (EMNLP)*. pages 1532–1543. http://www.aclweb.org/anthology/D14-1162.

L. Ratinov and D. Roth. 2009. Design challenges and misconceptions in named entity recognition. In *CoNLL*. http://cogcomp.org/papers/RatinovRo09.pdf.

Marek Rei. 2017. Semi-supervised multitask learning for sequence labeling. *CoRR* abs/1704.07156. http://arxiv.org/abs/1704.07156.

Marek Rei, Gamal Crichton, and Sampo Pyysalo. 2016. Attending to characters in neural sequence labeling models. *CoRR* abs/1611.04361. http://arxiv.org/abs/1611.04361.

Koichi Takeuchi and Nigel Collier. 2002. Use of support vector machines in extended named entity recognition. In *Proceedings of the 6th Conference on Natural Language Learning - Volume 20*. Association for Computational Linguistics, Stroudsburg, PA, USA, COLING-02, pages 1–7. https://doi.org/10.3115/1118853.1118882.

Ralph et al. Weischedel. 2013. Ontonotes release 5.0. *Linguistic Data Consortium, Philadelphia, PA* LDC2013T19. https://catalog.ldc.upenn.edu/docs/LDC2013T19/OntoNotes-Release-5.0.pdf.

A   Configuration

Parameter	Value
Glove word embeddings	300 dim
PoS embedding	15 dim
Morphological embedding	20 dim
First dense layer	40 dim
LSTM memory	$(2\times)$ 160 dim
Second dense layer	160 dim
GCN layer	$(2\times)$ 160 dim
Final dense layer	160 dim
Output layer	16 dim
Dropout	0.8 (*keep probability*)

Table 2: Summary of the configuration used for training the network.

Extensions to the GrETEL Treebank Query Application

Jan Odijk
Utrecht University / Utrecht
j.odijk@uu.nl

Martijn van der Klis
Utrecht University / Utrecht
m.h.vanderklis@uu.nl

Sheean Spoel
Utrecht University / Utrecht
s.j.j.spoel@uu.nl

Abstract

In this paper we describe the extensions we made to an existing treebank query application (GrETEL). These extensions address user needs expressed by multiple linguistic researchers and include (1) facilities for uploading one's own data and metadata in GrETEL; (2) conversion and cleaning modules for uploading data in the CHAT format; (3) new facilities for analysing the results of the treebank queries in terms of data, metadata and combinations of them. These extensions have been made available in a new version (Version 4) of GrETEL.

1 Introduction

In this paper we describe the extensions we made to an existing treebank query application (GrETEL) in the context of the AnnCor project, in which we are (inter alia) developing a treebank for the Dutch CHILDES corpora (MacWhinney, 2000).[1] The AnnCor treebank and the treebank query application are being developed in the Utrecht University AnnCor project, which we describe in section 2.[2] We briefly describe the treebank in section 3. We describe the extensions of the treebank query application GrETEL in section 4. We illustrate the extensions by means of an example in section 5. In section 6 we discuss related work, and we end with conclusions and plans and suggestions for future work in section 7.

This paper (1) presents facilities for uploading one's own data and metadata in GrETEL; (2) describes the conversion and cleaning modules for uploading data in the CHAT format; and (3) presents new facilities for analysing the results of the treebank queries in terms of data, metadata and combinations of them.

2 The AnnCor Project

The AnnCor project is an Utrecht University internal research infrastructure project that aims to create linguistically annotated corpora for the Dutch language and to enhance and extend an existing treebank query application in order to query the annotated corpora. Various types of corpora are being annotated, and various types of annotations are being added. The corpora include learner corpora, news corpora, narrative corpora, and language acquisition corpora. Annotations include annotations for learners' errors and their corrections, discourse annotations, and full syntactic structures. In this paper we focus on the application for querying the corpora, in particular treebanks (i.e. text corpora in which each utterance is assigned a syntactic structure) and analysing the search results.

Sagae et al. (2007) state for CHILDES corpora that 'linguistic annotation of the corpora provides researchers with better means for exploring the development of grammatical constructions and their usage'. The research described in (Odijk, 2015, 2016a) illustrates this for the study of the acquisition of particular syntactic modification phenomena using the Dutch CHILDES corpora. It is clear from these papers that such research cannot be done properly and efficiently without treebanks for these corpora. The AnnCor project aims to create exactly such treebanks, which, together with a query application, will

---

[1]The Dutch CHILDES Corpora are accessible via http://childes.talkbank.org/access/Dutch/.

[2]This paper contains many hyperlinks hidden under terms and acronyms. The presence of a hyperlink is visible in digital versions of the paper but may be badly visible or invisible in printed versions of the paper.

Proceedings of the 16th International Workshop on Treebanks and Linguistic Theories (TLT16), pages 46–55,
Prague, Czech Republic, January 23–24, 2018. Distributed under a CC-BY 4.0 licence. 2017.

Keywords: treebank, querying, GrETEL, CHILDES

become an integrated part of the Dutch part of the CLARIN research infrastructure (Odijk, 2016b; Odijk
and van Hessen, to appear 2017). These treebanks and the associated search and analysis applications
can then contribute to an acceleration of language acquisition research and to a larger empirical basis for
testing theories or hypotheses.

3   The AnnCor CHILDES Treebank

The AnnCor CHILDES Treebank is created with the help of the Alpino parser (Bouma et al., 2001),
which automatically assigns a syntactic structure to each utterance in the corpus. Since Alpino has
been developed for written adult language such as newspapers, it is not surprising that it creates many
wrong parses when applied to the CHILDES corpora.[3] The problem is twofold: CHILDES contains
transcriptions of spoken utterances from dialogues, and many of them are uttered by children that are still
in the process of acquiring the language. In the AnnCor project we create a manually verified subcorpus,
sampled in a representative manner. In addition, we manually verified and, if needed, corrected parse
trees for which it was very likely that they contain errors, as determined on the basis of a variety of
heuristics for identifying potential errors. For more details about this manually verified subcorpus, we
refer the reader to (Odijk et al., 2017).

3.1   Cleaning

CHILDES corpora are represented in the CHAT format (MacWhinney, 2015). Utterances in a CHAT
file are enriched with all kinds of annotations. Many of these annotations are in-line annotations. Some
examples are given in (1):[4]

(1)   Example in-line annotations in CHILDES CHAT files:

    a.   < ik wi   > [//] ik wil   xxx bekertje   doen.
        < I   wan > [//] I   want xxx cup-DIM do

        'I want to do the little cup'

    b.   < doe maar even > [/] doe maar even op tafel.
        < put PRT PRT > [/] put PRT PRT on table

        'Just put on the table'

    c.   knor knor [=! pig sound] , ik heb   honger.
        oink oink [=! pig sound] , I   have hunger

        'Oink oink, I am hungry'

These examples illustrate annotations for retracing ([//]) and repetition ([/]), both with scope over the
preceding part between angled brackets, for unintelligible material (xxx) and for paralinguistic material
([=! ...]).

The Alpino parser cannot deal with these annotations. A cleaning programme has been developed to
remove the annotations and send a cleaned utterance to the Alpino parser.

The cleaned variants of the utterances in (1) are:

(2)   Example cleaned utterances:

    a.   ik wil xxx bekertje doen.

    b.   doe maar even op tafel.

    c.   knor knor , ik heb honger.

The cleaning program is available on GitHub[5] and has been integrated in the GrETEL upgrade described
in section 4.

---

[3]Though even a fully automatically parsed treebank can be fruitfully used in linguistic research, as illustrated by (Odijk,
2015).

[4]The sources are indicated by the session name (e.g. Sarah35) followed by the utterance number (e.g. 224), starting counting
at 1. The examples here are the utterances Sarah35.015, Sarah35.023 and Sarah35.224 from the Van Kampen corpus.

[5]https://github.com/JanOdijk/chamd.

3.2 Annotation Conventions

The utterances used by the children contain many phenomena that are considered ill-formed in the adult language. In addition, as in any annotated corpus, many phenomena can be analysed in multiple ways, none of which can be considered better than any other on purely linguistic grounds. It is important to analyse each construction in a consistent and uniform manner, so that it can be easily automatically identified and distinguished from other constructions in a treebank query application when the data are used in research. For this reason, it is important to develop and adhere to annotation conventions and guidelines.

We illustrate this with some examples of phenomena that are not part of the adult language. The following examples appear to contain a finite verb form (*lees* and *kocht*, respectively) where a participle is expected:[6]

(3)   a. ik heb niet lees
         I   have not read-PRES

         'I have not read'

    b. Ik heb bolletjes   kocht
         I   have roll-DIM-PL buy-PAST

         'I have bought little rolls'

It is not a priori clear how such examples should be analysed: the child might produce forms that do not conform to the adult language due to syntactic reasons, morphological reasons or phonological reasons. One can decide among them only after an intensive investigation of the phenomena. In constructing the treebank we do not take a stand as to how such examples should be analysed, but we do treat each of them in a uniform way, so that each can be easily and automatically identified by researchers using a treebank query application. The examples in (3) are analysed in the treebank as participial verbal complements (*vc/ppart*) that contain a finite verb.

For more examples and how they are dealt with, we refer to (Odijk et al., 2017).

4   Treebank Querying

For querying the treebanks we started from the existing treebank query application *GrETEL*, which was developed in Leuven (Augustinus et al., 2012). This application comes in three versions,[7] and we started from version 3.[8] We extended this treebank search application with functionality that was requested by many linguists: they want to be able to upload their own data with metadata, in formats that they actually use (in the context of language acquisition and related fields the most frequently used format is CHAT), and not only get a list of sentences as a result of their queries but facilities for analysing the query results in terms of the relevant parts of the structures in combination with metadata. Initial versions of these extensions have been incorporated in GrETEL Version 4, and are being further refined.[9]

The existing treebank search application GrETEL allows researchers to search in Dutch treebanks and to perform a limited analysis of the search results. GrETEL has a very user-friendly example-based interface, but also allows queries in the XML query language XPath.

The example-based search interface enables one to query the treebank by providing an example sentence that illustrates the construction one is interested in, plus some information on which aspects of this sentence are crucial for the construction. The system parses the example sentence (using the same parser as the one used to create the treebank) and enables the user to select the substructure of this parse relevant for the construction.

In GrETEL 4, the corpus upload functionality was added as a separate application and allows users to upload an archived collection (zip file) of text files. The collection is subdivided in multiple components (on the basis of the folder structure). The software will tokenise and parse these files using the Alpino

---

[6]Utterances Laura09.527 and Laura13.042 from the VanKampen Corpus.

[7]See http://nederbooms.ccl.kuleuven.be/eng/gretel and references there for versions 1 and 2.

[8]GrETEL Version 3 can be found here: http://gretel.ccl.kuleuven.be/gretel3/index.php.

[9]GrETEL Version 4 is currently still under development but can already be used here: http://gretel.hum.uu.nl/gretel4/.

dependency parser (Bouma et al., 2001), and import them into the XML database BaseX (Grün, 2010) for querying with GrETEL. Users can specify their corpus as private (only searchable for them) or publicly available. Figure 1 shows a screenshot of the upload interface.

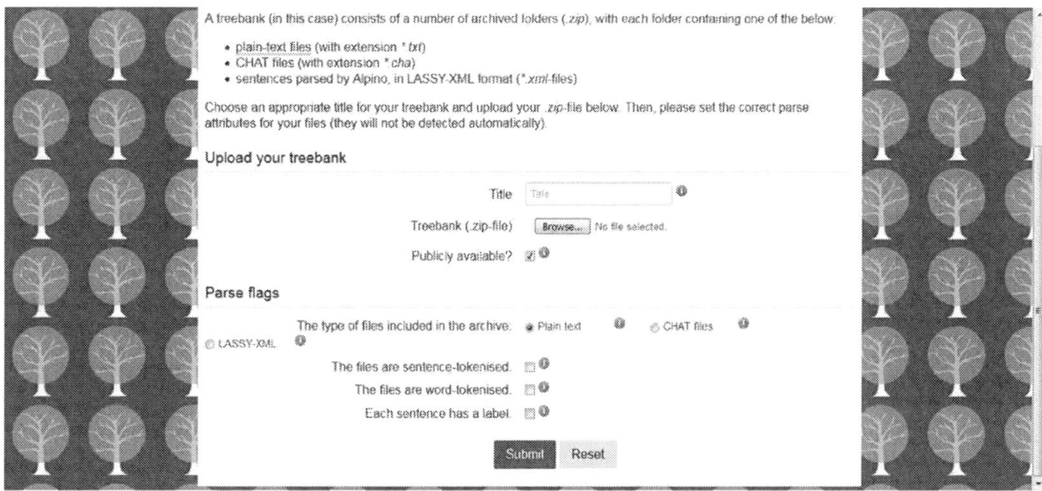

Figure 1: Screenshot of the GrETEL corpus upload page.

An interface is available to the researcher for managing the uploaded corpora. It offers buttons for viewing detailed information on the uploaded corpora, for viewing the uploading logfile, for making the corpora public, for downloading the treebank and for deleting it. A screenshot of this interface is given in Figure 2.

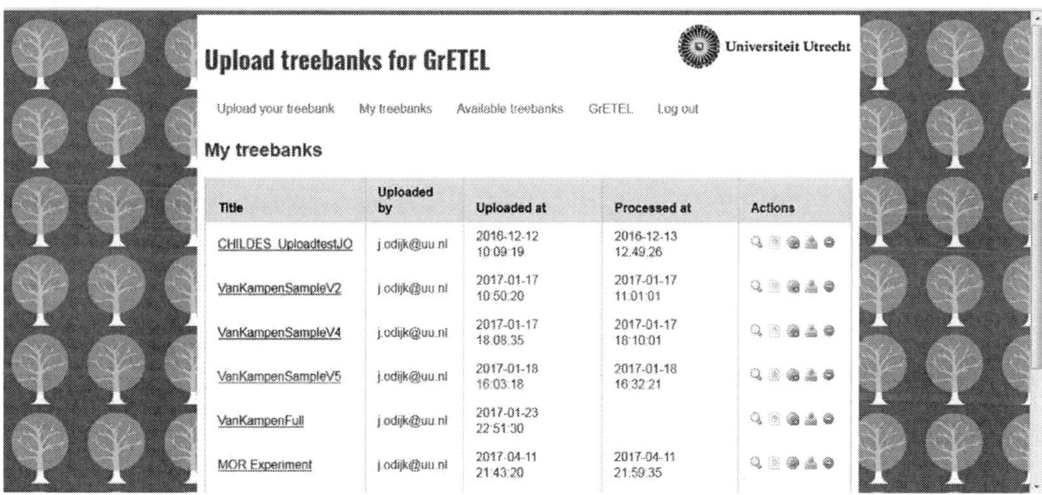

Figure 2: Screenshot of the GrETEL corpus managing page ('My treebanks').

The corpus details page (see Figure 3 for a screenshot) contains information about the components the treebank consists of and about the size of each component of the treebank (# sentences, # word occurrences). It also offers the user the option to select which metadata elements will occur in the analysis component and which user interface option is used for selecting values for a specific metadata element, e.g. to use a range filter instead of checkboxes for numeric metadata.

In GrETEL 4, one can upload a treebank parsed with Alpino (with XML files in accordance with the

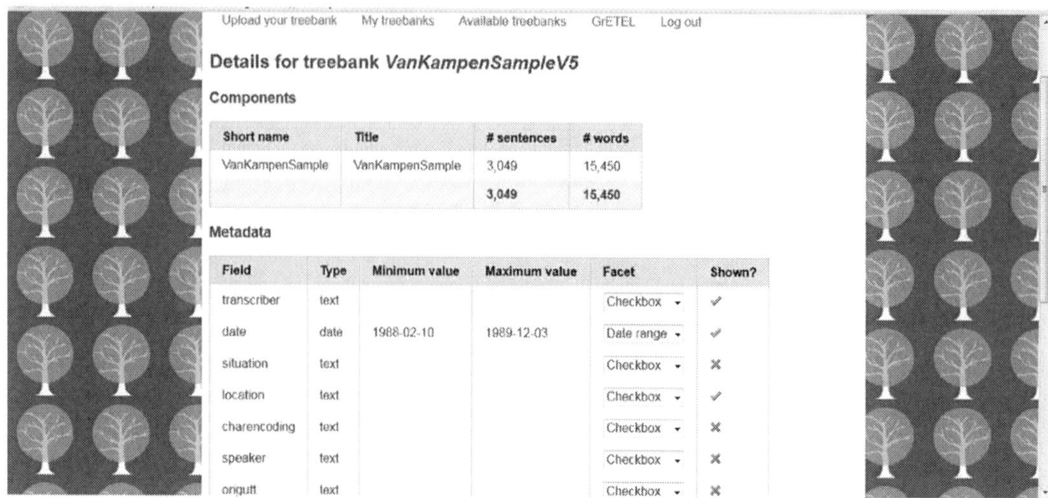

Figure 3: Screenshot of the details page of a particular treebank.

Alpino_ds DTD[10]), or a text corpus. The text files of a text corpus can be in plain text format, or in the CHAT format. In the latter case, the software uses, inter alia, the cleaning algorithm described in section 3.1. We are currently working on providing a wider range of input formats (in particular, FoLiA (van Gompel and Reynaert, 2013) and TEI).[11] Files in plain text or CHAT format are automatically parsed by Alpino. If needed, one can download the automatically parsed corpus, manually correct it or a part of it, and then upload the improved treebank in GrETEL.

Uploading a corpus requires authentication. Currently, this is restricted to users with an Utrecht University account, though a guest account is provided as well. When the extensions are complete, the application (and the treebanks) will be hosted by a certified type B CLARIN centre, most probably the Dutch Language Institute,[12] which will provide CLARIN-compatible federated login.

The maximum size of uploaded corpora will be determined by the CLARIN centre that will host the application. It is likely that a size restriction will be imposed allowing only corpora of maximally a few million words.[13] For larger corpora, it makes more sense to make special arrangements with the CLARIN centre. Very large corpora may require dedicated indexing techniques, e.g. the ones proposed by (Vandeghinste and Augustinus, 2014) and (Vanroy et al., 2017) for dealing with the 510 million word occurrences (41 million utterances) SoNaR corpus.

For representing metadata of corpora, we use a format defined during the development of PaQu that allows users to incorporate metadata in the running text (see http://www.let.rug.nl/alfa/paqu/info.html#cormeta for details). Metadata in CHAT files are converted to this format. The software reads in the metadata and will create faceted search in GrETEL to allow users to both analyse and filter their search results.

GrETEL 4 offers new functionality (not present in earlier versions) to further analyse a result set of interest via an analysis interface. This interface enables the creation of pivot tables and graphs such as a heatmap and a table bar map, which allows rapid insight into the data. The result set can also be exported to a tab-separated value text format to allow further analysis in other tools.

The user can not only select metadata elements and their values in this analysis interface but also select words that match with a node in the query tree, as illustrated in section 5.

---

[10]http://www.let.rug.nl/vannoord/alp/Alpino/versions/binary/latest.tar.gz.
[11]http://www.tei-c.org/.
[12]http://ivdnt.org/.
[13]The XML database BaseX has a theoretical limit of 500GB of XML, according to (Grün, 2010, section 2.4).

5   Example query and analysis

We will illustrate the query and analysis options with an example. We are interested in constructions with three bare[14] verbs in the children's speech. An example sentence illustrating this construction is given in (4), which contains the 3 bare verb forms *zal*, *willen* and *doen*:

(4)   Hij zal dat willen doen
      He will that want   do

      'He will want to do that'

In this sentence, the words *hij* 'he' and *dat* 'that' are not essential for the construction that we are interested in, so we mark them as optional. As to the three verbs in this sentence, they are crucial for this construction, but we are not interested in these specific verbs but in any word of category verb that can occur in this construction. Therefore we indicate for these words that we want any word here with the same part of speech. The example sentence is a main clause, but we want to find examples of this construction in any type of clause. Therefore we mark the option 'ignore properties of the dominating node'.

Specifying this results in the XPath query (6), visualised by the query tree (5):

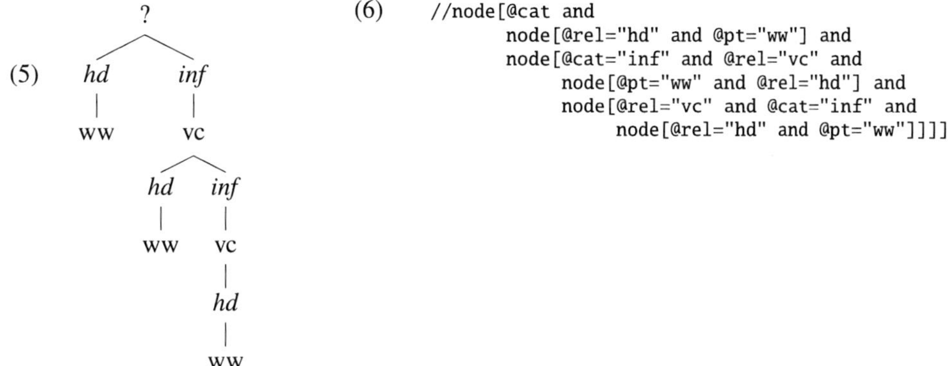

(6)
```
//node[@cat and
       node[@rel="hd" and @pt="ww"] and
       node[@cat="inf" and @rel="vc" and
            node[@pt="ww" and @rel="hd"] and
            node[@rel="vc" and @cat="inf" and
                 node[@rel="hd" and @pt="ww"]]]]
```

Executing the query on the corpus VKLaura ('Van Kampen Corpus LAURA') yields 325 matches in 325 utterances. A screenshot of the results is shown in Figure 4.

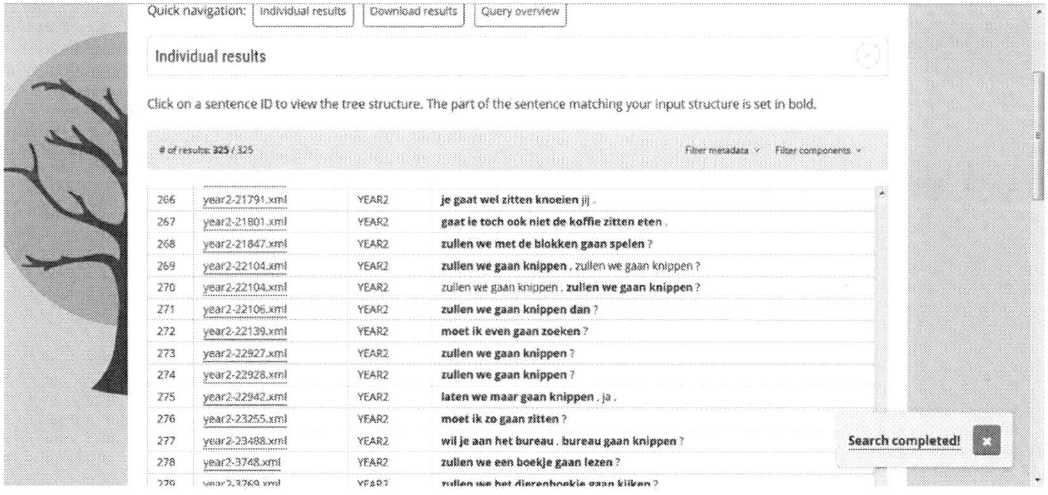

Figure 4: Screenshot of the results page of the query.

---

[14]i.e. verbs without *te* (cf. English 'to').

We can now filter by metadata and by components. If we filter by *speaker* and select only the (child) speaker LAU (Laura), we obtain 12 matches in 12 utterances (see Figure 5).[15]

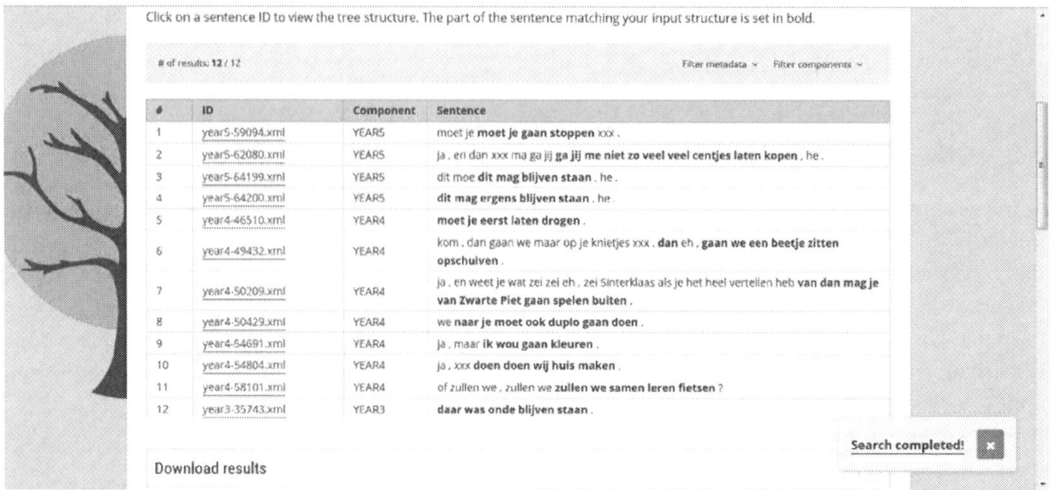

Figure 5: Screenshot of the results page of the query after filtering for speaker=LAU.

The search application allows a more detailed analysis of the search results, in particular selecting parts of the result data and metadata, grouping, filtering and sorting them, and represent them in pivot tables or frequency lists, with various visualisation options. For example, we can make a table that shows at what age the speaker LAU has uttered such constructions (as of month 43); or we can create a frequency list of the verb combinations that occur in the results, grouped by speaker (see Figure 6).

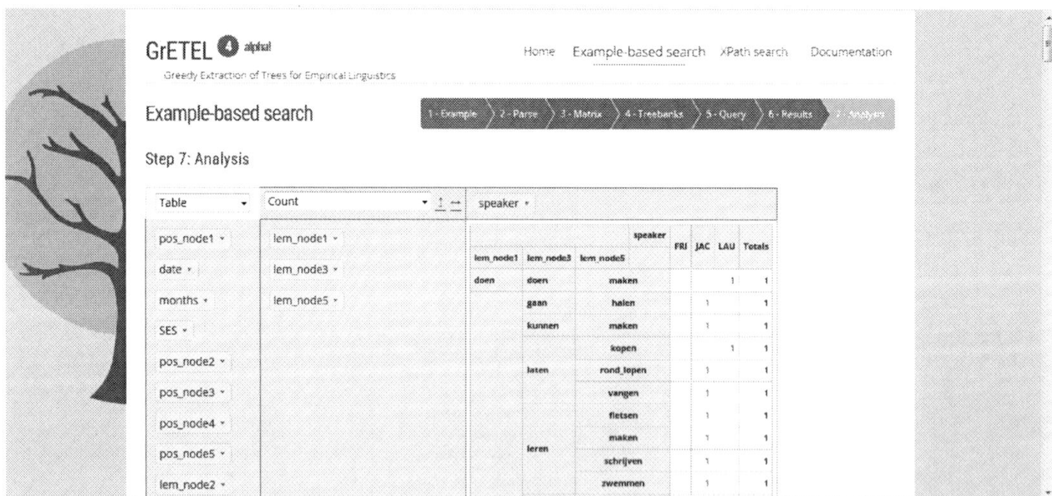

Figure 6: Analysis: verb lemmas used grouped by speaker

These data show that the child uses combinations of three bare verbs, and in only 4 out of the 12 examples the child uses a verb combination that also occurs in the adult's utterances in the corpus. In addition, the ones that the child uses are not from the most frequent verb combinations used by the adult. All of this suggests that the child fully commands the use of such constructions and can creatively use

---

[15]In the result set three speakers occur, with codes JAC (in the role of mother), LAU (with role target child), and FRI (another adult).

them.[16] Possibly the child has made a generalisation on the basis of the use of constructions with two bare verbs (which occur much more frequently: 6,645 in total, 1,363 uttered by Laura) and are used by the child much earlier (as of month 23).

6 Related Treebank Query Applications

We had two requirements on a treebank query application: (1) it must be compatible with the format generated by the Alpino parser and used in Dutch treebanks such as LASSY (van Noord et al., 2013) and the Spoken Dutch Treebank (Oostdijk et al., 2002)); (2) it must provide a user friendly interface that enables a researcher to query the treebank without having to write a query in a formal query language.

There are several treebank query applications, e.g. PMLTQ (Pajas et al., 2009); the WebLicht application Tündra (Hinrichs et al., 2010), and INESS (Rosén et al., 2012). However, only two treebank query applications meet these requirements: PaQu[17] (Odijk et al., to appear 2017) and GrETEL[18] (Augustinus et al., 2012).

The PaQu (Parse and Query) application enables upload of one's own corpus and provides a user-friendly interface for searching for syntactic dependency relations between words. It also offers facilities for analysis of the query results. PaQu was actually developed on the basis of the LASSY Word Relations application (Tjong Kim Sang et al., 2010) at the request of one of the authors of this paper. In addition, when we started our work on the AnnCor project, the PaQu developers made available a treebank for the Dutch CHILDES corpora with fully automatically parsed utterances in the PaQu application.

Nevertheless, we selected the GrETEL application because it makes it possible to search for arbitrary constructions using example-based querying (e.g. the construction with three verbs can only be queried in PaQu by writing an XPATH query from scratch), and we wanted to offer more sophisticated analysis options than PaQu provides, in particular more sophisticated ways of selecting parts of query results. Furthermore, the analysis interface is more user-friendly by allowing the creation of pivot tables through dragging attributes into a table.

7 Conclusions and Future Work

We have described the extensions to the GrETEL treebank query application we made in the context of the AnnCor project and illustrated it with a query in (a preliminary version of) the AnnCor CHILDES Treebank for Dutch. The extensions involve functionality for uploading one's own corpus with metadata, and functionality for analysing data, subparts of data and metadata in combination. The treebank query application and the treebank are still under development, but the extensions to the GrETEL query application described here are already available.[19] The source code is available on GitHub.[20]

There are a number of aspects of the treebank query application that we would like to work on in the future: (1) extend input formats (FoLiA and TEI); (2) allow more complex metadata that specify properties of spans of text such as retracings, repetitions, pronunciation, paralinguistic material etc. as in example (1);[21] (3) extend the analysis component with frequencies of constructions relative to the size of a subpart of the corpus (e.g. component, session) measured in terms of the number of tokens or number of utterances; and (4) provide a graphical interface for selecting nodes from a query tree in the analysis component.

Acknowledgements

This work was financed by the Utrecht University internal AnnCor research infrastructure project and by the CLARIAH-CORE project funded by the Dutch National Science Foundation (NWO).

---

[16]Though of course, it is no conclusive evidence, if only because the corpus is just a small sample of the full input of the child and its own production.

[17]http://portal.clarin.nl/node/4182.

[18]http://portal.clarin.nl/node/1967.

[19]via the url http://gretel.hum.uu.nl/gretel4/.

[20]https://github.com/UUDigitalHumanitieslab/gretel, https://github.com/UUDigitalHumanitieslab/GrETEL-upload.

[21]See (MacWhinney, 2015) for many more examples.

References

Liesbeth Augustinus, Vincent Vandeghinste, and Frank Van Eynde. 2012. Example-based treebank querying. In Nicoletta Calzolari, Khalid Choukri, Thierry Declerck, Mehmet Uğur Doğan, Bente Maegaard, Joseph Mariani, Asunción Moreno, Jan Odijk, and Stelios Piperidis, editors, *Proceedings of the Eight International Conference on Language Resources and Evaluation (LREC'12)*. European Language Resources Association (ELRA), Istanbul, Turkey.

Gosse Bouma, Gertjan van Noord, and Robert Malouf. 2001. Alpino: Wide-coverage computational analysis of Dutch. *Language and Computers* 37(1):45–59.

C. Grün. 2010. *Storing and querying large XML instances*. Ph.D. thesis, University of Konstanz, Konstanz, Germany. http://nbn-resolving.de/urn:nbn:de:bsz:352-opus-127142.

Erhard W. Hinrichs, Marie Hinrichs, and Thomas Zastrow. 2010. WebLicht: Web-Based LRT Services for German. In *Proceedings of the ACL 2010 System Demonstrations*. pages 25–29. http://www.aclweb.org/anthology/P10-4005.

Brian MacWhinney. 2000. *The CHILDES Project: Tools for Analyzing Talk*. Lawrence Erlbaum Associates, Mahwah, NJ, 3rd edition.

Brian MacWhinney. 2015. Tools for analyzing talk, electronic edition, part 1: The CHAT transcription format. Technical report, Carnegie Mellon University, Pittsburg, PA. `http://childes.psy.cmu.edu/manuals/CHAT.pdf`.

Jan Odijk. 2015. Linguistic research with PaQu. *Computational Linguistics in the Netherlands Journal* 5:3–14. http://www.clinjournal.org/sites/clinjournal.org/files/odijk2015.pdf.

Jan Odijk. 2016a. A Use case for Linguistic Research on Dutch with CLARIN. In Koenraad De Smedt, editor, *Selected Papers from the CLARIN Annual Conference 2015, October 14-16, 2015, Wroclaw, Poland*. CLARIN, Linköping University Electronic Press, Linköping, Sweden, number 123 in Linköping Electronic Conference Proceedings, pages 45–61. `http://www.ep.liu.se/ecp/article.asp?issue=123&article=004`, `http://dspace.library.uu.nl/handle/1874/339492`.

Jan Odijk. 2016b. Linguistic research using CLARIN. *Lingua* 178:1 – 4. Linguistic Research in the CLARIN Infrastructure. https://doi.org/http://dx.doi.org/10.1016/j.lingua.2016.04.003.

Jan Odijk, Alexis Dimitriadis, Martijn van der Klis, Marjo van Koppen, Meie Otten, and Remco van der Veen. 2017. The AnnCor CHILDES Treebank. Unpublished paper, AnnCor project, Utrecht University. accepted for LREC 2018.

Jan Odijk and Arjan van Hessen, editors. to appear 2017. *CLARIN in the Low Countries*. Ubiquity Press, London, UK. To appear as Open Access.

Jan Odijk, Gertjan van Noord, Peter Kleiweg, and Erik Tjong Kim Sang. to appear 2017. The parse and query (PaQu) application. In Jan Odijk and Arjan van Hessen, editors, *CLARIN in the Low Countries*, Ubiquity, London, UK, chapter 23. DOI: `http://dx.doi.org/10.5334/bbi.23`. License: CC-BY 4.0.

N. Oostdijk, W. Goedertier, F. Van Eynde, L. Boves, J.P. Martens, M. Moortgat, and H. Baayen. 2002. Experiences from the Spoken Dutch Corpus project. In M. González Rodriguez and C. Paz Suárez Araujo, editors, *Proceedings of the third International Conference on Language Resources and Evaluation (LREC-2002)*, ELRA, Las Palmas, pages 340–347.

Petr Pajas, Jan Štěpánek, and Michal Sedlák. 2009. PML tree query. LINDAT/CLARIN digital library at the Institute of Formal and Applied Linguistics, Charles University, Prague. `http://hdl.handle.net/11858/00-097C-0000-0022-C7F6-3`.

Victoria Rosén, Koenraad De Smedt, Paul Meurer, and Helge Dyvik. 2012. An open infrastructure for advanced treebanking. In Jan Hajič, Koenraad De Smedt, Marko Tadić, and António Branco, editors, *META-RESEARCH Workshop on Advanced Treebanking at LREC2012*. ELRA, Istanbul, Turkey, pages 22–29.

Kenji Sagae, Eric Davis, Alon Lavie, Brian MacWhinney, and Shuly Wintner. 2007. High-accuracy annotation and parsing of CHILDES transcripts. In *Proceedings of the Workshop on Cognitive Aspects of Computational Language Acquisition*. Association for Computational Linguistics, Stroudsburg, PA, USA, CACLA '07, pages 25–32. http://dl.acm.org/citation.cfm?id=1629795.1629799.

Erik Tjong Kim Sang, Gosse Bouma, and Gertjan van Noord. 2010. LASSY for beginners. Presentation at CLIN 2010, Utrecht. http://ifarm.nl/erikt/talks/clin2010.pdf.

Maarten van Gompel and Martin Reynaert. 2013. FoLiA: A practical XML format for linguistic annotation - a descriptive and comparative study. *Computational Linguistics in the Netherlands Journal* 3:63–81.

Gertjan van Noord, Gosse Bouma, Frank Van Eynde, Daniël de Kok, Jelmer van der Linde, Ineke Schuurman, Erik Tjong Kim Sang, and Vincent Vandeghinste. 2013. Large scale syntactic annotation of written Dutch: Lassy. In Peter Spyns and Jan Odijk, editors, *Essential Speech and Language Technology for Dutch*, Springer Berlin Heidelberg, Theory and Applications of Natural Language Processing, pages 147–164. https://doi.org/10.1007/978-3-642-30910-6_9.

Vincent Vandeghinste and Liesbeth Augustinus. 2014. Making large treebanks searchable. the SONAR case. In *Proceedings of the LREC 2014 2nd workshop on Challenges in the Management of Large Corpora (CMLC-2)*. Reykjavik, pages 15–20. http://www.lrec-conf.org/proceedings/lrec2014/workshops/LREC2014Workshop-CMLC2%20Proceedings-rev2.pdf.

Bram Vanroy, Vincent Vandeghinste, and Liesbeth Augustinus. 2017. Querying large treebanks: Benchmarking GrETEL indexing. *Computational Linguistics in the Netherlands Journal* 7:145–166.

The Relation of Form and Function
in Linguistic Theory and in a Multi-layer Treebank

Eduard Bejček   **Eva Hajičová**   **Marie Mikulová**   **Jarmila Panevová**
Charles University, Faculty of Mathematics and Physics,
Institute of Formal and Applied Linguistics
Malostranské náměstí 25, 118 00 Prague 1, Czech Republic
`{bejcek,hajicova,mikulova,panevova}@ufal.mff.cuni.cz`

Abstract

The aim of our contribution is to introduce a database of linguistic forms and their functions built with the use of the multi-layer annotated corpora of Czech, the Prague Dependency Treebanks. The purpose of the Prague Database of Forms and Functions (ForFun) is to help the linguists to study the form-function relation, which we assume to be one of the principal tasks of both theoretical linguistics and natural language processing. We will also demonstrate possibilities of the exploitation of the ForFun database.

1   Introduction

The study of the relation of (linguistic) forms and their functions or meanings is one of the fundamental tasks of linguistics, with important implications for natural language understanding. As Katz (1966, p. 100) says, to understand the ability of natural languages to serve as an instrument to the communication of thoughts and ideas we must understand what it is that permits those who speak them consistently to connect the right sounds with the right meanings. This, however, is obviously not an easy task as the relation between form and function is a many-to-many relation. At present, the availability of richly annotated corpora helps the linguist to analyze the given relation in its variety, and it is a challenging task to provide linguists with useful tools for their study.

One of the most useful types of corpora for this task are treebanks based on a stratificational (multi-layer) approach, where the form-function relation may be understood as a relation between units of two layers of the system. The aim of our contribution is to introduce a database of language forms and their linguistic functions built with the use of the multi-layer annotated corpora of Czech, the Prague Dependency Treebanks (PDTs), with the purpose to help the linguists to study the form-function relation. We offer a new tool ForFun which gives a possibility to search in a user-friendly way all forms (almost 1 500 items) used in PDTs for particular functions and vice versa to look up all functions (66 items) expressed by the particular forms.

The research question we follow by constructing the database and the new tool can be illustrated e.g. by the example of the Czech preposition *po* + Locative case of a noun (translated to English as *along, on, about, at, ... +* noun) in Figure 1. The blue colour indicates the forms, the pink colour the functions, identified in the PDTs by the functors attached to the nodes representing the given item (see below Section 2).[1] The prepositional case *po* + Locative (see the inner circle) may express the following eight functions (see the middle circle): TWHEN (when), THL (how long), ORIG (origin), MEANS, MANN (manner), EXT (extent), DIR2 (direction which way), DPHR (idiomatic meaning). Each of these functions, in turn, may be expressed by a number of forms (see the outer circle) one of which is *po* + Locative. Thus for example, the function labelled THL (how long) may be expressed by an adverb, or Accusative of a

---

[1]Throughout the paper, we use the term functor for the label of the type of the dependency relation between the governor and its dependent; in the dependency tree structure representing the sentence on the deep (underlying, tectogrammatical; see Section 2) layer this label is a part of the complex label attached to the dependent node. The term prepositional case is used for a combination of a preposition and a noun or a nominal group in a morphological case. In the figures and tables, morphological cases are indicated by numbers, i.e. 2 for Genitive, 3 for Dative, 4 for Accusative, 6 for Locative, 7 for Instrumental. When the noun or nominal group is not accompanied by a preposition, we use the term prepositionless case.

Proceedings of the 16th International Workshop on Treebanks and Linguistic Theories (TLT16), pages 56–63,
Prague, Czech Republic, January 23–24, 2018. Distributed under a CC-BY 4.0 licence. 2017.

Keywords: form-function relation, prepositions, functors

noun (prepositionless case), or prepositional cases *za* + Genitive, *za* + Accusative, *po* + Accusative, and, of course, by the already mentioned *po* + Locative.

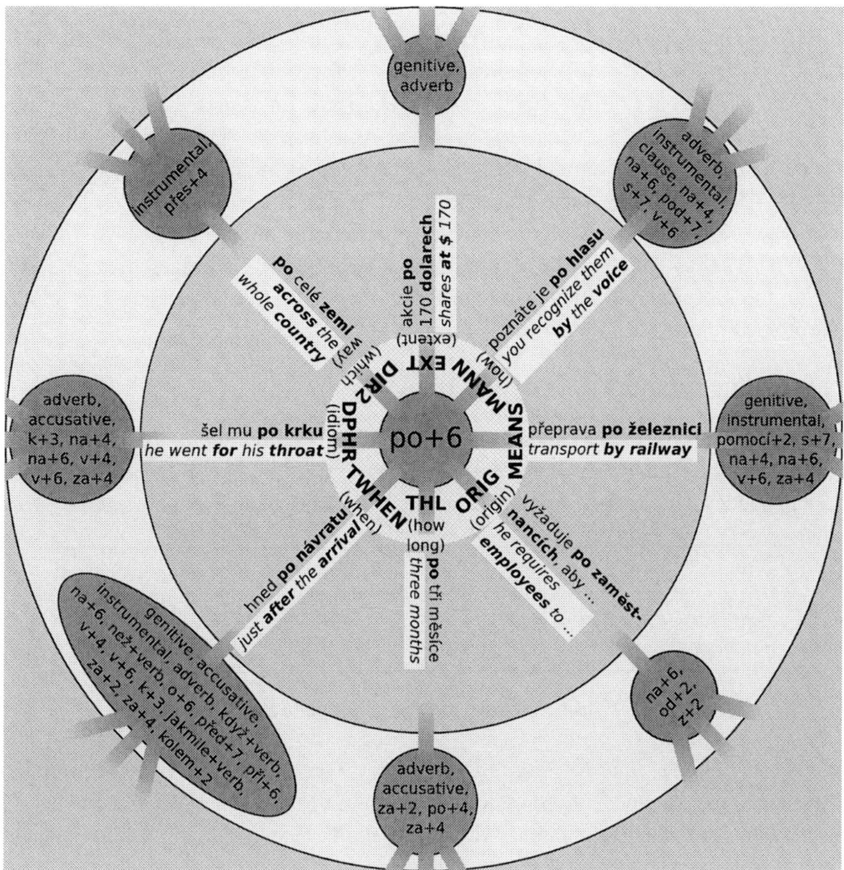

Figure 1: Many-to-many relation between forms and functions: prepositional case *po* + Locative.

2 Multi-layer Architecture of Prague Dependency Treebanks

PDTs (on which our ForFun database is based) are complex linguistically motivated treebanks based on the dependency syntactic theory of the Functional Generative Description (see Sgall et al. 1986). The original annotation scheme has the following multi-layer architecture:[2]

- **morphological layer**: all tokens of the sentence get a lemma and a (disambiguated) morphological tag,

- **surface syntax layer** (analytical): a dependency tree capturing surface syntactic relations such as subject, object, adverbial; a (structural) tag reflecting these relations is attached to the nodes as one component of their (complex) labels,

- **deep syntax layer** (tectogrammatical) capturing the semantico-syntactic relations: on this layer, the dependency structure of a sentence is a tree consisting of nodes only for autonomous meaningful units (function words such as prepositions, subordinating conjunctions, auxiliary verbs etc. are not represented as separate nodes in the structure, their contribution to the meaning of the sentence is captured within the complex labels of the autonomous units). The types of dependency relations are captured by means of the so-called functors.

---

[2]The PDTs annotation scenario is described in detail in Mikulová et al. (2006) and Hajič et al. (2017).

Functors (66 in total) are classified according to different criteria. The basic subdivision is based on the
the valency criterion, which divides functors into the argument functors and adjunct functors. There are
five arguments: Actor/Bearer (ACT), Patient (PAT), Addressee (ADDR), Origin (ORIG) and Effect (EFF).
The repertory of adjuncts is much larger than that of arguments. Their set might be divided into several
subclasses, such as temporal (TWHEN for "when?", TSIN for "since when?", TTILL for "till when?",
THL for "how long?", THO for "how often?", etc.), local (LOC for "where?", DIR1 for "where from?",
DIR2 for "which way?", DIR3 for "where to?"), causal (such as CAUS for "cause", AIM for "in order to",
COND for "condition", etc.), and other adjuncts (MANN for general "manner", ACMP for "accompaniment",
EXT for "extent", MEANS for "means or instrument", INTF for "intensifier", BEN for "benefactor", RSTR
for "attribute", etc.). For a full list of all dependency relations and their labels see Mikulová et al. (2006).

For the ForFun database, we use the annotations of the nodes on the deep syntactic layer and their
counterparts on the morphological layer, which has made it possible to retrieve the relations between
functions (expressed on the deep level by functors) and forms and vice versa.

3   List of available Prague Dependency Treebanks

For Czech, the following four treebanks are now available, each of them contains data of a different
source: the Prague Dependency Treebank 3.0,[3] the Prague Czech-English Dependency Treebank 2.0,[4]
the Prague Dependency Treebank of Spoken Czech 2.0,[5] and the PDT-Faust corpus.[6]

	PDT 3.0	PCEDT 2.0	PDTSC 2.0	Faust	Total
Tokens	833 195	1 162 072	742 257	33 772	2 771 296
Sentences	49 431	49 208	73 835	3 000	175 474

Table 1: Volume of data in Prague Depencency Treebanks

It is obvious (see Table 1) that the Prague Dependency Treebank family provides rich language data
for our purpose, i.e. for the study of the relation of forms and their functions since every content word
there is assigned one of those 66 functors. Altogether, the treebanks contain around 180 000 sentences
with their morphological, syntactic and semantic annotation.

4   Prague Database of Forms and Functions

ForFun 1.0—Prague Database of Forms and Functions—is a rich database of syntactic functions and their
formal realizations with a large amount of examples coming from both written and spoken Czech texts.
Since the database is extracted from the PDTs (see Section 3), it takes over the list of syntactic functions as
well as the terminology (they are called *functors*). ForFun is provided as a digital open source accessible
to all scholars via the LINDAT/CLARIN repository.[7]

4.1   Design

We have already mentioned that in general the relation between forms and functions is a many-to-many
relation. As such, it has to be explored from both sides: a given form has several functions and any of
these functions may again be realized by several forms (the given one among them). When such relations

---

[3]https://ufal.mff.cuni.cz/prague-dependency-treebank
In the PDT 3.0 (see Hajič et al., 2006, Bejček et al., 2013), the data consist of articles from Czech daily newspapers.

[4]https://ufal.mff.cuni.cz/pcedt2.0/
In the parallel PCEDT 2.0 (see Hajič et al., 2012), the English part consists of the Wall Street Journal sections of the Penn
Treebank (Marcus et al., 1993), and the Czech part, which is used in ForFun, was manually translated from the English original.

[5]https://ufal.mff.cuni.cz/pdtsc2.0
The PDTSC 2.0 (see Mikulová et al., 2017b) contains dialogs from the Malach project (https://ufal.mff.cuni.cz/cvhm/
vha-info.html, slightly moderated testimonies of Holocaust survivors) and from the Companions project (http://cordis.
europa.eu/project/rcn/96289_en.html, two participants chat over a collection of photographs).

[6]PDT-Faust is a small treebank containing short segments (very often with vulgar content) typed in by various users on the
reverso.net webpage for translation.

[7]http://hdl.handle.net/11234/1-2542

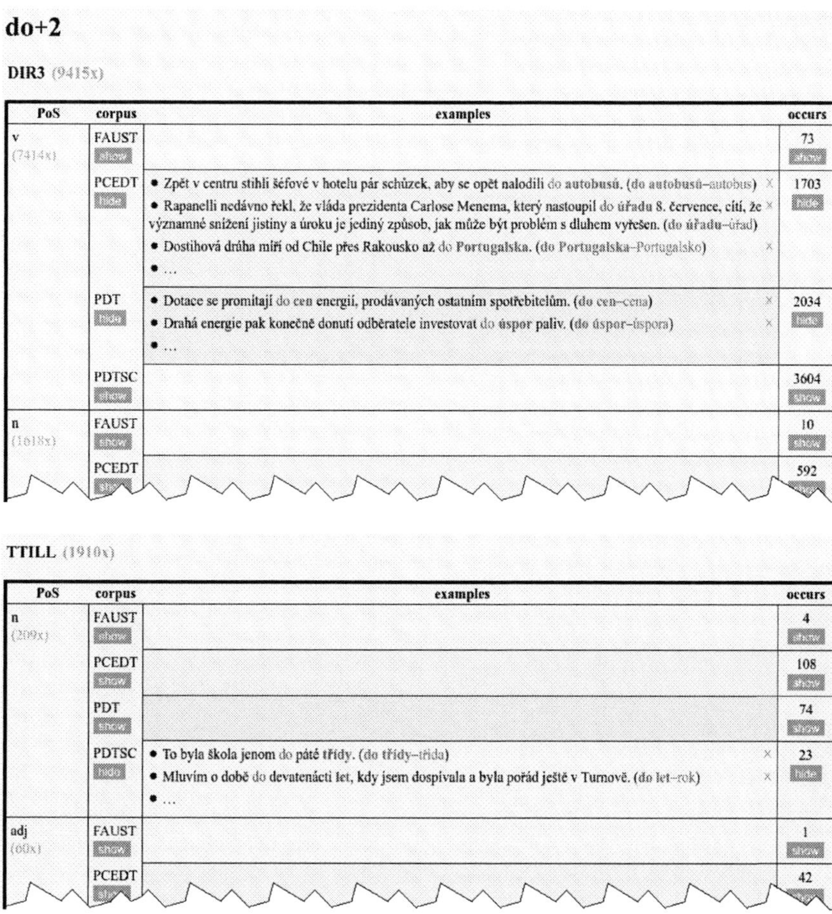

do+2

DIR3 (9415x)

PoS	corpus	examples	occurs
v (7414x)	FAUST show		73 show
	PCEDT hide	• Zpět v centru stihli šéfové v hotelu pár schůzek, aby se opět nalodili do autobusů. (do autobusů–autobus) × • Rapanelli nedávno řekl, že vláda prezidenta Carlose Menema, který nastoupil do úřadu 8. července, cítí, že × významné snížení jistiny a úroku je jediný způsob, jak může být problém s dluhem vyřešen. (do úřadu–úřad) • Dostihová dráha míří od Chile přes Rakousko až do Portugalska. (do Portugalska–Portugalsko) × • …	1703 hide
	PDT hide	• Dotace se promítají do cen energií, prodávaných ostatním spotřebitelům. (do cen–cena) × • Drahá energie pak konečně donutí odběratele investovat do úspor paliv. (do úspor–úspora) × • …	2034 hide
	PDTSC show		3604 show
n (1618x)	FAUST show		10 show
	PCEDT		592

TTILL (1910x)

PoS	corpus	examples	occurs
n (209x)	FAUST show		4 show
	PCEDT show		108 show
	PDT show		74 show
	PDTSC hide	• To byla škola jenom do páté třídy. (do třídy–třída) × • Mluvím o době do devatenácti let, kdy jsem dospívala a byla pořád ještě v Turnově. (do let–rok) × • …	23 hide
adj (60x)	FAUST show		1 show
	PCEDT		42

Figure 2: A screenshot of the ForFun web interface: From Form to Function.

have to be explored, ForFun is a perfect choice, since it is designed exactly for this kind of traversing through data.

Although the annotated example sentences are the same, they can be retrieved by asking either for their forms or for their functions. The ForFun database provides two entry points (cf. Figures 2 and 3):

- The user can choose one of almost 1 500 formal realizations of sentence units (i.e. prepositionless and prepositional cases, subordinated and coordinate conjunctions, adverbs, infinitive and finite verb forms, etc.) and obtains all functions it can represent.
- The user can choose one of 66 syntactic functions (i.e. LOC, TTILL, CAUS etc.) and obtains all forms used to express it.

The view can be always switched from a list of forms to a list of functions of one of them and vice versa.

For each form-function relation there are plenty of examples in the form of a sentence with the highlighted expression representing the relation. All these examples are sorted by various criteria:

- the word class of the parent node,
- the particular forms for the function or particular functions for the form, and
- the source of text data (written, spoken, translated texts and texts from internet users).

The number of examples available in the database is displayed for each pair form+functor, or functor+word class, each combination functor+form+word class and each specified 4-combination (form+functor+word class+source), see Figures 2 and 3. Either first ten examples or all of them are displayed on demand.

On top of that, examples can be also first filtered by their source, which allows the user to hide e.g. all

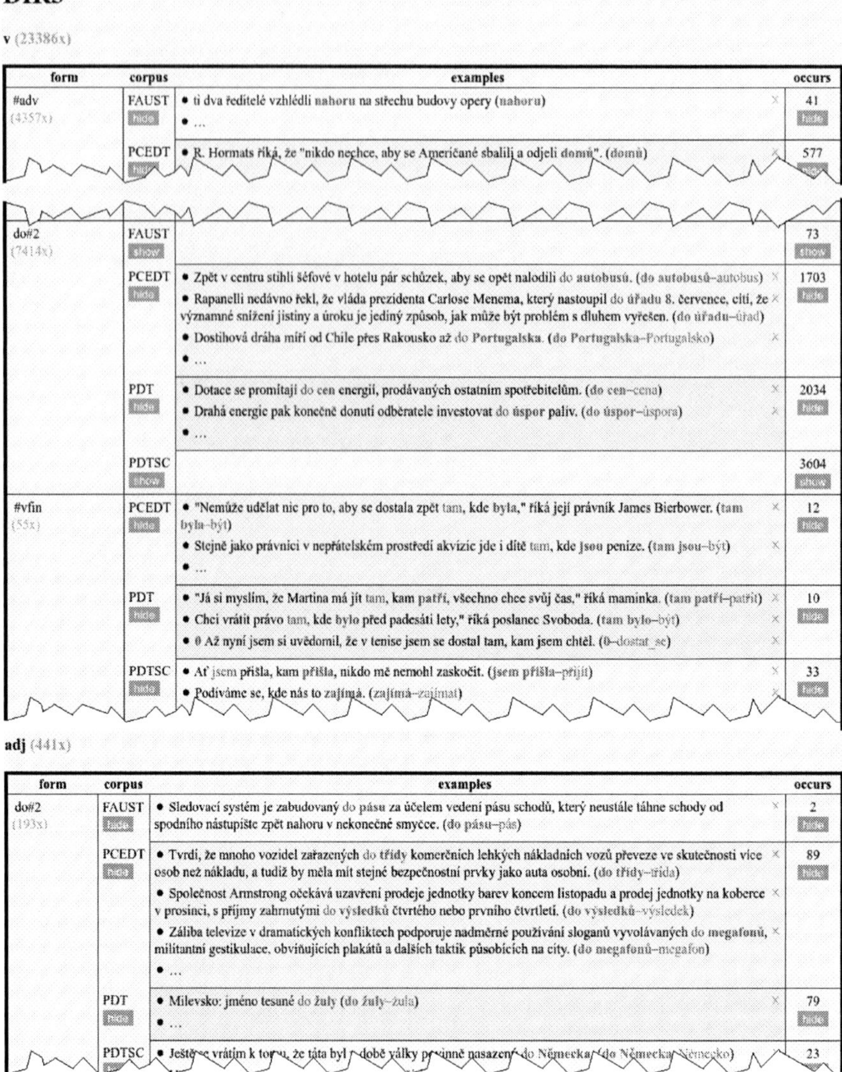

Figure 3: A screenshot of the ForFun web interface: From Function to Form.

forms used only in the spoken language.

An illustration of how the result of user's search for the functions of the prepositional case *do* + Genitive looks like is given in Figure 2. In the upper part, there are 9 415 occurrences in all PDTs of the form *do* + Genitive representing the functor DIR3. The occurrences of *do* + Genitive are divided according to their heads (be it a v(erb) or a n(oun), see the first column); their distribution within particular treebank is given in the second column followed by real examples from the corresponding treebank. A few of them are displayed on demand whereas many (see the last column) stay hidden. In the lower part of Figure 2, the same form *do* + Genitive in the function TTILL is exemplified in the same style.[8] For the opposite direction "from function to form" see Figure 3, where (among others) the same sentences for *do* + Genitive as the functor DIR3 can be found searching for all representations of the functor DIR3. Other forms include a finite verb (#vfin) or an adverbial.

---

[8] Figure 2 presents only a part of the full response obtained from the ForFun database for the given query. The other functions of *do* + Genitive (PAT, EXT, EFF and others) are also not included in this shortened sample.

4.2 Volume

The database contains 2.2 million examples altogether for all forms (and the same number from the function point of view), split approx. 3:1 between written and spoken text (see Table 2). Each example is one sentence long.[9] They can be examined from the function side (66 functors) or the form side (1 469 forms). All examples are split into 13.5 thousand of 4-combinations, each with 163 examples in average.

examples from written text	1 608 061
examples from spoken text	593 400
examples altogether	2 201 461
number of functions	66
number of forms	1 469
number of 4-combinations	13 514
avg. examples for a function	33 355
avg. examples for a form	1 500
avg. examples for a 4-combination	163
max. number of examples for a function	490 121
max. number of examples for a form	370 586
max. number of examples for a 4-combination	97 469

Table 2: Volume of the ForFun database

While the average number is high, median is only two examples. The reason is that there is a long tail of 4-combinations used very rarely. These occurences with very low frequencies in the data are one of the main benefits of the large volume of database, but they have to be used carefully. Every result has to be always understood solely as an input for a subsequent research, as the ForFun database may contain errors (caused by annotators as well as speakers/writers) considering its volume.

5 What Can We Find Out about Form-Function Relations in the ForFun Database?

To display the richness of the material we work with, we present several examples connected with the studies of the form-function relation what the user can find out in the ForFun database.

prep.	number	list of functors
na+4	42	ACT ADDR AIM APP ATT BEN CAUS COMPL COND CPHR CPR CRIT DIFF DIR1 DIR3 DPHR EFF EXT ID INTF INTT LOC MANN MAT MEANS MOD ORIG PAT PREC REG RESL RESTR RHEM RSTR SUBS TFHL TFRWH THL TOWH TPAR TTILL TWHEN
v+6	36	ACMP ACT AIM APP ATT BEN CAUS COMPL COND CPR CRIT DENOM DIR2 DIR3 DPHR EFF EXT ID LOC MANN MAT MEANS MOD PAT PREC REG RESL RESTR RHEM RSTR SUBS TFHL THL THO TPAR TWHEN
k+3	34	ACMP ACT ADDR AIM APP ATT BEN CAUS COMPL CPHR CRIT DIR1 DIR2 DIR3 DPHR EFF EXT ID INTT LOC MANN PAR PAT PREC REG RESL RESTR RHEM RSTR TOWH TPAR TSIN TTILL TWHEN

Table 3: The prepositional cases with the highest number of functions.

5.1 Multi-functionality of Forms

A rather straightforward use of the ForFun database is to retrieve which functions can be expressed by the particular form. Table 3 contains three prepositional cases with the highest number of functions they

---

[9]One sentence typically contains many different functions and serves for many examples (once for each of its parts).

express: *na* + Accusative, *v* + Locative and *k* + Dative. The *po* + Locative case from Figure 1 with 32 functions would be the seventh prepositional case in this Table.

5.2 Absolute Frequency of Forms and Functions (in both written and spoken texts)

An observation of frequency has an important place in the description of language because it quantifies linguistic choices made by speakers and writers. Theoretical statements are often of a little value for generalizations about language use unless they can be corroborated by observations of frequency.

For each form and function, ForFun provides information about absolute frequency in all the PDTs as well as in each corpus separately. The users can search quickly and in a user-friendly way which formal means are the most frequent in Czech sentences and which ones are rarely used. (See Table 4 for five most frequent prepositional cases in Czech in comparison with the class of adverbs and the clause with the conjunction *že* [*that*].) They can find out the distribution of a particular function (various arguments or adjuncts) in the sentences. For both forms and functions, they can compare their absolute frequencies in written and spoken texts.

form	occurences
v+6	51 682
na+4	22 444
s+7	19 747
z+2	19 502
na+6	17 870
adverb	93 824
že[that]+verb	26 831

Table 4: The most frequent prepositional cases

5.3 Material for Detailed Linguistic Studies

In addition to valuable statistical data, the ForFun database provides an extremely rich material for detailed linguistic studies of individual language phenomena and for their description and classification. One of the first linguistic studies based on the database is the analysis and subclassification of the original functors denoting space (Mikulová et al., 2017a).

6 Conclusion

The ForFun database has been built as a rich and user-friendly resource for those researchers who (want to) use corpora in their everyday work and look for various occurrences of specific forms or patterns in relation to their syntactic functions etc. but they are not interested or just do not need to deal with various technical, formal and annotation issues. ForFun brings a rich and complex annotation in PDTs based on a sound linguistic theory closer to common researchers. It will be further developed, though it should be borne in mind that it is designed to provide only a limited number of most useful features, rather than a full interface to everything PDTs can offer. There are other complex tools for that[10] and ForFun does not aim to substitute them. In its simplicity and clarity, it is a user-friendly source of examples for various explorations especially in syntax.

Acknowledgments

The research reported in the paper has been supported by the Czech Science Foundation under the projects GA17-12624S and GA17-07313S and by the LINDAT/CLARIN project of Ministry of Education, Youth and Sports of the Czech Republic (project LM2015071). This work has been using language resources developed, stored and distributed by the latter project (LM2015071).

---

[10]E.g. PML Tree Query https://lindat.mff.cuni.cz/services/pmltq/, INESS Search http://clarino.uib.no/iness, etc.

References

Eduard Bejček, Eva Hajičová, Jan Hajič, Pavlína Jínová, Václava Kettnerová, Veronika Kolářová, Marie Mikulová, Jiří Mírovský, Anna Nedoluzhko, Jarmila Panevová, Lucie Poláková, Magda Ševčíková, Jan Štěpánek, and Šárka Zikánová. 2013. Prague Dependency Treebank 3.0. Data, http://hdl.handle.net/11858/00-097C-0000-0023-1AAF-3.

Jan Hajič, Eva Hajičová, Marie Mikulová, and Jiří Mírovský. 2017. *Handbook on Linguistic Annotation*, Springer Verlag, Dordrecht, Netherlands, chapter Prague Dependency Treebank, pages 555–594.

Jan Hajič, Eva Hajičová, Jarmila Panevová, Petr Sgall, Ondřej Bojar, Silvie Cinková, Eva Fučíková, Marie Mikulová, Petr Pajas, Jan Popelka, Jiří Semecký, Jana Šindlerová, Jan Štěpánek, Josef Toman, Zdeňka Urešová, and Zdeněk Žabokrtský. 2012. Announcing Prague Czech-English Dependency Treebank 2.0. In *Proceedings of the 8th International Conference on Language Resources and Evaluation (LREC 2012)*. European Language Resources Association, Istanbul, Turkey, pages 3153–3160. https://aclanthology.info/pdf/L/L12/L12-1280.pdf.

Jan Hajič, Jarmila Panevová, Eva Hajičová, Petr Sgall, Petr Pajas, Jan Štěpánek, Jiří Havelka, Marie Mikulová, Zdeněk Žabokrtský, Magda Ševčíková-Razímová, and Zdeňka Urešová. 2006. Prague Dependency Treebank 2.0 (LDC2006T01).

Jerrold J. Katz. 1966. *The philosophy of language*. Studies in languages. Harper & Row, New York.

Mitchell P. Marcus, Beatrice Santorini, and Mary Ann Marcinkiewicz. 1993. Building a large annotated corpus of English: The Penn Treebank. *Computational Linguistics* 19(2):313–330. https://aclanthology.info/pdf/J/J93/J93-2004.pdf.

Marie Mikulová, Eduard Bejček, Veronika Kolářová, and Jarmila Panevová. 2017a. Subcategorization of adverbial meanings based on corpus data. *Journal of Linguistics / Jazykovedný časopis* 68(2):268–277.

Marie Mikulová, Alevtina Bémová, Jan Hajič, Eva Hajičová, Jiří Havelka, Veronika Kolářová, Lucie Kučová, Markéta Lopatková, Petr Pajas, Jarmila Panevová, Magda Razímová, Petr Sgall, Jan Štěpánek, Zdeňka Urešová, Kateřina Veselá, and Zdeněk Žabokrtský. 2006. Annotation on the tectogrammatical level in the Prague Dependency Treebank. Annotation manual. Technical Report 30, ÚFAL MFF UK, Prague, Czech Rep.

Marie Mikulová, Jiří Mírovský, Anna Nedoluzhko, Petr Pajas, Jan Štěpánek, and Jan Hajič. 2017b. PDTSC 2.0 – spoken corpus with rich multi-layer structural annotation. In *Text, Speech, and Dialogue 20th International Conference, TSD 2017*. Charles University, Springer International Publishing, Cham / Heidelberg / New York / Dordrecht / London, Lecture Notes in Computer Science, pages 129–137.

Petr Sgall, Eva Hajičová, and Jarmila Panevová. 1986. *The Meaning of the Sentence and Its Semantic and Pragmatic Aspects*. Academia/Reidel Publishing Company, Prague/Dordrecht.

Literal readings of multiword expressions: as scarce as hen's teeth

Agata Savary
Université François Rabelais Tours, France
University of Düsseldorf, Germany
agata.savary@univ-tours.fr

Silvio Ricardo Cordeiro
Aix-Marseille Université, France
silvio.cordeiro@lif.univ-mrs.fr

Abstract

Multiword expressions can have both idiomatic and literal occurrences. Distinguishing these two cases is considered one of the major challenges in MWE processing. We suggest that literal readings should be considered in both semantic and syntactic terms, which motivates their study in a treebank. We propose heuristics to automatically pre-identify candidate sentences that might contain literal readings of verbal VMWEs, and we apply them to an existing Polish treebank. We also perform a linguistic study of the literal readings extracted by the different heuristics. The results suggest that literal readings constitute a rare phenomenon. We also identify some properties that may distinguish them from their idiomatic counterparts.

1 Introduction

Multiword expressions (MWEs) are word combinations, such as ***all of a sudden***, *a **hot dog***, *to **pay** a **visit*** or *to **pull** one's **leg***, which exhibit lexical, syntactic, semantic, pragmatic and/or statistical idiosyncrasies. They encompass closely related linguistic objects such as idioms, compounds, light verb constructions, rhetorical figures, institutionalised phrases or named entities. A prominent feature of many MWEs, especially of verbal idioms such as *to **pull** one's **leg***, is their non-compositional semantics, i.e. the fact that their meaning cannot be deduced from the meanings of their components, and from their syntactic structure, in a way deemed regular for the given language. For this reason, MWEs pose special challenges both to linguistic modeling (e.g. as linguistic objects crossing boundaries between lexicon and grammar) and to Natural Language Processing (NLP) applications, especially those which rely on semantic interpretation of text (e.g. information retrieval, information extraction or machine translation).

Another challenging property of many MWEs, as in example (1), is that we can encounter their literally understood counterparts, as in (2). However, it is not clear what should be considered an occurrence of a literal reading of an MWE. Should "coincidental" co-occurrences of its lexicalized components,[1] like in (4) as opposed to (3), also be considered its literal occurrences? Should variants like (6), which considerably change the "canonical" syntactic dependencies between the components, compared to (5), still be considered idiomatic occurrences? Finally, what should be the status of word plays which deliberately refer to both the idiomatic and the literal reading of an MWE, as in (7)?

(1) *The man was **pulling my leg** but I didn't believe him.*

(2) *The kid was pulling my leg to make me play with him.*

(3) *The preparations were not thoroughly planned **after all**.*

(4) *After all the preparations we finally left.*

(5) *The Samsung boss can still **pull** the **strings** from prison.*

(6) *The article addresses the political **strings** which the journalist claimed that the senator **pulled**.*

(7) (Polish) *Wyciągnięcie rąk uchroniło go od **wyciągnięcia nóg*** 'Stretching hands prevented him from stretching legs' ⇒ STRETCHING HIS HANDS PREVENTED HIM FROM DYING

For a given MWE E with lexicalized components $e_1, \ldots, e_n$, we define its *literal reading occurrence*, or *literal reading* (LR) for short, as a co-occurrence of the lexemes $e_1, \ldots, e_n$ in a context in which:

---

[1]The lexicalized components of an MWE are those which are always realized by the same lexeme. For instance in *to **pay** a **visit*** the head verb is always a form of *pay* but the determiner *a* can be freely replaced, as in ***paid** many **visits***. In this paper the lexicalized components of MWEs are highlighted in boldface.

Proceedings of the 16th International Workshop on Treebanks and Linguistic Theories (TLT16), pages 64–72,
Prague, Czech Republic, January 23–24, 2018. Distributed under a CC-BY 4.0 licence. 2017.

Keywords: multiword expressions, literal reading, idiomaticity rate, treebank, Polish

(i) it is not a MWE; and (ii) one of the typical senses of each of $e_1, \ldots, e_n$ is activated; and (iii) the syntactic constraints among $e_1, \ldots, e_n$ are preserved, i.e. either the same or equivalent dependencies hold between E's components as in its canonical (citation) form. Dependencies are equivalent if the syntactic variation can be neutralized while preserving the overall meaning. For instance (6) can be reformulated into: *The journalist claimed that the senator **pulled** political **strings**, and this article addresses them.* Therefore, the syntactic constraints between $e_1 = pull$ and $e_2 = strings$ visible in (5) are preserved in (6). According to this definition, only example (2) above is considered an LR.[2] Example (4) does not fulfill condition (iii), while (1), (3), (5) and (6) do not fulfill (i-ii), since their are idiomatic readings (IRs). In example (7), the expression *wyciągnięcie rąk* STRETCHING HANDS points to a typical meaning of the verb *wyciągnąć* STRETCH. By analogy, the reader is also induced to think of a literal meaning of the noun *nogi* LEGS. However, the idiomatic meaning of *wyciągnięcie nóg* 'stretching legs' $\Rightarrow$ DYING is still intact and thus it fails condition (i). Note that, due to the presence of condition (iii), the study of literal readings of MWEs is best done in a treebank.

The motivation to study the phenomenon of LRs of MWEs, and of its frequency in particular, is both of linguistic and of computational nature. Firstly, psycholinguistic studies put special interest in the interplay between LRs and IRs, as well as their distributional and statistical properties, when discovering how idioms are stored and processed in human mind (Cacciari and Corradini, 2015). Secondly, the links between LRs and IRs readings can inform us which morpho-syntactic variation is allowed or prohibited by some MWEs, and why (Sheinfux et al., 2017; Pausé, 2017). Additionally, an opposition of the contexts in which LRs and IRs readings occur may yield better methods to automatically distinguish them (Peng et al., 2014; Peng and Feldman, 2016).

This last task is considered one of the major challenges in automatic processing of MWEs (Constant et al., 2017). Its quantitative importance can be estimated by measuring the *idiomaticity rate*, i.e. the ratio of occurrences of an MWE with idiomatic reading to both its idiomatic and literal occurrences in a corpus (El Maarouf and Oakes, 2015). If the overall (i.e. aggregated for all MWEs) idiomaticity rate is relatively low, distinguishing IRs and LRs readings becomes, indeed, a major challenge, as claimed by Fazly et al. (2009). If, conversely, it is high, or even close to 100%, the task can be neglected for many applications. Also, as shown by (Waszczuk et al., 2016), a high idiomaticity rate can considerably speed up parsing, if appropriately taken into account by a parser's architecture.

In this paper we are interested in verbal MWEs (VMWEs), in which syntactic flexibility can be particularly rich. We exploit an existing multilingual corpus (Savary et al., 2017) in which VMWE annotations are accompanied by morphological and dependency annotations, but literal occurrences are not tagged (Sec. 2). We propose several heuristics to automatically detect possible literal occurrences of known, i.e. manually annotated, VMWEs (Sec. 3). Then we manually categorize the resulting occurrences using a typology which accounts for true and false positives, as well as for linguistic properties of LRs as opposed to IRs (Sec. 5). We report on results in a Slavic language: Polish (Sec. 5). Finally, we conclude and discuss perspectives for future work (Sec. 6).

2 Corpus

We use the openly available PARSEME corpus[3] manually annotated for VMWEs in 18 languages (Savary et al., 2017). Among its 5 VMWE categories, three are relevant to this Polish-dedicated study:

- *Idioms* (IDs) are verbal phrases of various syntactic structures, mostly characterized by non-compositional meaning, as in (8). Due to the fact that many idioms were conceived as metaphors, they maintain a large potential of LRs, as exemplified in (9).
  - (8)   *dawno już powinien był **wyciągnąć nogi** 'long-ago already should-he have stretched legs'* $\Rightarrow$ HE SHOULD HAVE DIED LONG AGO
  - (9)   *położyłem się na trawie i wyciągnąłem nogi 'I-lay-down on the-grass and stretched legs'*
- *Light-verb constructions* (LVCs) are *VERB (PREP) (DET) NOUN* combinations in which the verb V is semantically void and the noun N is a predicate expressing an event or a state, as in (10). The

---

[2]Henceforth, we use wavy and dashed underlining for true and false LRs, respectively. Straight underlining denotes focus.
[3]http://hdl.handle.net/11372/LRT-2282

idiomatic nature of LVCs lies in the fact that the verb may be lexically constrained and does not contribute any semantics to the whole expression. LVCs are mostly semantically compositional, therefore the notion of a LR is less intuitively motivated for them. A LR of an LVC should be understood as a co-occurrence of its lexemes which does not have all the required LVC properties. This occurs, for instance, when N is not predicative or does not express and event or a state, as in (11), where *udziały 'shares'* denotes an amount of financial assets. Figures 1a and 1b present another occurrence of this VMWE, and of its LR, respectively.

(10)   ***mieć swój udział*** w debacie *'have one's share in debate'* $\Rightarrow$ TO TAKE PART IN THE DEBATE
(11)   *mieć udziały w spółce 'have shares in company'* $\Rightarrow$ TO HAVE SHARES IN A COMPANY

- *Inherently reflexive verbs* (IReflVs), pervasive in Romance and Slavic languages but not in English, are combinations of a verb V and a reflexive clitic $RCLI$, such that one of the 3 non-compositionality conditions holds: (i) V never occurs without $RCLI$ as is the case for the VMWE in (12); (ii) $RCLI$ distinctly changes the meaning of V, like in (13); (iii) $RCLI$ changes the subcategorization frame of V, like in (15) as opposed to (16). IReflVs are semantically non-compositional in the sense that $RCLI$ is not an argument of the verb. LRs never occur for type (i) but they do occur for types (ii) and (iii), due to homonymy with compositional V-RCLI combinations which express true reflexive or reciprocal meanings, as in (14), or impersonal or middle passive alternation, as in (17).

(12)   ***bał się*** wody *'feared RCLI water'* $\Rightarrow$ HE WAS AFRAID OF WATER
(13)   *nie **oglądaj się** na innych 'not watch RCLI on others'* $\Rightarrow$ DO NOT COUNT ON THE OTHERS
(14)   *oglądam się w lustrze 'I-am-watching myself in the mirror'*
(15)   ***spotykać się*** z przyjaciółmi *'meet RCLI with friends.INST'* $\Rightarrow$ MEET FRIENDS
(16)   *spotykać przyjaciół 'to meet friends.ACC'*
(17)   *nie spotyka się takich ludzi 'not meets RCLI such people'* $\Rightarrow$ SUCH PEOPLE ARE NEVER MET

The Polish part of the training corpus contains 11,578 sentences, for a total of 191,239 tokens and 3,149 annotated instances of VMWEs.[4] For most languages, including Polish, the VMWE annotation layer is accompanied by morphological and syntactic layers (ML and SL, respectively), as shown in Fig. 1a and 1b. In ML, a lemma, a POS and morphological features are assigned to each token. SL represents syntactic dependencies between tokens. For Polish, both ML and SL use the Universal Dependencies (UDs) tagsets.[5] ML was created partly manually and partly automatically, and SL automatically, using UDPipe[6] with its pre-trained Polish model. While the PARSEME corpus is manually annotated and categorized for IRs of VMWEs, it is not annotated for their LRs. Therefore, we developed several heuristics which allow us to identify them automatically.

3 Identifying literal readings

We use no external resources, therefore we can only identify LRs for VMWEs which are annotated at least once in the corpus. In order to fully reliably perform this task, we would have to ensure that conditions (i), (ii) and (iii) from page 1 hold. Condition (i) can be automatically fulfilled by discarding predictions that coincide with annotated VMWEs. Condition (ii) cannot be checked automatically, given that the available annotation layers do not account for semantics. It must, thus, be subject to manual verification. Condition (iii) is closely linked to the SL annotations but checking it fully reliably can be hindered by at least two factors. Firstly, some dependency annotations in SL can be incorrect, especially if SL was constructed automatically. Secondly, defining conditions under which two sets of dependency relations are equivalent seems challenging and highly language-dependent. Given the large number of possible syntactic structures of VMWEs, an exhaustive catalog of such equivalences would be huge, or

---

[4]The annotation was performed by a single native Polish annotator. The inter-annotator agreement (IAA) in VMWE identification was measured in terms of the F-measure and κ, with the scores of 0.529 and 0.434, respectively. The IAA in VMWE categorisation (based on the VMWE identified jointly by two annotators) assessed in terms of the F-measure, and equal to 0.939. All IAA scores were based on a small sample of the corpus, anotated in parallel by another Polish speaker who only had few experience with the guidelines and did not annotate the final corpus. Therefore, these IAA scores are rather weak indicators of the annotation quality.

[5]http://universaldependencies.org/guidelines.html
[6]https://ufal.mff.cuni.cz/udpipe

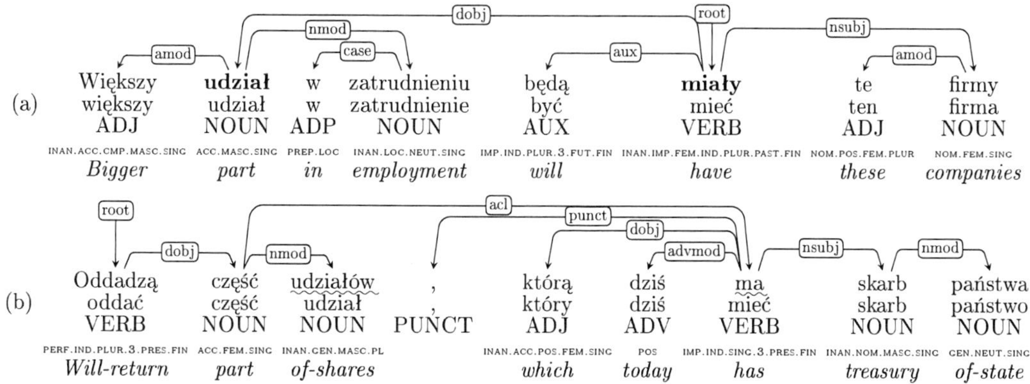

Figure 1: Morphosyntactic annotations for an occurrence context of the VMWE *mieć udział* 'have share'
⇒ TAKE PART (a) and its LR (b). Translations: (a) *These companies will participate in employment more intensively.* (b) *They will return the part of the shares that the treasury has today.*

even potentially infinite, due to long-distance dependencies in recursively embedded relative clauses, as illustrated in example (6). In order to cope with these obstacles, we designed four heuristics which should cover a large majority of LRs in complementary ways, while maintaining the amount of false positives relatively low (i.e. the heuristics are skewed towards high recall). They rely on the following definitions.

Each *sequence* of words is a function $s : \{1, 2, \ldots, |s|\} \to W$, where W are word forms. The sequence s can be noted as $s := \{s_1, s_2, \ldots s_{|s|}\}$, where $s_i := (i, w_i)$ is a single *token*. A sequence can thus be denoted as a set of pairs: $s = \{(1, w_1), (2, w_2), \ldots, (|s|, w_{|s|})\}$. For example, the sentence in Fig. 1a can be represented as a sequence $s = \{(1, \text{Większy}), (2, \text{udział}), \ldots, (8, \text{firmy})\}$. For a given token $s_i = (i, w_i)$, lemma(s_i) is its case-folded lemma form (or nil if unavailable in ML), and surface(s_i) is its case-folded surface form. For instance in Fig. 1a, lemma$(s_6) = $ mieć, surface$(s_6) = $ miały, and surface$(s_1) = $ większy. As not every token may have lemma information, we define lemmasurface(s_i) as the lemma if available, and as the surface form otherwise. If s is a sentence, each token s_i is associated with its parent, denoted as parent(s_i), through a syntactic label, denoted as label(s_i). Some tokens may have parent nil (and label root). In Fig. 1a, label$(s_2) = $ dobj, parent$(s_2) = s_6$, label$(s_6) = $ root, and parent$(s_6) = $ nil. For a given sequence s, its *subsequence* q is an injection defined as an order-preserving sequence over tokens of s, i.e. $q : \{1, 2, \ldots, |q|\} \to s$ such that, if $i < j$, $q(i) = s_k$ and $q(j) = s_l$, then $k < l$. The definitions of lemmas and surface forms extend straightforwardly to tokens of a subsequence: lemma$((i, s_k)) := $ lemma(s_k) and surface$((i, s_k)) := $ surface(s_k). For instance in Fig. 1a, the subsequence corresponding to the tokens in bold can be formalized as $q = \{(1, s_2), (2, s_6)\} = \{(1, (2, \text{udział})), (2, (6, \text{miały}))\}$, and lemma$(q_2) = $ lemma$((2, s_6)) = $ lemma$(s_6) = $ mieć, etc.

In a subsequence q, the definition of a parent still relies on the dependencies in the underlying sequence s but is restricted to the tokens in q. Formally, for a given $1 \leqslant i \leqslant |q|$, if there exists $1 \leqslant j \leqslant |q|$ such that parent$(q(i)) = q(j)$, then parent$_{sub}(q_i) := q_j$. Otherwise parent$_{sub}(q_i) := nil$. For instance in Fig. 1a, $q_1 = (1, s_2)$, $q_2 = (2, s_6)$, parent$_{sub}(q_1) = q_2$ and parent$_{sub}(q_2) = $ nil. In Fig. 1b, where the subsequence consisting of the underlined tokens forms a non-connected graph, the parents of both components are nil, i.e. $q_1 = (1, s_3)$, $q_2 = (2, s_7)$, and parent$_{sub}(q_1) = $ parent$_{sub}(q_2) = $ nil.

In the pre-processing step we extract each occurrence of an annotated VMWE in a sentence s as a subsequence of s, noted $m = \{m_1, m_2, \ldots, m_{|m|}\}$. For each known VMWE m extracted in this way, and for each sentence $s' = \{s'_1, s'_2, \ldots, s'_{|S|}\}$, we then look for literal matches of m in s'. We define a *literal match* as an injection $\phi : m \to s'$, where for every $t \in m$, we have lemmasurface$(t) \in \{$lemma$(\phi(t)), $ surface$(\phi(t))\}$, and the image of m is not annotated as a VMWE itself. For instance, for the VMWE $m = \{(1, s_2), (2, s_6)\}$ from Fig. 1a, we obtain the following literal match in the sentence from Fig. 1b: $\phi = \{((1, s_2), s'_3), ((2, s_6), s'_7)\}$. The set of such bijections can be huge and include a large number of false positives, i.e. coincidental co-occurrences of m's components in the same sentence.

Figure 2: True and false LRs of *mieć udział* 'have share' ⇒ TAKE PART, with extracts of SL.

Therefore, we restrain the set of such injections with the following criteria.

- **WindowGap**: Under this criterion, all matched tokens must fit into a sliding window with no more than g external elements. Formally, let J be the set of all matched indexes in the sentence s', i.e. $J = \{\, j \mid m_i \in m,\ s'_j = \phi(m_i) \,\}$. Then ϕ is only considered to match if $\max(J) - \min(J) + 1 \leqslant g + |m|$. For m in Fig. 1a and s' in Fig. 1b we have $J = \{3, 7\}$ and $|m| = 2$. Thus, the tokens corresponding to *udziałów ma* are a literal match only if $g \geqslant 3$. In the case of Fig. 2, every reading can be matched with $g \geqslant 2$.

- **BagOfDeps**: Under this criterion, a literal match must be a connected graph, but the directions and the labels of the dependencies are ignored. Formally, there must be a token $m_{\text{root}} \in m$ for which $\text{parent}(m_{\text{root}}) = \text{nil}$. Moreover, for every token $m_i \in m \setminus \{m_{\text{root}}\}$, there exists a token $m_k \in m$ such that $\text{parent}(\phi(m_i)) = \phi(m_k)$. For instance, the readings in Fig. 2a, 2b and 2d are matched under this criterion, but not those in Fig. 2c and Fig. 1b.

- **UnlabeledDeps**: Under this criterion, a literal match must be a connected directed graph in which the dependency labels are ignored but the parent relations are preserved. Formally, this criterion adds a restriction to BagOfDeps: m_k must be such that $m_k = \text{parent}_{sub}(m_i)$. For instance, the readings in Fig. 2b and 2d are matched under this criterion, but not those in Fig. 2a, 2c and Fig. 1b.

- **LabeledDeps**: Under this criterion, a literal match must be a connected directed graph in which both the parent relations and the dependency labels are preserved. Formally, this criterion adds a restriction to UnlabeledDeps: For every $m_i \in m \setminus \{m_{\text{root}}\}$, we must have $\text{label}(m_i) = \text{label}(\phi(m_i))$. Only the reading in Fig. 2b is matched under this criterion.

4 Results

The above heuristics, which are language-independent, were used to automatically pre-select LR candidates of VMWEs occurring in the training part of the Polish PARSEME corpus. For each of the 3,149 annotated VMWE instances, each of the four heuristics (with $g = 2$)[7] was used to extract literal matches, their POS sequences and the sentences in which they occur. We then performed a manual tagging of each LR candidate.[8] Out of the resulting 416 literal matches, 72 (17.3%) were manually tagged as true LRs, i.e. conforming to the definition in Sec. 1. These 72 occurrences correspond to 32 distinct VMWEs. The remaining 344 matches were due to one of these 3 reasons: (i) coincidental co-occurrences of VMWE components, as in example (4) and Fig. 2c–d, (ii) true VMWEs, wrongly omitted in the original annotation (29 such cases were detected), (iii) false VMWEs, which should have never been annotated (8 occurrences of 3 such expressions were detected).

Tab. 1 shows the per-category and the overall efficiency of the four heuristics from Sec. 3 in the task of finding LRs of VMWEs (the best results are highlighted in bold).[9] The overall F-scores (even if more than twice better for IDs than for other categories) indicate that automatic identification of LRs is a hard task. Obviously, mixing all heuristics gives optimal recall (since only those occurrences which were extracted by at least one of them are examined here). In particular, WindowGap and BagOfDeps are

---

[7] The average length of a gap in a VMWE in the Polish PARSEME corpus is equal to 0.53 and its mean absolute deviation (MAD) is equal to 0.77. Since the LRs had not been manually annotated, analogous data for the gaps contained in LRs were not available in advance. But when the LRs identified in this study (see below) are concerned, the average length of a gap and its MAD are equal to 1.1 and 1.2 respectively.

[8] One Polish native speaker, a co-author of this paper, participated in this task. She was also the main annotator of the VMWE layer in the Polish PARSEME corpus.

[9] Matches due to errors in the VMWE annotations were kept in Tab. 1. Correcting these errors would require a re-execution of the heuristics, which could bias our evaluation towards the underlying tool.

Category	WindowGap			BagOfDeps			UnlabeledDeps			LabeledDeps			All		
	P	R	F	P	R	F	P	R	F	P	R	F	P	R	F
ID	0.41	0.88	0.56	**0.50**	0.19	0.27	0.67	0.13	0.21	n/a	0.00	n/a	0.43	**1.00**	**0.60**
IReflV	0.15	1.00	**0.26**	0.14	0.63	0.23	**0.15**	0.63	0.25	0.14	0.37	0.20	0.13	**1.00**	0.23
LVC	0.17	0.73	0.28	**0.20**	0.65	**0.30**	0.15	0.38	0.21	0.14	0.19	0.16	0.17	**1.00**	0.29
ALL	**0.18**	0.88	**0.30**	0.17	0.54	0.26	0.16	0.43	0.23	0.14	0.22	0.17	0.17	**1.00**	0.30

Table 1: Precision, recall and F-measure of the four heuristics.

largely complementary: only 41,7% of LRs are extracted by both of these methods. Also expectedly, the WindowGap method outperforms each other individual method as far as recall is concerned. It also has optimal overall scores, even if it remains behind BagOfDeps and UnlabeledDep in precision for individual VMWE categories. Not surprisingly, the recall of the BagOfDeps is systematically higher than the recall of UnlabeledDeps, which in turn is systematically higher than the recall of LabeledDeps – since these heuristics rely on increasing degrees of syntactic constraints. However, this does not result in higher precision scores. To the contrary: BagOfDeps has the best precision of the three methods. This phenomenon may be partially explained by the presence of errors in SL.

All the results shown here rely on a maximum-coverage hypothesis (MCH), i.e. the assumption that the four heuristics, with $g = 2$, allow us to extract all LRs of the previously annotated VMWEs. This hypothesis is strong. Potentially, there could be a LR whose components have a gap longer than 2, and which was not extracted e.g. due to non-connectivity in the dependency graph as in Fig. 1b, or due to an error in the SL. Ideally, we should, thus, examine all co-occurrences of the lexicalized components of a given VMWE, whatever their distance in the sentence. However, we estimate that this would triple the number of exact matches and require a much higher manual annotation effort. We thus performed a less labor-intensive experiment to assess the reliability of MCH. We applied the WindowGap heuristic with a gap length of 9,999 (which exceeds all sentence lengths in the corpus) to the first 1,000 sentences of the corpus, which yielded 41 literal matches. Then, the matches previously seen (i.e. extracted by any of the four previously used heuristics) were eliminated, and the resulting 30 occurrences were manually labeled according to the same scenario as above. All of them were false positives, which suggests that the four heuristics would hardly ever miss any LRs among their literal matches.

As seen in Sec. 3, our heuristics are skewed towards high recall, which makes them practical for pre-identifying and manually validating LR candidates, but not optimal for automatic classification of IRs and LRs. Previous methods proposed for the latter task include (Fazly et al., 2009), where unsupervised MWE identification is based on statistical measures of lexical and syntactic flexibility of MWEs. The notion of a LR seems to have a much larger scope than in our approach: it notably includes variants stemming from replacement of lexicalized components by automatically extracted similar words, e.g. *spill corn* vs. **spill the beans**. The test data are restricted to the 28 most frequent verb-object pairs, and their manually validated IRs and LRs, i.e. accidental co-occurrences of the MWE components are excluded from performance measures (unlike in our approach). Their precision and recall in LR identification range from 0.18 to 0.86 and from 0.11 to 0.61, respectively. These results are hard to compare to Tab. 1, due to the very different understanding of the task and its experimental settings.

5 Corpus study

Given the manually identified true LRs, we can estimate the idiomaticity rate ($IdRate$) as follows:

$$IdRate_{CAT} = \frac{|IR_{CAT}|}{|LR_{CAT}| + |IR_{CAT}|} \tag{18}$$

where IR_{CAT} is the set of (idiomatic) VMWE occurrences of category CAT[10], LR_{CAT} is the set of true LRs of VMWEs of category CAT, and $CAT \in \{\text{ID}, \text{IReflV}, \text{LVC}, \text{ALL}\}$. As shown in Tab. 2, LRs of VMWEs in Polish are rare: the overall $IdRate$ amounts to 0.978. This score is consistent with

---

[10]This number was updated by accounting for the VMWE annotation errors identified during the manual validation (cf. Sec. 4).

(Waszczuk et al., 2016), where the *IdRate* of Polish verbal, nominal, adjectival and adverbial MWEs is estimated at 0.95. It is, however, in sharp contrast to (Fazly et al., 2009), where the proportion of LRs of the most frequent English verb-object MWEs was estimated at 40%. This is probably due to the different understanding of LRs by these authors, and their relatively restricted experimental scope (cf. Sec. 4). Important cross-language factors might also influence the *IdRate*, such as the pervasiveness of lexicalized determiners like *the/a* in Germanic and Romance languages vs. the lack of their equivalents in Slavic ones.

Tab. 2 also shows the per-category *IdRate*. Many IDs originated as metaphors, and this is reflected in the fact that IDs have the lowest *IdRate*, even if only slightly lower than other categories. IReflVs, conversely, have the highest *IdRate*, despite homonymy, shown in examples (14) and (17).

Category	# LRs		# IRs		IdRate
	tokens	types	tokens	types	
ID	16	5	322	219	0.953
IReflV	30	19	1547	368	0.981
LVC	26	8	1301	662	0.980
ALL	72	32	3170	1249	0.978

Table 2: Idiomaticity rate per VMWE category and overall.

Category	MORPH		SYNT		OTHER	
	tokens	types	tokens	types	tokens	types
ID	7	3	8	2	1	1
IReflV	8	3	1	1	21	16
LVC	18	2	2	1	6	5
ALL	(46%) 33	8	(15%) 11	4	28	22

Table 3: LRs distinguishable from VMWEs by constraints of various types

A close-up study of the 32 distinct VMWEs corresponding to the 72 LR tokens reveals that their individual *IdRate* varies greatly: from 0.20 for **daje się** *(zauważyć X)* 'allows RCLI (notice X)' ⇒ IT IS POSSIBLE (TO NOTICE X) to 0.94 for **czuć się** *(dobrze)* 'feel RCLI (well)' ⇒ TO FEEL (WELL).

In view of automatically distinguishing LRs from IRs, we studied the morphological and syntactic constraints imposed by VMWEs. We manually tagged the 72 LRs with one of the following labels:

- **MORPH**: the LR does not respect the morphological constraints imposed by the corresponding VMWE on one of its lexicalized components. For instance, the VMWE in example (10) requires the nominal component *udział 'share'* to occur in singular. If this constraint were known, the occurrence in (11) could be automatically classified as literal. Morphological constraints can also concern the head verb, e.g. the VMWE in (19) allows no overt subject and restricts the finite forms of its head verb *dać 'allow'* to 3rd person singular. Knowing this constraint would allow us to automatically identify (20), where the verb is inflected in 2nd person imperative, as an LR.

- **SYNT**: the LR violates the syntactic constraints – other than the dependencies between its lexicalized components – imposed by the VMWE. This typically concerns dependencies between lexicalized components and external arguments or adjuncts. E.g., while the VMWE in (19) admits no overt subject, the LR in (21) does take a subject *pięćdziesięciolatka '50-year-old-woman'*. Also, the VMWE from (22) requires an infinitive complement and its noun *stan 'state'* allows no modifier. If this constraint were known, the dependent of this noun in (23) would automatically imply a LRs.

- **OTHER**: in order to distinguish an LR from IRs, more advanced (e.g. semantic) constraints would have to be verifiable. E.g., an LVC with the light verb *mieć 'to have'* in present tense and occurring under the scope of negation, as in (24), is homonymic with the existential *być 'to be'*, whose negation in present tense is realized in Polish precisely by *mieć 'to have'*, as in (25). Since Polish is a pro-drop language, the subject in (24) can be skipped, which makes both occurrences look identical. Also, IReflVs like in (26) are polysemic with reflexive, reciprocal, impersonal or middle alternation uses, as in (27), and divergences in syntactic constraints are inexistent or unverifiable (e.g. due to dropped arguments). Only powerful pragmatic mechanisms would allow these cases to be distinguished.

(19) *dokładnich kwot nie **da się** wyliczyć* 'exact amounts not allows.3.SING.FIN.PRES RCLI calculate'
⇒ THE EXACT AMOUNTS CANNOT BE CALCULATED

(20) *nie **daj się** zbywać ogólnikami* 'not allow.2.SING.IMPER RCLI dispose-of with-commonplaces' ⇒
DON'T BE DISPOSED OF WITH COMMONPLACES

(21) *Pięćdziesięciolatka nie **da się** na to złapać* '50-year-old-woman not allows.3.SING.FIN.FUT RCLI
on this catch' ⇒ A 50-YEAR-OLD WOMAN WILL NOT FALL INTO THIS TRAP

(22)   *więcej nie **jestem w stanie** <u>dokonać</u>* 'more not am in state <u>to-do</u>' ⇒ I AM NOT ABLE TO DO MORE

(23)   *trzech żołnierzy <u>było w stanie</u> krytycznym* 'three soldiers were in state <u>critical</u>' ⇒ THREE SOLDIERS WERE IN A CRITICAL STATE

(24)   *(klient) nie **ma powodów** do satysfakcji* '(client) not has reasons for satisfaction' ⇒ (THE CLIENT) HAS NO REASONS TO BE SATISFIED

(25)   *nie <u>ma powodów</u> do satysfakcji* 'not has reasons for satisfaction' ⇒ THERE ARE NO REASONS TO BE SATISFIED

(26)   *kadydaci **znaleźli się** w trudnej sytuacji* 'candidates found RCLI in hard situation' ⇒ THE CANDIDATES FOUND THEMSELVES IS A DIFFICULT SITUATION

(27)   *kadydaci <u>znaleźli się</u> dopiero po tygodniu* 'candidates found RCLI only after week' ⇒ CANDIDATES WERE FOUND ONLY A WEEK LATER

As shown in Tab. 3, 61% of the LRs can be automatically distinguished in the treebank from IRs if morphological and syntactic constraints imposed by VMWEs are known, e.g. encoded in a lexical resource (Przepiórkowski et al., 2017) or learned from a corpus. The remaining 39% of LRs call for powerful mechanisms which go beyond sentence boundaries and most lexical encoding frameworks. Note also that the percentage of the VMWE types which exhibit any literal readings is relatively low (32 types out of 1249, i.e. 2.6%). This suggests that methods for MWE identification might benefit from language-specific components explicitly targeting those few expressions.

6 Conclusions and future work

The main contribution of this paper is a close examination of several aspects of literal readings (LRs) of VMWEs. Firstly, we defined the notion of an LR in terms of both the semantics of their components, and of their syntactic dependencies, which motivates their study in a treebank. We proposed four language-independent heuristics, oriented towards high recall and a reasonable precision, for the task of automatically identifying LRs, given their manually performed annotations in a treebank. We applied these heuristics to Polish data stemming from a multilingual corpus annotated for VMWEs following universal guidelines, and we manually validated the extracted LR candidates. The resulting dataset, available under an open license[11], allowed us to show that automatic identification of LRs is a hard task, especially when syntactic annotations are created automatically. We also discovered that up to 61% of the LRs can be automatically distinguished from their idiomatic counterparts if data on morphological and syntactic constraints imposed by VMWEs are available (e.g. lexically encoded or learned from a corpus). Last but not least, we showed that LRs are relatively rare in Polish: the idiomaticity rate of VMWEs is equal to 0.978, and only 2.6% of all VMWE types exhibit literal readings in our corpus.

The proposed heuristics can also be used as part of MWE annotation methods. In the context of PARSEME, a similar tool was used to check the consistency of VMWE annotations in the corpus, and to detect VMWE occurrences that were possibly missed during the annotation phase.

Future work could investigate the extent to which the results from the different heuristics are statistically significant. The heuristics could also be extended to handle long-distance dependencies such as the one in (6). We also plan to apply this study to other languages from various languages families, concerned by the PARSEME corpus, so as to check the discovered tendencies. Preliminary studies in Portuguese show that the definition of an LR needs enhancements: not only the syntactic dependencies between the lexicalized components are to be preserved but also their POS. This condition is necessary to avoid ambiguities, notably between the reflexive pronoun *se* '*RCLI*' in IReflVs and the conjunction *se* '*if*'. Further enhancement, useful for Slavic languages, might consist in merging aspectual pairs (perfective/imperfective) of VMWEs such as ***da się*** '*let.PERF RCLI*' ⇒ IT WILL BE POSSIBLE (TO) vs. ***daje się*** '*let.IMP RCLI*' ⇒ IT IS POSSIBLE (TO). Finally, the findings on LRs may enhance MWE identification methods. They may for instance yield useful hints for feature engineering, or may be used in a post-processing step to eliminate LRs wrongly recognized as variants of VMWEs seen in the training corpus.

---

[11]http://clip.ipipan.waw.pl/MweLitRead

References

Cristina Cacciari and Paola Corradini. 2015. Literal analysis and idiom retrieval in ambiguous idioms processing: A reading-time study. *Journal of Cognitive Psychology* 27(7):797–811. https://doi.org/10.1080/20445911.2015.1049178.

Mathieu Constant, Gülşen Eryiğit, Johanna Monti, Lonneke van der Plas, Carlos Ramisch, Michael Rosner, and Amalia Todirascu. 2017. Multiword expression processing: A survey. *Computational Linguistics* to appear.

Ismail El Maarouf and Michael Oakes. 2015. Statistical Measures for Characterising MWEs. In *IC1207 COST PARSEME 5th general meeting*. http://typo.uni-konstanz.de/parseme/index.php/2-general/138-admitted-posters-iasi-23-24-september-2015.

Afsaneh Fazly, Paul Cook, and Suzanne Stevenson. 2009. Unsupervised type and token identification of idiomatic expressions. *Computational Linguistics* 35(1):61–103. https://doi.org/10.1162/coli.08-010-R1-07-048.

Marie-Sophie Pausé. 2017. *Structure lexico-sentaxique des locutions du français et incidence sur leur combinatoire*. Ph.D. thesis, Université de Lorraine, Nancy, France.

Jing Peng and Anna Feldman. 2016. Automatic idiom recognition with word embeddings. In *SIMBig (Revised Selected Papers)*. Springer, volume 656 of *Communications in Computer and Information Science*, pages 17–29.

Jing Peng, Anna Feldman, and Ekaterina Vylomova. 2014. Classifying idiomatic and literal expressions using topic models and intensity of emotions. In *Proceedings of the 2014 Conference on Empirical Methods in Natural Language Processing (EMNLP)*. Association for Computational Linguistics, Doha, Qatar, pages 2019–2027. http://www.aclweb.org/anthology/D14-1216.

Adam Przepiórkowski, Jan Hajič, Elżbieta Hajnicz, and Zdeňka Urešová. 2017. Phraseology in two Slavic valency dictionaries: Limitations and perspectives. *International Journal of Lexicography* 30(1):1–38.

Agata Savary, Carlos Ramisch, Silvio Cordeiro, Federico Sangati, Veronika Vincze, Behrang QasemiZadeh, Marie Candito, Fabienne Cap, Voula Giouli, Ivelina Stoyanova, and Antoine Doucet. 2017. The PARSEME Shared Task on Automatic Identification of Verbal Multiword Expressions. In *Proceedings of the EACL'17 Workshop on Multiword Expressions*.

Livnat Herzig Sheinfux, Tali Arad Greshler, Nurit Melnik, and Shuly Wintner. 2017. *Representation and Parsing of Multiword Expressions*, Language Science Press, Berlin, chapter Verbal MWEs: Idiomaticity and flexibility, pages 5–38.

Jakub Waszczuk, Agata Savary, and Yannick Parmentier. 2016. Promoting multiword expressions in A* TAG parsing. In *COLING 2016, 26th International Conference on Computational Linguistics, Proceedings of the Conference: Technical Papers, December 11-16, 2016, Osaka, Japan.* pages 429–439. http://aclweb.org/anthology/C/C16/C16-1042.pdf.

Querying Multi-word Expressions Annotation with CQL

Natalia Klyueva
The Hong Kong Polytechnic University
Hong Kong
`natalia.klyueva@polyu.edu.hk`

Anna Vernerová
Charles University
Prague, Czech Republic
`vernerova@ufal.mff.cuni.cz`

Behrang QasemiZadeh
Heinrich-Heine University
Düsseldorf, Germany
`zadeh@phil.hhu.de`

Abstract

This paper demonstrates a solution for querying corpora with multi-word expression (MWE) annotation using a concordance system. Namely, the PARSEME multilingual corpora, which contain manually annotated verbal multi-word expression (VMWE) in 18 languages, are converted to a suitable *vertical format* so that they can be explored using the Corpus Query Language (CQL). VMWEs encompass a range of categories such as idioms, light verb constructions, verb-particle constructions, and so on. Although these corpora were mainly developed for the purpose of developing automatic methods for the identification of VMWEs, we believe they are a valuable source of information for corpus based studies. The solution proposed in this paper is an attempt to provide a linguist/non-tech-savvy friendly method for exploring these corpora. We show how CQL-enabled concordancers such as NoSke or KonText can be exploited for this purpose. Despite several limitations, such as problems related to discontinuous and coordinated MWEs, CQL still is an enabling tool for basic analysis of MWE-annotated data in corpus-based studies.

1 Introduction

Multi-word expressions (MWEs) are structures that cross word boundaries and thus present challenges to a variety of NLP tasks such as syntactic analysis and machine translation, etc. The PARSEME (PARSing and Multi-word Expressions) EU COST action (Savary et al., 2015) addressed these problems by organizing a shared task on automatic identification of verbal MWEs (Savary et al., 2017)[1]. Verbal MWEs (VMWEs) were annotated in corpora in 18 languages according to common guidelines (Candito et al., 2017). Several categories of VMWEs were defined: idioms (ID), light verb constructions (LVC), inherently reflexive verbs (IReflV), verb-particle constructions (VPC), and OTH (other).

The data for each of the languages is distributed in two files: **.conllu** and **.parsemetsv**. The first one contains morphosyntactic annotation in the CoNLL-U format[2] and the second one contains the MWE annotation in the parseme-tsv format (example follows). These representation are mainly optimized for machine readability and particularly for training predictive models. The data in these two files is not presented in an intuitive and suitable form for search and retrieval scenarios involving human users. We present one of the approaches that can be used for this purpose (i.e., as a query system for MWE annotated corpora). For example, one may easily retrieve frequency lists of MWEs and study them as key words in context.

The problem we face is not well-studied, though we can find some works related to the topic. Klyueva and Straňák (2016) introduce a mechanism for basic queries over syntactic trees by copying selected attributes of a node's parent to attributes of the child node itself, e.g. `p_form`, `p_lemma`, `p_tag`. A corpus with terminology (above all, multi-word terminology) annotation was represented in a vertical format with structural attributes used for encoding MWEs (QasemiZadeh and Schumann, 2016)[3]. Another web service that allows to query for MWEs is based on CQPWeb[4], but the texts as well as the manual are only

---

[1] `http://multiword.sourceforge.net/sharedtask2017`
[2] `http://universaldependencies.org/format.html`
[3] Online search at `http://lindat.mff.cuni.cz/services/kontext/first_form?corpname=aclrd20_en_a`.
[4] `http://yeda.cs.technion.ac.il/HebrewCqpWeb/`

Proceedings of the 16th International Workshop on Treebanks and Linguistic Theories (TLT16), pages 73–79,
Prague, Czech Republic, January 23–24, 2018. Distributed under a CC-BY 4.0 licence. 2017.

Keywords: verbal multiword expressions, Sketch Engine, corpus query

in Hebrew which did not let us make a full study of the functionality. A survey of MWEs in treebanks is presented by Rosén et al. (2015), but the paper does not contain any directions on how to access and query MWEs.

This paper is structured as follows. Section 2 is devoted to corpus query systems suitable to querying corpora with annotation of MWEs. Section 3 introduces the data format in which the data is distributed and the necessary conversion to the vertical format behind CQL. Example queries can be found in Section 4.

Our conversion scripts[5] are intended for a subgroup of 15 PARSEME corpora that also feature syntactic annotation, thus excluding Bulgarian, Hebrew and Lithuanian which are distributed without a **.conllu** file.

2 Corpus Query Systems

Tools to search corpora—corpus query systems—present a powerful and popular concept for digital humanities. We can distinguish several types of engines depending on their functionalities. The first group treats text in a linear manner (as a string of annotated words), e.g. SketchEngine[6] (Rychlý, 2007) or IMS Corpus Workbench[7] (Evert and Hardie, 2011); the second group sees text as a group of trees, e.g. PML-TQ[8] (Štěpánek and Pajas, 2010), INESS[9] (Rosén et al., 2012) or Tündra[10] (Martens, 2013). While the first group of tools is easier to maintain, and from the user's point of view the query language (CQL/CQP) is simpler than that of the second group, the treebank query languages of the tools in the second group have much greater expressive power.

Concerning data preparation and compilation, treebank query systems use much more complex data formats, e.g. the native format of PML-TQ is an XML-based format called PML (Štěpánek and Pajas, 2010); for the web search, the data is indexed using a relational database and high level queries are internally translated to SQL. In contrast, the vertical format required for concordance systems such as Sketch Engine or IMS almost corresponds to the original format of our corpora and requires less effort to make them available for search and retrieval.

Multi-word units pose problems for both categories of corpus querying tools since in both paradigms the basic unit that carries annotation is a token. In this paper, we work with the open source corpus management system Manatee that applies the linear paradigm; the suggested representation of data can then be exploited through either of the two open-source front-ends for Manatee, i.e. either through the NoSke[11] (a free edition of the Sketch Engine) or through KonText[12] (a front-end developed by the Institute of the Czech National Corpus based on NoSke); the PARSEME corpora in this paper are available via both platforms.

3 Vertical Encoding of the Data

As mentioned earlier, the PARSEME corpora come in two files in two different formats for each language, one with morphosyntactic annotations (**.conllu**) and another with MWE annotation (**.parsemetsv**). Both formats represent a challenge to the 'linear'-based corpus management tools as they contain hierarchal or graph annotations (e.g., syntactic dependencies in CoNLL-U and discontinuous structures in parseme-tsv). In order to provide unified querying over both morphosyntactic and MWE annotations, we combine these two resources into a single file.

The following is a sentence fragment in the **.parsemetsv** format:[13]

---

[5]`https://github.com/natalink/mwe_noske`
[6]`http://sketchengine.co.uk`
[7]`http://cwb.sourceforge.net`
[8]`http://hdl.handle.net/11858/00-097C-0000-0022-C7F6-3`
[9]`http://iness.uib.no`
[10]`http://weblicht.sfs.uni-tuebingen.de/Tundra`
[11]`https://nlp.fi.muni.cz/trac/noske`, Parseme data `http://corpora.phil.hhu.de/parseme`
[12]`https://github.com/czcorpus/kontext`, Parseme data `http://lindat.mff.cuni.cz/services/kontext`
[13]The four columns contain the word id, the word form, information whether the token is followed by a space, and the MWE annotation.

```
 1    Delegates   _  _
 2    are         _  1:LVC
 3    in          _  1
 4    little      _  _
 5    doubt       _  1
 6    that        _  _
 7    the         _  _
 8    shadow      _  2:ID
 9    cast        _  2
10    over        _  _
11    the         _  _
12    city        _  _
...
```

The fourth column encodes the MWE annotation of a token as follows. Tokens belonging to the same MWE are labeled with the same numerical identifier so that they can be distinguished as independent MWE unit in a sentence. The first token in a particular MWE is additionally labeled the category of the MWE. In case that a token belongs to several MWEs, the respective tags are separated by a semi-colon (e.g. `1:VPC;2:VPC`).

In our previous work (QasemiZadeh and Schumann, 2016), we have been able to encode MWEs by structural[14] attributes. In doing so, we were relying on annotation that was based on the largest span policy—there data did not annotate MWEs that are part of other MWEs, nor overlapping MWEs. However, in case of VMWEs, modeling overlapping structures is inevitable, and the use of structural attributes leads to complexities which can be avoided by the use of positional attributes. In our proposed format, the CoNLL-U attributes and the MWE annotations are both encoded as positional attributes (columns themselves).

We use the following attributes to encode MWEs:

- **mwe** specifies the type of the MWE, e.g. LVC for a light verb construction or `IReflV` for an inherently reflexive verb;

- **mwe_order** has two possible values, `first` for the first word in the MWE and `cont` for all remaining ("continuation") words;

- **mwe_id** gives the consecutive number of the MWE within the sentence; we shall show later how this attribute helps to distinguish overlapping MWEs;

- **mwe_lemma** is just a concatenation of the lemmas of all words that are part of the MWE, in the order in which they appear in the sentence, e.g. `be in doubt`.

In case one token is annotated as part of multiple MWEs, the MWE annotations attached to it are treated as *multivalue*. For instance, the sentence above will be represented as

```
1 Delegates Delegates NOUN  NNS Number=Plur                      5 nsubj _ _  _  _    _ _
2 are       be        AUX   VBP Mood=Ind|Tense=Pres|VerbForm=Fin 5 cop   _ _  LVC first 1 be in doubt
3 in        in        ADP   IN  _                                5 case  _ _  LVC cont  1 be in doubt
4 little    little    ADJ   JJ  Degree=Pos                       5 amod  _ _  _  _    _ _
5 doubt     doubt     NOUN  NN  Number=Sing                      0 root  _ _  LVC cont  1 be in doubt
6 that      that      SCONJ IN  _                                9 mark  _ _  _  _    _ _
```

The attributes to search for are named exactly as in the CoNLL-U scheme (e.g. **upostag**) with an exception for the word-form, which is called **word** in our concordance system instead of **form** as in CoNLL-U; they can be queried using the standard CQL syntax (see the screenshot from the UI on Figure 1).

4 Example Queries

In this section we provide basic examples showing how to query the PARSEME corpora using CQL queries. We concentrate on a few examples that we believe can be most helpful in several scenarios.

---

[14]Definitions of structural and positional attributes can be found at https://www.sketchengine.co.uk/corpus-configuration-file-all-features/.

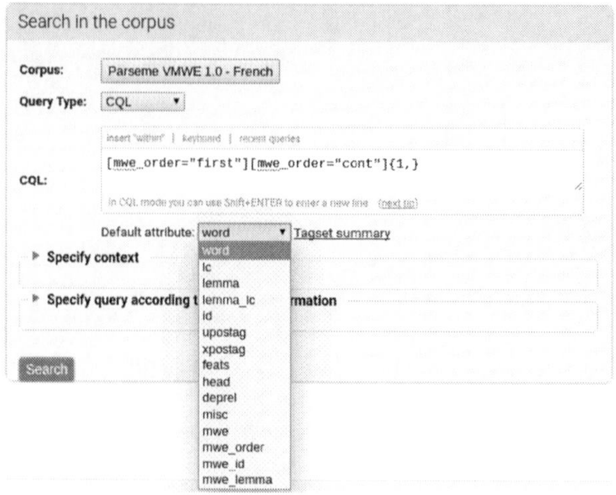

Figure 1: Search interface, attribute menu

The aim is to provide a range of examples to demonstrate both pros and cons of using CQL queries for exploring MWE annotated corpora, given our representation structure using positional attributes.

CQL queries are composed of blocks of the form of `[attribute="value"]`, in which the value expresses a condition over the given attribute. In its simplest form, a CQL query consists of only one pair of attribute-value, and the value is an exact string, e.g., `[word="test"]`, which in turn returns all the occurrences of the word-form *test* in the corpus under investigation. However, these building blocks can be concatenated to form a more complex query involving a sequence of one or more tokens. Additionally, the attribute values may be specified through regular expressions and simple logical operators such as 'and' (&) and or (|) are also available.

All queries in the following examples are linked to the KonText search tool and the result for them can be seen online by clicking on them. In our examples, we use the French, Spanish and German corpora; however, all the queries are valid for other languages in the PARSEME collection. These queries (and more) are also available in the online tutorial at `https://ufal.mff.cuni.cz/lindat-kontext/ parseme-mwe`.

4.1 Continuous MWE Fragments

We start with a simple example:

`[mwe_order="first"]`

which results in a KWIC[15] view containing the first word of each MWE in the corpus. Note that if the same word happens to be the first word of several MWEs (such as the word *letting* in *they were letting us in and out*), it will appear in the KWIC output only once.

The query below will display and highlight continuous MWEs:

`[mwe_order="first"][mwe_order="cont"]{1,}`

In case of MWEs with more than two tokens, this resulting concordance contains the same location more than once. For example, for a 3 token MWE, the KWIC view contains two lines: one with two tokens highlighted and another – the same sentence – with three tokens, as displayed in Figure 2. One immediate solution to remove unwanted duplicates in the output is to use the so-called *overlaps/sub-hits filter*, which is supported in the NoSke system: only one of the matches is kept, whilst the other lines matching around the same position are omitted from the output.[16]

---

[15]key word in context

[16]Another solution is to use an additional positional attribute to specifically mark the last token of MWEs. In this case, the corresponding attribute–value pair can be added to the end of the proposed query.

| adéquates afin d' assurer le rendement qui | s' appuie | exclusivement sur l' activité de pêche |
| Herman De Croo et de ses deux collègues soit | couronnée de | succès . </s><s> Monsieur le Commissaire |
| Herman De Croo et de ses deux collègues soit couronnée de succès . </s><s> Monsieur le Commissaire , j' ai |
| le sein de l' Union européenne ? </s><s> | Y a | -t-il des circonstances dans lesquelles |
| le sein de l' Union européenne ? </s><s> | Y a -t-il | des circonstances dans lesquelles la Commission |

Figure 2: The same occurrence of MWE retrieved twice.

4.2 MWEs with Discontinuity

Intuitively when creating a query we want to see only tokens belonging to MWEs in the concordance. This is not straightforward in a 'linear' corpus query system and we can not reach the state when all MWEs will be highlighted as a whole in discontinuous constructions through only one interaction with the underlying corpus management system. In current implementations of KWIC, the intermediate words (not belonging to the MWE) will be highlighted as well in this case.

In order to show not only the first word of the MWE, but also its continuation, a more complex query that matches also the nodes in between must be executed:

```
1:[mwe_order="first"] []* 2:[mwe_order="cont"] & 1.mwe_id=2.mwe_id within <s/>
```

This query will match the first token in an expression, anything in between and the continuation of the MWE. To avoid greedy matching ([]* overshoot and match other MWEs in the sentence) we make the condition that the MWE id tag of the first token and continuation part should be the same (as stipulated by the condition & `1.mwe_id=2.mwe_id` which uses 1 and 2 as the names previously given to the two nodes in `1:[...]` and `2:[...]`); because the values of `mwe_id` are only unique within a sentence, we also make sure both tokens belong to the same sentence through the `within <s/>` condition.

The previous query will match only two tokens in each MWE. In case more tokens needed to be highlighted, the following query has to be evaluated:

```
1:[mwe_order="first"] []* 2:[mwe_order="cont"] []*  3:[mwe_order="cont"] &
1.mwe_id=2.mwe_id & 1.mwe_id=3.mwe_id within <s/>
```

Another method for highlighting just the two tokens belonging to the same MWE but not the intermediate words is through the use of `meet` operator:

```
(meet 1:[mwe_order="first"] 2:[mwe_order="cont"] 0 5) & 1.mwe_id=2.mwe_id within <s/>
```

The `meet` operator with parameters 0 5 then formulates the condition that node 2 must be at most 0 words to the left and at most 5 words to the right of node 1.

4.3 Overlapping and Embedded MWEs

A single token may be part of multiple MWEs in two cases.

In the first case, one MWE is embedded in another one, as in the case of the Czech LVC *dát se v let* 'begin flying', which contains the inherently reflexive verb *dát se* 'enter into, begin'.

In the second case, two MWEs overlap without being embedded in each other. This happens particularly in cases of coordination mixed with ellipsis, as in this sentence fragment:

```
1 They      _  _
2 were      _  _
3 letting   _  1:VPC;2:VPC
4 us        _  _
5 in        _  1
6 and       _  _
7 out       _  2
```

Here a full linguistic analysis would first expand this fragment to *they were letting us in and they were letting us out*, in which case the two MWEs would not overlap. However, the Parseme annotation style does not attempt to restore elided tokens and instead annotates the token that is present in the sentence as belonging to both coordinated MWEs.

The following query matches all nodes that belong to multiple MWEs simultaneously:

```
[mwe=".*;.*"]
```

In case of coordinated MWEs, we further expect that both MWEs are of the same type, which translates into

```
[mwe="(.*);\1"]
```

On the other hand, two tokens that share the same pair of MWE ids typically (although not necessarily) belong to a pair of overlapping MWEs:

```
(meet 1:[mwe_id="(.*;.*)"] 2:[] 1 5) & 1.mwe_id=2.mwe_id within <s/>
```

4.4 Queries Involving Morphosyntactic Information

Evidently, CQL queries can be formulated to simultaneously make use of annotations that are specific to MWEs and those that express other linguistic information such as morphosyntactic about their building blocks. For example, the following query:

```
1:[mwe_order="first" & upostag="VERB" & mwe="LVC"] []* 2:[mwe_order="cont" & upostag="NOUN"] &
   1.mwe_id=2.mwe_id within <s/>
```

finds all light verb constructions where the real syntactic head goes first.

Similarly, a simple query such as

```
[mwe="LVC" & upostag="VERB"]
```

followed by a request for a frequency list (through the user interface) returns the frequency list of verbs used in LVCs.

Above we listed basic queries which do not involve constraints on word forms, lemmas, or language-specific morphological tags—examples of this sort can be found at `https://ufal.mff.cuni.cz/lindat-kontext/parseme-mwe`.

5   Conclusion and future work

Concordance systems (in our paper KonText and NoSke, but also their ancestors such as the Sketch Engine, and the IMS Open Corpus Workbench) for exploring corpora using CQL queries are well known tools among linguists for applications such as lexicography. We believe that these systems are also effective tools for exploring MWE-annotated corpora, particularly at the absence of sufficient resources for developing specialized tools for their manipulation. To this end, we show a method to encode and query an MWE annotated corpus in a concordance system; this can facilitate the search and retrieval of MWEs in corpus based studies.

One possible area of future work is to extend the current interfaces' capability to handle search and retrieval of discontinuous structures, e.g. by extending the concept of the "key word in context" to "key *words* in context" (KWsIC), with "context" denoting not just the left and right context, but also intermediate context between the KWIC words. The `meet` operator goes some way towards this goal, but is not sufficient for more complex cases such as KWsIC consisting of three or more tokens; we propose to add a new operator of the form (all `[attribute="value"] within <structure/>`).

Acknowledgments

The first author has been supported by the postdoctoral fellowship grant of the Hong Kong Polytechnic University, project code G-YW2P. The second author has been supported by the LINDAT/CLARIN project of the Ministry of Education, Youth and Sports of the Czech Republic (project LM2015071); the data is shared through services developed and/or maintained within the same project.

References

Marie Candito, Fabienne Cap, Silvio Cordeiro, Vassiliki Foufi, Polona Gantar, Voula Giouli, Carlos Herrero, Mihaela Ionescu, Verginica Mititelu, Johanna Monti, Joakim Nivre, Mihaela Onofrei, Carla Parra Escartín, Manfred Sailer, Carlos Ramisch, Monica-Mihaela Rizea, Agata Savary, Ivelina Stonayova, Sara Stymne, and Veronika Vincze. 2017. Parseme shared task on automatic identification of verbal MWEs - edition 1.0. Annotation guidelines.

Stefan Evert and Andrew Hardie. 2011. Twenty-first century Corpus Workbench: Updating a query architecture for the new millennium. In *Proceedings of the Corpus Linguistics 2011 conference*. University of Birmingham, UK.

Natalia Klyueva and Pavel Straňák. 2016. Improving corpus search via parsing. In Nicoletta Calzolari, Khalid Choukri, Thierry Declerck, Marko Grobelnik, Bente Maegaard, Joseph Mariani, Asunción Moreno, Jan Odijk, and Stelios Piperidis, editors, *Proceedings of the 10th International Conference on Language Resources and Evaluation (LREC 2016)*. European Language Resources Association, Paris, France, pages 2862–2866.

Scott Martens. 2013. TüNDRA: A Web Application for Treebank Search and Visualization. In *Proceedings of The Twelfth Workshop on Treebanks and Linguistic Theories (TLT12)*. pages 133–144.

Behrang QasemiZadeh and Anne-Kathrin Schumann. 2016. The ACL RD-TEC 2.0: A language resource for evaluating term extraction and entity recognition methods. In *Proceedings of the Tenth International Conference on Language Resources and Evaluation LREC 2016, Portorož, Slovenia, May 23-28, 2016.*. http://www.lrec-conf.org/proceedings/lrec2016/summaries/681.html.

Victoria Rosén, Gyri Smørdal Losnegaard, Koenraad De Smedt, Eduard Bejček, Agata Savary, Adam Przepiórkowski, Petya Osenova, and Verginica Barbu Mititelu. 2015. A survey of multiword expressions in treebanks. In *Proceedings of the 14th International Workshop on Treebanks & Linguistic Theories conference*. Warsaw, Poland.

Victoria Rosén, Koenraad De Smedt, Paul Meurer, and Helge Dyvik. 2012. An open infrastructure for advanced treebanking. In Jan Hajič, Koenraad De Smedt, Marko Tadić, and António Branco, editors, *META-RESEARCH Workshop on Advanced Treebanking at LREC2012*. pages 22–29.

Pavel Rychlý. 2007. Manatee/bonito - a modular corpus manager. In *1st Workshop on Recent Advances in Slavonic Natural Language Processing*. Masaryk University, pages 65–70.

Agata Savary, Carlos Ramisch, Silvio Cordeiro, Federico Sangati, Veronika Vincze, Behrang QasemiZadeh, Marie Candito, Fabienne Cap, Voula Giouli, Ivelina Stoyanova, and Antoine Doucet. 2017. The PARSEME Shared Task on Automatic Identification of Verbal Multi-word Expressions. In *Proceedings of the 13th Workshop on Multiword Expressions (MWE 2017)*. Valencia, Spain.

Agata Savary, Manfred Sailer, Yannick Parmentier, Michael Rosner, Victoria Rosén, Adam Przepiórkowski, Cvetana Krstev, Veronika Vincze, Beata Wójtowicz, Gyri Smørdal Losnegaard, Carla Parra Escartín, Jakub Waszczuk, Matthieu Constant, Petya Osenova, and Federico Sangati. 2015. PARSEME – PARSing and Multi-word Expressions within a European multilingual network. In *7th Language & Technology Conference: Human Language Technologies as a Challenge for Computer Science and Linguistics (LTC 2015)*. Poznań, Poland. https://hal.archives-ouvertes.fr/hal-01223349.

Jan Štěpánek and Petr Pajas. 2010. Querying diverse treebanks in a uniform way. In *Proceedings of the International Conference on Language Resources and Evaluation, LREC 2010, 17-23 May 2010, Valletta, Malta*. http://www.lrec-conf.org/proceedings/lrec2010/summaries/381.html.

REALEC learner treebank: annotation principles and evaluation of automatic parsing

Olga Lyashevskaya
School of Linguistics
National Research University
Higher School of Economics,
Vinogradov Institute of the Russian
Language RAS Moscow
olesar@yandex.ru

Irina Panteleeva
School of Linguistics
National Research University
Higher School of Economics
Moscow
impanteleyeva@gmail.com

Abstract

The paper presents a Universal Dependencies (UD) annotation scheme for a learner English corpus. The REALEC dataset consists of essays written in English by Russian-speaking university students in the course of general English. The original corpus is manually annotated for learners' errors and gives information on the error span, error type, and the possible correction of the mistake provided by experts. The syntactic dependency annotation adds more value to learner corpora since it makes it possible to explore the interaction of syntax and different types of errors. Also, it helps to assess the syntactic complexity of learners' texts.

While adjusting existing dependency parsing tools, one has to take into account to what extent students' mistakes provoke errors in the parser output. The ungrammatical and stylistically inappropriate utterances may challenge parsers' algorithms trained on grammatically appropriate academic texts. In our experiments, we compared the output of the dependency parser Ud-pipe (trained on ud-english 2.0) with the results of manual parsing, placing a particular focus on parses of ungrammatical English clauses. We show how mistakes made by students influence the work of the parser. Overall, Ud-pipe performed reasonably well (UAS 92.9, LAS 91.7). We provide the analysis of several cases of erroneous parsing which are due to the incorrect detection of a head, on the one hand, and with the wrong choice of the relation type, on the other hand. We propose some solutions which could improve the automatic output and thus make the syntax-based learner corpus research and assessment of the syntactic complexity more reliable.

The REALEC treebank is freely available under the CC BY-SA 3.0 licence.[1]

1   Introduction

The diversity of research based on learner corpora is increasing in the fields of language acquisition and language teaching methodology. The manual and automatic analysis of texts written by learners leads to the creation of various tools used for pedagogical purposes, namely, for improvements in teaching techniques achieved by paying attention to frequent errors that have been made by generations of learners. Linguistic data obtained in the analysis of the learner corpora texts serve as a basis not only for teaching but also for evaluating the works written by people learning a language.

Using different automatic tools in learner corpus is a frequent idea of works aimed at checking the progress of language learning. For example, Cobb and Horst point out the importance of such analysis of learners' essays (Cobb and Horst, 2015). Berzak et al. (2016) introduce a publicly available syntactic treebank for English as a Second Language (ESL), which provides manually annotated POS tags and Universal Dependency (UD), with which the data obtained from the parser can be checked. Moreover, ESL annotation allows for consistent syntactic treatment of ungrammatical English texts. Many applications based on syntactic parsing have been created in cooperation with Daniella McNamara, cf. (Graesser

---

[1] https://github.com/olesar/REALECtreebank

80

Proceedings of the 16th International Workshop on Treebanks and Linguistic Theories (TLT16), pages 80–87,
Prague, Czech Republic, January 23–24, 2018. Distributed under a CC-BY 4.0 licence. 2017.

Keywords: learner corpus, dependency annotation of learner treebank, UD, evaluation of parser quality

et al. (2011), in which the results on linguistic evaluation of complexity are presented. One more complexity analyzer is made by (Lu and Haiyan, 2016). This work provides a set of simple criteria such as the length of each clause, the number of dependent clauses, and so on. In ((Ragheb and Dickinson, 2017) authors discuss how to improve syntactic annotation for learner language by dint of clarifying the properties which the layers of annotation refer to. They also show the mistakes of annotation that could be corrected with the help of some tools. The list of the studies in learner data syntactic parsing also includes (Rosén and Smedt, 2010), who explore how dependency annotation complements the annotation of errors, and (Schneider and Gilquin, 2016), who focus on innovations in learner's grammar revealed by parsing, to name just a few. In (Rooy and Schäfer, 2002) Bertus van Rooy and Lande Schäfer present the idea that spelling errors cause errors in parsing. Also they show how learners' errors influence the performance of the taggers. Our research, as we hope to show, also confirms this.

In (Vinogradova et al., 2017) syntax complexity is discussed with the examples from REALEC. The paper presents the results of the syntactic analysis made by parsing the sentences and taking into account the mean sentence depth and the average number of relative clauses, other adnominal clauses, and adverbial clauses. There we cleared up how much these criteria influence the syntactic complexity of the essay. The analysis showed that the mean sentence depth is insignificant for evaluation of a text, and the average number of clauses, on the contrary, is considered to be the feature distinguishing better works (scored 75% and higher) from all others.

In the section 'Original data' we present data on which we based for this research. The next part of the text named 'Dependency annotation scheme' shows how we worked on the examples from the corpus. Section 'Choice among alternatives' explains how we chose the option of the annotation. The next chapter presents the sample of our research and also reports which tool we have used. In the section 'Confusion matrix and causes of errors' we show the relations which are confused frequently in students' essays. In 'Constructions that require attention' the examples from corpus that cause the errors in the parser's work are brought in.

2   Original data

The treebank annotations reported in this article are based on the materials from the publicly available corpus REALEC (Russian Error-Annotated English Learner Corpus), see (Vinogradova, 2016; Vinogradova et al., 2017).[2] It is an open-access collection of English texts written by Russian-speaking students of English. The resource consists of more than 3,500 pieces written by Bachelor students while preparing for the English examination. Students' errors are annotated manually by experts (EFL instructors and trained students). Error labels are divided into groups depending on the type of error (spelling, punctuation, grammar, vocabulary, and discourse, with the last three further subdivided according to a detailed categorisation scheme). Experts mark the error span, assign to it one error tag or a few tags, and suggest the corrected version of the span. The original corpus is also equipped with tools for searching and downloading.

3   Dependency annotation scheme

We have chosen Universal Dependencies framework ((Nivre et al., 2016) since it allows one to present typologically diverse treebanks in a comparable format and provides certain matching of different types of dependency relations in different languages. There are 32 dependency relation types provided by parsers trained on english ud 2.0 data, among them subject and object, relative, adverbial and adnominal clauses, conjunction, auxiliary and copula, parataxis).

There exist two common approaches to syntactic annotation of learner and other insufficiently edited data: 'literal' labeling describe the way the two words are related given their formal properties (Lee et al., 2017)), whereas an alternative design bears on the notion of 'intended' usage, and experts are asked to consider functional rather than formal side of the utterance and to try and reconstruct what the intended meaning of the author was. (1) and (1') below illustrate an original sentence and its 'intended'

---

[2]http://realec.org

reading (a partly corrected version). In (1), the phrases *On the other hand is Tokyo* and *Tokyo situated in Japan* present two locally well-formed syntactic structures, but their combination within the whole tree is problematic for the 'literal' approach. As for the 'intended-usage' approach, it is prone to the word order related issues that reflect native patterns of Russian speakers. What is convenient, the corpus is already annotated for students' errors, so our experts can get use of 'the suggested corrections' provided in that layer. However, we do not ask the treebank annotators to rewrite sentences in the correct way, as the intended reading is only implied.

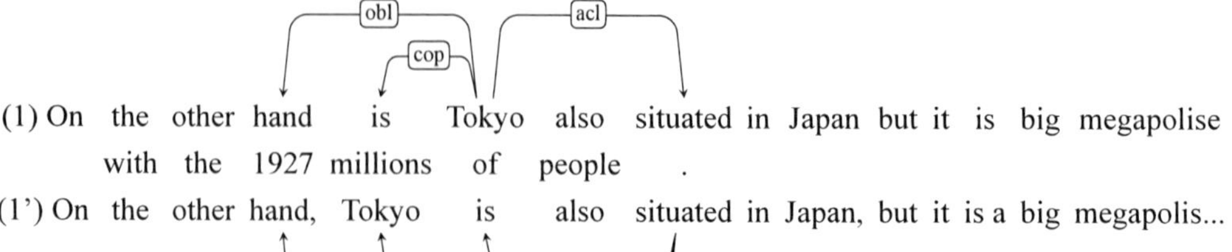

(1) On the other hand is Tokyo also situated in Japan but it is big megapolise with the 1927 millions of people .

(1') On the other hand, Tokyo is also situated in Japan, but it is a big megapolis...

In schemes that follow we show the automatic output (edges above the text) and gold parses (edges below the the text), respectively.

4 Choice among alternatives

There can be multiple alternatives for possible corrections, in which case the principle of minimal editing distance seems to be relevent. For example, in sentence (2), two readings can evoke.

(2) *In the second part if the 20th century, there were founded another three major railway systems, which although had significantly worse harasteristics.*

The first one is the situation that is chosen by the automatic parser but grammarwise it is not quite correct. We have chosen the option where we change *if* for *of*. In this case we also have to change the label of the primary relation 'mark' for 'case'.

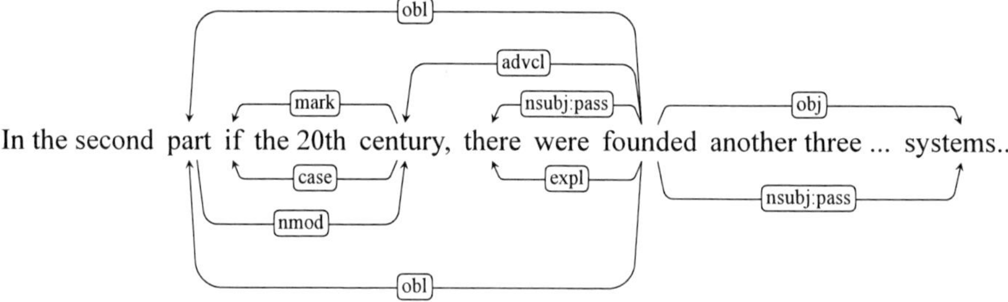

5 Parsing and manual corrections

We needed an easy-to-use parser which would provide the information about part-of-speech, syntactical groups, dependency relation between words and which would represent the syntax trees for more convenient counting, so the choice fell on Ud-pipe (Straka et al., 2016; Straka and Straková, 2017)[3] trained on english ud 2.0 treebank. Like any parser, Ud-pipe makes mistakes, and it was important to evaluate the output for the purposes of our project and assess to what extent these mistakes are imposed by students' errors in orphography, morphology, and syntax. For the research, 373 random sentences (7196 tokens, including 756 punctuation marks) from students' essays were processed with the Ud-pipe parser. The parser detected the heads correctly for 6688 out of 7196 nodes (UAS 92,9 %), of which 6600 were labeled corectly (LAS 91,7 %). Overall, 6894 nodes (95,8 %) were labeled correctly, which suggests that it was the disfluencies that affected the tree structures, rather than functions.

---

[3]http://ufal.mff.cuni.cz/Parsing

6 Confusion matrix and causes of errors

Table 1 illustrates the confusion matrix for the most frequent mismatches in relation types. The totals are calculated for all relations.

	acl	nsubj	num mod	amod	case	obj	obl	root	nmod	com pound	conj	others
acl	36					1		4			1	
nsubj		475		1		5	1	9	1	2	7	5
num-mod			227				3		2	1	1	
amod		3		387	1		1	4		6		1
case					994							7
obj	2	2				246	1	1	2	4	7	1
obl		1	1			1	405	1	10		1	
root	1	1	1					348	5	3	8	9
nmod	3	1	4	1		1	15	1	465	6	6	6
com-pound		1		5			1		5	141	3	
conj	2			2	4	2	2	3	1	5	270	7
others	2	4	2	3	7	9		2		4	15	

Table 1: Confusion matrix of relation types.

The most frequent relation errors are mismatches between root and adjectival modifier, root and nominal subject, object and nominal modifier, root and nominal modifier, conjunction and root, adnominal modifier and conjunction. There are different causes of incorrect detection of relation type, some of them depend on failures in other parsing stage - for example, incorrect detection of the head of the sentence (confusion between root and other relations), incorrect detection of the syntactic group, incorrect detection of part of speech, while still others are the result of learner errors.

7 Constructions that require attention

We have identified the cases in which the parser most often makes mistakes. The following examples present the errors that arise because of ungrammatical nature of sentences, or because of the parser's deficiency.

7.1 Typical errors made by Russian students

In a learner corpus essay, L1-interference mistakes often occur. In our sample we also have such cases. The errors can be connected with calques, or the possibility of omitting the auxiliary verb in Russian when in English it is not possible, or the absence of category in L1, for example, articles, uses of perfect forms of the verb, several types of relative clauses are all absent in Russian, to name just a few.

For example, sentence (3) has a calque mistake critical to building an appropriate syntactic structure: there is a conjunction (*but*) between the noun phrase and the clause, and there is a double coordinating conjunction *but and* between two adjectives, *oldest* and *longest*.

(3) *The oldest railway system in London, but it is not only the oldest, but and the longest – three hundred ninety four kilometres of route.*

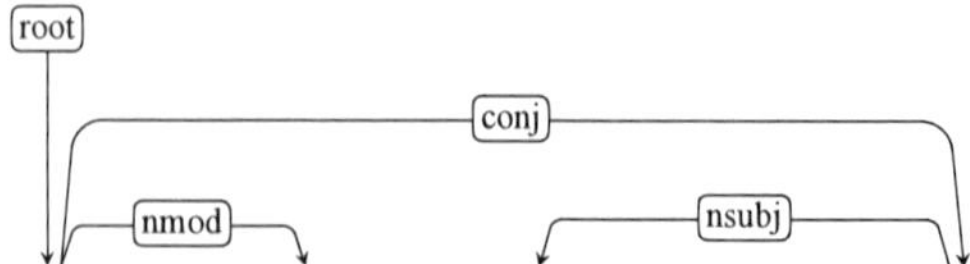

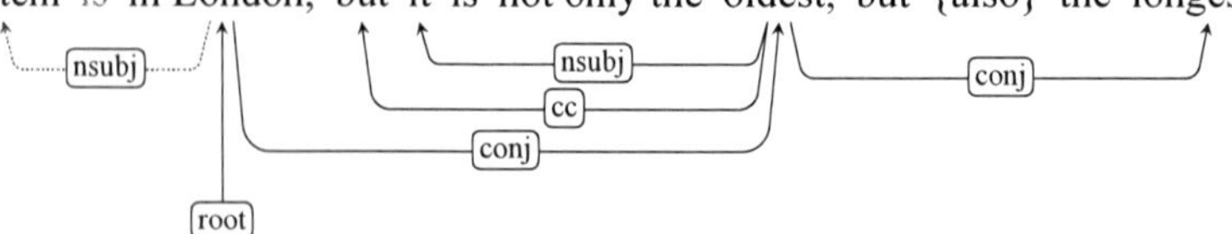

The phrase *The oldest railway system in London* can be considered as (a) an appositive linked to the pronoun *it* in the main clause; (b) a part of the concessive clause (with *being* being omitted), or (c) a part of the main clause where the copula is omitted after the subject *The oldest railway system*).

The next example presents the frequent mistake made by Russian students - the usage of large amount of specifying words. Because of them the parser determines the head of the sentence incorrectly.

(4) *Accordingly, the same situation as in the proportion of skilled vocational diploma is in postgraduate diploma.*

The parser determines the noun *situation* as the head of the word *accordingly*, but the right choice here is the root of the whole sentence - *diploma*. As the head of the introductory phrase is too far, parser take the closest possible word as a head. The head of the introductory word should be always the root of the whole sentence.

7.2   Errors influenced by word order

Sentence (5) demonstrates the wrong SV word order typical of students' writing. In a gold representation, this mistake is reflected in a non-projective tree.

(5) *On the other hand is Tokyo also situated in Japan but it is big megapolise with the 1927 millions of people.*

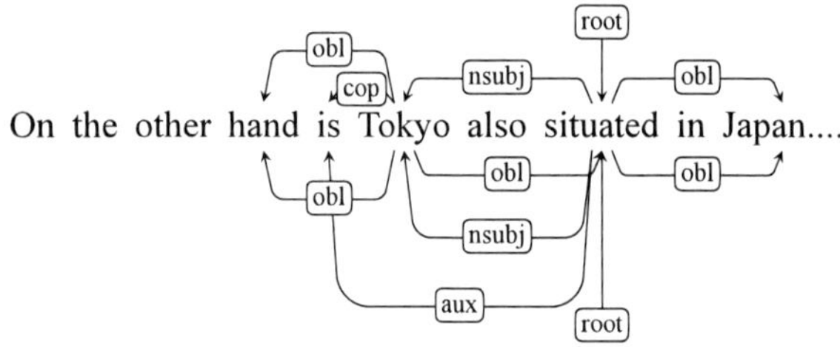

However, it can be seen that even in well-formed sentences the parsing errors can be explained by non-standard word order patterns. Sentence (6) has an ambiguity in reading *presents* as a noun or as a verb, the former being provided by the parser. As a result, the adverbial modifier *below* comes after its nominal head (*graph*), thereby evoking the reading of the segment *below present* as PP.

(6) *The graph below presents to us, that between 1983 and 2030 in Japan it rise from 3 procent to 10 procent, but in Sweden it is a little fall to 13 procent , but there was a high growth to 20 procent in 2010.*

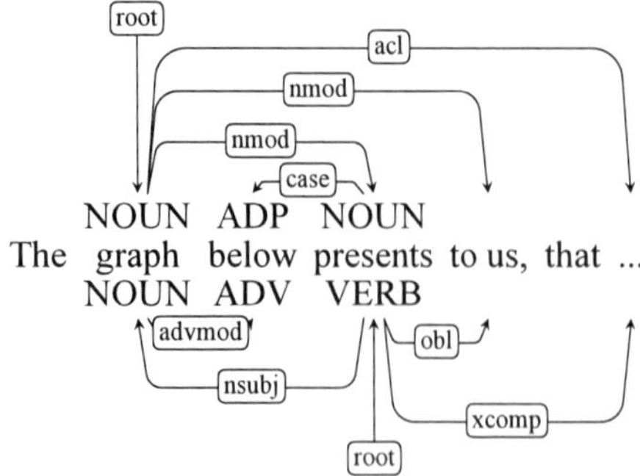

7.3 Spelling and grammar mistakes made by students

We investigated to what extent misspelt words affect the parser's quality. Comparison of automatic and gold parses in (7) with those of its 'improved' version (7') demonstrates that verb agreement is critical for parsing.

(7) *The persent of old people in the USA stay constant (14 %) from 1980 to 2020 and rising quicly (23%) during next 20 years.*

(7') *The percentage of old people in the USA stays constant (14 %) from 1980 to 2020 and rises quickly (23%) during the next 20 years.*

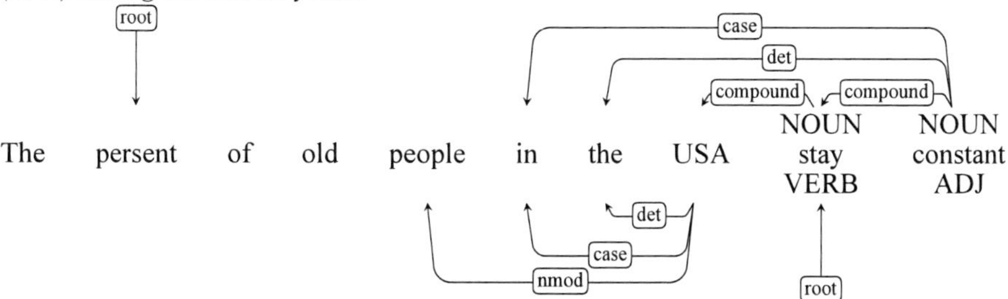

The schemes show that grammatically correct sentences are parsed better than those with spelling and grammatical mistakes. We suggest that this problem could for the most part be solved with the help of a common spellchecker. It will allow us to analyze the syntactic structure of the sentences ignoring the students' grammar and spelling errors that do not influence syntactic complexity.

Generally, the modification in grammar showed that the grammatically correct statements are parsed more accurately than those that contain errors. The main mistake of the parser is the wrong detection of part of speech. It causes the wrong detection of sentence root, which is considered critical for parsing and entails other errors (in head detection and consequently in type of relation). Accordingly, spelling correction made before parsing would reduce the number of errors made by the parser.

7.4 Participial construction not recognized by the parser

(8) *Tokyo railway, opened in 1927, was only 155 kilometres on route but, compare to previous system, helped to travel to almost 2000 millions passengers.*

In (8), the participle *opened* is parsed as the root of the sentence. As the parser chooses the part of speech incorrectly, the error arises: *opened* is defined as a verb and it becomes more and more probable that this word will be the root of the sentence. The probability of choosing *opened* as a verb and the head of the sentence is higher than the probability of choosing *kilometres* as the head of the sentence.

7.5 Syntactic homonymy

(9) *Meanwhile, in USA there was 9 procent of people aged 65 and over in 1940, then in 1960 it increased by 10 procent.*

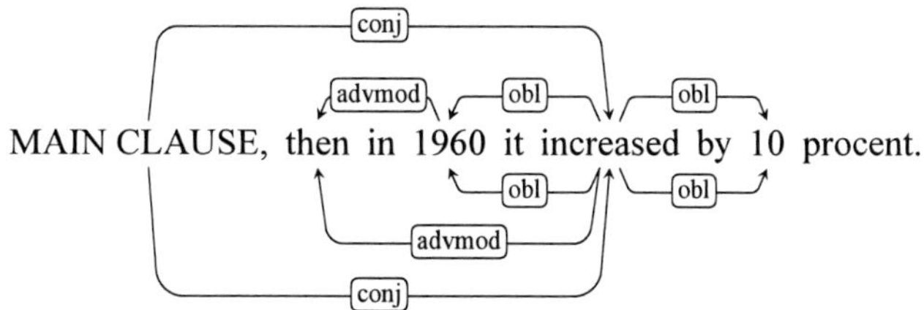

Here we can see that the linking word *then* refers not to the whole sentence. It is parsed as the clarification of the adverbial modifier of time *in 1960*. This is not a critical mistake but the automatic parsing slightly changes the meaning of the statement.

8   Conclusion

This paper presents the REALEC learner treebank automatically annotated by Ud-pipe and then manually corrected. We provide evaluation of the automatic parsing output and explore what types of learners' errors are critical for the parser.

We confirmed the idea of van Rooy and Schäfer, who claimed that if we check the spelling in essays before applying a parser, errors that are not related to the syntax will not affect the evaluation of the syntactic complexity. This conclusion leads to the idea that advanced annotated learner corpora should have a spellchecker which analyses not only the spelling, but also improves the work of various automatic tools.

Studying the output of the Ud-pipe parser, we found out that phrases like *a chart below* or *7 years old*, which occur frequently in academic register of English, are parsed incorrectly. In such cases, the parser fails to identify the head of the phrase, which is in turn the cause of further parser errors, and involves a large amount of manual corrections.

The obtained results will help to improve the quality of the parser and the annotation in the learner corpora. Firstly, we have identified a list of typical error-provoking patterns based on the collection of reannotated sentences. In the future the inventory of such patterns will be expanded. Secondly, as the amount of annotated learner data in the open access grows, we will conduct a series of experiments on parser training and compare the models trained on grammatically correct texts vs. those involving learner data.

For future work, we also plan to increase the size of our treebank taking more samples from the learner corpus REALEC. We would also like to use dependency parsing to improve the quality of corpus annotation.

Acknowledgements

The paper was prepared within the framework of the Academic Fund Program at the National Research University Higher School of Economics (HSE) in 2016–17 (grant No 16-05-0057) and by the Russian Academic Excellence Project «5-100». We would like to thank the participants of the Research Team Project "Learner corpus REALEC: Lexicological observations" and in particular, Olga Vinogradova for discussions and suggestions.

References

Berzak, Y., Kenney, J., Spadine, C., Wang, J. X., Lam, L., Mori, K. S., Garza, S., and Katz, B. (2016). Universal dependencies for learner English. In *Proceedings of the 54th Annual Meeting of the Association for Computational Linguistics*, volume 1, pages 737–746.

Cobb, T. and Horst, M. (2015). Learner corpora and lexis. In *The Cambridge Handbook of Learner Corpus Research*, pages 185–206. Cambridge University Press.

Graesser, A., McNamara, D., and Kulikowich, J. (2011). Coh-metrix: Providing multilevel analyses of text characteristics. *Educational Researcher*, 40(5):223–234.

Lee, J., Leung, H., and Li, K. (2017). Towards universal dependencies for learner Chinese. In *Proceedings of the NoDaLiDa 2017 Workshop on Universal Dependencies, 22 May 2017*, volume 135.

Lu, X. and Haiyan, A. (2016). Universal dependencies for learner English. In *Journal of Second Language Writing*, volume 29, pages 16–27.

Nivre, J., de Marneffe, M.-C., Ginter, F., Goldberg, Y., Hajič, J., Manning, C., McDonald, R., Petrov, S., Pyysalo, S., Silveira, N., Tsarfaty, R., and Zeman, D. (2016). Universal dependencies v1: A multilingual treebank collection. In *Proceedings of Language Resources and Evaluation Conference (LREC'16)*.

Ragheb, M. and Dickinson, M. (2017). Defining syntax for learner language annotation. In *Proceedings of the 24th International Conference on Computational Linguistics (COLING 2012), Poster Session*, pages 965–974.

Rooy, B. V. and Schäfer, L. (2002). Universal dependencies for learner English. In *Southern African Linguistics and Applied Language Studies, 20(4)*, pages 325–335.

Rosén, V. and Smedt, K. D. (2010). *Syntactic Annotation of Learner Corpora*, pages 120–132.

Schneider, G. and Gilquin, G. (2016). Detecting innovations in a parsed corpus of learner English. *International Journal of Learner Corpus Research*, 2(2):177–204.

Straka, M., Hajič, J., and Strakova, J. (2016). Ud-pipe: Trainable pipeline for processing Conll-u files performing tokenization, morphological analysis, pos tagging and parsing. In *Proceedings of the 10th International Conference on Language Resources and Evaluation (LREC 2016)*, pages 4290–4297.

Straka, M. and Straková, J. (2017). Tokenizing, pos tagging, lemmatizing and parsing UD 2.0 with UDPipe. In *Proceedings of the Conll 2017 Shared Task: Multilingual Parsing from Raw Text to Universal Dependencies*.

Vinogradova, O. (2016). The role and applications of expert error annotation in a corpus of English learner texts. In *Computational Linguisitics and Intellectual Technologies. Proceedings of Dialog 2016*, volume 15, pages 740–751.

Vinogradova, O., Lyashevskaya, O., and Panteleeva, I. (2017). Multi-level student essay feedback in a learner corpus. In *Computational Linguisitics and Intellectual Technologies. Proceedings of Dialog 2017*, volume 16, pages 382–396.

A semiautomatic lemmatisation procedure for treebanks.
Old English strong and weak verbs.

Darío Metola Rodríguez
University of La Rioja
Edificio Filologías
26004, Logroño (La Rioja) Spain
dario.metola@unirioja.es

Marta Tío Sáenz
University of La Rioja
Edificio Filologías
26004, Logroño (La Rioja) Spain
marta.tio@unirioja.es

Abstract

The aim of this paper is to present a semiautomatic lemmatisation procedure implemented on database software that is compatible with the morphological tagging of treebanks. The language of analysis is Old English, for which parsed corpora are available but they are not lemmatised. The scope of the paper includes both strong and weak verbs. After describing the lemmatisation procedure, the paper discusses the results of automatic searches and compares them with the lists of inflectional forms by lemma provided by other lexicographical sources. The conclusions insist on the limits of automatic lemmatisation and the compatibility with treebank parsing.

1   Introduction

This paper deals with lemmatisation in a corpus of Old English and focuses on the seven classes of strong verbs, and classes 1 and 2 of weak verbs. The analysis reported here is based on the lemmatiser *Norna*, a building block of the lexical database of Old English *Nerthus* (www.nerthusproject.com). *Norna*, in turn, draws on the information available from the *Dictionary of Old English Corpus* (hearafter DOEC, Healey et al., 2004), the *Helsinki Corpus* (Rissanen et al., 1991), the *York-Toronto-Helsinki Parsed Corpus of Old English Prose* (Taylor et al., 2003) and the *York-Helsinki Parsed Corpus of Old English Poetry* (Pintzuk and Plug, 2001). Of these, only the *York-Toronto-Helsinki Parsed Corpus of Old English Prose* (Taylor et al., 2003) and the *York-Helsinki Parsed Corpus of Old English Poetry* (Pintzuk and Plug, 2001) are parsed. The parsing includes syntactic categories and functions as well as lexical and morphological tagging. For this reason, these corpora are commonly known as *treebanks*. In their current state, these treebanks are unlemmatised. That is to say, the attestations of the inflections of a given lemma are not related to the dictionary word, which results in a lower descriptive power, especially as regards paradigmatic analysis and the quantification of morphological and lexical aspects.

Moreover, the standard dictionaries of Old English, including *An Anglo-Saxon Dictionary, A Concise Anglo-Saxon Dictionary* and *The student's Dictionary of Anglo-Saxon,* constitute valuable sources of philological data, although they are not based on an extensive corpus of the language but on the partial list of texts listed in their prefaces or introductions. On its part, *The Dictionary of Old English* (henceforth DOE) is based on the corpus mentioned above, but is still in progress (the letter H was published in 2016). All in all, neither the textual nor the lexicographical sources of Old English are fully lemmatised. At the same time, treebanks could improve their descriptive power and searchability by incorporating lemma tags. For these reasons, the aim of this paper is to present a semiautomatic lemmatisation procedure implemented on database software that is compatible with the morphological tagging of treebanks. The first step was to carry out a concordance of the texts that the *Dictionary of Old English* provides in its corpus. The concordance by word consists of three million lines, one per word in the corpus. The concordance by fragment, in contrast, contains around two hundred thousand fragments of texts identified with the short title with which they appear in the DOEC, as in *Eala ðu cleric ne wana ðu æfre wexbreda fram sidan* [Abbo 000100 (103.1)]. The target of the analysis is the data retrieved from the word concordance to the DOEC, which turns out an index of approximately one hundred and ninety thousand inflectional forms. Once the data has been identified and extracted from the concordance, the process of lemmatisation starts. The different types of verbs are lemmatised in turn, depending on their formal transparency. That is to say, strong verbs have been lemmatised in the first

Proceedings of the 16th International Workshop on Treebanks and Linguistic Theories (TLT16), pages 88–94,
Prague, Czech Republic, January 23–24, 2018. Distributed under a CC-BY 4.0 licence. 2017.

Keywords: semi-automatic lemmatisation, treebanks, Old English, weak verbs

place and then weak verbs from the second class have been processed. The former can be identified by stem and inflectional ending, the latter by inflectional ending only, but their inflectional paradigm is more transparent that the one of the weak verbs from the first and the third class. Then, weak verbs from class 1 have been lemmatised. Weak class 3, anomalous, contracted and preterite-present verbs will be dealt with in further research.

2 Lemmatisation procedure for strong verbs

On the lemmatiser *Norna*, inflectional forms of strong verbs are assigned a lemma on the basis of a reference list of verbs from each strong class that has been retrieved from the lexical database Nerthus and supplemented with information from Krygier (1994) and Hogg and Fulk (2011).

The second step in the process of lemmatisation in *Norna* has already been implemented for the seven classes of strong verbs of Old English. Query strings are defined and launched in the database, so that the results are compared with the existing sources, and the conclusions of such comparison are used to refine the query strings.

After these query strings have been inputed to the lemmatiser, the assignments of lemmas to attestations are filed and compared with the lexicographical and philological sources, so that the feedback of previous searches is used to improve subsequent query strings.

With this method, the design of the search algorithm is stepwise. The target of the first step is the simplex word. The underived verbs in the reference list of the seven strong classes have been inflected for the infinitive, inflected infinitive, present participle and past participle; present indicative singular and plural, present subjunctive singular and plural, preterite indicative singular and plural, preterite subjunctive singular and plural, imperative singular and plural.

The second step in the creation of the algorithm is focused on the complex word. It consists on the compilation of a list of elements that may be attached to simplex strong verbs to form derived or compound verbs. Originally, the inventory of preverbal elements, retrieved from the lexical database of Old English *Nerthus*, includes affixes with a very specific meaning, such as the negative prefix *un-*, the pejorative prefix *mis-* as well as the aspectual prefixes *eft-* and *ed-*; the Germanic pure prefixes *ā-*, *be-*, *for-*, *ge-*, *of-*, *on-*, *tō-* (de la Cruz 1975); the spatial and temporal adverbs and prepositions that are going through grammaticalisation resulting in a telic marker (Brinton and Traugott 2005; Martín Arista and Cortés Rodríguez 2014), including *adūn-*, *æfter-*, *æt-*, *āweg-*, *beforan-*, *betwux-*, *ðurh-*, *forð-*, *fore-*, *fram-*, *geond-*, *in-*, *niðer-*, *oð-*, *ofer-*, *onweg-*, *under-*, *ūp-*, *ūt-*, *wið-*, *wiðer-*, and *ymb-*; and fully free forms that appear in compound verbs such as *āgēn-*, *and-*, *ðri-*, *dyrn-*, *efen-*, *ful-*, *hearm-*, *mæg-*, *mān-*, *nyd-*, *riht-*, *twi-*, *wyrg-*. Having the preverbal elements, the roots and the set of inflections presented above, the third step in the design of the search algorithm is the definition of query strings that can be applied on Filemaker. Four query strings (QS) have been defined. QS1 is devoted to the stems and inflections by using the operator (wild card) for exact matches in Filemaker (==). The part of QS1 that searches the corpus for the inflections of *bēodan* can be seen in (1).

(1)

> ==beodan, ==bead, ==budon, ==beode, ==bead, ==biedest, ==biedst, ==bietst, ==biest, ==bude, ==beodeð, ==beodeþ, ==biett, ==bietð, ==bietþ, ==bead, ==beodaþ, ==beodað, ==budon, ==beode, ==bude, ==beoden, ==buden, ==beod, ==beodað, ==beodaþ

The target of the second QS (QS2) is prefix *ge-*, the most frequent in Old English (Martín Arista 2012b), to such an extent that most strong verbs present a simplex and complex form prefixes with *ge-*. QS2 for *gebēodan* is shown in (2).

(2)

> ==gecimban, ==gecamb, ==gecumbon, ==gecumben, ==gecimbe, ==gecamb, ==gecimbst, ==gecimbest, ==gecumbe, ==gecimbð, ==gecimbþ, ==gecimbeð, ==gecimbeþ, ==gecamb, ==gecimbaþ, ==gecimbað, ==gecumbon, ==gecimbe, ==gecambe, ==gecimben, ==gecumben, ==gecimb, ==gecimbaþ, ==gecimbað, ==gecimbanne, ==gecimbenne, ==gecimbende

QS3 has been created for accounting the existence of complex strong verbs with preverbs different from *ge-*. The wild card (*) in (3) represents any preverbal elements attached to the base and its inflections.

(3)

==*beodan, ==*bead, ==*budon, ==*beode, ==*bead, ==*biedest, ==*biedst, ==*bietst, ==*biest, ==*bude, ==*beodeð, ==*beodeþ, ==*biett, ==*bietð, ==*bietþ, ==*bead, ==*beodaþ, ==*beodað, ==*budon, ==*beode, ==*bude, ==*beoden, ==*buden, ==*beod, ==*beodað, ==*beodaþ

QS4 is the least specific of all the query strings. It looks in the corpus for the stems of strong verbs with any preverbal element and inflectional ending, hence the addittion of the wild card (*) to both sides of the stem, as in (4).

(4)

==*beod*, ==*bead*, ==*bud*, ==*bod*, ==*bied*, ==*biet*, ==*biest*

The previous query strings have been launched in a sequential manner: QS1, QS2, QS3, QS4. After the submission of each query, the resulting hits have been tagged on the lemmatiser *Norna*, with the result that the tags from previous queries could aid the tagging of the hits resulting from subsequent queries. This brings about a simplification of the overall task because, in spite of being likely to find some unexpected spellings, QS4 is redundant with respect to QS1 (endings), QS2 and QS3 (preverbs). Moreover, due to its wide scope, it is predictable that this query strings turns out a remarkably high number of results. For this, the final step in the design of this algorithm is the definition of filters to put aside at least part of the undesired results of QS4, so that manual revision can be diminished dramatically.

Four filters have been designed for this purpose. Filter (F) 1 is intended to isolate verbal forms. It cuts down the hits of QS4 to inflectional forms that end with -odon-, -ast, -est, -ost, -ð, -þ, -iað and-iaþ, thus the operators == and *. The application of F1 to the 17,138 hits of SQ4 reduces this figure to 1,939. F1 is presented in (5).

(5)

==*-on, ==*-odon-, ==*-ast, ==*-est, ==*-ost, ==*-ð, ==*-þ, ==*-iað, ==*-iaþ

F2 is aimed at finding spelling variations in the consonantal endings of verbal forms. It is applied in two steps. The first selects the inflectional forms that end in a consonant, as can be seen in (6).

(6)

==*b, ==*c, ==*d, ==*f, ==*g, ==*h, ==*l, ==*m, ==*n, ==*p, ==*r, ==*s, ==*t, ==*w, ==*x, ==*y, ==*ð, ==*þ

The second step of F2 targets members of the non-verbal classes as well as weak verbs by deleting inflectional forms that end in -on, -en, -an, -es, -um, -end, -as, -est, -ost, -ed, -od, -ig, -ic, -ing, -ung, -un, -us, -nes, -er, -or, -ur, -iað, -iaþ. It must noted that F2 also puts aside the endings -iað, -iaþ, which are selected by F1. When applied to the outcome of SQ4, the first step of F2 reduces its hits from 17,138 to 10,305, which, after the application of the second step of F2, result in 3,533 hits. The second step of F2 is displayed in (7).

(7)

==*on, ==*en, ==*an, ==*es, ==*um, ==*end, ==*as, ==*est, ==*ost, ==*ed, ==*od, ==*ig, ==*ic, ==*ing, ==*ung, ==*un, ==*us, ==*nes, ==*er, ==*or, ==*ur, ==*iað, ==*iaþ

Turning to the comparison with lexicographical sources, the comparison with the inflectional forms provided by the DOE (A-H) has shown that the accuracy of the search algorithm is around 80%.

As regards the comparison with textual sources, the lemmatiser *Norna* has been modified so that it gives access to the inflectional forms that appear both in the DOEC and the YCOE.

A comparison of YCOE and the lemmatiser *Norna* has been carried out. As an illustration, for the letter L the forms in (8a) can be retrieved from the YCOE (165), while those in (8b) appear in *Norna* (148).

(8)
a. lacað, lacan, laceð, lacende, laðaþ, ladigan, laðod, laðode, lædað, lædan, Læddan, lædde, læddest, læddon, læde, læded, lædeð, lædeþ, Læf, læfan, læfde, læg, lægon, lægun, lær, læran, lærde, lærde, lærdes, lære, læreð, lærest, læs, læst, læstan, læste, læston, læt, læt, læt, Lætað, lætað, lætan, læte, læte, læteð, lætst, lagan, lagon, lah, lata, laþaþ, leag, leanað, leanast, leanige, leccað, leccaþ, lecgað, lecgan, lecge, legde, legdun, legeð, lengde, lengeð, leofa, leofað, leofaþ, leogan, leoge, leohte, leolc, leordan, leorde, Leort, leoþode, lepeþ, Let, Letan, lete, lete, Leton, letton, liban, libban, licað, licgað, licgan, licge, licgean, , lician, licode, licodon, liðan, liðan, liden, liden, lifað, Lifde, lifdon, lifdon, lifgað, lifgan, lifgaþ, lifge, lifiaþ, lifige, ligeð, ligeð, lihteð, limpeð, linnan, linneð, linnið, lixað, lixan, lixeð, lixtan, lixte, lixton, liþ, liþan, locað, locade, locast, locen, lociað, Lofiað, lofian, log, logon, lomp, Longað, losað, losade, losaþ, losian, lucan, ludon, lufast, lufaþ, lufiað, lufian, lufiaþ, lufie, lufien, lufige, lufu, lunnon, lycð, Lyfað, lyfað, lyfde, lyhð, lyhte, lyhteð, lysan, lyst, lyste, lyste, lysteð, lysteð, lysteþ.
b. lac, lace, lece, lec, lacað, lacan, leolc, lecc, laceð, læceð, Læt, let, læte, lætan, Lætað, Leton, lete, læst, læten, læteð, letan, lætst, lett, lætt, læton, lætest, lætaþ, leten, læteþ, leto, leteð, lætenne, Leort, lettes, leteþ, lætæð, lætoð, lætæst, lætin, lætene, Læt.þ, leode, lead, leod, leodan, leoden, lude, ludon, liet, leogað, leoge, lugon, leogan, leag, leoh, luge, leogaþ, lugen, liehð, leogeð, leogendan, leogð, liegeð, lieht, , leah, leore, leoreð, leoran, leor, leorað, lure, leoren, leord, leorest, lorene, leorad, lierest, liereð, loren, les, List, lese, lesan, lisð, lesað, lest, lisseð, lað, liðe, liþe, liðan, liþan, laþ, liðon, liþon, liþ, lið, liðað, lif, life, laf, lifað, lifeð, lifæs, lifæþ, lifen, lifaþ, lifð, lifast, lifeþ, lift, limpð, limpeð, lamp, limpe, limpað, limpes, limpa, limpeþ, lumpe, limpan, lin, lan, linnan, linnen, lunnon, linne, linnið, linneð, leac, Lucan, Luce, locen, lucon, lucað, luc, lycð, leat, luton, lutan, luteð, lute, lut, loten, lutaþ, lutað.

The discrepancies in the number of forms can be attributed to the compilations of the DOEC and the YCOE. An avenue of future research in this respect is the identification of forms in the YCOE that has been deleted in the different editions of the DOEC. Apart from this question, the search algorithm has to be modified to include, at least, three aspects: <g> followed by a front vowel in the same syllable, as is the case with ladigan, legde, legdun, legeð, lifige and lufige; <y> for <i> in accented syllables, as in lyfað and lyfde; -an/-un for -on in unaccented (inflectional) syllables, as in lægun and legdun.

3   Lemmatisation procedure for weak verbs

Weak verbs correspond to the modern 'regular' verbs. The changes in their inflection take place in the suffixal part of the word rather than in the stem, as is the case with strong verbs, counterparts of the modern 'irregular verbs'. In order to find the inflectional forms of weak verbs in the database, it is necessary to list a set of inflectional endings of class 1 and class 2 weak verbs that includes the endings of finite forms (indicative, subjunctive and imperative) and non-finite forms (infinitive, inflected infinitive, present participle, past participle and past participle forms inflected as adjective). The choice of forms has been made by comparing Old English verbal paradigms of the three subclasses of weak verbs in four Old English grammars (Campbell, 1987; Hogg and Fulk, 2011; Sievers, 1903; Stark, 1992). The compilation of these inflectional endings will guide the automatic searches in subsequent steps of the analysis. The result of this task is an inventory of 24 different endings for the paradigm of class 1 and 29 different endings for the paradigm of class 2.
On the lemmatiser, the query strings for each of the endings selected are defined as follows: two equal signs followed by a wild card (an asterisk) and the spelling of the ending. Thus, we will obtain all inflectional forms in the database with the requested ending. For example, we use the query string ==*ianne, the canonical inflectional ending of the inflected infinitive of class 2 weak verbs, and obtain 160 inflectional forms included in the database, most of which are likely to be lemmatised under a lemma from the second weak class. We launch 24 different queries for the canonical endings of class 1 weak verbs and another 29 for the counterparts of the second class of weak verbs. Then, all the hits are checked with the lists of weak verbs available in *Nerthus*. These lists of reference contain more than 2,000 verbs each. To achieve the maximum degree of accuracy in the initial stages of the project, the

criterion was to assign lemma only to combinations of stems of the weak verbs as they appear in the reference lists and canonical endings.

The results of this lemmatisation process consist of more than 4,680 inflectional forms lemmatised with class 1 weak verbs and more than 6,600 inflectional forms for class 2 weak verbs. The lemmatisation of these forms provides paradigmatic information on weak verbs that can contribute to the development of treebanks, since lemmatisation relates the syntactic analysis of the inflectional forms that are lemmatised under the same headword, thus allowing for extensive descriptive analysis as well as quantification. For instance, the inflectional forms lemmatised in the database for class 2 weak verb *lufian* are the following: *lufað, lufiað, lufode, lufige, lufast, lufie, lufaþ, lufodon, lufodest, lufiað, lufien, lufigen, gelufiað, gelufode, gelufie, lufian, gelufod, lufianne, lufiende, lufienne, lufodes, lufiendum, lufodan, gelufoda, lufod, gelufian, gelufodes, gelufodne, lufoden*. All these inflectional forms belong to different parts of the paradigm of the same lemma; therefore, lemmatisation is proved to be an effective tool for linking together syntactic analysis of a given lemma. In turn, we are able to take a look at all the inflectional forms for a given lemma with the click of a button, as shown in Figure 1. The two leftmost columns list the number of occurrences and the inflectional forms, and the column *Headword* shows the lemma assigned to them.

Occurrences	InflectionalForm	Headword	Weak_Verb_1	Weak_Verb_2	DOE	DOE_head...	Strong_Verb_I
26	gelangian	langian(ge) 2		langian(ge) 2			
8	gelangode	langian(ge) 2		langian(ge) 2			
5	langað	langian(ge) (2)		langian(ge) (2)			
3	langian	langian(ge) 2		langian(ge) 2			
2	langode	langian(ge) 2		langian(ge) 2			
2	langaþ	langian(ge) (2)		langian(ge) (2)			
1	gelangað	langian(ge) (2)		langian(ge) (2)			
1	gelangien	langian(ge) (2)		langian(ge) (2)			
1	gelangod	langian(ge) (2)		langian(ge) (2)			
1	gelangodest	langian(ge) (2)		langian(ge) (2)			
1	Gelangiað	langian(ge) (2)		langian(ge) (2)			
1	gelangige	langian(ge) (2)		langian(ge) (2)			
1	gelangast	langian(ge) (2)		langian(ge) (2)			
1	gelangie	langian(ge) 2		langian(ge) 2			

Figure 1: Inflectional forms for the lemma *langian(ge)* (2) 'to grieve' in *Norna*.

The lemmatisation of Old English weak verbs with this procedure needs checking. The DOE (A-H) is the lexicographical source used for this task. As stated above, this dictionary is still in progress but the information listed for verbs from A-H is detailed and central to this investigation. Through the online version of this dictionary, it is possible to search inflectional forms by lemma. For this reason, the lemmatiser *Norna* permits to compare the attested spellings for weak verbs from A to H with those that appear in the DOE. Many unpredictable spellings of weak verbs are available in the DOE that cannot be found by means of automatic lemmatisation, since most of them include spelling variations in prefixes, stems and endings. For instance, for the lemma *bǣdan(ge)* (1) 'to force', seven inflectional forms can be obtained by automatic lemmatisation: *bædað, baedde, bædde, bæddon, bæde, bædeð, bæden*. However, the DOE includes eight extra attested spellings in the entry to this verb: *bæddan, baedendrae, baedendre, bædendre, bædendum, bædt, beadcætþ* and *bedændræ*. The feedback of previous searches are input into the database and used to refine subsequent searches, so that the amount of manual revision can be reduced.

This task of comparison results in the identification of 12,000 extra inflectional forms for weak verbs, on the grounds of the information found in the DOE verb entries in the letters A-H. The analysis of these extra forms will allow to compile a list of the recurrent variants of canonical forms of weak verbs and, eventually, normalisations patterns (by prefix, stem or ending). This correspondence will be applied to the search for the inflectional forms of the verbs beginning with the letters I-Y. As illustration, the inflectional form *aflemde* is lemmatised under the headword *āflyman* (1) 'to put to fly' in the DOE. This change of vowel < e > ≈ < y > will be included in the normalisation patterns for the stem of the verbal form. Similarly, the DOE includes the inflectional form *aredad* in the paradigm of the lemma *āredian* (2) 'to arrange', which is a variant of *aredod*, the past participle form. This pattern <o> ≈ <a> is consequently added to the normalisation patterns taking place in the endings of the inflectional forms. In this context, the prefix of the inflectional form *gifered* from the lemma *ferian(ge)* (1) 'to carry' shows the recurrent pattern of variation <gi> ≈ <ge>, which is added to the list of normalisation patterns for the prefixal segment of the attested form. The application of these three types of patterns in the study of inflectional forms I-Y, with the same queries as in the search for the canonical endings of weak verbs, will undoubtedly lead to the lemmatisation of a larger number of inflectional forms for class 1 and class 2 weak verbs and, more importantly, will result in the reduction of manual revision.

The lemmatisation procedure has limitations that need to be taken into account. There are many unexpected spellings within the paradigms of weak verbs, not foreseeable abbreviations, as well as many ambiguities that can only be lemmatised with the help of dictionaries. Gemination and simplification of consonants are also recurrent in verbal forms, thus excluding the automatic lemmatisation of several inflectional forms. This is the case with *cunedon*, from *cunnian(ge)* (2) 'to try', which gets consonant simplification. In addition, and according to the DOE, some inflectional forms lemmatised with this method belong to different categories and to other verbs classes. The explanation for this phenomenon is the overlapping of endings among verbs, nouns, adjectives and adverbs, like the ending -e. The inflectional form *dere* was initially lemmatised under the lemma *derian(ge)* (1) 'to hurt', given that it includes the stem of a weak verb of the first class and one of the canonical endings of this class; but the comparison with the DOE showed that, in fact, *dere* is a nominal rather than a verbal form. Finally, the unpredictable forms *auandod*, from *āfandian* (2) 'to test', and *hergendne*, from *erian* (1) 'to plough', which are also available from the DOE, are hard to find by automatic means, at least in this stage of the project.

4 Conclusion

The lemmatisation procedure for the strong verbs of Old English presented in this paper has an accuracy of around 80% before manual revision. After checking the results with lexicographical and textual sources, search strings can be refined and manual revision reduced. The compatibility with treebanks has been addressed with respect to the YCOE. As for weak verbs, the lemmatisation procedure has allowed for the identification of more than 20,000 inflectional forms of weak verbs. However, the comparison with the DOE, as the main lexicographic source, has also proved a crucial step of the lemmatisation procedure because it turns out more inflectional forms but, above all, because it identifies recurrent spelling variants with which normalisation patterns can be defined and subsequent searches can be refined. The inclusion of additional patterns of normalisation and the gradual improvement of searches are likely not only to find more lemmas and inflectional forms but also to reduce the necessary amount of manual revision. In spite of the limitations of semiautomatic lemmatisation, this procedure has allowed us to find a large amount of inflectional forms from weak verbs in Old English.

It will be necessary, therefore, to check the inflectional forms of the DOEC and the YCOE, but further guidelines for search strings have been obtained. To conclude, a step has been taken towards the inclusion of lemma tags into treebanks, which could reinforce the paradigmatic dimension of these parsed corpora and contribute to the retrievability of the information that they contain, including the important aspect of the quantification of the occurrences of a given lemma.

References

Bosworth, J. and T. N. Toller. 1973 (1898). *An Anglo-Saxon Dictionary*. Oxford: Oxford University Press.

Brinton, L. and E. Closs Traugott. 2005. *Lexicalization and Language Change*. Cambridge: Cambridge University Press.

Campbell, A. 1987. *Old English Grammar*. Oxford: Oxford University Press.

Clark Hall, J. R. 1996 (1896). *A Concise Anglo-Saxon Dictionary*. Toronto: University of Toronto Press.

de la Cruz, J. 1075. Old English Pure Prefixes: Structure and Function. *Linguistics* 13: 47-82.

Healey, A. diPaolo (ed.) 2016. *The Dictionary of Old English in Electronic Form A-H*. Toronto: Dictionary of Old English Project, Centre for Medieval Studies, University of Toronto.

Healey, A. diPaolo (ed.) with J. Price Wilkin and X.Xiang. 2004. *The Dictionary of Old English Web Corpus*. Toronto: Dictionary of Old English Project, Centre for Medieval Studies, University of Toronto. Available online at http://www.doe.utoronto.ca/pages/pub/web-corpus.html.

Hogg, R. M. and R. D. Fulk 1992 (2011). *A Grammar of Old English*. Oxford, Wiley-Blackwell.

Krygier, M. 1994. *The Disintegration of the English Strong Verb System*. Frankfurt am Main: Peter Lang.

Martín Arista, J. 2012b. The Old English Prefix *Ge-*: A Panchronic Reappraisal. *Australian Journal of Linguistics* 32(4): 411-433.

Martín Arista, J. and F. Cortés Rodríguez. 2014. From directional to telics: meaning construction, word-formation and grammaticalization in Role and Reference Grammar. In M. A. Gómez González, F. Ruiz de Mendoza Ibáñez and F. Gonzálvez García (eds.), *Theory and Practice in Functional-Cognitive Space*. Amsterdam: John Benjamins. 229-250.

Martín Arista, Javier (ed.), Laura García Fernández, Miguel Lacalle Palacios, Ana Elvira Ojanguren López and Esaúl Ruiz Narbona. 2016. *NerthusV3. Online Lexical Database of Old English*. Nerthus Project. Universidad de La Rioja. [www.nerthusproject.com]

Pintzuk, S. and L. Plug (ed.) 2001. *The York-Helsinki Parsed Corpus of Old English Poetry*. Department of Language and Linguistic Science, University of York.

Rissanen M., M. Kytö, L. Kahlas-Tarkka, M. Kilpiö, S. Nevanlinna, I. Taavitsainen, T. Nevalainen and H. Raumolin-Brunberg (eds.) 1991. *The Helsinki Corpus of English Texts*. Department of Modern Languages, University of Helsinki.

Sievers, E. 1903 (1885). *An Old English Grammar*. Boston: The Athenaeum Press.

Taylor, A., A. Warner, S. Pintzuk and F. Beths (eds.) 2003. *The York-Toronto-Helsinki Parsed Corpus of Old English Prose*. Department of Language and Linguistic Science, University of York.

Data point selection for genre-aware parsing

Ines Rehbein
Leibniz ScienceCampus
Heidelberg/Mannheim
rehbein@cl.uni-heidelberg.de

Felix Bildhauer
Institut für Deutsche Sprache
Mannheim
bildhauer@ids-mannheim.de

Abstract

In the NLP literature, adapting a parser to new text with properties different from the training data is commonly referred to as *domain* adaptation. In practice, however, the differences between texts from different sources often reflect a mixture of *domain* and *genre* properties, and it is by no means clear what impact each of those has on statistical parsing. In this paper, we investigate how differences between articles in a newspaper corpus relate to the concepts of *genre* and *domain* and how they influence parsing performance of a transition-based dependency parser. We do this by applying various similarity measures for data point selection and testing their adequacy for creating genre-aware parsing models.

1 Introduction

The work of Biber (1988; 1995) and Biber & Conrad (2009) on language variation has brought valuable insights into the concepts of genre and register and the linguistic features that define them. It has also triggered many studies on genre classification (Kessler et al., 1997; Feldman et al., 2009; Passonneau et al., 2014), trying to automatically predict the genre or register for a particular text. However, despite the amount of work dedicated to genre prediction, the theoretical concept of *genre* remains vague and no agreement has been reached within the NLP (and linguistics) community on how to define it.[1]

This is even more surprising as concepts like *genre* and *domain* seem to be of crucial importance to our field and it is well known that the accuracy of NLP tools trained on one type of text will decrease noticeably when applying the same tools to another type of text with underlying properties that are different from the training data (Sekine, 1997; Gildea, 2001; McClosky et al., 2006). This might be due to either domain or genre differences, however, in NLP we usually refer to both as *out-of-domain* effects. While many studies have successfully shown how we can adapt tools to new domains (or genres) (Blitzer et al., 2006; Titov, 2011; Mitchell and Steedman, 2015), less is known about the underlying properties that are responsible for the decrease in performance. Out-of-domain (including out-of-genre) effects might be due to a large amount of unknown words introduced by topic shifts but might also be caused by a higher structural complexity in the data, by longer dependencies or a higher amount of non-projectivity.

Intuitively, we assume that domain differences can be captured by content-related features (e.g. from topic modelling) while we expect that functional differences between genres are reflected in structural features such as part-of-speech n-grams and other morpho-syntactic features. In the paper, we address these issues and investigate how differences between articles in a newspaper corpus relate to the concepts of *genre* and *domain* and how they impact parsing performance of a transition-based dependency parser.

---

[1]This is especially true for distinguishing *genre* from closely related concepts such as *register* and *text type*, which is why we will use *genre* in a broad sense here, i. e., as a cover term for *genre, register, text type* and similar.

Proceedings of the 16th International Workshop on Treebanks and Linguistic Theories (TLT16), pages 95–105,
Prague, Czech Republic, January 23–24, 2018. Distributed under a CC-BY 4.0 licence. 2017.

Keywords: genre and register variation, parser adaptation, dependency parsing

2 Related work

2.1 Register, Genre and Topic

It is hard to find a clear definition for concepts such as *register, genre* or *domain* in the literature.[2] We follow Biber and Conrad (2009) and consider *register* and *genre* not as different concepts but rather as different perspectives on the same thing. On this view, *genre* focusses on the "linguistic characteristics that are used to structure complete texts" (Biber and Conrad, 2009, p. 15). Passonneau et al. (2014) follow the functional view of Biber and Conrad and describe *genre* as a "set of shared regularities among written or spoken documents that enables readers, writers, listeners and speakers to signal discourse function, and that conditions their expectations of linguistic form". The *domain* concept, on the other hand, is orthogonal to the concept of *register* and *genre*. It reflects the main topic of the text (e. g., the sports domain) and can include texts from various genres with different communicative functions, such as soccer news, a report of a tennis match or an interview with a golf player.

While genre/register classification of documents can be a daunting task for humans, automatic genre/register classification of unrestricted text does not even reach 50% classification accuracy in recent state-of-the-art experiments (Biber and Egbert, 2015). One reason for this is, of course, the fact that there is no general consent about the number and boundaries of relevant categories to be included in a taxonomy of genres/registers. Moreover, as Petrenz and Webber (2011) point out, a text can not only have more than one topic but can also belong to multiple genres, which makes the *genre* concept even more complex and also casts some doubt on the validity of the task of genre classification on the document level. The authors discuss the correlation between genre and topic and show for a large newspaper corpus that there is a substantial correlation between the two, and that this correlation is not stable over time but undergoes significant changes. Petrenz and Webber (2011) also show that linguistic features that correlate with topic can decrease results in a genre prediction task. The authors argue that a meaningful evaluation of genre classification should thus control for topic, to avoid overly optimistic results that do not generalise to new texts with a topic distribution different from the one in the training data.

These observations are relevant also for adapting a parser to text from a new genre or domain, as most studies do not distinguish between content-based and structural features when measuring domain and genre similarity but use both evenhandedly. To our best knowledge, there are no studies on parser adaptation that try to separate domain from genre effects.

2.2 Adapting parsers to new genres and domains

Many parsing studies have addressed the problem of parser adaptation to new genres or domains, often focussed on adapting a Penn treebank-trained parser to biomedical text or to web data.[3] Different techniques have been tested for parser adaptation, such as transformations applied to the target data (Foster, 2010), ensemble parsing (Dredze et al., 2007) or co-training (Baucom et al., 2013). Other studies have tried to distinguish between features specific to the source data and general features that also occur in the target data (Dredze et al., 2007), or to create domain- or genre-specific parsing models and select the model combination that most probably will maximise parsing scores on the target data (McClosky et al., 2010; Plank and Sima'an, 2008). Plank and van Noord (2011) and Mukherjee et al. (2017) create new training sets that reflect the distribution in the target data by identifying the source data most similar to the target, based on measures that assess structural or topic similarity between both.

Features used in these experiments (McClosky et al., 2010; Plank and van Noord, 2011; Mukherjee et al., 2017) include known and unknown words, character n-grams and LDA topics but do not (or only implicitly) capture *structural* similarity. The authors show that content and surface features are successful in selecting appropriate training data for the new domain and also work better than using genre labels assigned by humans (Plank and van Noord, 2011). Søgaard (2011), however, has shown that data point selection based on structural similarity can improve parsing accuracy significantly in a cross-lingual parser adaptation setting and Rehbein (2011) shows a similar effect for in-domain self-training. Based

---

[2]A full survey of work on register, genre or domain variation is beyond the scope of this paper. We refer to Biber (1988) and especially Lee (2001) for a review of how these terms have been used in various theoretical frameworks.

[3]See, e. g., the CoNLL 2007 Shared Task on Domain Adaptation (Nivre et al., 2007) and the SANCL 2012 Shared Task on Parsing the Web (Petrov and McDonald, 2012).

	# articles	# sent	# token	avg. sent length	# sent train pool	# sent testset
portrait	42	1,195	24,035	20.1	695	500
letter	102	1,789	34,923	19.5	1,289	500
documentary	72	3,162	61,534	19.5	2,662	500
agency	617	5,278	84,944	16.1	4,750	528
interview	102	7,585	120,215	15.8	6,826	759
commentary	333	9,613	178,347	18.5	8,652	961
taz report	2,376	66,973	1,283,803	19.2	66,973	–

Table 1: Distribution of different genres in the TüBa-D/Z and training/test sizes.

on these results, we are interested in comparing the adequacy of *surface* and *content* features for data point selection with features that capture *structural* similarity in the data.

We evaluate the features in a setting where we try to improve the performance of a dependency parser on different genres in a newspaper corpus by training genre-aware parsing models. We would like to know whether the different feature types capture similar properties in the data. We consider content-related features to be characteristic for certain domains while we expect that functional differences between genres are reflected in structural differences between texts and can be captured by features such as part-of-speech n-grams. In addition, we compare the potential of content and structural features to measure domain and genre similarity with linguistically defined features, inspired by the work of Biber (1988; 1995) on register variation.

3   Experiments

In our experiments, we use the TüBa-D/Z treebank (Telljohann et al., 2004), a corpus of German newspaper text from the *taz*, a German daily newspaper, that includes more than 95,000 sentences annotated with constituency trees and grammatical function labels. The data has been automatically converted to dependencies. Webber (2009) has shown for the Penn treebank (Marcus et al., 1994) that even newspaper corpora should not be considered as homogeneous objects but typically also consist of multiple genres. Similar to the Penn treebank, the TüBa-D/Z (v10) includes articles from a variety of genres. The genre labels in the TüBa-D/Z have been assigned by the editors of the *taz* and are: *reports, commentaries, documentaries, letters to the editor, interviews, portraits* and messages from *news agencies*. It is, however, not clear to what extend these labels correspond to linguistically well-defined categories, i. e., whether documents within a specific genre category share "linguistic characteristics that are used to structure complete texts" as suggested by Biber and Conrad (2009). The vast majority of the articles in the treebank is labelled as *taz reports* (Table 1).

3.1   Genre differences

The first question we are interested in is whether we can cluster the data according to the labels assigned by the *taz*, to see whether these labels reflect systematic linguistic differences in the data. For this, we divide the data into genre-specific samples of 10,000 tokens each. First, we concatenate all articles from the same genre and split them into smaller samples of 10,000 tokens, so that sentences from the same article end up in the same sample most of the time. Then we run a Principle Components Analysis (PCA), a) based on the frequency of POS tags in the data (Figure 1 left), and b) based on topic distributions from an LDA (Figure 1 right).[4]

Figure 1 (left) shows crucial differences between samples taken from articles that have been assigned different labels. Interviews and agency messages are separated from the other samples along the second principal component (Dim2) while both can be separated from each other along the first component (Dim1). Reports and documentaries are positioned more central, with the reports a bit more to the left and the documentaries a bit more to the right. The commentaries cluster together in the lower part of the space and the letters are at the boundary between documentaries and commentaries. While we can

---

[4]For topic modelling we use the Mallet implementation from `http://mallet.cs.umass.edu/` and learn 100 topics on the lemmatised version of the TüBa-D/Z. We compute the PCA using the R PCA function from the `FactoMineR` package. To increase readability, we only include the first 20 samples from the *report* genre.

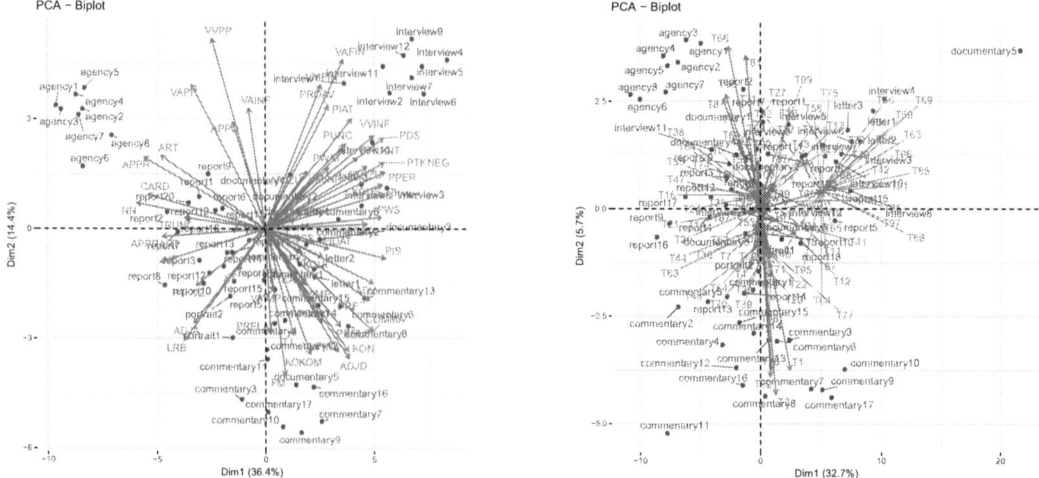

Figure 1: PCA based on frequency of POS (left) and on topic distributions (right) from LDA topic modelling in samples of 10,000 tokens from the TüBa-D/Z.

observe strong tendencies, the distinction between these samples is not as pronounced as the one between the interviews and the agency messages.

Most interestingly, we can see similar trends for the PCA based on the LDA topics (Figure 1, right). The most important difference, however, is that topic-wise we observe a similarity between the interviews and the letters while in the PCA based on POS tags the letters are positioned between the commentaries. The PCA shows the strong correlation between topics and genres that has already been pointed out by Petrenz and Webber (2011). It also shows that the labels assigned by the *taz* correspond to systematic differences between the texts and can be used at least as an approximation to linguistically defined genres.

3.2 Impact of genre differences on parsing

Given that we are able to discriminate documents from different genres based on the distribution of POS in the data, we expect that the genre differences also impact parsing accuracy. To investigate this, we split the texts into a pool of training data and test data as follows. From each genre, we create test sets with 10% of the tokens for this genre or, for genres with less than 50,000 sentences, we select 500 sentences from the pool for the test set. For the test sets we also control for topic by selecting articles so that the similarity with regard to topic distribution is maximised.[5] The rest of the data is used as a pool from which we create different-sized training sets (see Table 1).

For the first experiment, we create training sets of size $N = \{10000, 20000, 380000\}$ tokens by *randomly* selecting articles from the *report* data that constitute the largest part of the training pool.[6] We would like to know whether we can observe systematic differences between the genres with regard to their "parsability", i. e., how hard it is to predict the correct parse. We train the IMSTrans parser (Björkelund and Nivre, 2015), a transition-based dependency parser, on the randomly extracted training sets and report LAS for the different genres. All results are based on automatic POS and morphological tags predicted by Marmot (Mueller et al., 2013)[7] and include punctuation in the evaluation (Table 2). We report average LAS and standard deviation (σ) over 5 runs.

As expected, we observe substantial differences in parsing scores between the genres. Over all sample sizes, agency messages achieve the highest parsing accuracy, followed by portraits and documentaries while letters and commentaries seem to be more difficult to parse.

---

[5]We compute the topic distribution for articles in the TüBa-D/Z, based on LDA and then compute the Manhattan distance between the topic distribution for each pair of articles from the same genre. Then we select articles for each genre in the test set so that the accumulated distance between the articles for each genre is minimised.

[6]We count tokens instead of sentences as the differences in sentence length between the genres would impact results.

[7]We also use predicted POS/morphological information in the training data. We use the pre-trained SPMRL models kindly provided by the developers: http://cistern.cis.lmu.de/marmot/models/CURRENT.

size (token)		agency	commentary	documentary	interview	letter	portrait
10,000	*avg.*	85.65	78.47	79.20	78.64	77.61	80.06
	σ	0.31	0.47	0.31	0.23	0.36	0.33
50,000	*avg.*	89.87	83.31	84.61	83.95	83.08	85.66
	σ	0.24	0.26	0.24	0.17	0.21	0.28
380,000	*avg.*	93.15	87.71	89.40	88.41	87.96	89.58
	σ	0.22	0.13	0.17	0.14	0.28	0.12

Table 2: LAS for different genres: ***random*** training sets from reports (avg. LAS over 5 runs and std dev.)

3.3 Genre effects as an out-of-domain problem

In the next set of experiments, we investigate whether the performance changes when we train the parser on the same amount of data, but this time using sentences from the same genre (according to the *taz* labels) as in the test set. In other words, we would like to know whether the differences in parsing accuracy reflect an out-of-domain problem and will vanish when we train on "in-domain" (or rather, *in-genre*) data. As before, we randomly select articles from the pool of training data, but now we control for genre. This is possible only for the smaller training set sizes ($N = 2500, 4500$) and we also have to exclude the genres for which we do not have enough data in the pool (*letter*, *portrait*).

Table 3 shows the improvements we obtain when training the parser on data from the same genre, as opposed to training it on a randomly selected dataset from the *taz* reports. An exception are the *documentaries* which seem to be closer to the *reports* (see figure 1) so that the effect of training on in-genre data is levelled out. As before, we note substantial differences between the parsing scores for the different genres. This shows that the gap in results is not due to missing in-domain (or *in-genre*) training data but that certain genres are in fact harder to parse than others. To find out what it is that makes agency texts so much easier to parse than the commentaries and letters, we compare linguistic properties of the texts in the different genres that have been associated with syntactic complexity and parsing difficulty in the literature (Roark et al., 2007; McDonald and Nivre, 2007; Gulordava and Merlo, 2016).

size (token)		agency	commentary	documentary	interview	letter	portrait
10,000	*random*	85.65	78.47	**79.20**	78.64	77.61	80.06
10,000	*in-domain*	**86.30**	**79.01**	79.13	**78.83**	**79.53**	**80.52**
50,000	*random*	89.87	83.31	84.61	83.95	83.08	85.66
50,000	*in-domain*	**90.68**	**83.80**	**84.82**	**84.47**	n.a.	n.a.

Table 3: LAS for *random* training sets from reports and *in-domain* training sets (avg. LAS over 5 runs).

Table 4 shows the average sentence length, the number of finite verbs per sentence (as an approximation of the complexity of the sentence structure), the number of unknown words, the average dependency length, the average entropy in arc direction (Liu, 2010) (whether the head of a dependent is found to its left, to its right, or can be positioned either way), and the percentage of non-projective sentences in the test sets. When fitting a linear regression model to the data, arc direction entropy was the only significant predictor for parsing accuracy (β = -2.44, $p < .01$). However, given the small size of the test sets we used, we prefer to consider our results as preliminary pending confirmation on larger data sets.

genre	LAS	sent.len	Vfin/sent	# unk	dep.len	arc.ent	non-proj
agency	93.15	16.1	1.2	16.3	2.7	13.1	7.0
portrait	89.58	19.5	1.8	16.2	2.6	14.7	9.2
documentary	89.40	21.9	1.6	14.7	3.1	14.9	13.0
interview	88.41	19.2	1.5	19.0	2.7	15.1	10.0
letter	87.96	17.7	1.5	13.4	2.6	15.1	11.1
commentary	87.71	18.3	1.6	12.9	2.8	14.7	10.2

Table 4: Differences between test sets (avg. sentence length, no. of finite verbs per sentence, % of unknown tokens, avg. dependency length, entropy of arc direction, % of non-projective trees) and LAS for each test set when training the parser on a randomly selected training set from reports (N =380,000).

	setting	feature types				raw data	description	no. of features
		surface	structural	content	linguistic			
Exp01	KNS	✓				✓	Text statistics and word frequencies	33
Exp02	POS n-gram		✓			✓	LM perplexity based on pos n-grams	n.a.
Exp03	LDA topics			✓			Distance from topic distribution	100
Exp04	COReX	✓			✓		Text statistics, morpho-syntactic features	40

Table 5: Overview of the settings and features used for data point selection.

3.4 Data point selection for genre-aware parsing

We now explore whether we can train genre-aware parsing models on larger data by selecting out-of-genre data points that are similar to the *target* genre. To that end, we test the adequacy of different feature types for measuring similarity.

Kessler et al. (1997) (KNS) have obtained consistently good results for genre prediction across topics (Petrenz and Webber, 2011), based only on *surface* features.[8] Plank and van Noord (2011) and Mukherjee et al. (2017) have trained domain-specific parsing models based on *content* (LDA topics) and *surface* features (word frequencies and character n-gram frequencies). In our experiments, we would like to compare the adequacy of *content* and *surface* features with data selection based on *structural* similarity (where similarity is operationalised as the perplexity of a language model (LM) based on POS n-grams) and features that take into account the *linguistic* properties of a text, relying on Biber-style features. Table 5 gives an overview over the different settings and features used for data selection.

3.5 Selecting the training sets

For our different settings, we select training data from the pool as follows. For the structural setting, we make use of additional unannotated data from the *taz* with articles from 1989-1999, with information on article boundaries and genre labels. We select all articles from 1989, 1992, 1995, 1997, 1999 and remove those that are included in the TüBa-D/Z treebank from the raw text corpus. We automatically predict POS tags and lemma forms, using the Treetagger (Schmid, 1994) with the standard parameter file provided by the developer.

Exp01 We create a version of the raw newswire data where we replace all words with their POS and divide the data so that we have one sample per genre. We use the CMU SLM toolkit (Clarkson and Rosenfeld, 1997) to train a LM for each genre, based on POS n-grams in the samples. Then we compute the perplexity for each article in the training pool of the TüBa-D/Z and assign articles to the genre for which they show the lowest perplexity, i. e., to which they are most similar. Based on this, we extract one training set per genre with N=380,000 tokens from the most similar articles. Please note that the articles do not need to come from the same genre but only need to be similar to the raw text files in this genre.

Exp02 For the next experiment, we extract the features described in Kessler et al. (1997) from the large, POS tagged newswire corpus. We aggregate the scores for each feature over all files from the same genre and normalise by the number of articles. Then we extract the same features from the articles in the TüBa-D/Z training pool and compute the similarity of each article in the training pool to the genres in the raw text corpus, based on the aggregated feature scores, using the Manhattan distance as similarity measure. We select the most similar articles for each genre and extract the first N=380,000 tokens for the genre-specific training sets.

Exp03 For topic modelling, we use a lemmatised version of all articles in the TüBa-D/Z data. The test data for each genre has been merged into one document per genre while the articles from the training pool are included as separate documents (each article is one document).[9] We use the topic distributions for each document to compute the similarity of each article in the training pool to the different genre testsets, and create genre-specific training sets by selecting the most similar articles for each test set. As a similarity measure we use the Manhattan distance. Please note that –in contrast to the other settings–

---

[8] We reimplemented the KNS features (text statistics and frequencies for particular word forms) described at `http://homepages.inf.ed.ac.uk/s0895822/SCTG/features.html` for German.

[9] We set the number of topics to N=100. We use standard settings und remove stopwords but do not lowercase the lemmas.

	Setting	agency	commentary	documentary	interview	letter	portrait
Baseline	*random*	93.15	87.71	89.40	88.41	87.96	89.58
Exp01	POS n-gram LM	93.38	87.68	89.40	88.61	88.57*	89.45
Exp02	KNS	**93.83***	87.52	89.26	88.31	88.50*	89.32
Exp03	LDA topics	93.67*	**88.19***	89.61	89.15**	**88.60***	**90.05**
Exp04	CoReX	93.70*	87.93	**89.80**	**89.25***	88.14	89.50

Table 6: Results for different data selection methods for genre-aware parsing (LAS; * indicates a significant improvement over the baseline with $p < 0.05$; ** with $p < 0.01$).

here we directly maximise the similarity between training and test data, while in the other settings we use the unannotated newspaper data as a proxy for determining genre similarity. This means that a direct comparison of the results might not be fair. On the other hand, this approach allows us to investigate the interaction between topic and genre. We will get back to this issue in Section 3.6.

Exp04   For the CoReX setting, training sets are created based on the linguistic properties of each genre. We use a fine-grained set of 40 linguistic features obtained from CoReX (Bildhauer and Schäfer, 2017), a framework for lexico-grammatical document annotation for large German corpora. The CoReX features we use inlcude frequencies for POS, morphosyntactic features, named entity-based features and stylistic markers in the text, inspired by Biber (1988). We extract these features for each article in the training pool[10] and aggregate the scores over all articles in the same genre. We then compute the similarity (or, rather, the distance) of the feature vector for one article to the aggregated vectors for each genre, again using Manhattan distance as similarity measure. For each genre, we select the documents that showed the highest genre similarity, based on the distance between the feature vectors, and create new training sets for each genre with N=380,000 tokens.

We create genre-aware parsing models by training the parser on the different datasets and evaluate the different models on the test sets from each genre (based on the human-assigned genre labels, see Table 1). Another possible approach would be to select the best model for each text that we want to parse based on its similarity to the different training sets. We refrain from doing so as extracting the CoReX features is costly and includes several preprocessing steps such as POS and morphological tagging, topological parsing and NER. In our setup, we only have to run the pipeline once for creating the genre-aware parsing models. Doing the same again for each text that we want to parse seems exorbitant. Our setup, however, assumes that we have genre information for the texts we want to parse. In a different scenario where genre labels are not given we could either refer to the CoReX pipeline or test how far we get when using similarity measures based on simple POS and surface frequencies. We leave this to future work.

3.6   Results for genre-aware parsing

Table 6 shows parsing results for the genre-aware models based on different similarity measures. The *structural* model (Exp01) fails to outperform the random baseline for all genres but the letters.[11] The KNS model (Exp02) that is based on *surface* features gives a significant improvement for agency messages and letters but also fails to improve LAS for the other genres. Most interestingly, the topic setting (Exp03) is the only model where we see an improvement over the baseline for *all* genres. The CoReX features improve results for nearly all genres, however not always significantly.

As already pointed out above, the success of the topic model might be due to the fact that we directly optimised the selection of training instances based on their similarity to the articles in the test set (and not, as done for the other settings, by approximating genres via unlabelled data (Exp01-02) or by computing similarity against an averaged score obtained from all articles in the treebank (Exp04).

We thus run another experiment where we create additional test data for each genre by selecting articles from this particular genre but with a topic distribution different from the one in the previous test data. We do this by selecting new articles so that we maximise the Manhattan distance to the articles in the old test sets. Then we use the same parsing models (Exp03) to parse the data and compare the results to the

---

[10]Feature counts are normalised per 1,000 words.
[11]For significance testing we use Bikel's Randomized Parsing Evaluation Comparator.

size (token)		agency	commentary	documentary	interview	letter	portrait
380,000	*random*	93.80	**90.62**	**90.44**	92.54	87.13	90.26
	σ	0.09	0.17	0.27	0.09	0.13	0.29
380,000	*topic*	**94.54***	90.37	90.15	92.55	**87.71**	**90.46**

Table 7: LAS for baseline (*random* training sets from reports; avg. LAS over 5 runs and standard deviation) and for *topic* setting where data selection is *not* optimised on the test set.

ones we get when parsing the new test sets with the baseline parsing models from Exp01.

Table 7 shows that the parsing models we trained based on topic similarity do not necessarily generalise well to other data from the same genre. Only for agency messages results improve, while for all other genres results are in the same range or even decrease.

3.7 Discussion

Our results showed that our initial hypothesis about the *structural* similarity being more suitable for capturing genre similarity than *surface* and *content* features does not seem to bear out. We take this as evidence that the concept of genre can not easily be defined (or reduced to) structural properties in the texts, at least not in the way as operationalised in our experiments.

We also showed that data selection based on LDA topics in the data can improve parsing scores, as has been shown before by Plank and van Noord (2011) and Mukherjee et al. (2017). This approach, however, requires to compute topics over the joint training and test data which might not always be possible in practice. In addition, our experiments showed that while there is a correlation between topic and genre, the topics we learn are by no means representative for a particular genre. Our results are in line with the results of Petrenz and Webber (2011) for genre prediction. We thus argue that LDA topic modelling might be appropriate for domain adaptation for highly diverse sources such as biomedical data and data from the newswire. For more homogeneous source texts as we have in our setup, however, relying on content similarity might not be the right approach.

This brings us back to our original research question: How can we model genre distinctions for parsing? So far, our experiments showed that distinguishing genre from domain is by no means an easy task. We argue that the human-labelled categories in the TüBa-D/Z reflect both, genre and domain properties, and both seem to have an impact on parsing. We also showed that content similarity based on LDA topics might be useful for parser adaptation to new domains but not for adapting the parser to a new genre.

4 Conclusions

We presented an approach to genre-aware parsing where we only have access to small amounts of annotated training data for each genre. Our approach tests several ways to operationalise similarity and makes use of large unannotated data to learn genre-specific distributions of features. Based on this, we extract training sets for each genre by selecting sentences from the pool of annotated training data that are similar to the target genre. We computed similarity based on surface features, structural features, text topic and fine-grained linguistic features, and showed that different feature types work best for different datasets. We take that as evidence that for parser adaptation we have to deal with a mixture of genre and domain effects, and to obtain optimal results we need to model both. However, using content features such as topics for modelling genre similarity might be dangerous as those features do not generalise well.

In future work we would like to test our approach in a setting where no human-assigned genre labels are available, and also apply self-training to extend the training data size for genre-aware parsing.

Acknowledgments

This research has been partially supported by the Leibniz Science Campus "Empirical Linguistics and Computational Modeling", funded by the Leibniz Association under grant no. SAS-2015-IDS-LWC and by the Ministry of Science, Research, and Art (MWK) of the state of Baden-Württemberg.

References

Eric Baucom, Levi King, and Sandra Kübler. 2013. Domain adaptation for parsing. In *Proceedings of the International Conference Recent Advances in Natural Language Processing RANLP 2013*. Hissar, Bulgaria, pages 56–64.

Douglas Biber. 1988. *Variation across speech and writing*. Cambridge: Cambridge University Press.

Douglas Biber. 1995. *Dimensions of register variation: A cross-linguistic comparison*. Cambridge: Cambridge University Press.

Douglas Biber and Susan Conrad. 2009. *Register, genre, and style*. Cambridge: Cambridge University Press.

Douglas Biber and Jesse Egbert. 2015. Using grammatical features for automatic register identification in an unrestricted corpus of documents from the open web. *Journal of Research Design and Statistics in Linguistics and Communication Science* 2(1):3–36.

Felix Bildhauer and Roland Schäfer. 2017. COReX und COReCO: A lexico-grammatical document annotation framework for large German corpora. Poster at the Computational linguistics poster session at the DGfS 2017.

Anders Björkelund and Joakim Nivre. 2015. Non-deterministic oracles for unrestricted non-projective transition-based dependency parsing. In *Proceedings of the 14th International Conference on Parsing Technologies*. Bilbao, Spain, pages 76–86.

John Blitzer, Ryan McDonald, and Fernando Pereira. 2006. Domain adaptation with structural correspondence learning. In *Proceedings of the 2006 Conference on Empirical Methods in Natural Language Processing*. Sydney, Australia, EMNLP '06, pages 120–128.

Philip Clarkson and Ronald Rosenfeld. 1997. Statistical language modeling using the CMU-Cambridge toolkit. In *ESCA Eurospeech*. pages 2707–2710.

Mark Dredze, John Blitzer, Partha Pratim Talukdar, Kuzman Ganchev, João V. Graça, and O Pereira. 2007. Frustratingly hard domain adaptation for dependency parsing. In *Proceedings of the CoNLL Shared Task Session of EMNLP-CoNLL 2007*. EMNLP-CoNLL.

S. Feldman, M. A. Marin, M. Ostendorf, and M. R. Gupta. 2009. Part-of-speech histograms for genre classification of text. In *Proceedings of the 2009 International Conference on Acoustics, Speech and Signal Processing*. Washington, DC, IEEE'09, pages 4781–4784.

Jennifer Foster. 2010. "cba to check the spelling" investigating parser performance on discussion forum posts. In *Human Language Technologies: The 2010 Annual Conference of the North American Chapter of the Association for Computational Linguistics*. Los Angeles, California, HLT '10, pages 381–384.

Daniel Gildea. 2001. Corpus variation and parser performance. In *Empirical Methods in Natural Language Processing*. EMNLP '01, pages 167–202.

Kristina Gulordava and Paola Merlo. 2016. Multi-lingual dependency parsing evaluation: a large-scale analysis of word order properties using artificial data. *TACL* 4:343–356.

Brett Kessler, Geoffrey Nunberg, and Hinrich Schütze. 1997. Automatic detection of text genre. In *Proceedings of the 35th Annual Meeting of the Association for Computational Linguistics*. Morristown, NJ, ACL'97, pages 32–38.

David Yw Lee. 2001. Genres, registers, text types, domains and styles: clarifying the concepts and navigating a path through the bnc jungle. *Technology* 5:37–72.

Haitao Liu. 2010. Dependency direction as a means of word-order typology: A method based on dependency treebanks. *Lingua* 120(6):1567–1578.

Mitchell Marcus, Grace Kim, Mary Ann Marcinkiewicz, Robert MacIntyre, Ann Bies, Mark Ferguson, Karen Katz, and Britta Schasberger. 1994. The penn treebank: Annotating predicate argument structure. In *Proceedings of the Workshop on Human Language Technology*. Plainsboro, NJ, HLT '94, pages 114–119.

David McClosky, Eugene Charniak, and Mark Johnson. 2006. Reranking and self-training for parser adaptation. In *Proceedings of the International Conference on Computational Linguistics and the Association for Computational Linguistics*. Sydney, Australia, COLING-ACL, pages 337–344.

David McClosky, Eugene Charniak, and Mark Johnson. 2010. Automatic domain adaptation for parsing. In *Human Language Technologies: The 2010 Annual Conference of the North American Chapter of the Association for Computational Linguistics*. Los Angeles, California, HLT '10, pages 28–36.

Ryan McDonald and Joakim Nivre. 2007. Characterizing the errors of data-driven dependency parsing models. In *Proceedings of the 2007 Joint Conference on Empirical Methods in Natural Language Processing and Computational Natural Language Learning*. EMNLP-CoNLL '07, pages 122–131.

Jeff Mitchell and Mark Steedman. 2015. Parser adaptation to the biomedical domain without re-training. In *Proceedings of the Sixth International Workshop on Health Text Mining and Information Analysis*. Lisbon, Portugal, pages 79–89.

Thomas Mueller, Helmut Schmid, and Hinrich Schütze. 2013. Efficient higher-order CRFs for morphological tagging. In *Proceedings of the 2013 Conference on Empirical Methods in Natural Language Processing*. Association for Computational Linguistics, Seattle, Washington, USA, pages 322–332. http://www.aclweb.org/anthology/D13-1032.

Atreyee Mukherjee, Sandra Kübler, and Matthias Scheutz. 2017. Creating POS tagging and dependency parsing experts via topic modeling. In *Proceedings of the 15th Conference of the European Chapter of the Association for Computational Linguistics*. Valencia, Spain, EACL'17, pages 347–355.

Joakim Nivre, Johan Hall, Sandra Kübler, Ryan McDonald, Jens Nilsson, Sebastian Riedel, and Deniz Yuret. 2007. The CoNLL 2007 Shared Task on Dependency Parsing. In *Proceedings of the CoNLL Shared Task Session of EMNLP-CoNLL 2007*. Prague, Czech Republic, pages 915–932.

Rebecca J. Passonneau, Nancy Ide, Songqiao Su, and Jesse Stuart. 2014. Biber Redux: Reconsidering Dimensions of Variation in American English. In *Proceedings of the 25th International Conference on Computational Linguistics*. COLING'14, pages 565–576.

Philipp Petrenz and Bonnie Webber. 2011. Stable classification of text genres. *Computational Linguistics* 37(2):385–393.

Slav Petrov and Ryan McDonald. 2012. Overview of the 2012 shared task on parsing the web. Notes of the First Workshop on Syntactic Analysis of Non-Canonical Language (SANCL).

Barbara Plank and Khalil Sima'an. 2008. Subdomain sensitive statistical parsing using raw corpora. In European Language Resources Association (ELRA), editor, *Proceedings of the Sixth International Language Resources and Evaluation (LREC'08)*. Marrakech, Morocco.

Barbara Plank and Gertjan van Noord. 2011. Effective measures of domain similarity for parsing. In *Proceedings of the Second International Conference on Human Language Technology Research*. San Francisco, CA, pages 82–86.

Ines Rehbein. 2011. Data point selection for self-training. In *Proceedings of the Second Workshop on Statistical Parsing of Morphologically Rich Languages*. Dublin, Ireland, SPMRL '11, pages 62–67.

Brian Roark, Margaret Mitchell, and Kristy Hollingshead. 2007. Syntactic complexity measures for detecting mild cognitive impairment. In *Proceedings of the ACL 2007 Workshop on Biomedical Natural Language Processing*. BioNLP, pages 1–8.

Helmut Schmid. 1994. Probabilistic part-of-speech tagging using decision trees. In *International Conference on New Methods in Language Processing*. Manchester, UK, pages 44–49.

Satoshi Sekine. 1997. The domain dependence of parsing. In *Applied Natural Language Processing*. ANLP '01, pages 96–102.

Anders Søgaard. 2011. Data point selection for cross-language adaptation of dependency parsers. In *Proceedings of the 49th Annual Meeting of the Association for Computational Linguistics: Human Language Technologies: Short Papers - Volume 2*. Portland, Oregon, HLT '11, pages 682–686.

Heike Telljohann, Erhard Hinrichs, and Sandra Kübler. 2004. The Tüba-D/Z Treebank: Annotating German with a Context-Free Backbone. In *In Proceedings of the Fourth International Conference on Language Resources and Evaluation*. Lisbon, Portugal, LREC'04, pages 2229–2235.

Ivan Titov. 2011. Domain adaptation by constraining inter-domain variability of latent feature representation. In *Proceedings of the 49th Annual Meeting of the Association for Computational Linguistics: Human Language Technologies - Volume 1*. Portland, Oregon, HLT '11, pages 62–71.

Bonnie Webber. 2009. Genre distinctions for discourse in the penn treebank. In *Proceedings of the Joint Conference of the 47th Annual Meeting of the ACL and the 4th International Joint Conference on Natural Language Processing of the AFNLP: Volume 2 - Volume 2*. Association for Computational Linguistics, Suntec, Singapore, ACL '09, pages 674–682.

Error Analysis of Cross-lingual Tagging and Parsing

Rudolf Rosa and **Zdeněk Žabokrtský**
Charles University, Faculty of Mathematics and Physics,
Institute of Formal and Applied Linguistics,
Malostranské náměstí 25, 118 00 Prague, Czech Republic
{rosa,zabokrtsky}@ufal.mff.cuni.cz

Abstract

We thoroughly analyse the performance of cross-lingual tagger and parser transfer from English into 32 languages. We suggest potential remedies for identified issues and evaluate some of them.

1 Introduction

In this case study, we try to answer several questions one might have about the performance of cross-lingual tagging and parsing. We do that by extensively evaluating a state-of-the-art cross-lingual setup, with a single source language (English) and 32 target languages.

A researcher in cross-lingual parsing might ask what the strengths and weaknesses of the system are, which information is transferred well from the input knowledge, which information is lost in the transfer, and which information is already missing or confusing on the input – and why that probably is and how this might potentially be addressed.

Furthermore, a user of the cross-lingual parsing, such as a computational linguist interested in utilising the outputs of the cross-lingual parsing in subsequent automatic processing, or a formal linguist interested in the syntax of low-resource languages, may still ask a somewhat different set of questions, such as how trustworthy the outputs of the system are, and how likely to be correct which parts of the outputs are.

We try to answer questions of both of these kinds, analysing errors in cross-lingual parsing along various dimensions. We focus on a state-of-the-art cross-lingual parsing setup, based on translating training data with a 1:1 machine translation (MT) system – this is the approach used in SFNW (Rosa et al., 2017), the winning system of the VarDial cross-lingual parsing shared task (Zampieri et al., 2017).

We make sure our setup is realistic for the supposed low-resource scenario, by only requiring a dependency treebank for a source language (we use English) and source-target parallel data to perform the cross-lingual parser transfer; in particular, we do not assume the availability of a target language tagger (or data to train one), contrary to a lot of previous work in the field.

In practice, significantly better results can be achieved by carefully selecting one or more appropriate source languages for each target language, but this would add too much complexity to our analysis, and we thus leave this for future work. Using a fixed source language makes it easier to generalise in our observations over some or all of the target languages. Moreover, choosing English specifically, which we understand well both theoretically and practically, allows us to perform a more in-depth analysis than with a source language we do only have a limited knowledge of.

Note that we do require supervised target language treebanks to be able to perform the error analysis. However, we hope that our observations can be used to provide a more general insight into the mechanisms of cross-lingual processing, driving intuitions and seeding expectations valid even for languages that we did not cover, thus facilitating a researcher to informedly choose a particular setup for this scenario, knowing what to be careful about and what to expect. We hope this to be especially useful with truly under-resourced target languages, where performing an error analysis of the outputs is costly.

We review previous work in Section 2 and describe our setup in Section 3. We then proceed with error analysis of cross-lingual tagging (Section 4) and parsing (Section 5), evaluate some of our suggested remedies in Section 6, and conclude with Section 7.

Proceedings of the 16th International Workshop on Treebanks and Linguistic Theories (TLT16), pages 106–118,
Prague, Czech Republic, January 23–24, 2018. Distributed under a CC-BY 4.0 licence. 2017.

Keywords: cross-lingual parsing, cross-lingual tagging, Universal Dependencies

2   Cross-lingual parsing

Cross-lingual parsing is the task of performing syntactic analysis of a *target* language with no treebank available for that language by using annotated data for a different *source* language and a method for transferring the knowledge about syntactic structures from that source language into the target language. It has already been studied for over a decade, starting with the works of Hwa et al. (2005) and Zeman and Resnik (2008), and then continued by many others, such as McDonald et al. (2011), Täckström et al. (2012), Georgi et al. (2013), Agić et al. (2015), Søgaard et al. (2015), and Duong et al. (2015).

A thorough overview, analysis and comparison of existing methods can be found in (Tiedemann et al., 2016). The authors also include a detailed analysis of the performance of the systems based on various factors, such as part-of-speech (POS) labelling accuracy or size of training data. Another work dealing with error analysis of cross-lingual parsing systems is that of Ramasamy et al. (2014).

The system evaluated in this paper is a new version of the aforementioned SFNW (Rosa et al., 2017), improved and generalised according to our experiments and findings of other researchers, such as Tiedemann (2014). The core of our approach is to translate the source treebank into the target language by a word-by-word statistical MT system (Moses in an adapted setup), resulting in a pseudo-target treebank, which is then used to train a standard tagger and parser. Limiting the MT system in this way leads to a lower quality of the translations, but allows us to use an extremely simple 1:1 cross-lingual transfer strategy. This approach has been shown to achieve results competitive to high quality phrase-to-phrase translation followed by complex many-to-many transfer strategies, as usually done by other authors.

For simplicity, we use a setup with a fixed source language (English) in this work. This allows us to keep the experimental space at a manageable scale, as well as to provide a more in-depth analysis thanks to our knowledge of the shared English source. However, we admit that this also significantly reduces the achieved scores – in practice, one should always carefully select appropriate source language(s) for each target language, as shown e.g. by Rosa and Žabokrtský (2015), or more recently and comprehensively by Agić (2017). Admittedly, the value of our analysis is thus somewhat limited from that perspective.

3   Setup

3.1   Cross-lingual tagger and parser transfer

We use the following approach to obtain a tagger and a parser for the target language t, assuming the availability of a treebank for a source language s (English), and s-t sentence-aligned parallel data:

1. Train a word-based MT system on the parallel data
2. Obtain a synthetic t treebank by translating the words in the s treebank
3. Train a tagger on the t treebank
4. Re-tag the t treebank with the tagger
5. Train a parser on the re-tagged treebank

As the cross-lingual transfer happens already in the training phase, the prediction phase is then trivial:

1. Tag the t text with the t tagger
2. Parse the tagged text with the t parser

We only use the word forms and the POS tags predicted by the tagger, as the other features (lemma, morphological features) are usually too specific for each language and do not transfer well cross-lingually, typically bringing only very moderate improvements or even deteriorations.

We also trained fully supervised monolingual taggers and parsers to provide reference scores; these were trained with the same settings, but using existing target treebanks instead of the synthetic ones.

3.2   Languages and dataset

We used the Universal Dependencies v1.4 treebanks[1] (Nivre et al., 2016) – *train* for training and *dev* for evaluation – and parallel OpenSubtitles2016 data from the Opus collection[2] (Tiedemann, 2012). We used all UD 1.4 languages except for those that had no or too small parallel data (*cop, cu, ga, got, grc, kk,*

---

[1]http://universaldependencies.org/docsv1/index.html
[2]http://opus.lingfil.uu.se/

la, sa, swl, ta, ug) and those that do not use spaces to separate words (*ja, zh*), thus limiting ourselves to 32 target languages.[3] For the analysis, we sorted and grouped the languages into three groups according to cross-lingual tagging accuracy. A detailed overview of the languages and datasets can be found in Table 4 in the Appendix; a brief overview of the emergent language groups follows:

High *pt, no, it, fr, da, de, sv*
  European languages closely related to English, from the Germanic and Romance language families, with sufficient parallel data to provide high-quality machine translation, and thus high accuracy in cross-lingual tagging and parsing.

Med *bg, ca, gl, nl, sk, cs, ru, id, el, hr, ro, pl, et, lv, sl*
  Mostly European languages from the Indo-European family (with the exception of *id* and *et*) which are more distant from English and/or lower on parallel data, but still achieving competitive translation quality and mediocre accuracy of cross-lingual methods.

Low *fi, he, hi, uk, tr, ar, fa, vi, eu, hi*
  Distant non-European or non-Indo-European languages (with the exception of *uk*, which is extremely low on parallel data), achieving very low quality of both MT and cross-lingual methods.

3.3 Tools

We used the following tools in the cross-lingual analysis pipeline in the following ways:
- a rule-based Treex tokenizer[4] (Popel and Žabokrtský, 2010) to tokenize the parallel data,
- UDPipe tagger and parser bundle[5] (Straka et al., 2016) to train the taggers and parsers,
- word2vec[6] (Mikolov et al., 2013) to pre-compute target word embeddings for the parser,
- MGiza[7] to compute intersection-symmetrized word alignment links (`-alignment intersect`),
- Moses SMT system[8] (Koehn et al., 2007) to translate the treebank data, constrained to perform word-to-word translation with no reordering (`-max-phrase-length 1 -dl 0`),
- KenLM language model (Heafield et al., 2013) as a component of Moses.

Our source codes are freely available on GitHub,[9] containing both the cross-lingual parsing pipeline, as well as evaluation scripts which can produce detailed accuracy breakdowns along various dimensions for both tagging and parsing and which provided data for the tables in this paper.

To manually inspect the CoNLLU files, we used the `conll_view` tool (Rosa, 2017).

4 Tagging error analysis

As parsing heavily depends on the UPOS tags, we will first analyse errors in tagging. Cross-lingual Universal POS (UPOS) tagging accuracies for several most frequent UPOS tags are shown in Table 1. For an interested reader, a larger table can be found in the Appendix (Table 5), showing UPOS tagging accuracies for all UPOS tags, as well as most common errors in cross-lingual tagging together with their frequencies. However, the presented analysis is also based on other, more detailed numbers, which are not shown here for space reasons, as well as on direct inspection of the inputs and outputs in some cases.

Note that we are mainly interested in tagging as a pre-processing step for parsing – achieving high-quality tagging is expected to improve the parsing quality, but is not our primary goal in itself.

4.1 Nouns

Cross-lingual tagging of both common nouns (*NOUN*) and proper nouns (*PROPN*) is very successful, with accuracies usually notably above the average across all language groups – a noun in one language seems to usually correspond 1:1 to a noun in the other language, making nouns highly suitable for the selected lexical transfer method.

---

[3]This was done mostly for simplicity – *ja* and *zh* tokenizers do exists and/or can be trained, and *some* parallel data could presumably be found even for the omitted languages; we leave re-including those languages for future work.
[4]`https://github.com/ufal/treex/blob/master/lib/Treex/Block/W2A/Tokenize.pm`
[5]`http://ufal.mff.cuni.cz/udpipe`
[6]`https://code.google.com/archive/p/word2vec/`
[7]`https://github.com/moses-smt/mgiza`
[8]`http://www.statmt.org/moses/`
[9]`https://github.com/ptakopysk/crosssynt`

Setup	Languages	all	*NOUN*	*VERB*	*PRON*	*ADP*	*DET*	*PROPN*	*ADJ*	*ADV*	*AUX*
Cross-lingual	Low	58%	63%	55%	57%	57%	59%	61%	34%	39%	38%
	Med	73%	79%	74%	57%	75%	61%	78%	51%	56%	52%
	High	82%	86%	81%	73%	87%	80%	75%	62%	60%	70%
Supervised	English	94%	93%	95%	98%	97%	99%	85%	89%	88%	97%

Table 1: Macro-averaged tagging accuracy of the cross-lingual tagging, factored along gold UPOS tags (only several most frequent shown) and language groups; also listing the fully supervised English tagger.

The most common error in tagging of nouns is mistaking one of the types for the other (*NOUN* for *PROPN* or *PROPN* for *NOUN*) – specifically, 30% of words predicted to be *PROPN*s are actually *NOUN*s, which is a rather high error rate. Many of these errors happen at the sentence-initial word, in parts of titles, and at nouns that are capitalised in English (months, days of the week, titles) – these could probably be at least partially avoided by truecasing the data.

As the capitalisation of *PROPN*s is an important feature for the tagger, we saw a huge drop in *PROPN* tagging accuracy for German (capitalises all nouns) and Hindi (does not capitalise anything). For such languages, it might make sense to abandon the *NOUN/PROPN* distinction (as is common in other tagsets), leading to a less granular but more accurate tagging which the parser could better rely on; a new feature could be added to the parser input capturing information about the casing of the word (e.g. lowercase/uppercase/capitalised/mixed) so that this information is not lost.

4.2 Adjectives

The overall most frequent error is an adjective (*ADJ*) confused for *NOUN*. This seems to be mostly caused by the fact that in English, *NOUN*s are often used as adjectives – as in e.g. "fruit salad", where the noun "fruit" in this context would be expressed by an adjective in many languages. Because of that, the translation of the treebank often contains much noise in the form of adjectives labelled as nouns, hence the error.

Other than choosing a different source language which does not have this property, one could try to alleviate this problem by e.g. identifying such cases in the source data and forcibly relabelling them with the UPOS of the expected translation; or, more straightforwardly, by simply removing all sentences containing such trap words. As suggested by Reviewer 2, even a more fine-grained approach could be used, by only deleting the confusing adjective-like nouns but keeping the modified sentences in the training data. We note that although this problem seems to be rather specific for English, similar confusing situations with words of unclear POS exist in other languages.

Moreover, *ADJ*s perform particularly badly in target languages with the *NOUN ADJ* word order, with all Romance languages (*pt, it, fr, ca, gl, ro*) constituting a prominent example – if the error distribution is computed only on Romance languages, only 40% of *ADJ* labels get actually assigned to *ADJ*s, while 45% of words predicted to be *ADJ*s are actually *NOUN*s or *PROPN*s. This shows the tremendous importance of word order for tagging. Primarily, one should try to use a source language with similar word order to the target language. Otherwise, it may be possible to handle these cases by employing a reordering model within the MT system (which we explicitly disallowed in our setup), or by pre-reordering the source sentences to resemble more closely the target word order, as done e.g. by Aufrant et al. (2016). A simpler but potentially interesting approach could also be to modify the word order randomly, by locally shuffling parts of the sentences, thus making the tagger more robust to differences in word order.

4.3 Verbs

Auxiliaries (*AUX*) are often confused with verbs (*VERB*), with the accuracy on *AUX* quite low even for many of the High group languages (with the exception of the Romance languages), and falling quickly for the other language groups. As different languages use different verbs as auxiliaries and in different ways, they get very easily mistranslated by the MT system.

Of course, as always, one should choose a source language that uses *AUX*es in the same way as the target language. However, if this is not possible, it may help to discard the *VERB/AUX* distinction and label everything as *VERB*s. This theoretically means loosing some information, but, looking at the accuracies of *AUX* tagging, in many cases the information is already lost anyway. On the other hand, it could make the subsequent parser more robust and thus more successful than a parser that learns to trust the *AUX* labels.

Furthermore, some languages do not seem to use auxiliaries much (or at all). In such cases (as in all cases where a source data label is not relevant for the target language), the cross-lingual parsing might be improved by deleting the *AUX* tokens from the source data altogether.

4.4 Pronouns, Determiners and Adpositions

Pronouns (*PRON*) seem to be rather difficult, with a very low accuracy even in the High languages, as even similar languages tend to use pronouns differently (this may still partially be due to unresolved inter-lingual annotation inconsistencies).

A common error is confusing *PRON*s with determiners (*DET*) both ways, especially in languages where the same word form can be used both as a *DET* and as a *PRON* (e.g. *fr, it*). We believe that it may help to relabel all *DET*s as *PRON*s in such cases, thus postponing the decision to parsing.

Another frequent error is related to reflexive pronouns, which are very common in many languages but not very prominent in English, leading to misalignments, mistranslations, and then mistaggings – e.g. the reflexive pronoun in the target language gets often aligned to an *AUX* in English (which may or may not be appropriate). We have also noticed frequent mistranslations of English *PRON*s with pro-drop target languages; again, this time the source *PRON* gets typically aligned to some other word, such as an *AUX* (which, again, might be the best thing to do in some cases, but not always).

If a source language matching in the aforementioned characteristics cannot be used, it may be possible to modify the source to correspond better to the target. However, these cases clearly show the limitations of the selected word-by-word MT approach, in contrast to the classical phrase-based one, which inherently learns to add/remove words that do not have a proper counterpart in the other language by using variable-length phrases, and thus should suffer from such problems much less.

Tagging of adpositions (*ADP*) is relatively accurate, but they are sometimes confused for *DET*s; this happens more often in languages that are low on *DET*s (e.g. Russian), where the word aligner is likely to misalign one of the *DET*s that are abundant in English onto a target *ADP*. In such cases, it might be beneficial to remove some of the *DET*s from the source data – e.g. "a" and "the" if the target language does not use similar determiners – but keep the other *DET*s ("this", "some", etc.). Still, in some target languages, *DET*s seem to be so rare (or possibly even non-existent) that the cross-lingual parsing might by improved by simply deleting all *DET* tokens from the source data.

5 Parsing errors analysis

Labelled Attachment Scores (LAS) for several most frequent dependency relation labels are shown in Table 2. For an interested reader, a larger table can be found in the Appendix (Table 6), showing accuracies for more labels, as well as most common labelling errors together with their frequencies.

The least frequent dependency relations are not included in any of the tables, as the evaluation results have little meaning there – mostly the scores are computed over very small numbers of instances, and the measured accuracies are thus rather random numbers. A general remark regarding the low-frequency labels is that they mostly should not be trusted, as even the parser has very little training support for them. It is definitely worth considering to remove them altogether from the training data in the cross-lingual scenario, replacing them by some more general relations (even *dep*), as with the accuracy of the cross-lingual parsing as low as it is, these come out mostly as random noise.

5.1 Nouns

With nouns, the dependency relation (usually *nmod*, *compound*, *nsubj*, or *dobj*) is often incorrectly distinguished. It should be noted that for other parts of speech, it is usually easier to correctly identify the relation label than the head – the label is often determined by the POS already, sometimes including some simple local context. For nouns, however, the situation is different, as there are 4 very common

Setup	Langs	ALL	*punct*	*nmod*	*case*	*nsubj*	*det*	*root*	*dobj*	*compound*	*advmod*	*amod*
Cross-lingual	Low	20%	28%	8%	21%	21%	36%	35%	10%	16%	17%	21%
	Med	34%	38%	22%	48%	32%	46%	55%	32%	15%	33%	41%
	High	51%	49%	45%	75%	48%	66%	63%	49%	23%	41%	55%
Supervised	English	80%	75%	74%	92%	87%	95%	88%	84%	74%	74%	83%

Table 2: Macro-averaged LAS of the cross-lingual parsing, factored along gold-standard dependency relations (only several most frequent shown) and language groups; also including LAS for the fully supervised English parser.

dependency labels, and they can be very hard to correctly identify, especially in a cross-lingual setting – different languages use different means of distinguishing them (e.g. word order, adpositions, determiners, or morphology), and so they are often mislabelled even when the head is identified correctly. For languages from the High group, the problem is not that severe, since they mostly use similar distinguishing features as English; however, we observe a huge drop in accuracy when moving to the Med group, and we even see low results for some of the High languages, such as German.

Detailed investigation showed that the most frequent mistake is mislabelling an *nmod* relation as a *compound*. *Nmod*s in English are nearly always marked by adpositions (as in "the house **of** the lady"), while a sequence of nouns without a preposition is typically a *compound* (as in "investment firm"). However, many languages (e.g. German) use case marking for *nmod*s, where the case may be expressed e.g. by a determiner (as in "das Haus **der** Frau") – which, due to an adposition not being present, the parser usually mislabels as a *compound*. Most of the noun labelling errors are actually *compound*s mislabelled as other relations, or other relations mislabelled as *compound*s. What hugely adds to this is the fact that the *compound* relation is much more frequent in English than in most of the target languages, where it is usually rare or not present (again, this may partially be an inter-lingual inconsistency of the annotation). Due to this, it may be sensible to either relabel the *compound*s as other relations (presumably *nmod*s, which they are on average most frequently confused with), or delete the *compound* tokens from the source data altogether. While this would inevitably cut the *compound*-labelling accuracy to zero, it may still increase the overall parsing accuracy thanks to the rareness of this label in most target languages.

Other labels get frequently confused as well, such as switching *nsubj* and *dobj*, especially in languages which mark the subject and object morphologically rather than with word order.

Thus, it seems highly important when choosing a source language for a given target language to observe the way they mark noun-based relations and the way they join together chains of nouns, as the mismatches in this aspect led to the largest number of errors on our dataset.

Moreover, *amod*s also get often mislabelled as *compound*s, due to the difficulty in correctly identifying the *NOUN* or *ADJ* category when translating from English, as explained in Section 4.2.

Furthermore, the parsing of *PROPN*s also shows very low accuracies across all of the language groups. However, this seems to be at least partially caused by inter-treebank annotation inconsistencies, as the v1 of the UD guidelines seems not to have been explicit enough in the correct way of annotating names (later noting e.g. that "The *name* label is another one that has led to confusion."). Therefore, UD decided to redesign name annotation in UD v2, as explained online,[10] which will hopefully suppress this problem significantly.

However, a real problem with *PROPN*s in the source data remains that they are necessarily often unknown to the MT system and thus remain untranslated in the training treebank, which may confuse the subsequent tools. It is therefore probably worth considering to pre-process the data in some way. One option would be to replace the specific names (which are bound to be unknown to all the tools) by some generic placeholders (which the tools can be trained to be able to process), provided this can be done on the target side as well (e.g. using cross-lingual or language-independent named entity recognisers). A slightly different approach could be to replace uncommon names with more common ones (so e.g. we could rename "Pervaiz Musharraf" and "Velupillai Prabhakaran" to "John Smith" and "Martin Jones").

---

[10]http://universaldependencies.org/v2/semantic-categories.html

Experiment	Low group		Med group		High group		All languages	
Base		19.6%		34.1%		51.2%		33.3%
NOUN+PROPN	4/10	-0.6%	6/15	-0.2%	2/7	-0.4%	12/32	-0.4%
VERB+AUX	7/10	0.0%	10/15	0.3%	2/7	0.0%	19/32	0.1%
PRON+DET	6/10	-0.3%	9/15	0.1%	3/7	-0.2%	18/32	-0.1%
nmod+compound	5/10	0.8%	9/15	0.8%	4/7	-0.1%	18/32	0.6%
Reordering	6/10	1.0%	2/15	-3.7%	0/7	-10.4%	8/32	-3.7%

Table 3: Number of target languages for which improvement was observed and absolute improvement in macro-averaged LAS when various modifications are applied, as compared to Base (Table 2).

5.2 Easy regular phenomena

Unsurprisingly, phenomena that behave quite regularly – *case, nummod, punct, det, amod, advmod* – are rather easy to parse correctly, as long as they bear the correct POS tag. As explained in Section 4, correctly tagging some of them is often tricky, especially with *amod* (*ADJ* tag), *advmod* (*ADV* tag), and *det* (*DET* tag); however, if their tagging succeeds, it is usually not difficult for the parser to identify the correct head for them, and to identify the correct dependency relation label is mostly trivial. In particular, the *amod* accuracies are quite low for Romance languages, which prefer the *NOUN ADJ* order.

As could be expected, the head assignment accuracy for the *case* relation drops near zero for target languages that strongly prefer postpositions while the source language strongly prefers prepositions. This is manifested by the relatively very low *case* accuracy for the Low language group, which contains several such languages.

As already discussed in Section 4.2, the problems related to differences in word order may be solvable by employing a reordering component, either before or during the translation.

5.3 Verbs

In general, parsing of *VERB*s is quite successful over all language groups. However, the auxiliary verbs (*aux, cop*) are only parsed well in the High group, i.e. in languages with sufficiently similar grammar (the ideal source language should use auxiliary verbs similarly to the target language).

Moreover, clausal relations (*advcl, acl, xcomp, ccomp*) are very hard to get right, even for the High languages (and often even for a fully supervised parser) – both in assigning the correct head, as they tend to form long-distance relations, as well as in assigning the correct label, as all of these are frequently confused for each other. Thus, these should not be trusted much on the output of cross-lingual parsing.

6 Preliminary experiments

Implementing, fine-tuning and evaluating all of the modifications of the base approach that we suggest would clearly be beyond the scope of this work. Nevertheless, we include at least a brief experimental part, evaluating the effects of several of the suggested modifications – merging a pair of UPOS labels (*NOUN+PROPN, VERB+AUX, PRON+DET*), merging a pair of dependency relation labels (*nmod* and *compound*),[11] and allowing reordering in Moses.[12] Note that these are rather preliminary results, without the usual several iterations of experimentation and evaluation.

Table 3 shows the number of languages for which LAS improved when the modifications were applied, and the average improvement/deterioration in LAS for each language group.

We see that even the very noisy *PROPN* signal from the tagger is useful for the parser, probably because the main distinguishing feature (capitalization) is not directly available to the parser, and it thus cannot easily make the distinction itself. We thus believe that other approaches are to be tried out, such as truecasing the data and/or explicitly including information about the casing into the parser input.

Merging the other label pairs usually behaved quite expectedly, slightly improving the results for the low and med groups, but not for the high group. The results for merging of *DET* and *PRON* are rather

---

[11]The labels were not merged in the test data – the parser is still "expected" by the evaluator to output the *compound* label.

[12]We used the setting recommended in the documentation (`-reordering msd-bidirectional-fe`). Moses decoding was set to output the word alignment (`-alignment-output-file file.a`), which was used to correctly transfer the annotations.

mixed, as the language groups do not sufficiently differentiate the usage of determiners in the target language; one should be more careful when deciding whether to merge these labels or not. The very frequent *compound* label, on the other hand, is something very specific for English, while in most target languages it is rare or non-existent; thus, removing it helped even for many languages in the high group.

Surprisingly, enabling reordering in Moses led to deteriorations (often large) in LAS for all languages, except for a few of the most dissimilar ones (8/32), even though the BLEU score actually improved in most cases (24/32). This clearly requires a thorough further investigation, as our previous experiments (unpublished) indicated a positive correlation between BLEU and LAS. Based on a quick inspection of the data, we currently hypothesise that disallowing reordering forces the MT system to produce more literal translations, which better preserve the sentence structure (POS and dependency relations).

7 Conclusion

We thoroughly analysed a particular cross-lingual tagging and parsing setup, investigating the behaviour of the tools factored along labels and language groups.

We found that the properties of the source and target language have a huge impact on the way the tools work and the kinds of errors we encounter. It is not surprising that best results are obtained when the source and target languages are close. However, we believe it is not straightforward to determine which aspects of the language similarity will have what effect on the analysis of which language phenomena; here, we see the value of our work.

In particular, we saw a high importance of grammatical similarity, especially in terms of word order and auxiliary words usage, such as auxiliary verbs, determiners, pronouns, and adpositions. Except for adpositions, the interlingual variation in usage of the auxiliaries often causes severe problems already in the translation step, with the auxiliaries being frequently misaligned, then necessarily mistranslated, and subsequently mishandled by the tagger and parser.

We spent much of our analyses with understanding the errors that revolve around nouns. However, it seems that the nouns themselves do not cause the problems; it is rather the words around them (especially the auxiliaries), which different languages use differently to mark the roles fulfilled by the nouns.

The question of the word order similarity is less subtle – we clearly saw well-known word order patterns, such as *ADJ NOUN* vs *NOUN ADJ*, or prepositions vs postpositions, to cause severe drops in accuracy in case of a mismatch of the preferred word order between the source and target language.

We hope that this analysis can be used to provide more insight into cross-lingual tagging and parsing, and to help develop better-performing cross-lingual tools in future.

Acknowledgments

This work has been supported by the grant No. DG16P02B048 of the Ministry of Culture of the Czech Republic, the grant No. CZ.02.1.01/0.0/0.0/16_013/0001781 of the Ministry of Education, Youth and Sports of the Czech Republic, the SVV 260 453 grant, and the grant 15-10472S of the Czech Science Foundation. This work has been using language resources and tools developed, stored and distributed by the LINDAT/CLARIN project of the Ministry of Education, Youth and Sports of the Czech Republic (project LM2015071).

We would also like to thank the anonymous reviewers for many helpful observations and suggestions.

References

Željko Agić, Dirk Hovy, and Anders Søgaard. 2015. If all you have is a bit of the Bible: Learning POS taggers for truly low-resource languages. In *The 53rd Annual Meeting of the Association for Computational Linguistics and the 7th International Joint Conference of the Asian Federation of Natural Language Processing (ACL-IJCNLP 2015)*. Hrvatska znanstvena bibliografija i MZOS-Svibor. http://aclweb.org/anthology/P15-2044.

Željko Agić. 2017. Cross-lingual parser selection for low-resource languages. In *Proceedings of the NoDaLiDa 2017 Workshop on Universal Dependencies, 22 May, Gothenburg Sweden*. Linköping University Electronic Press, Linköpings universitet, 135, pages 1–10. htp://aclweb.org/anthology/W17-0401.

Lauriane Aufrant, Guillaume Wisniewski, and François Yvon. 2016. Zero-resource dependency parsing: Boosting delexicalized cross-lingual transfer with linguistic knowledge. In *Proceedings of COLING 2016, the 26th International Conference on Computational Linguistics: Technical Papers*. The COLING 2016 Organizing Committee, Osaka, Japan, pages 119–130. http://aclweb.org/anthology/C16-1012.

Long Duong, Trevor Cohn, Steven Bird, and Paul Cook. 2015. Cross-lingual transfer for unsupervised dependency parsing without parallel data. In *Proceedings of the Nineteenth Conference on Computational Natural Language Learning*. Association for Computational Linguistics, Beijing, China, pages 113–122. http://www.aclweb.org/anthology/K15-1012.

Ryan Georgi, Fei Xia, and William D. Lewis. 2013. Enhanced and portable dependency projection algorithms using interlinear glossed text. In *Proceedings of the 51st Annual Meeting of the Association for Computational Linguistics (Volume 2: Short Papers)*. Association for Computational Linguistics, Sofia, Bulgaria, pages 306–311. http://www.aclweb.org/anthology/P13-2055.

Kenneth Heafield, Ivan Pouzyrevsky, Jonathan H. Clark, and Philipp Koehn. 2013. Scalable modified kneser-ney language model estimation. In *Proceedings of the 51st Annual Meeting of the Association for Computational Linguistics (Volume 2: Short Papers)*. Association for Computational Linguistics, Sofia, Bulgaria, pages 690–696. http://www.aclweb.org/anthology/P13-2121.

Rebecca Hwa, Philip Resnik, Amy Weinberg, Clara Cabezas, and Okan Kolak. 2005. Bootstrapping parsers via syntactic projection across parallel texts. *Natural Language Engineering* 11:11–311. https://doi.org/10.1017/S1351324905003840.

Philipp Koehn, Hieu Hoang, Alexandra Birch, Chris Callison-Burch, Marcello Federico, Nicola Bertoldi, Brooke Cowan, Wade Shen, Christine Moran, Richard Zens, Chris Dyer, Ondřej Bojar, Alexandra Constantin, and Evan Herbst. 2007. Moses: Open source toolkit for statistical machine translation. In *ACL 2007, Proceedings of the 45th Annual Meeting of the Association for Computational Linguistics Companion Volume Proceedings of the Demo and Poster Sessions*. Association for Computational Linguistics, Prague, Czech Republic, pages 177–180. http://www.aclweb.org/anthology/P07-2045.

Ryan McDonald, Slav Petrov, and Keith Hall. 2011. Multi-source transfer of delexicalized dependency parsers. In *Proceedings of Empirical Methods in Natural Language Processing (EMNLP)*. https://www.aclweb.org/anthology/D11-1006.

Tomas Mikolov, Kai Chen, Greg Corrado, and Jeffrey Dean. 2013. Efficient estimation of word representations in vector space. In *Proceedings of Workshop at ICLR*. https://arxiv.org/abs/1301.3781.

Joakim Nivre et al. 2016. Universal dependencies 1.4. LINDAT/CLARIN digital library at the Institute of Formal and Applied Linguistics (ÚFAL), Faculty of Mathematics and Physics, Charles University. http://hdl.handle.net/11234/1-1827.

Martin Popel and Zdeněk Žabokrtský. 2010. TectoMT: Modular NLP framework. In *Proceedings of IceTAL, 7th International Conference on Natural Language Processing, Reykjavík, Iceland, August 17, 2010*. Springer, pages 293–304. https://doi.org/10.1007/978-3-642-14770-8_33.

Loganathan Ramasamy, David Mareček, and Zdeněk Žabokrtský. 2014. Multilingual dependency parsing: Using machine translated texts instead of parallel corpora. *The Prague Bulletin of Mathematical Linguistics* 102:93–104. http://ufal.mff.cuni.cz/pbml/102/art-ramasamy-marecek-zabokrtsky.pdf.

Rudolf Rosa. 2017. Terminal-based CoNLL-file viewer, v2. LINDAT/CLARIN digital library at the Institute of Formal and Applied Linguistics (ÚFAL), Faculty of Mathematics and Physics, Charles University. http://hdl.handle.net/11234/1-2514.

Rudolf Rosa, Daniel Zeman, David Mareček, and Zdeněk Žabokrtský. 2017. Slavic Forest, Norwegian Wood. In Preslav Nakov, Marcos Zampieri, Nikola Ljubešić, Jörg Tiedemann, Shervin Malmasi, and Ahmed Ali, editors, *Proceedings of the Fourth Workshop on NLP for Similar Languages, Varieties and Dialects (VarDial4)*. Association for Computational Linguistics, Association for Computational Linguistics, Stroudsburg, PA, USA, pages 210–219. http://www.aclweb.org/anthology/W17-1226.

Rudolf Rosa and Zdeněk Žabokrtský. 2015. KL_{cpos^3} - a language similarity measure for delexicalized parser transfer. In *Proceedings of the 53rd Annual Meeting of the Association for Computational Linguistics and the 7th International Joint Conference on Natural Language Processing (Volume 2: Short Papers)*. Association for Computational Linguistics, Beijing, China, pages 243–249. http://www.aclweb.org/anthology/P15-2040.

Anders Søgaard, Željko Agić, Héctor Martínez Alonso, Barbara Plank, Bernd Bohnet, and Anders Johannsen. 2015. Inverted indexing for cross-lingual NLP. In *The 53rd Annual Meeting of the Association for Computational Linguistics and the 7th International Joint Conference of the Asian Federation of Natural Language Processing (ACL-IJCNLP 2015)*. http://www.aclweb.org/anthology/P15-1165.

Milan Straka, Jan Hajič, and Jana Straková. 2016. UDPipe: trainable pipeline for processing CoNLL-U files performing tokenization, morphological analysis, POS tagging and parsing. In *Proceedings of the Tenth International Conference on Language Resources and Evaluation (LREC'16)*. European Language Resources Association (ELRA), Paris, France. http://www.lrec-conf.org/proceedings/lrec2016/pdf/873_Paper.pdf.

Oscar Täckström, Ryan McDonald, and Jakob Uszkoreit. 2012. Cross-lingual word clusters for direct transfer of linguistic structure. In *Proceedings of the 2012 Conference of the North American Chapter of the Association for Computational Linguistics: Human Language Technologies*. Association for Computational Linguistics, Stroudsburg, PA, USA, NAACL HLT '12, pages 477–487. http://www.aclweb.org/anthology/N12-1052.

Jörg Tiedemann. 2012. Parallel data, tools and interfaces in OPUS. In *LREC*. pages 2214–2218. http://lrec.elra.info/proceedings/lrec2012/pdf/463_Paper.pdf.

Jörg Tiedemann. 2014. Rediscovering annotation projection for cross-lingual parser induction. In *Proceedings of COLING 2014, the 25th International Conference on Computational Linguistics: Technical Papers*. pages 1854–1864. http://www.aclweb.org/anthology/C14-1175.

Jörg Tiedemann, Željko Agić, et al. 2016. Synthetic treebanking for cross-lingual dependency parsing. *Journal of Artificial Intelligence Research* 55:209–248. http://dx.doi.org/10.1613/jair.4785.

Marcos Zampieri, Shervin Malmasi, Nikola Ljubešić, Preslav Nakov, Ahmed Ali, Jörg Tiedemann, Yves Scherrer, and Noëmi Aepli. 2017. Findings of the VarDial evaluation campaign 2017. In *Proceedings of the Fourth Workshop on NLP for Similar Languages, Varieties and Dialects (VarDial)*. Valencia, Spain. http://aclweb.org/anthology/W17-1201.

Daniel Zeman and Philip Resnik. 2008. Cross-language parser adaptation between related languages. In *Workshop on NLP for Less-Privileged Languages, IJCNLP*. Hyderabad, India. http://www.aclweb.org/anthology/I08-3008.

A Detailed Evaluation Results

Target group	iso	Target language name	Para data (en tokens)	MT BLEU	Treebank tokens train	dtest	UPOS acc x-ling	sup	LAS x-ling	sup
Low	hi	Hindi	321,339	7.3%	281,057	35,217	48.5%	96.4%	10.4%	86.7%
	eu	Basque	1,082,072	6.1%	72,974	24,095	49.5%	94.1%	10.2%	63.4%
	vi	Vietnamese	13,582,467	8.8%	31,799	6,093	51.3%	88.2%	21.5%	52.0%
	fa	Farsi	23,653,954	1.3%	121,064	15,832	55.0%	96.7%	14.1%	79.2%
	ar	Arabic	149,458,897	3.7%	225,853	28,263	56.5%	95.7%	14.0%	72.5%
	tr	Turkish	234,219,925	3.6%	40,617	8,852	59.8%	93.4%	13.8%	69.5%
	uk	Ukrainian	3,797,579	1.4%	1,281	241	62.7%	68.0%	35.7%	31.5%
	hu	Hungarian	215,222,322	8.1%	33,016	4,781	63.0%	94.2%	21.3%	72.4%
	he	Hebrew	156,340,612	22.0%	135,496	11,234	66.0%	95.4%	28.5%	76.4%
	fi	Finnish	133,830,769	4.0%	162,721	9,161	66.3%	94.5%	26.8%	73.1%
		Average	93,150,994	6.6%	110,588	14,377	57.9%	91.7%	19.6%	67.7%
		Std. dev.	94,197,934	6.0%	92,061	11,313	6.7%	8.6%	8.6%	15.7%
Med	sl	Slovenian	106,842,127	11.5%	112,334	14,021	68.8%	95.0%	33.5%	80.3%
	lv	Latvian	2,548,465	7.3%	13,083	3,640	70.7%	91.2%	24.1%	57.4%
	et	Estonian	64,034,502	10.3%	187,814	22,867	71.6%	94.6%	29.4%	72.8%
	pl	Polish	183,401,406	8.7%	69,499	6,887	71.9%	95.3%	37.9%	80.0%
	ro	Romanian	249,781,321	16.3%	163,262	27,965	72.0%	96.8%	32.3%	76.1%
	hr	Croatian	174,234,575	18.6%	127,894	4,823	72.8%	98.0%	34.4%	78.9%
	el	Greek	205,382,482	13.4%	47,449	6,039	73.1%	97.9%	46.4%	77.5%
	id	Indonesian	31,382,075	16.5%	97,531	12,612	73.7%	93.3%	24.3%	72.0%
	ru	Russian	117,951,946	10.2%	79,772	10,044	73.9%	95.7%	30.4%	74.3%
	cs	Czech	217,464,167	10.2%	1,173,282	159,284	74.1%	98.3%	32.6%	79.7%
	sk	Slovak	44,334,287	11.5%	80,575	12,440	74.1%	94.1%	39.4%	75.6%
	nl	Dutch	197,441,086	20.5%	197,134	6,434	74.8%	94.3%	41.5%	74.1%
	gl	Galician	1,106,922	12.1%	79,329	29,777	75.2%	97.2%	18.9%	77.6%
	ca	Catalan	2,513,413	11.9%	429,157	58,020	75.6%	98.0%	41.2%	80.1%
	bg	Bulgarian	214,756,441	11.2%	124,474	16,111	76.3%	97.7%	45.2%	82.8%
		Average	120,878,348	12.7%	198,839	26,064	73.2%	95.8%	34.1%	75.9%
		Std. dev.	90,308,798	3.7%	286,467	39,435	2.0%	2.1%	8.0%	6.0%
High	sv	Swedish	81,231,502	12.7%	66,645	9,797	79.1%	95.0%	47.5%	72.9%
	de	German	88,261,445	15.9%	269,626	12,348	80.6%	90.1%	47.4%	76.2%
	da	Danish	73,620,273	15.0%	88,979	5,870	81.2%	95.5%	50.7%	74.1%
	fr	French	221,712,167	18.3%	356,419	38,758	81.2%	97.1%	51.8%	83.8%
	it	Italian	172,151,250	13.0%	270,598	10,921	81.8%	97.3%	51.4%	83.7%
	no	Norwegian	37,362,647	22.0%	243,887	36,369	83.3%	97.0%	58.6%	82.3%
	pt	Portuguese	160,033,555	14.7%	216,001	5,124	83.4%	96.7%	51.0%	81.9%
		Average	119,196,120	15.9%	216,022	17,027	81.5%	95.5%	51.2%	79.3%
		Std. dev.	66,022,248	3.2%	103,918	14,283	1.5%	2.5%	3.7%	4.7%
All		Average	111,845,562	11.5%	175,019	20,435	70.2%	94.5%	33.3%	74.1%
		Std. dev.	85,249,035	5.6%	208,818	28,439	9.9%	5.3%	13.6%	10.6%
Source	en	English			204,586	25,148		94.3%		79.6%

Table 4: List of all target languages divided into the three groups, reporting their source-target parallel data size (number of tokens in the English side of the parallel data), treebank size (number of tokens in training and development test set of the treebank), translation quality (BLEU measured on the last 10,000 sentences held out from the parallel data), UPOS accuracy and Labelled Attachment Score (for both cross-lingual and fully supervised monolingual tagging and parsing).
Averages are also included, together with standard deviations to illustrate the variance in the data.
The last line lists some of this information for the source language (English).

Gold tag	Actual predicted tag							
NOUN	75.5%	NOUN	8.0%	PROPN	6.7%	VERB	4.6%	ADJ
VERB	69.6%	VERB	12.0%	NOUN	6.2%	AUX	3.6%	ADJ
PUNCT	94.7%	PUNCT	2.2%	CONJ	0.9%	DET	0.6%	SYM
PRON	60.3%	PRON	9.9%	DET	4.4%	AUX	4.2%	VERB
ADP	72.0%	ADP	7.8%	DET	3.6%	PART	3.5%	NOUN
DET	65.2%	DET	16.3%	PRON	6.3%	ADJ	3.9%	ADP
PROPN	72.2%	PROPN	16.0%	NOUN	2.8%	PRON	2.6%	ADJ
ADJ	48.4%	ADJ	25.3%	NOUN	8.7%	VERB	6.8%	PROPN
ADV	52.3%	ADV	8.9%	NOUN	8.8%	ADJ	6.3%	VERB
AUX	52.3%	AUX	20.7%	VERB	8.9%	PRON	4.4%	NOUN
CONJ	78.0%	CONJ	4.5%	ADV	3.8%	SCONJ	2.6%	ADP
PART	32.3%	PART	17.7%	ADV	11.9%	PRON	9.2%	DET
NUM	79.1%	NUM	5.9%	DET	5.5%	NOUN	3.6%	ADJ
SCONJ	39.3%	SCONJ	14.7%	PRON	10.5%	ADP	8.8%	DET
X	33.3%	NOUN	27.1%	PROPN	7.4%	X	6.5%	ADP
INTJ	29.9%	INTJ	20.8%	NOUN	16.9%	ADV	11.0%	PROPN
SYM	36.7%	SYM	29.2%	PUNCT	25.0%	NOUN	3.0%	PROPN

Predicted tag	Actual gold tag							
NOUN	75.7%	NOUN	7.8%	ADJ	6.7%	VERB	4.1%	PROPN
VERB	66.8%	VERB	13.4%	NOUN	5.4%	ADJ	4.7%	AUX
PUNCT	96.7%	PUNCT	0.6%	AUX	0.5%	ADP	0.5%	VERB
PRON	56.2%	PRON	11.8%	DET	5.5%	SCONJ	4.9%	AUX
ADP	74.8%	ADP	3.7%	ADV	3.6%	VERB	3.3%	DET
DET	45.9%	DET	16.1%	ADP	10.0%	PRON	3.9%	VERB
PROPN	54.5%	PROPN	29.6%	NOUN	7.4%	ADJ	2.3%	VERB
ADJ	56.1%	ADJ	18.3%	NOUN	7.3%	VERB	6.0%	ADV
ADV	53.1%	ADV	8.7%	NOUN	7.7%	ADJ	5.3%	PART
AUX	34.1%	AUX	33.9%	VERB	8.9%	PRON	7.0%	PART
CONJ	88.0%	CONJ	3.9%	PUNCT	2.1%	SCONJ	2.0%	ADV
PART	31.2%	ADP	23.9%	PART	11.4%	ADV	9.1%	VERB
NUM	77.1%	NUM	6.5%	ADJ	6.3%	NOUN	3.4%	PROPN
SCONJ	38.4%	SCONJ	21.7%	ADP	10.3%	CONJ	8.2%	ADV
X	31.1%	NOUN	16.3%	NUM	12.8%	PROPN	9.1%	VERB
INTJ	19.7%	ADV	15.0%	NOUN	13.7%	PROPN	13.6%	VERB
SYM	35.1%	PUNCT	22.1%	NOUN	19.5%	SYM	4.3%	PRON

Table 5: Error distribution in cross-lingual UPOS tagging, each row listing an UPOS tag and the four most common tags found with it (i.e. usually showing the three most common errors), macro average over all target languages. The rows are ordered by the frequency of the UPOS tags in the English treebank.

Gold label	Actual predicted label							
punct	94.6%	punct	2.3%	cc	0.9%	case	0.8%	det
nmod	43.3%	nmod	19.0%	compound	8.3%	dobj	6.0%	nsubj
case	72.3%	case	7.7%	det	5.7%	mark	2.8%	advmod
nsubj	45.8%	nsubj	12.4%	compound	9.8%	dobj	5.6%	nmod
det	61.7%	det	10.4%	nmod	7.6%	amod	4.9%	nsubj
root	50.4%	root	5.7%	nsubj	4.3%	acl	4.2%	nmod
dobj	36.4%	dobj	12.9%	nmod	12.5%	compound	10.5%	nsubj
compound	23.6%	compound	17.5%	nmod	9.4%	nummod	9.2%	case
advmod	48.9%	advmod	6.0%	amod	6.0%	case	5.3%	nmod
amod	48.1%	amod	13.0%	compound	9.7%	nmod	4.3%	dobj
conj	50.4%	conj	9.0%	compound	5.8%	acl	5.5%	amod
mark	46.2%	mark	12.8%	case	9.0%	nsubj	6.8%	det
cc	82.8%	cc	3.4%	advmod	2.2%	case	1.9%	det
aux	45.1%	aux	8.1%	nsubj	6.9%	cop	6.4%	mark
cop	52.3%	cop	7.4%	aux	5.8%	root	5.5%	auxpass
advcl	33.7%	advcl	7.9%	root	7.7%	acl	6.3%	amod
acl	34.7%	acl	10.2%	amod	7.6%	advcl	6.7%	root
xcomp	16.4%	xcomp	13.3%	root	9.4%	ccomp	8.3%	dobj
nummod	73.4%	nummod	5.8%	det	5.3%	compound	4.5%	nmod
ccomp	22.8%	ccomp	10.3%	acl	9.9%	advcl	6.9%	root
neg	69.4%	neg	11.9%	nsubj	3.8%	aux	2.8%	punct
appos	22.2%	appos	17.5%	compound	12.2%	nmod	10.8%	name

Predicted label	Actual gold label							
punct	96.0%	punct	0.5%	nmod	0.5%	case	0.3%	auxpass
nmod	56.9%	nmod	7.0%	dobj	4.8%	amod	4.1%	det
case	72.4%	case	3.7%	nmod	3.7%	det	3.6%	advmod
nsubj	42.1%	nsubj	14.3%	nmod	7.6%	dobj	4.4%	root
det	49.4%	det	16.1%	case	4.2%	nmod	3.8%	mark
root	54.7%	root	6.6%	nmod	5.5%	nsubj	3.0%	amod
dobj	34.2%	dobj	22.6%	nmod	11.6%	nsubj	4.7%	amod
compound	37.4%	nmod	12.9%	amod	9.5%	nsubj	8.1%	dobj
advmod	53.5%	advmod	7.1%	nmod	5.3%	case	4.8%	amod
amod	49.0%	amod	11.8%	nmod	5.0%	det	4.8%	advmod
conj	46.3%	conj	11.3%	nmod	4.7%	amod	4.3%	dobj
mark	43.4%	mark	22.7%	case	6.7%	advmod	4.5%	aux
cc	84.9%	cc	4.3%	punct	3.1%	advmod	1.3%	discourse
aux	36.5%	aux	12.3%	root	7.2%	advmod	4.7%	cop
cop	47.6%	cop	11.6%	aux	9.2%	root	3.6%	auxpass
advcl	21.6%	advcl	11.5%	nmod	10.2%	root	8.6%	acl
acl	30.5%	acl	11.8%	root	10.1%	nmod	7.8%	conj
xcomp	17.2%	xcomp	10.0%	nmod	9.7%	root	8.4%	amod
nummod	59.8%	nummod	11.5%	nmod	7.4%	amod	2.2%	conj
ccomp	24.9%	ccomp	12.1%	root	8.5%	xcomp	7.5%	acl
neg	64.6%	neg	8.1%	advmod	4.9%	aux	3.9%	cop
appos	29.3%	nmod	12.6%	appos	11.0%	name	7.0%	nsubj

Table 6: Error distribution in cross-lingual parsing, each row listing a relation label and the four most common labels found with it (i.e. usually showing the three most common errors), reporting macro average of dependency relation label assignment over all target languages (disregarding the head assignment, i.e. this is not LAS). The rows are ordered by the frequency of the relations in the English treebank, and only the most frequent are included in this table.

A Dependency Treebank for Telugu

Taraka Rama
Department of Informatics
University of Oslo, Norway
tarakark@ifi.uio.no

Sowmya Vajjala
Applied Linguistics and Technology Program
Iowa State University, USA
sowmya@iastate.edu

Abstract

In this paper, we describe the annotation and development of Telugu treebank following the Universal Dependencies framework. We manually annotated 1328 sentences from a Telugu grammar textbook and the treebank is freely available from Universal Dependencies version 2.1.[1] In this paper, we discuss some language specific annotation issues and decisions; and report preliminary experiments with POS tagging and dependency parsing. To the best of our knowledge, this is the first freely accessible and open dependency treebank for Telugu.

1 Introduction

An annotated treebank is a pre-requisite for developing computational tools that support deeper language processing for any language. Treebanks are typically created with texts collected from specific genre such as news, fiction, Wikipedia, blogs, and Bible. There also exist treebanks for non-canonical text such as learner data (Berzak et al., 2016; Lee et al., 2017). While these treebanks have been used for the development of natural language parsers and other tools, they may not cover infrequent grammatical structures that do not occur in the specific domain of the training data. Grammar books provide an excellent set of examples for annotated sentences that cover a wide range of syntactic structures as these sentences are chosen to illustrate the interesting and unique features in a language. Additionally, such grammar book based treebanks can also be used to test the coverage of statistical parsers trained with a large amount of data from a specific domain or genre. Further, a typical grammar book features short sentences and allows rapid development of a treebank. Hence, they serve as a good starting point for developing a broad coverage treebank (Cöltekin, 2015).

Telugu is a Dravidian Language native to India with 74 million native speakers with a long history of written and oral literature. Despite some published research on development of part-of-speech taggers (PVS and Karthik, 2007) and a treebank (Vempaty et al., 2010), neither of the resources are publicly available. In this paper, we describe our efforts in developing a publicly available treebank for Telugu that covers a range of syntactic constructions and morphological phenomena. We manually annotated 1328 sentences from the Telugu grammar book by Krishnamurti and Gwynn (1985) with (universal) part-of-speech tags and dependency relations. We followed the Universal Dependencies (Nivre et al., 2016) framework for annotation, as it supports the development of treebanks for new languages through extensive documentation. We also report preliminary POS tagging and dependency parsing results using the treebank data and UDPipe (Straka et al., 2016).

The rest of the paper is organized as follows. We describe the related work in section 2. We provide a brief description of linguistic properties of Telugu in section 3. Then, we describe the corpus and annotation environment in section 4. We describe the annotation decisions during the annotation of POS tags in section 5. Section 6 briefly introduces Telugu morphology and is followed by section 7 that discusses dependency relations that are specific to Telugu . We present the results of our POS tagging and parsing experiments in section 8. Finally, we conclude the paper and discuss some directions for future work.

---

[1]http://universaldependencies.org/treebanks/te/

119

Proceedings of the 16th International Workshop on Treebanks and Linguistic Theories (TLT16), pages 119–128,
Prague, Czech Republic, January 23–24, 2018. Distributed under a CC-BY 4.0 licence. 2017.

Keywords: Telugu, Universal dependencies, adverbial clauses, relative clauses

2 Related Work

Treebanks for some South Asian languages were developed following the Paninian framework for dependency annotation (Begum et al., 2008) and some of them are publicly available.[2] There were some early efforts towards Telugu dependency treebank development following the Paninian framework (Vempaty et al., 2010). A Telugu treebank was also a part of an Indian language dependency tools contest (Husain et al., 2010). However, none of these resources are publicly available to the best of our knowledge. There have been efforts to convert some of the Indian language treebanks into Universal Dependencies (UD) framework (Tandon et al., 2016) and there is a reasonably large UD treebank for Hindi (Palmer et al., 2009; Bhat et al., 2017). However, except for Tamil (Ramasamy and Žabokrtský, 2012), converted from Prague dependency style (Hajič et al., 2017) to UD, there is no UD treebank for any other language from the Dravidian language family. In this scenario, the availability of free and open UD Telugu treebank would be a good starting point for the future of computational infrastructure support for Telugu and the Dravidian language family.

UD treebanks were developed from scratch for several low-resource languages such as Kazakh (Makazhanov et al.) and Buryat (Badmaeva and Tyers, 2017) in the recent years. Several existing treebanks are also being converted into UD. While there is no Dravidian language in UD other than Tamil, there exist treebanks for other agglutinative languages such as Finnish (Pyysalo et al., 2015), Hungarian (Vincze et al., 2017), Turkish (Çöltekin, 2015; Sulubacak et al., 2016), and Estonian (Muischnek et al., 2016) which provided us with useful insights in dealing with language-specific morphological and syntactic phenomena for Telugu.

3 Telugu

Telugu is one of the 22 languages with official status in India. Telugu belongs to the South-Central subgroup of the Dravidian language family[3] and is mainly spoken in Southern India. The Dravidian language family was the subject of both historical and comparative linguistic research in the later half of twentieth century (Krishnamurti, 2003). Telugu is an agglutinative language like other Dravidian languages such as Tamil or Malayalam. The dominant word order in Telugu is Subject-Object-Verb (SOV) with inclination towards pro-drop. Telugu verbs inflect for gender, number and person. The "be" (*vun-*, "existential") verb in Telugu shows agreement with the subject for gender, number, and person. The existential verb has a negative counterpart "not to be" (*le:-*) which can participate in both light and serial verb constructions and also act as the main verb.[4] Telugu does not have a dominant overt coordination as in English or Hindi. Telugu forms subordinate clauses through verbal nouns, verbal adjective, and converbs. Control constructions marked by xcomp relation are rare (less than ten instances in our treebank) in Telugu.

4 Corpus and Annotation

The Telugu treebank currently consists of 1328 sentences and 6465 tokens. The sentences were manually typed in Telugu script (derived from Brahmi script) from the examples in chapters 7–29 in (Krishnamurti and Gwynn, 1985). Many sentences in this book are collected from contemporary Telugu fiction of that time (1960s-80s). Both the authors manually annotated all the sentences, and disagreements were adjudicated after discussion. Annotation was done using the Brat (Stenetorp et al., 2012) tool and the conversion to CONLL format was done using a Python script. We annotated the sentences with UD POS tags and dependency relations (annotation guidelines available on the UD website[5]). The whole process of annotation and correction process took 4 months. The following sections outline our annotation decisions with examples.

---

[2]Available at `http://kcis.iiit.ac.in/`

[3]The Dravidian language family is one of the four language families spoken in India (the others being Indo-European, Austro-Asiatic, and Sino-Tibetan).

[4]The closest parallel of a negative verb is the negative auxiliary verb in Finnish `http://wals.info/chapter/112` and in Kurmanji (*tune*).

[5]`http://universaldependencies.org/guidelines.html`

5 Part-of-speech annotation

UD specification defines 17 POS tags, of which we used 14 tags in Telugu. We did not use the tags - X, SYM and AUX. X was not used as there were no instances of unanalyzable foreign words that are not loan words in the corpus. SYM was not used as there were no symbols in the sentences. Words that resemble auxiliary verbs in Telugu also function as main verbs in the sentence. Hence, we did not use the AUX tag in our annotations. While we largely followed UD guidelines for POS tagging, we also made accommodations for some language specific phenomena. Among the open-class words, while Nouns, Proper Nouns and Verbs are relatively straightforward to tag, we made specific annotation decisions for adjectives and adverbs. Verbs functioning as Nouns or Adjectives were tagged Verbs but annotated with appropriate dependency relation (e.g., *acl* for verbal adjectives) to the head. We mark the morphological feature `VerbForm` with `Vnoun` and `Part` respectively.

Adjectives (ADJ):   Adjectives in Telugu are indeclinable. Oblique nouns functioning as adjectives are tagged as NOUN with the relation `nmod:poss` to the head noun. Adjectives with a pronominal suffix (e.g., manci=vaːɖu good-3-SG-M. suffix, meaning: good one) are tagged as PRON and not adjective, as they refer to entities. Figure 1a illustrates a sentence with pronominalized adjective in predicate position with words transcribed in IPA. Adjectives denoting dimensions such as tall (*poɖugu*) or short (*poʈʈi*) do not need a pronominal suffix to function as the root of a sentence non-verbal construction. In such cases, we treat such as adjectives as abstract nouns and mark the POS tag as NOUN.

Adverbs (ADV):   Krishnamurti and Gwynn (1985) and Krishnamurti (2003) note that adverbs of time and place behave as nouns (can inflect with case markers) in Telugu. We adopt the judgment into our treebank and mark all adverbs of time and place as nouns. We annotate an inflected time or location noun as NOUN and annotate it as the dependent of the dependency relations `obl` or `obl:tmod`. This is shown in Figures 1b and 1c.

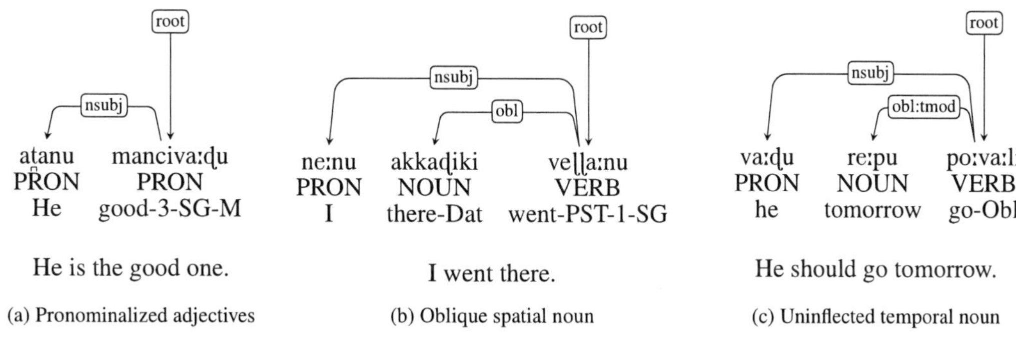

(a) Pronominalized adjectives

(b) Oblique spatial noun

(c) Uninflected temporal noun

Figure 1: Part-of-speech tag examples

In the case of closed class words – Adpositions, Determiners, Numerals – we made the following language specific decisions:

Adpositions (ADP):   Telugu uses postpositions and suffixes to denote cases. Postpositions are tagged as ADP and are dependent of nominals through `case` relation. Some adverbs indicating temporal or location information that appear as nominal modifiers are also tagged ADP.

Determiners (DET):   UD guidelines distinguish 6 kinds of determiners. Of those, Telugu does not have articles and possessive determiners. We mark distal/proximal demonstratives and interrogative determiners that precede a nominal as DET. Telugu does not have relative pronouns and forms relative clauses through nominalization or verbal adjectives.

Numerals (NUM):   Following UD guidelines, we tagged all numbers, fractions and multi-word numeric expressions with the NUM tag. However, numbers can also function as adjective, adverb or noun in Telugu, and can be inflected. Inflected numbers which do not appear in a multi-word numeric expression are marked according to their syntactic function. UD guidelines also describe the tagging of non-cardinal numbers according to their syntactic function.[6]

6 Morphology

Telugu verbs show agreement with the agent in number, gender and person. Telugu has two genders: masculine and non-masculine and we will annotate with the same categories. Telugu has two numbers: singular and plural. Telugu nominals show highly inflected case system with nominative, dative, instrumental, genitive, commitative, ablative, and locative cases. Postpositions also function as adessive (*mi:da* "on"), purposive and comparative cases. Complex cases are formed through a combination of base case markers and postpositions.

Telugu verbs show tense, aspect, and mood. Verbs are typically active voice and passive constructions are not common. Causative constructions (`Voice=Cau`) are formed by adding *-inc* to the transitive verb. Telugu also has a reflexive suffix *-kon* that is added to causative and transitive verb stems to denote that the agent is also the patient. We mark such a reflexive verb with `Reflex=Yes`. There are two tenses: past and non-past. Telugu does not have a negative particle and shows negation through *-a-* marker that occurs before index markers. Verb can show aspect: habitual (`Hab`), progressive (`Prog`), perfect (`Perf`), prospective (`Prosp`) which are available in UD. The mood features are imperative (`Imp`), conditional (`Cnd`), potential (`Pot`), necessitative (`Nec`), inceptive (`Inc`), hortative (`Hor`).[7] Morphological annotation is not a part of the UD 2.1 release for Telugu and is a part of future work.

7 Universal Dependency Relations

Our treebank has 42 dependency relations, of which 11 are language specific. They are listed below in Table 1. Relations that are not seen in other language UD treebanks are marked with ∗.

Relation	Description
acl:relcl	Relative clause
advcl:cond	Conditional Adverbial clause
compound:lvc	Light verb construction
compound:redup	Reduplicative construction
compound:svc	Serial verb construction
nmod:cmp∗	Nominal comparative modifier
nmod:poss	Nominal possessive modifier
nmod:tmod	Nominal temporal modifier
nsubj:nc	non-canonical subjects (e.g., dative subjects)
obl:tmod	Oblique case-temporal
obl:cau∗	Oblique case-causative (Section 6

Table 1: Language Specific Dependency Relations for Telugu

While some relations such as `acl:relcl` and `nmod:poss` exist in several other language treebanks, other relations are not very common. Some of them are discussed below.

Light verb constructions: Light verbs are noun-verb constructions where the semantic content is in the noun even if the syntactic head is the verb. These constructions are wide spread in Hindi-Urdu (Butt, 2010; Vaidya et al., 2016). However, the Hindi UD treebank (converted from Paninian dependency treebank) does not seem to tag this construction specifically though it is annotated with `pof` (part-of) relation in the original Paninian treebank. We tag this construction explicitly using `compound:lvc`. In UD 2.1, this construction is explicitly marked in Farsi, Kazakh, Kurmanji, Marathi, Turkish and Uyghur along with Telugu. Recent work in Hungarian (Vincze et al., 2017) described these constructions using the label `dobj:lvc`. Light verb construction is illustrated in figure 2 where a noun (start) followed by a verb is used as a light verb compound.

---

[6]http://universaldependencies.org/u/pos/NUM.html
[7]Inceptive and Hortative moods are not available in UD.

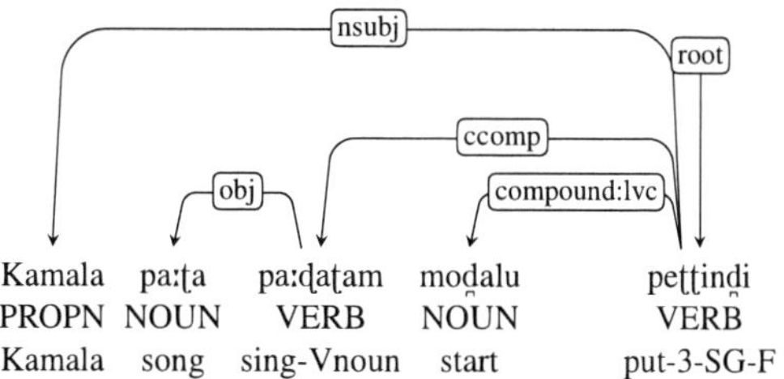

Kamala started singing a song.

Figure 2: Light verb construction with a nominalized clausal complement.

Reduplication: Reduplication is the morphological process in which whole or parts of the word are repeated to denote a syntactic function. Reduplication (both partial and complete) is a common phenomenon in several languages although it is explicitly marked in only five other UD 2.1 languages – Hindi, Kurmanji, Marathi, Turkish and Uyghur – with the relation `compound:redup`. We mark all reduplicated words with this relation and treat the final word as the head. In Telugu, reduplication can occur across POS categories such as determiner, verbs, adjectives, nouns, and adverbs. We show examples of verb and adjective reduplication in figure 3.

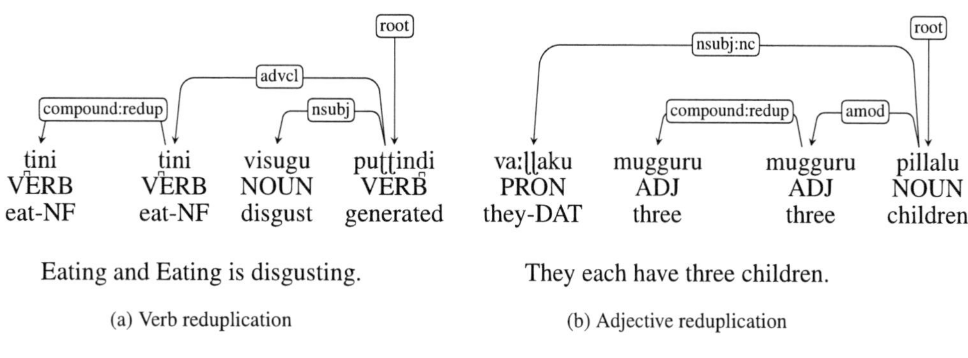

Eating and Eating is disgusting.

(a) Verb reduplication

They each have three children.

(b) Adjective reduplication

Figure 3: Reduplication in verbs and adjectives.

Serial Verbs: The Dravidian comparative literature defines serial verbs as a series of finite verbs which are present in Old Telugu but absent in Modern Telugu. There is no limit to the number of participating verbs in such a construction. We employ the definition of serial verbs from Velupillai (2012, 332) that a series of verbs referring to a single event is labeled as serial verb. These are different from other compound verbs such as V-V complex predicates in that they describe a sequence of actions. We mark such constructions with `compound:svc` (cf. Figure 4). The Dravidian comparative literature treats these constructions as adverbial clauses.

Non-verbal predication: In this paragraph, we present non-overt copula (cf. Figure 5a) and negative verb (cf. Figure 5b) which is specific to Telugu. Equative, attributive, possession, and benefaction constructions consist of NP+NP and lack an overt copula. Location construction (negation variant) shown in Figure 5b shows agreement and does not fall under the definition of non-verbal predication in UD.

Genitives: Genitive constructions can be formed through a preceding nominal dependent in nominative case, postposition (*yokka*), and oblique noun. We mark all these relations as `nmod:poss` (cf. figure 6).

Comparatives: Comparative constructions are formed through a special postposition *kaṇṭe* which is marked as a dependent of the second nominal through `case` relation (cf. figure 7). [8]

---

[8] At the time of submission of the paper, we marked the relation between the two nominals using `nmod:cmp` relation. We mark the relation between the second nominal and the root noun with `obl` relation. We thank one of the reviewers for pointing

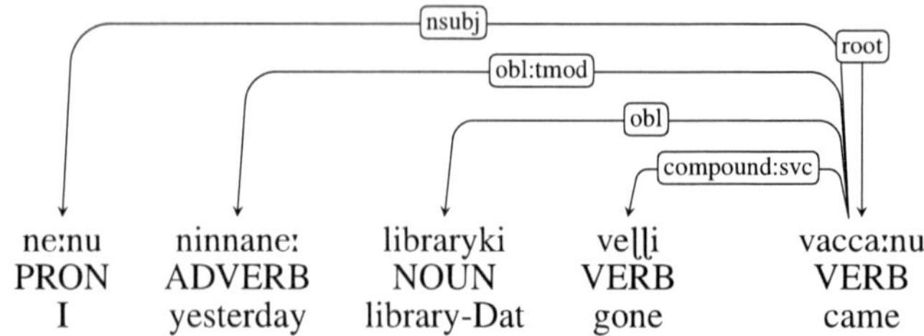

I went to the library yesterday.

Figure 4: Serial verb construction

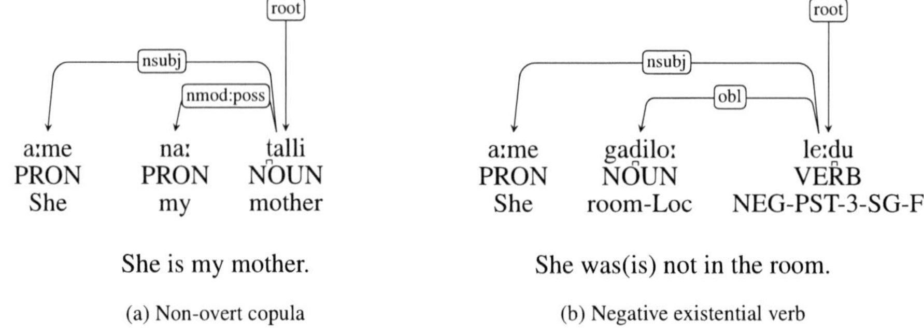

(a) Non-overt copula

(b) Negative existential verb

Figure 5: Non-verbal predication in Telugu.

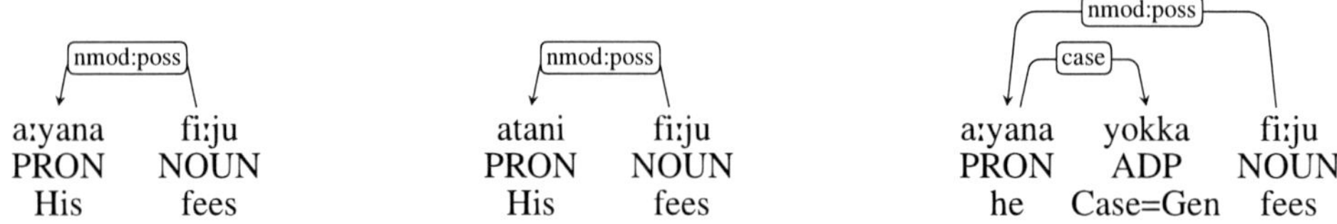

Figure 6: Genitive formation strategies

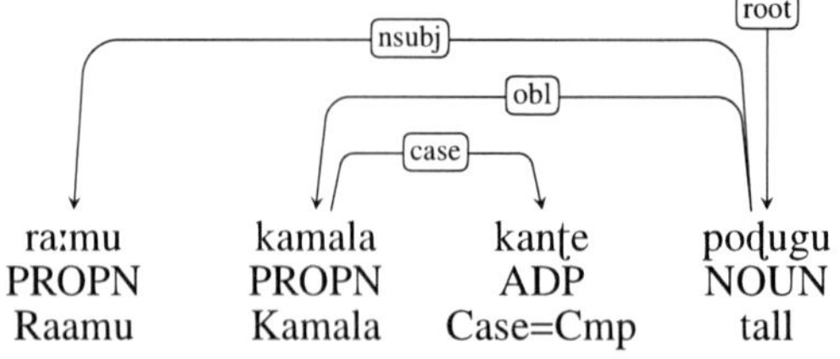

Ramu is taller than Kamala.

Figure 7: Comparative construction without an overt copula

Dative subjects: Typically, NPs that occur at the sentence-initial position are in nominative case (unmarked). However, stative verbs such as "to know" and intransitive verbs such as "to want" do not show any agreement with any of the NPs in the sentence. In such cases, the NP in initial position is marked with dative case (Sridhar, 1979; Nizar, 2010). We mark the syntactic relation between the verb and the dative NP with nsubj:nc. Although dative NP occurs in sentence initial position, the free word order allows the dative NP to be moved to a non-final position in the sentence. A dative NP (annotated as

this mistake.

124

`nsubj:nc`) can also occur as the experiencer NP in non-verbal sentences (cf. figure 3b).[9]

Adverbial clauses: Telugu forms adverbial clauses through converbs. The final verb in the sentence is a finite verb which is treated as the root of the sentence. The subject of the embedded clause can be co-referential (cf. Figure 8) when the non-finite verb is marked for perfective or progressive aspect. In such a case, we annotate the subject to be the dependent of the main verb. Subjects of the main and subordinate clauses cannot be co-referential when the non-finite verb is marked for conditional or concessive moods.

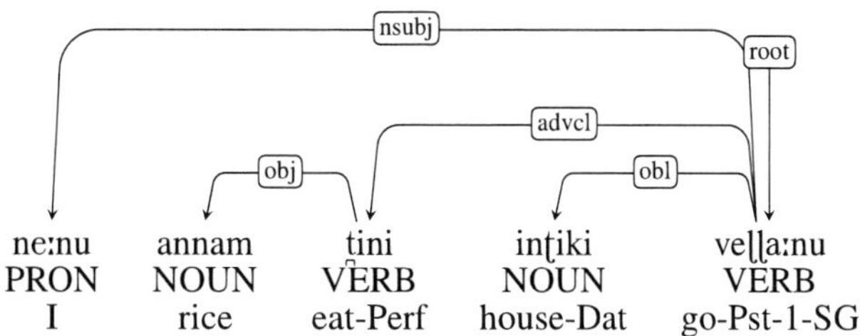

I ate rice and went home.

Figure 8: Adverbial clause

Relative clauses: There is no relative pronoun in Telugu and relative clauses are formed through verbal adjectives. There are no expletive nominals in Telugu and cleft constructions are formed through pronominalized verbal adjectives. We analyze cleft sentences as relative clauses (cf. figure 9).

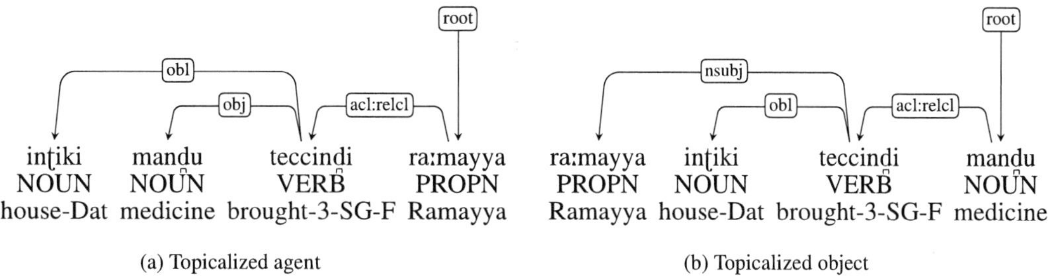

(a) Topicalized agent

(b) Topicalized object

Figure 9: Cleft constructions derived from a simple sentence: *raːmayya inṯiki manḍu teccaːḍu.* (Rammayya brought medicine home.)

Nominalized clauses: Non-finite verbs are nominalized by adding *-atam*. A nominalized verb can then be the head of a subordinate clause which can be the subject or object of the main verb (cf. figure 2). We annotate a nominalized verb clause as `csubj` (functions as subject) and `ccomp` (functions as object), respectively.

8   Tagging and Parsing Experiments

As a demonstration of the usefulness of our treebank in real world settings, we evaluated POS tagging and parsing models trained using UDPipe (Straka et al., 2016). UDPipe is a free, open-source, and language agnostic pipeline for training and evaluating NLP models for lemmatization, POS tagging and dependency parsing.

We split our treebank into 80-10-10 for training, development, and testing; and trained POS tagging and parsing models. Both training and evaluation was performed with UDPipe-1.2 on a Linux machine.

---

[9]We follow the Persian UD annotation guidelines (Seraji et al., 2016) in this case and name the dependency relation as `nsubj:nc`.

We report POS tagging accuracy, Labeled Attachment Score (LAS), and Unlabeled Attachment Score (UAS) on test set (after parameter tuning on development set) in Table 2. We also trained and evaluated a second parsing model on gold POS tags and found that the LAS and UAS scores are better than the joint model for predicting POS tags and dependency relations. We expect the POS tagging results to be high since nouns and verbs make the bulk of the part-of-speech tags in Telugu.

Input features	POS Acc.	LAS	UAS
Tagging + Parsing	90.43%	74.76%	87.79%
Parsing (Gold POS tags)	–	78.50%	89.74%

Table 2: Preliminary tagging and parsing results with UDPipe.

Previous work on Telugu dependency parsing – trained and evaluated with Paninian dependency labels – report the highest LAS of 70.15% (Husain et al., 2010) and best UAS of 90.5% (Kanneganti et al., 2016). While our LAS results are higher than both the previous results, the UAS results are slightly lower; however, a direct comparison is not possible due to the unavailability of the training data for these results and also due to different annotation schemes.

9 Conclusion

In this paper, we presented the first publicly available treebank for Telugu annotated in Universal Dependencies framework. We annotated POS tags and dependency relations from scratch for 1328 sentences. We trained and evaluated two parser models using UDPipe on the training split of the treebank and found that the parser performs within the range reported in the previous experiments.

As a part of future work, we intend to add morphological annotations to the treebank. It would also be interesting to compare different parsers on this treebank data. We are currently working towards expanding the treebank to include at least 100,000 tokens from Telugu Wikipedia. We plan to achieve this in a semi-automated fashion by running a trained parser model on Wikipedia sentences and then, manually checking and correcting for errors. We are also in the process of augmenting the treebank with fine-grained POS tags designed for Indian languages (Choudhary and Jha, 2011). The average sentence length in our treebank corpus is rather small ($\sim$ 5 tokens per sentence) whereas Wikipedia sentences are typically much longer. We intend to analyze how accurate can an automatic parser trained on grammar book examples would be when faced with longer sentences, with possibly complicated syntactic structures.

Acknowledgments

The first author was supported by ERC Advanced Grant 324246 EVOLAEMP and a NRC LightHouse grant which is gratefully acknowledged. We thank Çağrı Çöltekin, Lilja Øvrelid, and Viswanath Naidu for all the discussions and input which proved useful in the development of the treebank. Finally, we thank the anonymous reviewers for the comments that helped improve the paper.

References

Elena Badmaeva and Francis M Tyers. 2017. A Dependency Treebank for Buryat. In *15th Internationtal Workshop on Treebanks and Linguistic Theories (TLT15)*. pages 1–12.

Rafiya Begum, Samar Husain, Arun Dhwaj, Dipti Misra Sharma, Lakshmi Bai, and Rajeev Sangal. 2008. Dependency Annotation Scheme for Indian Languages. In *Proceedings of the Third International Joint Conference on Natural Language Processing: Volume-1*. pages 721–726.

Yevgeni Berzak, Jessica Kenney, Carolyn Spadine, Jing Xian Wang, Lucia Lam, Keiko Sophie Mori, Sebastian Garza, and Boris Katz. 2016. Universal Dependencies for Learner English. In *Proceedings of the 54th Annual Meeting of the Association for Computational Linguistics (Volume 1: Long Papers)*. Association for Computational Linguistics, Berlin, Germany, pages 737–746. http://www.aclweb.org/anthology/P16-1070.

Riyaz Ahmad Bhat, Rajesh Bhatt, Annahita Farudi, Prescott Klassen, Bhuvana Narasimhan, Martha Palmer, Owen Rambow, Dipti Misra Sharma, Ashwini Vaidya, Sri Ramagurumurthy Vishnu, and Fei Xia. 2017. The Hindi/Urdu Treebank Project. In *Handbook of Linguistic Annotation*, Springer, pages 659–697.

Miriam Butt. 2010. The Light Verb Jungle: Still Hacking Away. *Complex predicates in cross-linguistic perspective* pages 48–78.

Narayan Choudhary and Girish Nath Jha. 2011. Creating Multilingual Parallel Corpora in Indian languages. In *Language and Technology Conference*. Springer, pages 527–537.

Cagrı Cöltekin. 2015. A Grammar-book Treebank of Turkish. In *Proceedings of the 14th workshop on Treebanks and Linguistic Theories (TLT 14)*. pages 35–49.

Jan Hajič, Eva Hajičová, Marie Mikulová, and Jiří Mírovskỳ. 2017. Prague Dependency Treebank. In *Handbook of Linguistic Annotation*, Springer, pages 555–594.

Samar Husain, Prashanth Mannem, Bharat Ambati, and Phani Gadde. 2010. The ICON-2010 tools contest on Indian language dependency parsing. *Proceedings of ICON-2010 Tools Contest on Indian Language Dependency Parsing, ICON* 10:1–8.

Silpa Kanneganti, Himani Chaudhry, and Dipti Misra Sharma. 2016. Comparative Error Analysis of Parser Outputs on Telugu Dependency Treebank. *Proceedings of CICLING 2016* .

Bhadriraju Krishnamurti. 2003. *The Dravidian Languages*. Cambridge University Press.

Bhadriraju Krishnamurti and John Peter Lucius Gwynn. 1985. *A Grammar of Modern Telugu*. Oxford University Press, USA.

John Lee, Herman Leung, and Keying Li. 2017. Towards Universal Dependencies for Learner Chinese. In *Proceedings of the NoDaLiDa 2017 Workshop on Universal Dependencies (UDW 2017)*. Association for Computational Linguistics, Gothenburg, Sweden, pages 67–71. http://www.aclweb.org/anthology/W17-0408.

Aibek Makazhanov, Aitolkyn Sultangazina, Olzhas Makhambetov, and Zhandos Yessenbayev. ???? Syntactic Annotation of Kazakh: Following the Universal Dependencies Guidelines- A Report.

Kadri Muischnek, Kaili Müürisep, and Tiina Puolakainen. 2016. Estonian Dependency Treebank: From Constraint Grammar tagset to Universal Dependencies. In *Proceedings of the Tenth International Conference on Language Resources and Evaluation (LREC)*. pages 1558–1565.

Joakim Nivre, Marie-Catherine de Marneffe, Filip Ginter, Yoav Goldberg, Jan Hajic, Christopher D Manning, Ryan T McDonald, Slav Petrov, Sampo Pyysalo, Natalia Silveira, Reut Tsarfaty, and Daniel Zeman. 2016. Universal Dependencies v1: A Multilingual Treebank Collection. In *Proceedings of the Tenth International Conference on Language Resources and Evaluation (LREC 2016)*. pages 1659–1666.

Milla Nizar. 2010. Dative Subject Constructions in South-Dravidian Languages. *Unpublished master's thesis, University of California, Berkeley, Berkeley, CA.* .

Martha Palmer, Rajesh Bhatt, Bhuvana Narasimhan, Owen Rambow, Dipti Misra Sharma, and Fei Xia. 2009. Hindi Syntax: Annotating Dependency, Lexical Predicate-Argument Structure, and Phrase Structure. In *The 7th International Conference on Natural Language Processing*.

Avinesh PVS and Gali Karthik. 2007. Part-of-speech Tagging and Chunking Using Conditional Random Fields and Transformation Based Learning. *Proceedings of the Workshop on Shallow Parsing for South Asian Languages* .

Sampo Pyysalo, Jenna Kanerva, Anna Missilä, Veronika Laippala, and Filip Ginter. 2015. Universal dependencies for Finnish. In *Proceedings of the 20th Nordic Conference of Computational Linguistics (NODALIDA 2015)*. Linköping University Electronic Press, 109, pages 163–172.

Loganathan Ramasamy and Zdeněk Žabokrtský. 2012. Prague Dependency Style Treebank for Tamil. In Nicoletta Calzolari (Conference Chair), Khalid Choukri, Thierry Declerck, Mehmet Uğur Doğan, Bente Maegaard, Joseph Mariani, Asuncion Moreno, Jan Odijk, and Stelios Piperidis, editors, *Proceedings of Eighth International Conference on Language Resources and Evaluation (LREC 2012)*. İstanbul, Turkey, pages 1888–1894. http://www.lrec-conf.org/proceedings/lrec2012/summaries/456.html.

Mojgan Seraji, Filip Ginter, and Joakim Nivre. 2016. Universal dependencies for persian. In *LREC*.

Shikaripur N Sridhar. 1979. Dative Subjects and the Notion of Subject. *Lingua* 49(2-3):99–125.

Pontus Stenetorp, Sampo Pyysalo, Goran Topić, Tomoko Ohta, Sophia Ananiadou, and Jun'ichi Tsujii. 2012. BRAT: A Web-based Tool for NLP-assisted Text Annotation. In *Proceedings of the Demonstrations at the 13th Conference of the European Chapter of the Association for Computational Linguistics*. Association for Computational Linguistics, pages 102–107.

Milan Straka, Jan Hajic, and Jana Straková. 2016. UDPipe: Trainable Pipeline for Processing CoNLL-U Files Performing Tokenization, Morphological Analysis, POS Tagging and Parsing. In *Proceedings of the Tenth International Conference on Language Resources and Evaluation (LREC 2016)*. pages 4290–4297.

Umut Sulubacak, Memduh Gokirmak, Francis Tyers, Çağrı Çöltekin, Joakim Nivre, and Gülşen Eryiğit. 2016. Universal Dependencies for Turkish. In *Proceedings of COLING 2016, the 26th International Conference on Computational Linguistics: Technical Papers*. pages 3444–3454.

Juhi Tandon, Himani Chaudhry, Riyaz Ahmad Bhat, and Dipti Sharma. 2016. Conversion from Paninian Karakas to Universal Dependencies for Hindi Dependency Treebank. In *Proceedings of the 10th Linguistic Annotation Workshop held in conjunction with ACL 2016 (LAW-X 2016)*. Association for Computational Linguistics, Berlin, Germany, pages 141–150. http://anthology.aclweb.org/W16-1716.

Ashwini Vaidya, Sumeet Agarwal, and Martha Palmer. 2016. Linguistic Features for Hindi Light Verb Construction Identification. In *COLING*. pages 1320–1329.

Viveka Velupillai. 2012. *An introduction to linguistic typology*. John Benjamins Publishing.

Chaitanya Vempaty, Viswanatha Naidu, Samar Husain, Ravi Kiran, Lakshmi Bai, Dipti Sharma, and Rajeev Sangal. 2010. Issues in Analyzing Telugu Sentences towards Building a Telugu Treebank. *International Conference on Intelligent Text Processing and Computational Linguistics (CICLING)* pages 50–59.

Veronika Vincze, Katalin Simkó, Zsolt Szántó, and Richárd Farkas. 2017. Universal Dependencies and Morphology for Hungarian-and on the Price of Universality. In *Proceedings of the 15th Conference of the European Chapter of the Association for Computational Linguistics: Volume 1, Long Papers*. volume 1, pages 356–365.

Recent Developments within BulTreeBank

Petya Osenova
IICT-BAS,
Sofia, Bulgaria
petya@bultreebank.org

Kiril Simov
IICT-BAS,
Sofia, Bulgaria
kivs@bultreebank.org

Abstract

The paper discusses recent developments in BulTreeBank (BTB). First of all, these developments include the preparatory steps for transferring richer linguistic knowledge from the original BTB into BTB-UD in order to for the enhanced dependencies to be added in the next release in May 2018. The new line of research also handles the extension of the BTB valency lexicon with subatom-based embeddings for English. The aim is to check automatically how good they are for detecting the core participants in an event. Since there are not enough resources for Bulgarian, we rely on transferring the embeddings trained on English data but enhanced with mappings to the Bulgarian WordNet and evaluated over BTB as gold standard.

1 Introduction

The original BulTreeBank (BTB) is an HPSG-based treebank including constituent annotation that reflects the HPSG hierarchy of phrases, annotation of the head constituent in each phrase, coreference annotation, named entities, ellipsis and discontinuous elements. Later on, the annotated sentences have been transferred into two different dependency formats: (1) CoNLL 2006 format where we used our own list of dependency relations and (2) Universal Dependency (UD) format where we focused rather on universal mappings of our data than on the language specific relations. As a follow-up, all newly annotated sentences adhere directly to the UD format. In addition to the mainly syntactic information, in the last few years we annotated the treebank with senses from the BulTreeBank Bulgarian WordNet (BTB-WN), aligned to Princeton WordNet (Osenova and Simov, 2017), and with valency frames (Osenova et al., 2012).

On the basis of the available rich linguistic information within the original HPSG-based treebank as well as the semantic annotation and valency frames information, new extensions were performed in two directions: (1) transferring linguistic information from the HPSG-based annotation to the UD format with the goal to facilitate the addition of the so-called *enhanced dependencies*; and (2) assigning sense embeddings to valency slots in the valency lexicon for supporting better feature representations that are learned from huge corpora. In this paper we discuss these two developments as well as the preliminary results from them.

The paper is structured as follows: next section presents related works. Section 3 describes the strategies behind the transfer of the linguistic information from the original treebank to the UD one. Section 4 focuses on the syntactic roles transfer from English to Bulgarian with the help of word embeddings. Section 5 concludes the paper.

2 Related Work

Many treebanks in Universal Dependencies (UD) initiative have been converted from already existing ones that were not necessarily dependency-based. This is also the case of BulTreeBank. Thus, initially the main focus was put on the mapping and proper transfer of parts-of-speech, grammatical and syntactic information from the existing annotation scheme into the UD one. As described in (Osenova and Simov,

Proceedings of the 16th International Workshop on Treebanks and Linguistic Theories (TLT16), pages 129–137,
Prague, Czech Republic, January 23–24, 2018. Distributed under a CC-BY 4.0 licence. 2017.

Keywords: enhanced dependencies, grammatical role embeddings, transfer between languages

2015) this transfer was performed by rules of two kinds: (1) lexical head identifier moving up the constituent tree; and (2) relation assignment for a constituent node of the dependent child when all children of the parent node have lexical identifiers. The example, given in that paper, was as follows: Let us have the following constituent, whose lexicalized example might be this one: tvarde visok zelen stol 'too tall green chair' [NPA [APA too tall] [NPA green chair]].

```
NPA -> APAid1 NPAid2
```

where id1 is a lexical head identifier for the adjectival phrase APA and id2 is a lexical head identifier for the noun phrase NPA. Then we establish the relation `amod` from `NPAid2` to `APAid1` and the identifier for the child NPA is moved up, because the lexical head of the child NPA is the lexical head for the whole phrase. After the application of these two rules we have the constituent tree annotated with lexical identifiers and dependency relations in this way:

```
NPAid2 -> APAid1 amod NPAid2.
```

However, it became clear that richer annotation in treebanks is needed to capture syntax-semantics-pragmatics interfaces. It should be noted that there already exist a number of semantically and discourse annotated treebanks (for example Prague Dependency Treebank annotated on discourse level — (Zikánová et al., 2015) and Italian Syntactic-Semantic Treebank (Montemagni et al., 2003), among others). However, they are not so many considering the multilinguality dimensions. At the same time, the NLP applications started to require the availability of richer cross-level linguistic knowledge.

Hence, the idea of the enhanced dependencies reflects exactly the linguistic multilevel interfaces (syntax, semantics, discourse). More precisely, it aims "to make implicit relations between content words more explicit by adding relations and augmenting relation names." (Schuster and Manning, 2016). They build on the basic dependencies and include the following phenomena:[1]

- *Null nodes for elided predicates.* This dependency involves the addition of special null nodes in clauses with an elided predicate. An example is: 'I go to Varna, and you [NULL NODE] to Sofia'. With this ellipsis recovery the grammatical relations are maintained also in the clause without an explicit predicate.

- *Propagation of conjuncts.* Apart from attaching the governor and dependents of a conjoined phrase to the first conjunct, dependencies are established between the other conjuncts and the governor, and dependents of the phrase. An example of conjoined subjects is: [The boy and the girl] are walking.

- *Additional subject relations for control and raising constructions.* In the enhanced dependency there is a relation between the embedded verb and the subject of the matrix clause. An example is: *She* intends to *go*. Between 'she' and 'go' there is a relation.

- *Arguments of passives (and other valency-changing constructions).* Here the enhanced dependency assignes a type (passive or agent) to the subject or a complement in a passive sentence. An example is: The vase was broken by the child, where 'vase' is a nominal subject of type *passive*, and 'child' is an oblique of type *agent*.

- *Coreference in relative clause constructions.* The enhances dependencies add a relation between the relative pronoun and its antecedent as well as between this antecedent and the predicate in the relative clause. An example is: The man who came ran away quickly. 'Who' refers to 'man'. Also. between 'man' and 'came'.

- *Modifier labels that contain the preposition or other case-marking information.* This means that some modifier relations, such as nominal and adverbial modification, etc., reflect also the preposition involved either as a case or the preposition itself. An example is: He put the book on the table, where the relation between 'book' and 'table' is oblique and copies also 'on' in the relation label.

---

[1]http://universaldependencies.org/v2/enhanced.html and http://universaldependencies.org/u/overview/enhanced-syntax.html

Since BTB has been originally annotated with information additional to the grammatical functions on the syntactic level, its annotation can be transferred also into the UD enhanced dependencies. It should be noted, however, that some of these relations have been annotated explicitly in the original treebank, while others stayed implicit, but they might be derived when necessary from the present annotations. Such a case are the arguments of passive predicates. Subjects and obliques are not explicitly marked as passive/agent, but in some cases this information can be derived automatically on the base of the predicate form. Needless to say, not all mappings are straightforward and trivial.

The assignment of sense embeddings to valency slots in the valency lexicon follows our previous work on grammatical role embeddings for English — (Simov et al., 2018). In this work we used two corpora: real text corpora (RTC) and pseudo corpus generated over WordNet (PCWN). The RTC was annotated with POS tags and parsed with Stanford CoreNLP pipeline — (Manning et al., 2014). Then on the basis of syntactic information we substituted the subject, direct object and indirect object lemmas with pseudo words representing the corresponding grammatical roles for the corresponding verb. Then we mixed the RTC with PCWN in order to train sense embeddings for the senses represented in the joint corpus in the same vector space. This allowed us to compare the embeddings for the grammatical roles with the embeddings for noun senses. This approach proved to be successful for English and we evaluated it via an extension of the Princeton WordNet with new syntagmatic relations between synsets which improved the results for Knowledge-based Word Sense Disambiguation — (Simov et al., 2018).

A similar application of the same approach to Bulgarian is justified by the fact that the BTB Bulgarian WordNet (BTB-WN) does not have good coverage on Bulgarian texts — (Osenova and Simov, 2017). Thus, we exploited the mapping from BTB-WN to Princeton English WordNet (PWN) — (Fellbaum, 1998) — in order to transfer the grammatical role embeddings trained for English to Bulgarian and to assign them to valency slots in the Bulgarian valency lexicon. We consider these tasks as part of a bigger task of transferring lexical semantic relations from the English WordNet to the Bulgarian one, but we will not report on this issue here. We performed the training of sense embeddings and grammatical role embedding in a similar way as for English, but first we extended the English WordNet with Bulgarian Synsets that lack the same meanings among the English Synsets. Then we generated a pseudo corpus using the UKB system[2] for knowledge-based word sense disambiguation. The sense embeddings were trained again over a joint corpus real texts and pseudo corpus.

Our work seems similar to the work of (Vulić et al., 2017). In their paper they consider three research questions: (**Q1**) Given their fundamental dependence on the distributional hypothesis, to what extent can unsupervised methods for inducing vector spaces facilitate the automatic induction of VerbNet-style verb classes across different languages? (**Q2**) Can one boost verb classification for lower-resource languages by exploiting general-purpose cross-lingual resources to construct better word vector spaces for these languages? (**Q3**) Based on the stipulated cross-linguistic validity of VerbNet-style classification, can one exploit rich sets of readily available annotations in one language (e.g., the full English VerbNet) to automatically bootstrap the creation of VerbNets for other languages? Our work differs from theirs in the fact that in our case the valency lexicon already existed before the experiment. In this respect more relevant to us are Q2 and Q3 with the modification that our goal is not to construct a VerbNet-like-lexicon for Bulgarian, but to perform a sense-embeddings-transfer from English to Bulgarian. in this way we use the larger availability of data in one language to address the contexts of sentence participants in a language with less data availability. However, in future it will be interesting to apply the approach, decsribed in (Vulić et al., 2017), to our resources in order to transfer additional knowledge from VerbNet to our valency lexicon.

3   The BulTreeBank Annotation Scheme with regard to the enhanced dependencies

BulTreeBank in its original format is HPSG-based and it consists of 15 000 sentences (or 214 000 tokens). More information on the annotation strategies can be found in the BulTreeBank Stylebook.[3]

---

[2]`http://ixa2.si.ehu.es/ukb/`
[3]http://bultreebank.org/wp-content/uploads/2017/04/BTB-TR05.pdf

3.1 Glances at the BTB annotation scheme

The original BTB annotation scheme is constituency-based with indication of head-dependency relations. In spite of the fact that XML was used as a main encoding format, additional graph-forming relations had been also assigned. These include several semantics and discourse-oriented (named entities, intrasentential coreferences, ellipsis, etc.) phenomena. To start with, subject and object control were annotated when one or both elements are pro-drop. This relation was introduced by a co-indexation mechanism that binds the overt subject and the pro-ss element (as in Fig. 1, left part) or two (more) pro-drop elements. For example, the instances of elided subjects (marked as *pro-ss*) always being part a co-referential chain within a sentence, are 6953.

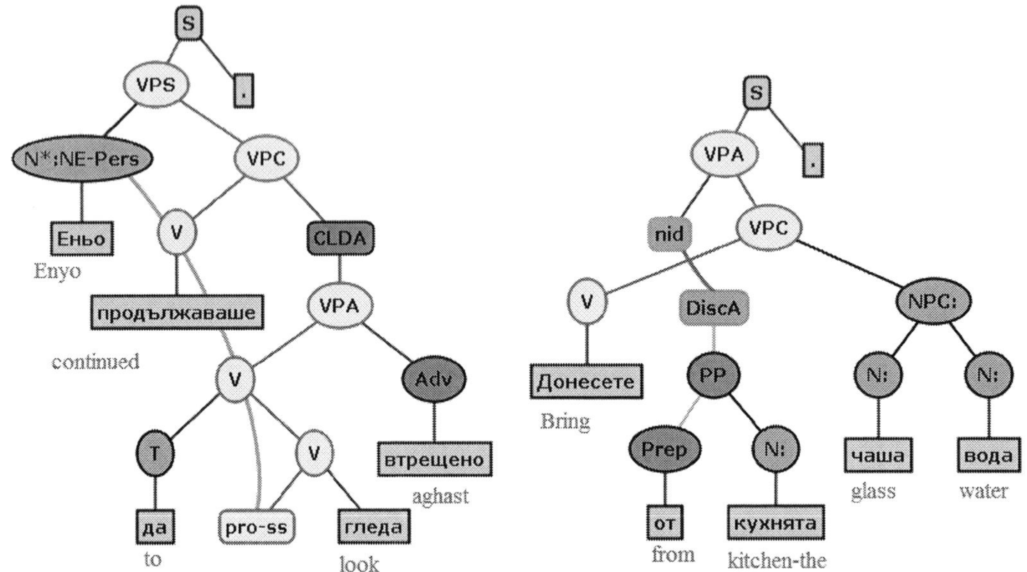

Figure 1: **Left:** Enyo [1] continued to [1] look aghast (Enyo kept looking aghast.) **Right:** Bring from kitchen-the glass water (Bring me from the kitchen a glass of water)

Another relation is the discontinuity one, introduced through three more specific relations: *DiscA*, *DiscM* and *DiscE*. The first one reflects scrambling. The second one — the so-called mixing arguments,[4] and the third one — topicalization. The most frequent type is scrambling *DiscA* (2447 instances), then comes topicalization *DiscE* (932 instances) and the rarest one, as expected, is *DiscM* (8 instances). See Fig. 1, right part, for an example of scrambling.

Further, ellipsis was added as well. It was marked on two levels: syntactic (V-Elip) and discourse (VD-Elip). The syntactic one has 262 instances in the treebank. It marks one verb form that is recoverable from the nearest context. It has subtypes only for marking equality of the missing element, its opposite or a different grammatical form. The discourse one has 255 instances. This type marks not only verb forms that are recoverable in a bigger context or even with the help of our common world knowledge. The subtypes represent existential verbs (to be, there is) with 120 instances, possessive verbs with 10 instances and a discourse element with 35 instances. It also marks whole VPs with a head and a complement. It can be seen that both types are almost equally represented. See Figure 2 for an example of syntactic ellipsis.

---

[4]By mixing arguments we mean a situation in which two constituents swap their elements. It can be found mainly in folklore and colloquial speech. For example: *Malki* **go** *momi beryaha* 'Little it-ACC girls picking-were' instead of *Malki momi* **go** *beryaha* 'Little girls were picking it'. The accusative clicic comes between the adjective and the head noun in the NP, while belonging to the VP and thus causing an extraction-like process in this VP.

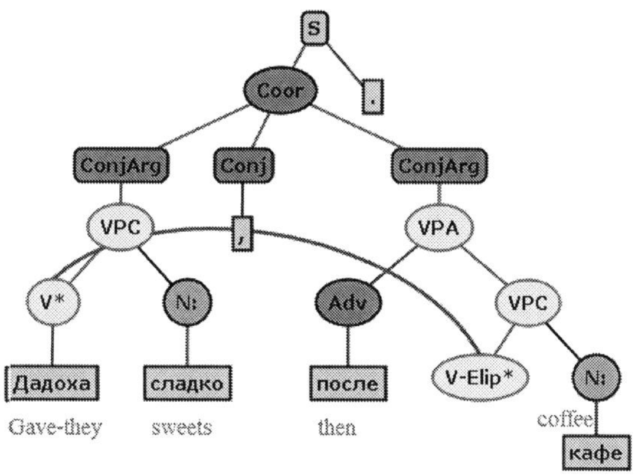

Figure 2: Gave-they sweets, then coffee (They gave sweets and then - coffee)

3.2 Towards enhanced dependencies

In this section the UD enhanced dependencies are considered with regard to the transfer procedure.

As it was mentioned above, there are two ways of transferring the information: implicit one in which the needed information is derived from the the linguistic annotation below the syntactic one, and explicit one in which the information can be directly processed through the represented syntactic nodes.

Similarly to our strategy for transferring basic graph information from the original BTB to the UD one, the same two types of rules are used, as described above: assigning a syntactic label to all nodes and then assigning appropriate relations among them.

Null nodes for elided predicates. In BTB such predicates are introduced as V-Elip or VD-Elip. Thus, both labels can be mapped directly into the so-called null nodes. V-Elip is the more straightforward one, while VD-Elip considers also cases of VP-ellipsis and copula ellipsis. While the latter is more systematic, the former varies in the length of the involved recovered material, such as different parts of a verb form or a head verb with a complement, etc. Apart from that VD-Elip provides discourse labels with the meaning that it is difficult to identify the type (let alone the form) of the missing element(s). These difficult cases can be processed only manually.

Propagation of conjuncts. Here we have to rely on the implicit but straightforward information, since in UD each dependant in a coordinated phrase has to be attached to its head (subject, object, modifier). In BTB the coordination phrases are considered head-less and thus - flat. However, the overall approach with respect to the treatment of conjuntcs is similar to the UD ideology. For example, two modifiers that modify the same head are coordinated as [**NP** [**CoordP** flat-the and lonely] voice]. Thus *amod* relations can be established on the base of the morphosyntactic and lexical information coming from the elements of the coordination phrase. The same holds for the core/non-core arguments. For example, the coordinated subjects can be assigned the *nsubj* relation per each subject with respect to the predicate.

Additional subject relations for control and raising constructions. In BTB the subject connects to the predicate in the main clause (i.e. the controller). Then the controller is connected with the unexpressed subject of the embedded verb. Thus, the *nsubj* relation between the subject of the main verb and the embedded verb can be established rather easily. Just the *pro-ss* element has to be substituted with *nsubj* and to be moved on the verb itself (see Fig. 1, left part, for the original tree).

Arguments of passives (and other valency-changing constructions). In BTB there are no special markings of these arguments. Some of them can be derived automatically (such as the participle passive due to its special morphological form), and some of them are not trivial, such as the se-passives (being formed with the originally reflexive accusative clitic 'se' attached to the tensed verb form), since they are ambiguous across types of voice as well as markers of intransitive/detranzivised verbs. In the present UD version these labels are already available.

Coreference in relative clause constructions. The representation in BTB is similar to the representation in the basic UD graph where the relative is connected to the predicate with a grammatical relation. Thus, the *ref* relation with its antecedent can be established automatically.

Modifier labels that contain the preposition or other case-marking information. Since Bulgarian is analytic language, the non-core or nominal dependants (nmod, obl, acl and advcl) would have labels with propagated prepositions. This step can be done automatically.

Thus, it seems that the necessary information for the preliminary list of enhanced dependencies can be covered in BTB-UD almost in a straightforward way, since this kind of information has been already encoded in the original treebank. The main problems would go to some types of ellipsis and some non-typical coordinations.

In our case the only fully non-covered phenomenon were the arguments of passives, but they were (semi)automatically added where needed. Some difficulties in the transfer are expected in the following directions: (a) lack of enough instruction documentation in UD on some very complex examples and interrelated phenomena, such as ellipsis and coordination, (b) attempts to expand the treebank automatically and (c) some errors or problematic cases in the original treebank.

4   Syntactic Role Embeddings over the BTB Valency Lexicon

In our view word embeddings have to reflect the relational structure of the corresponding word. Thus, for a verb having a subject, a direct object and an indirect object we expect that its word embedding will be formed by four parts: embedding for the whole verb reflecting the semantics of the event denoted by the verb; then embeddings for the subject, direct and indirect objects. Such embeddings have to represent the selectional restrictions for the corresponding grammatical roles. There are many possible applications of such embeddings such as in the coreference resolution task where embeddings for the used pronouns are provided, also in word sense disambiguation, parsing, etc.

Here we report on the first experiments for learning such vector representations for the verb valency slots in Bulgarian valency lexicon, that correspond to subject, direct objects and indirect objects of verbs. We perform this through a knowledge transfer from English-to-Bulgarian with the help of the WordNet alignments. Our long-term goal is to train such embeddings for all lexical items with a relational structure including adjectives, adverbs, nouns (plus relational nouns), etc. We call such embeddings *subatom embeddings* because they contain features only on some aspects of a given event (or state).

The training of such embeddings for Bulgarian is not so easy because of the lack of sufficient language resources especially with respect to the coverage of BTB-WN. Thus we decided to exploit the available resources and their alignment to English in order to transfer these sense embeddings back to Bulgarian. Hence, we reused most of the work that has been already done for English — (Simov et al., 2018). In this work we learned subatom semantic embeddings on the basis of dependency-parsed corpora. We determined the arguments as wordforms in the text. As an example, let us consider the following sentence:

```
Every dog chases some white cat.
```

The generalization over the various word forms (or lemmas) in the different examples in the corpus has been performed by substituting the word forms for the corresponding argument with a pseudoword form. For example, for the above sentence the following variations have been generated with pseudoword forms for the different arguments of the different predicates:

```
Every SUBJ_chase chases some white cat.
Every dog chases some white DOBJ_chase.
```

Having learned embeddings for these pseudowords, we assume that they represent the selectional features for the corresponding grammatical roles of the verbs.

The corpus for training the embeddings reported in the paper consists of two parts: (1) real text corpora (RTC); and (2) pseudo corpus generated over WordNet (PCWN). RTC is used to represent relevant contexts for learning embeddings of pseudo words for subjects, direct objects and indirect objects. PCWN is used to ensure that the embeddings represent features extracted from the knowledge within the WordNet and also the coverage is extended to all synsets in WordNet.

As RTC we have used WaCkypedia_EN corpus — (Baroni et al., 2009). The WaCkypedia_EN corpus was reparsed with a more recent version of the Stanford CoreNLP dependency parser. The dependency of type "collapsed-cc" was selected, which collapses several dependency relations in order to obtain direct dependencies between content words, and in addition propagates dependencies involving conjuncts. For instance, a parse of the sentence "the dog runs and barks" would result in the relations nsubj(dog, runs) and nsubj(dog, barks). This type of dependency allows for a token to have multiple head words.

The head word of each nominal subject, as well as direct and indirect object, is then replaced by its predicate role and its governing verb's lemma (SUBJ_run, SUBJ_bark — both for the noun 'dog'). When a token has more than one head word suitable for substitution, copies of the sentence are created for each alternative replacement.

For the relation `has-subj` we use the dependency relations 'nsubj' and 'nsubjpass'; for the relation `has-dobj` we use the dependency relation 'dobj'; and for the relation `has-iobj` we use the dependency relation 'iobj'. In order to minimize some errors we enforced a condition that the dependency word should be a noun.

Here is a real example from RTC that was processed:

```
few high-quality SUBJ_address address long-term DOBJ_address
```

In the example both subject and direct object are substituted with pseudo words. All of the word forms are substituted with lemmas because our goal is getting sense embeddings.

The PCWN consists of pseudo texts that are the output from the Random Walk algorithm, when it is set to the mode of selecting sequences of nodes from a knowledge graph (KG) — see (Goikoetxea et al., 2015) for generation of pseudo corpora from a WordNet knowledge graph and (Ristoski and Paulheim, 2016) for generation of pseudo corpora from RDF knowledge graphs such as DBPedia, GeoNames, FreeBase. Here we report results only for knowledge graphs based on WordNet and its extensions. The pseudo corpus is generated using the UKB system[5] for knowledge-based word sense disambiguation.

Here is an example of a pseudo sentence from PCWN:

```
unfit function use undertake disposal
```

The pseudo sentences in PCWN represent sequences of related words on the basis of relations within WordNet. Such pseudo corpora provide good basis for learning lemma embeddings — see (Goikoetxea et al., 2015) and (Simov et al., 2017).

The union of both corpora is used in the experiments. As said before, in RTC all the words were substituted with their lemmas. Punctuation marks and numbers were deleted. We used the Word2Vec tool[6] in order to train the embeddings. From the various models we selected the one with the best score on the similarity task. This model was trained with the following settings: context window of 5 words; 7 iterations; negative examples set to 5; and frequency cut sampling set to 7. This approach worked for English and we used it to extend Princeton WordNet which improved the results for Knowledge-based Word Sense Disambiguation — (Simov et al., 2018). As it was described already, the resulting embeddings are related to lemmas, but not to senses, which is actually our goal. In order to have sense embeddings we performed some additional processing. Thus, for each synset, we obtained its vector by averaging the vectors for all lemmas it can be expressed by (this information is retrieved from WordNet). For grammatical roles, we averaged the corresponding grammatical role vectors per each lemma in the particular verb synset.

For the transfer from English to Bulgarian we extended the corpus of English senses with Bulgarian senses. In the BTB-WN an alignment to the Princeton WordNet has been maintained. We have supported three main relations of mapping Bulgarian-to-English synsets: *equality*, *subsumption*, and *generalization*. Here are some examples: vertolet = helicopter; chicho[7] is-subsumed-by uncle; mafia[8] generalized-over Cosa Nostra and Sicilian Mafia. A new PCWN was generated using this extended knowledge graph. The new corpus includes enough examples of Bulgarian synsets. The sense embeddings were trained over

---

[5] `http://ixa2.si.ehu.es/ukb/`
[6] https://code.google.com/archive/p/word2vec/
[7] Brother of the father.
[8] Organized crime group using the mechanisms of power.

the new PCWN and the RTC from English WikiPedia. Here we assume that the new trained embeddings represent well enough the Bulgarian senses.

The evaluation of the approach was done over the sense annotation of BulTreeBank. From it we extracted 285 instances of the subject–verb relation (subj(NounSynset, VerbSynset)), 207 instances of the direct object–verb relation (dobj(NounSynset, VerbSynset)), and 98 instances of the indirect object–verb relation where VerbSynset is presented in the training corpus and also there are embeddings for the related grammatical roles. Thus we were able to calculate the cosine similarity between the NounSynset embedding vector and the embedding vector for the corresponding grammatical role. If there is an instance of the relation subj(NounSynset, VerbSynset) we calculated the cosine similarity between the embedding for NounSynset and the embedding for SUBJ_VerbSynset. The results from this evaluation are presented in Table 1. The threshold for a good relation is set to 0.40. This value was selected by empirical evaluation on the impact of adding new syntagmatic relations to WordNet. The results showed that the embeddings selected the correct relations: in one third of the Subject–Verb cases, almost half of the Direct Object–Verb cases and one third of the Indirect Object–Verb cases.

Grammatical Relation	Minimum	Maximum	Mean	Number over 0.40
Subject–Verb	0.2304	0.7463	0.3798	91
Direct Object–Verb	0.2387	0.5924	0.3947	96
Indirect Object–Verb	0.2199	0.5202	0.3698	28

Table 1: Evaluations for Grammatical Roles Embeddings.

Although the results are not very impressive we believe that they show the utility of aligning the slots of the frames in a valency lexicon with embeddings that generalize over the concrete words in real texts. In our future work we plan to extend the BTB-WordNet in order to create such embeddings directly from Bulgarian resources. The proposed evaluation approach needs to be made more precise with respect to the quality of the embeddings. We also plan to incorporate these embeddings in some mainstream NLP applications like parsing, coreference resolution and word sense disambiguation.

5 Conclusions

The paper presented two recent developments in BTB. The first one is the preparation work for transferring the knowledge from the original BTB in order to add enhanced dependencies into BTB-UD for the next release in May 2018. Our expectation is that the transfer will be done relatively smoothly, since the linguistic information in the original treebank covers the list of proposed UD enhanced dependencies.

The second one is the extension of the BTB valency lexicon with subatom-based embeddings for English with the aim to check automatically how good they are for detecting the core participants in an event. Due to the scarce Bulgarian resources for this task, we relied on transferring the embeddings trained on English data but enhanced with mappings to the Bulgarian WordNet. The evaluation was performed against BTB as gold standard. Our preliminary results showed the feasibility of the approach. There are many directions of future work, such as: better transfer from English to Bulgarian, exploiting of more Bulgarian resources, using approaches like retrofitting with respect to human created resources for tuning the initially assigned embeddings.

Acknowledgements

This research has received partial support by the grant 02/12 — *Deep Models of Semantic Knowledge (DemoSem)*, funded by the Bulgarian National Science Fund in 2017–2019. We are grateful to the anonymous reviewers for their remarks, comments, and suggestions. All errors remain our own responsibility.

References

Marco Baroni, Silvia Bernardini, Adriano Ferraresi, and Eros Zanchetta. 2009. The WaCky wide web: a collection of very large linguistically processed web-crawled corpora. *Language Resources and Evaluation* 43(3):209–226.

Christiane Fellbaum. 1998. *WordNet: An Electronic Lexical Database*. MIT Press.

Josu Goikoetxea, Aitor Soroa, and Eneko Agirre. 2015. Random walks and neural network language models on knowledge bases. In *Proceedings of the 2015 Conference of the North American Chapter of the Association for Computational Linguistics: Human Language Technologies*. Association for Computational Linguistics, Denver, Colorado, pages 1434–1439. http://www.aclweb.org/anthology/N15-1165.

Christopher D. Manning, Mihai Surdeanu, John Bauer, Jenny Finkel, Steven J. Bethard, and David McClosky. 2014. The Stanford CoreNLP natural language processing toolkit. In *Association for Computational Linguistics (ACL) System Demonstrations*. pages 55–60. http://www.aclweb.org/anthology/P/P14/P14-5010.

Simonetta Montemagni, Francesco Barsotti, Marco Battista, Nicoletta Calzolari, Ornella Corazzari, Alessandro Lenci, Antonio Zampolli, Francesca Fanciulli, Maria Massetani, Remo Raffaelli, Roberto Basili, Maria Teresa Pazienza, Dario Saracino, Fabio Zanzotto, Nadia Mana, Fabio Pianesi, and Rodolfo Delmonte. 2003. *Building the Italian Syntactic-Semantic Treebank*, Springer Netherlands, Dordrecht, pages 189–210.

Petya Osenova and Kiril Simov. 2015. Universalizing bultreebank: a linguistic tale about glocalization. In *The 5th Workshop on Balto-Slavic Natural Language Processing*. INCOMA Ltd. Shoumen, BULGARIA, Hissar, Bulgaria, pages 81–89. http://www.aclweb.org/anthology/W15-5313.

Petya Osenova and Kiril Simov. 2017. Challenges behind the Data-driven Bulgarian Wordnet (Bultreebank Bulgarian Wordnet). In *John P. McCrae, Francis Bond, Paul Buitelaar, Philipp Cimiano, Thierry Declerck, Jorge Gracia, Ilan Kernerman, Elena Montiel Ponsoda, Noam Ordan and Maciej Piasecki (eds): Proceedings of the LDK 2017 Workshops*. pages 152–163.

Petya Osenova, Kiril Simov, Laska Laskova, and Stanislava Kancheva. 2012. A treebank-driven creation of an ontovalence verb lexicon for bulgarian. In Nicoletta Calzolari (Conference Chair), Khalid Choukri, Thierry Declerck, Mehmet UÄŞur DoÄŞan, Bente Maegaard, Joseph Mariani, Asuncion Moreno, Jan Odijk, and Stelios Piperidis, editors, *Proceedings of the Eight International Conference on Language Resources and Evaluation (LREC'12)*. European Language Resources Association (ELRA), Istanbul, Turkey.

Petar Ristoski and Heiko Paulheim. 2016. *RDF2Vec: RDF Graph Embeddings for Data Mining*, Springer International Publishing, Cham, pages 498–514.

Sebastian Schuster and Christopher D. Manning. 2016. Enhanced english universal dependencies: An improved representation for natural language understanding tasks. In Nicoletta Calzolari (Conference Chair), Khalid Choukri, Thierry Declerck, Sara Goggi, Marko Grobelnik, Bente Maegaard, Joseph Mariani, Helene Mazo, Asuncion Moreno, Jan Odijk, and Stelios Piperidis, editors, *Proceedings of the Tenth International Conference on Language Resources and Evaluation (LREC 2016)*. European Language Resources Association (ELRA), Paris, France.

Kiril Simov, Petya Osenova, and Alexander Popov. 2017. *Comparison of Word Embeddings from Different Knowledge Graphs*, Springer International Publishing, Cham, pages 213–221.

Kiril Simov, Alexander Popov, Iliana Simova, and Petya Osenova. 2018. Grammatical Role Embeddings for Enhancements of Relation Density in the Princeton WordNet. In *Proceedings of the 9th Global Wordnet Conference*.

Ivan Vulić, Nikola Mrkšić, and Anna Korhonen. 2017. Cross-lingual induction and transfer of verb classes based on word vector space specialisation. In *Proceedings of the 2017 Conference on Empirical Methods in Natural Language Processing*. Association for Computational Linguistics, Copenhagen, Denmark, pages 2546–2558. https://www.aclweb.org/anthology/D17-1270.

Šárka Zikánová, Eva Hajičová, Barbora Hladká, Pavlína Jínová, Jiří Mírovský, Anna Nedoluzhko, Lucie Poláková, Kateřina Rysová, Magdaléna Rysová, and Jan Václ. 2015. *Discourse and Coherence. From the Sentence Structure to Relations in Text*. ÚFAL, Praha, Czechia.

Towards a dependency-annotated treebank for Bambara

Ekaterina Aplonova
School of Linguistics
ВШЭ
Moscow
aplooon@gmail.com

Francis M. Tyers
School of Linguistics
ВШЭ
Moscow
ftyers@hse.ru

Abstract

In this paper we describe a dependency annotation scheme for Bambara, a Mande language spoken in Mali, which has few computational linguistic resources. The scheme is based on Universal Dependencies. We describe part-of-speech tags, morphological features and dependencies and how we performed a rule-based conversion of an existing part-of-speech annotated corpus of Bambara, which contains approximately 900,000 tokens. We also describe the annotation of a small treebank of 116 sample sentences, which were picked randomly.

1 Introduction

One of the basic language resources has, for a long time, been a part-of-speech tagged (or morphologically disambiguated) corpus. In recent years, treebanks — collections of sentences annotated for syntactic structure — have become increasingly available and vital resources, both for natural-language processing and corpus linguistics. Current end-to-end pipelines like UDPipe (Straka et al., 2016), which perform each stage of the classic NLP pipeline from tokenisation to dependency parsing, make it easy to go from a situation where a language has no effective language resources to one where the language has a functional pipeline in a few months as opposed to a few years of work.

A crucial prerequisite for building a treebank is to have a set of annotation guidelines which describe how particular syntactic structures are to be represented. In our work on creating a treebank for Bambara we have chosen version 2.0 of the Universal Dependencies scheme (Nivre et al., 2016) as it provides ready-made recommendations on which to base annotation guidelines for part-of-speech tags, morphological features and dependency relations. This reduces the amount of time needed to develop bespoke annotation guidelines for a given language as where the existing *universal* guidelines[1] are adequate they can be imported wholesale into the language-specific guidelines. In addition, the Universal Dependencies project provides a free/open *pool* (in the terminology of Streiter et al. (2006)) which collects dependency corpora in a single place, allowing for economies of scale in maintenance and ensuring that resources can persist after any initial development effort.

The remainder of the paper is laid out as follows: In Section 2, we give a short typological overview of Bambara, in Section 3, we describe an existing annotated resource for Bambara, the *Corpus Bambara de Référence* (CBR). Section 4 describes the conversion process we used, Section 5 describes some constructions in Bambara, which are not typologically common, and how we intend to annotate them. Finally, Sections 6 and 7 describe future work and conclusions respectively.

2 Bambara

In the description of Bambara presented in this paper, we used as sources the Vydrin (2013) and Выдрин (2017).[2] Bambara is the most widely-spoken language of the Manding language group (Western Mande < Mande < Niger-Congo). It is spoken mainly in Mali by 13–14 million people; of these, around four

---

[1] http://universaldependencies.org/guidelines.html

[2] Abbreviations are as follows: PFV = perfective predicative marker; SG = singular; POSS = possessive postposition; ; AG.OCC = suffix, which denotes an occasional actor; PP = postposition; QUAL = special predicative marker for qualitative verbs; PRES

138

Proceedings of the 16th International Workshop on Treebanks and Linguistic Theories (TLT16), pages 138–145,
Prague, Czech Republic, January 23–24, 2018. Distributed under a CC-BY 4.0 licence. 2017.

Keywords: Bambara, Mande, treebank

Section	Sentences	Tokens
Unannotated	—	4,113,006
Disambiguated	—	903,585
Dependency annotated	116	1307

Table 1: Composition of the *Corpus Bambara de Référence* as of December, 2017

million are L1 speakers. There are two variants of naming this language: Bambara and Bamana, both of them are in use. Bambara is one of 13 "national languages" of Mali. Besides French, it is the major language on Malian radio and television, there are periodicals in Bambara, it is broadly used in literacy programmes and in primary schools; it is also taught at several universities in Europe and the US.

Bambara is a tonal language. It has two level tones and a down-drift. Tones can be lexical and grammatical, i.e. every lexeme has its lexical tone(s), which can change depending on the context into grammatical one(s). For instance, in the noun phrase *jíri fìn* 'black tree', the rule of tonal compactness is demonstrated when the recessive syllables take the tone of dominant ones. The lexical tone of *fìn* 'black' is low, however, in an attributive position, it takes the tone of its head *jíri* 'tree', whose tone is high. Moreover, in Bambara, there is a tonal definite article (indicated by a low floating tone). In the CBR it is not indicated. For this reason, in the present paper, we do not indicate it either. Tones are never marked in Bambara press and books published in Mali; tonal notation is present in publications of texts by linguists, however, even in the latter case it desperately lacks uniformity.

As described by Vydrin (2013), Bambara is an isolating language with certain elements of agglutination and incorporation. The basic word order is S AUX O V X. Therefore, in (1) *Fúla* is a subject, *ye* is an auxiliary, *á ká mìsi* is a direct object, *dí* is a verb, *í mà* is an oblique.

(1)

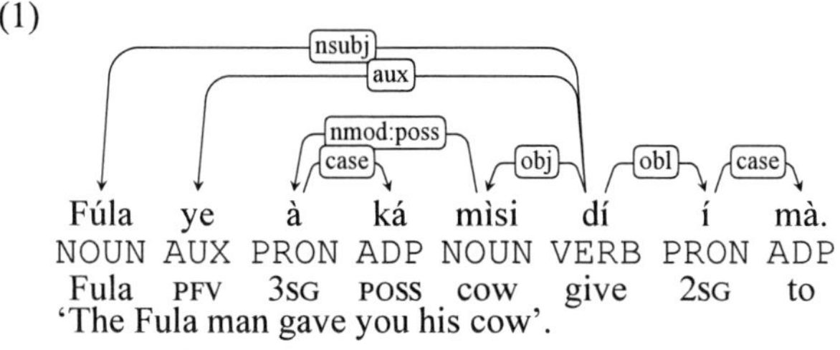

The word order is fixed, however it is possible to remove a topicalised NP in the beginning of the clause (see §5.5).

3   Corpus Bambara de Référence

Development of the Bambara Reference Corpus (usually known by its name in French, *Corpus Bambara de Référence*) was started in April 2012. It is composed of texts of different kinds e.g. periodicals, oral literature, manuals, religious publications, letters from newspaper readers, texts recorded and transcribed by researchers etc. Since the Bambara orthographic standard is relatively undeveloped, the corpus assumes different levels of orthographic normalisation. The corpus includes a non-disambiguated sub-corpus and a disambiguated one (see Table 1 for statistics about its composition). In the non-disambiguated sub-corpus, there is only Bambara texts without any annotation. Annotation in the disambiguated sub-corpus, consists of part-of-speech tags, glosses and a respective token in a normalized orthography (with tones). A user is able either to search the entire corpus or to limit their search to the disambiguated sub-corpus. Texts have been and continue to be disambiguated by volunteers using Daba (Maslinsky, 2014), a morphological analyser based on a language-independent framework dictionary and

---

= presentative copula; LOC = locative copula; EQU = equative copula; NEG = negative copula; IPFV = imperfective predicative marker; INF = infinitive predicative marker; QUOT = quotative 'copula'; PROH = prohibitive predicative marker; PL = plural; NP = noun phrase; REL = relative pronoun/determinative; PFV.NEG = negative perfective predicatve marker; DIN = suffix, which derives a dynamic verb from a qualitative verb.

A ye foli di jamanakuntigi ma ka da a ka hakili ɲuman kan.

A	ye	foli		di	jamanakuntigi			ma	ka	da	a	ka	hakili	ɲuman	kan	.
à	yé	fòli		dí	jàmanakuntigi			mà	kà	dá	à	ká	hákili	ɲùman	kàn	
pers	pm	n		v	n			pp	pm	v	pers	pp	n	adj	pp	
3SG	PFV.TR	salutation		donner	président			à	INF	poser	3SG	POSS	esprit	bon	sur	
		fò	li		jàmana	kùn	tìgi									
		v	mrph		n	n	n									
		saluer	NMLZ		pays	tête	maître									

Figure 1: Example of a disambiguated sentence. The output format is machine-readable HTML. A free translation of the sentence into English would be 'He greeted the president and swore that he has good thoughts'. The first line is the original text, the second line is the tokenised text, the third line are the lemmas, and the fourth line has the part-of-speech tags. The fifth line has a gloss following the Leipzig glossing rules. Subsequent lines give a morphemic breakdown and gloss.

a rule-based morphological analyser. Language-specific data used by the analyser consist of a dictionary and a list of rules for splitting words into morphemes. Its output consists of seven lines: sentence in the original orthography, separate tokens in the original orthography, separate tokens in normalised orthography, part of speech tags, separate morphemes and glosses (cf. Figure 1).

4 Data conversion

To convert the corpus we used a Python script which reads the HTML format of the CBR performed substitution of tags and wrote the output in CoNLL-U format. In order to generate the morphological features, it was necessary to look at both the glosses and the morphological breakdown of the words.

We were able to maintain the original tokenisation scheme for the sentences, with the exception of three auxiliaries, the affirmative progressive marker *bé kà*, the negative progressive marker *té kà*, and the emphatic perfective marker *yé kà*, which we treat as fixed units as it is not possible to give part-of-speech tags to the individual parts.[3]

Regarding the lemmas, we left them as in the original corpus, where they appear as word forms with the addition of tone marking. We do not treat compounding and derivation productively, so the lemma of the compound *jamanakuntigi* 'president' is not split into its component parts *jamana-kun-tigi* 'country-head-master'.

Part-of-speech tags were largely able to be converted deterministically using a simple translation table, however there was one tag, `conj` 'conjunction' which needed to be split into CCONJ 'co-ordinating conjunction' and SCONJ 'subordinating conjunction'. For this we made a list of lemmas for both types, and converted based on this.

In the original annotation scheme, some words were annotated with two part-of-speech tags. This was done in cases where a word could be annotated for part of speech differently according to syntactic context. For example, a word which could be a determiner or pronoun would receive the tag `dtm/prn` (determiner or pronoun). The majority of determinatives perform different syntactic functions, e.g. the same word can act as an argument or as an attribute. Another example would be the tag `conj/prep` (conjunction or preposition). Prepositions are closely connected to some subordinate conjunctions. There are only seven prepositions and each of them can also act as a subordinate conjunction. These lexemes are treated as preposition, if they introduce a NP. If they introduce a whole clause, they are treated as conjunctions. We manually resolved these ambiguities, annotating them with the appropriate universal tag according to context.

We used the following language-specific features for Bambara: `AdjType=Attr` was used for adjectives with the suffix -/man/ and `Valency=1` was used for intransitive verbs, while `Valency=2` was used for transitive verbs. The feature `AdjType=Attr` is also used in the Afrikaans treebank to mark attributive adjectives (in Afrikaans adjectives have separate attributive and predicative forms). The feature `Valency=1` has been proposed for use in the Ainu treebank (Senuma and Aizawa, 2017).

---

[3]A reviewer suggests that we could have these as separate tokens with the part of speech tag AUX for both parts and the dependency relation `fixed`. As this would allow us to maintain the same tokenisation as the original we are planning to implement this change.

In addition to converting the part-of-speech tags and morphological features a number of sentences were annotated for dependencies using the UD ANNOTATRIX annotation tool (Tyers et al., 2018) by a single annotator in discussion with various linguists while developing the guidelines.

5 Dependency scheme

In this section, we describe some of the features of Bambara, which are not typologically common, and how they are annotated. We use the original glosses (partly modified in order to make it clearer for readers, who are not familiar with Bambara) along with dependency relations from Universal Dependencies.

5.1 Qualitative verbs and adjectives

In Bambara, verbs are divided into two classes: dynamic verbs and qualitative verbs. Qualitative verbs have special predicative marker, glossed as *qual*. They cannot express tense, aspect, modality values (2a). Moreover, they cannot bear a direct object, but they can have adjuncts (2b). We annotated them as VERB.

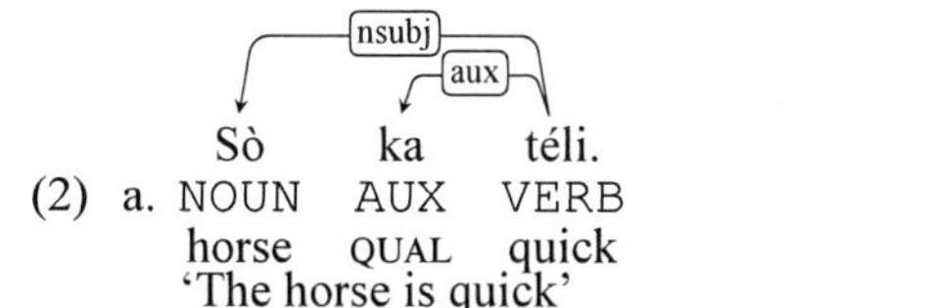
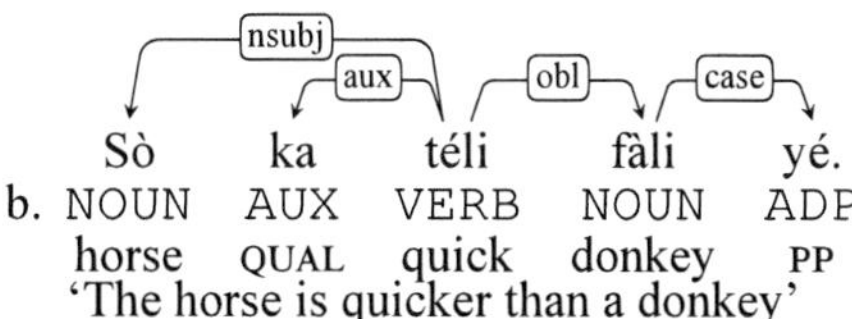

<table>
<tr><td></td><td></td><td>Sò</td><td>ka</td><td>téli.</td><td></td><td></td><td>Sò</td><td>ka</td><td>téli</td><td>fàli</td><td>yé.</td></tr>
<tr><td>(2)</td><td>a.</td><td>NOUN</td><td>AUX</td><td>VERB</td><td>b.</td><td></td><td>NOUN</td><td>AUX</td><td>VERB</td><td>NOUN</td><td>ADP</td></tr>
<tr><td></td><td></td><td>horse</td><td>QUAL</td><td>quick</td><td></td><td></td><td>horse</td><td>QUAL</td><td>quick</td><td>donkey</td><td>PP</td></tr>
<tr><td></td><td></td><td colspan="3">'The horse is quick'</td><td></td><td></td><td colspan="5">'The horse is quicker than a donkey'</td></tr>
</table>

In predicative position, adjectives can be used only as secondary predicates. In the main predicative position, there are only qualitative verbs.

A considerable number of adjectives are derived from qualitative verbs by adding a suffix -/man/: téli 'quick' → téliman. However, there are two other types of adjectives, which do not have a suffix -/man/. In the first type, there are adjectives derived from qualitative verbs by conversion: mɔ́gɔ fin 'black (adj) man (lit. 'black man')' → mɔ́gɔ ká fin 'a man is black (verb)'. In the second type, there are simple (non-derived) adjectives: *kúra* 'new', *gánsan* 'simple', *sὲbε* 'serious', *bὲlebele* 'fat, bai', *bánga* 'without sauce', etc.

5.2 Non-verbal predication

There are three main types of non-verbal predication: presentative (3a), locative (3b) and equative (3c).

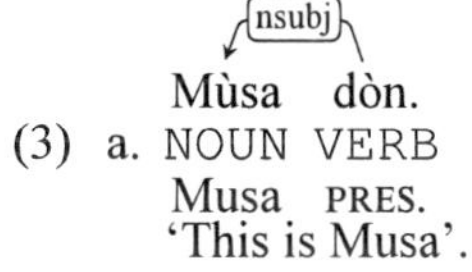
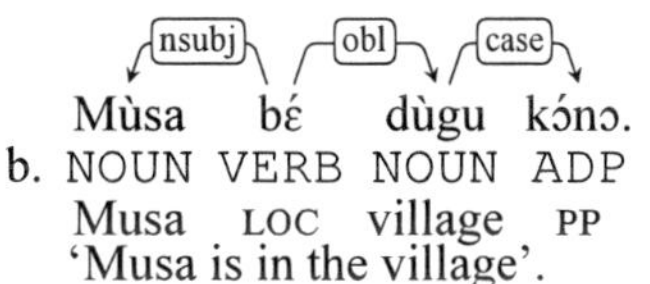
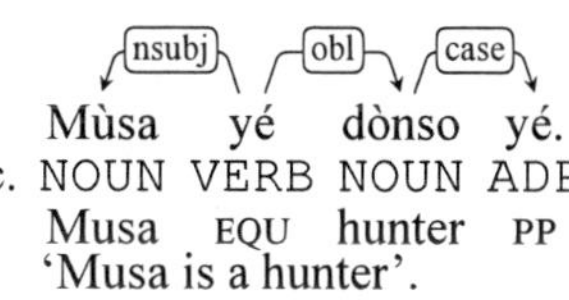

<table>
<tr><td></td><td></td><td>Mùsa</td><td>dòn.</td><td></td><td>Mùsa</td><td>bέ</td><td>dùgu</td><td>kɔ́nɔ.</td><td>Mùsa</td><td>yé</td><td>dònso</td><td>yé.</td></tr>
<tr><td>(3)</td><td>a.</td><td>NOUN</td><td>VERB</td><td>b.</td><td>NOUN</td><td>VERB</td><td>NOUN</td><td>ADP</td><td>c. NOUN</td><td>VERB</td><td>NOUN</td><td>ADP</td></tr>
<tr><td></td><td></td><td>Musa</td><td>PRES.</td><td></td><td>Musa</td><td>LOC</td><td>village</td><td>PP</td><td>Musa</td><td>EQU</td><td>hunter</td><td>PP</td></tr>
<tr><td></td><td></td><td colspan="2">'This is Musa'.</td><td></td><td colspan="4">'Musa is in the village'.</td><td colspan="4">'Musa is a hunter'.</td></tr>
</table>

We annotated all copulae as VERB. First of all, in presentative construction, the copula *dòn* is always the last element of a clause. We cannot postulate an ellipsis of a predicate, so this is the copula, which bears all predicative functions. Secondly, if we change an aspect in locative and equative constructions, the copula will be replaced by a verb *kέ* 'do' (4a, 4b).

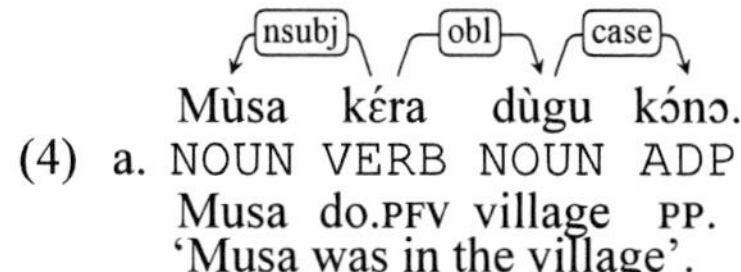
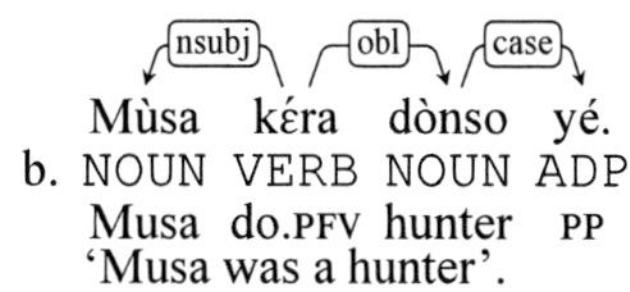

<table>
<tr><td></td><td></td><td>Mùsa</td><td>kéra</td><td>dùgu</td><td>kɔ́nɔ.</td><td></td><td>Mùsa</td><td>kéra</td><td>dònso</td><td>yé.</td></tr>
<tr><td>(4)</td><td>a.</td><td>NOUN</td><td>VERB</td><td>NOUN</td><td>ADP</td><td>b.</td><td>NOUN</td><td>VERB</td><td>NOUN</td><td>ADP</td></tr>
<tr><td></td><td></td><td>Musa</td><td>do.PFV</td><td>village</td><td>PP.</td><td></td><td>Musa</td><td>do.PFV</td><td>hunter</td><td>PP</td></tr>
<tr><td></td><td></td><td colspan="4">'Musa was in the village'.</td><td></td><td colspan="4">'Musa was a hunter'.</td></tr>
</table>

In negative clauses, in all these three types of predication, the negative copula *tέ* is used (5).

(5)

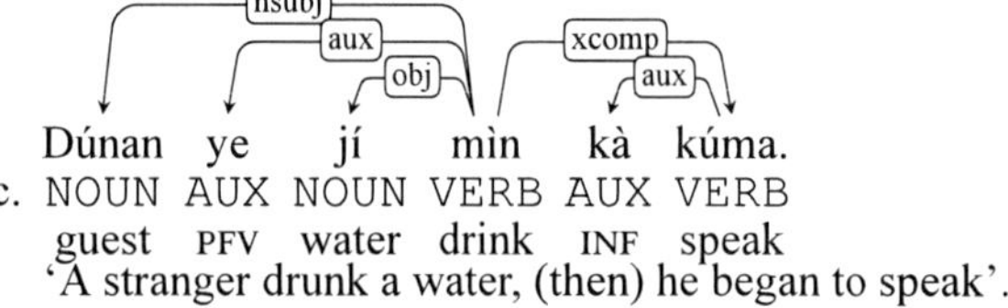

Mùsa   té   dònso   yé.
NOUN VERB NOUN ADP
Musa   EQU   hunter   PP
'Musa is not a hunter'

5.3   Infinitive marker

A verbal infinitive form is unmarked morphologically. It is introduced by a predicative marker *kà*. Verbs introduced by *kà* cannot bear their own subjects, but they can bear objects and obliques.

An infinitive construction can be an argument of the verb in the main clause (6a), its adjunct with the purpose meaning (6b) and it can express a sequential meaning (6c). We annotated *kà* as AUX.

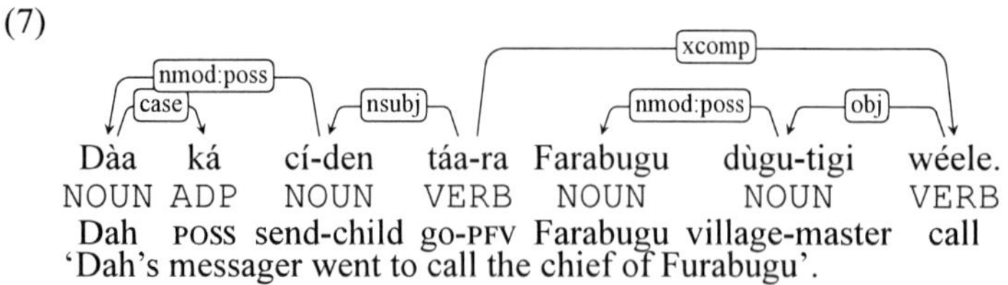

(6) a.

N̄   bɛ   sé   kà   móbili   bòli.
PRON AUX VERB AUX NOUN VERB
1SG   IPFV   arrive   INF   car   run
'I can drive'.

b.

U   ká   ɲɔ́gɔn   sɔ̀rɔ   kà   bɛ̀nkan   sɔ̀rɔ.
PRON AUX PART VERB AUX NOUN VERB
3PL   SUBJ together   find   INF   agreement   find
'They met together in order to find an agreement'.

c.

Dúnan   ye   jí   mìn   kà   kúma.
NOUN AUX NOUN VERB AUX VERB
guest   PFV   water   drink   INF   speak
'A stranger drunk a water, (then) he began to speak'.

Note that verbs of motion *táa* 'go' and *nà* 'come' take a verbal complement phrase without infinitive marker (7).

(7)

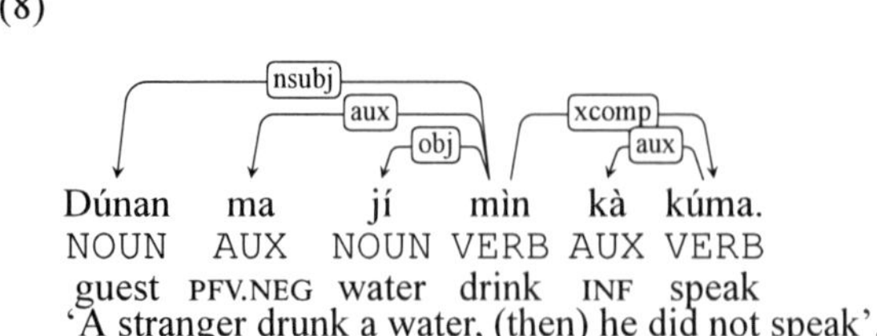

Dàa   ká   cí-den   táa-ra   Farabugu   dùgu-tigi   wéele.
NOUN ADP NOUN VERB NOUN NOUN VERB
Dah   POSS send-child   go-PFV   Farabugu   village-master   call
'Dah's messenger went to call the chief of Furabugu'.

The dependency relation is *xcomp*, because if a predicate of a main clause is negated, the subordinate clause is in the scope of negation (8).

(8)

Dúnan   ma   jí   mìn   kà   kúma.
NOUN   AUX   NOUN VERB AUX VERB
guest   PFV.NEG   water   drink   INF   speak
'A stranger drunk a water, (then) he did not speak'.

5.4 Quotative 'copula'

In CBR, *kó* is always annotated as a *quotative copula*, however, Выдрин (2017) mentions, that, perhaps, we could postulate several homonymous lexemes. In (9a), the word *kó* has its own subject and it introduces direct speech, but in (9b), it only introduces a subordinate clause.

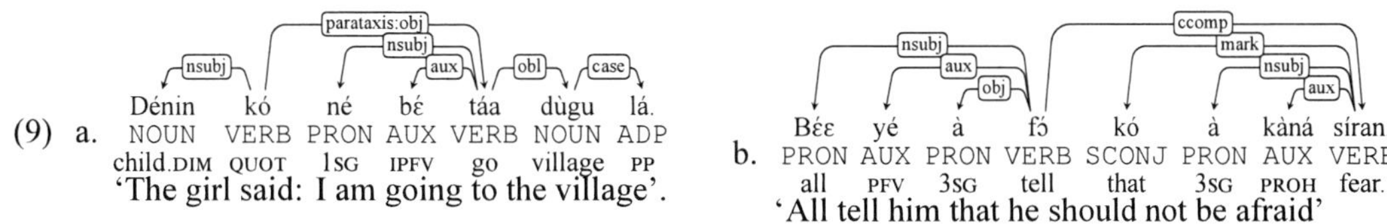

(9) a.
Dénin kó né bɛ́ táa dùgu lá.
NOUN VERB PRON AUX VERB NOUN ADP
child.DIM QUOT 1SG IPFV go village PP
'The girl said: I am going to the village'.

b.
Bɛ́ɛ yé à fɔ́ kó à kàná síran.
PRON AUX PRON VERB SCONJ PRON AUX VERB
all PFV 3SG tell that 3SG PROH fear.
'All tell him that he should not be afraid'

If *kó* has its own subject, we annotate it as VERB, unless it is annotated as SCONJ.

5.5 Topicalisation

Any NP can be placed in the beginning of the sentence and, thus, topicalised. A resumptive pronoun takes its place (10).

(10)

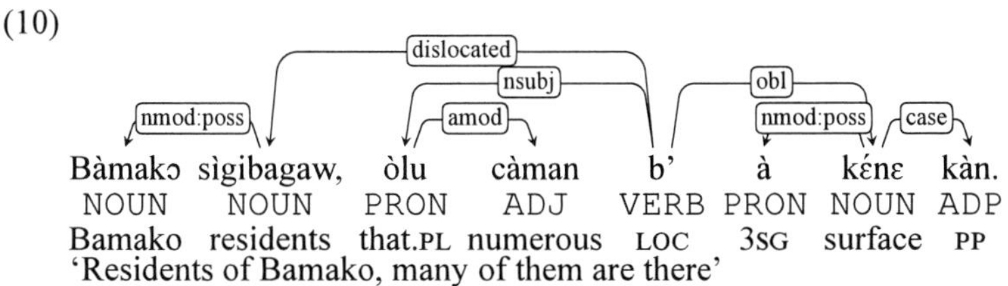

Bàmakɔ sìgibagaw, òlu càman b' à kɛ́nɛ kàn.
NOUN NOUN PRON ADJ VERB PRON NOUN ADP
Bamako residents that.PL numerous LOC 3SG surface PP
'Residents of Bamako, many of them are there'

This strategy is commonly used for introducing the subject of a main clause. We annotate the topicalised NP as dislocated and the resumptive pronoun gets the main function of the NP.

5.6 Adnominal clauses

Adnominal clauses include relative clauses and participle clauses. There are two main relativisation strategies. In the first strategy a dependent clause precedes the main clause (11), while in the second one a subordinate clause follows the main clause (12).

In the first strategy, the two clauses are combined into what, from a functional point of view, is a relativising construction: one of the clauses narrows the potential reference of a referring expression from the other clause.

(11)

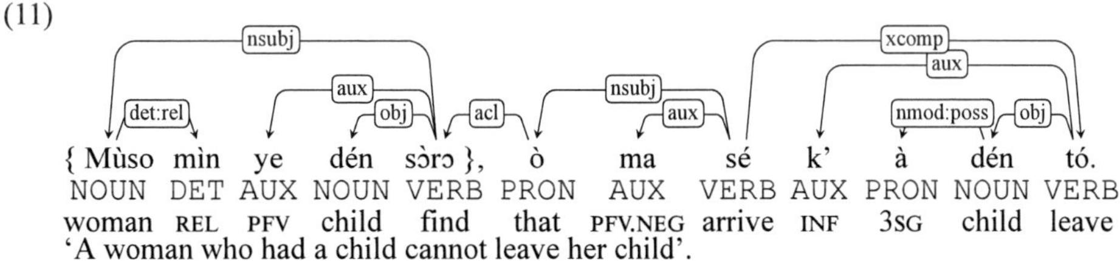

{ Mùso mìn ye dén sɔ̀rɔ }, ò ma sé k' à dén tó.
NOUN DET AUX NOUN VERB PRON AUX VERB AUX PRON NOUN VERB
woman REL PFV child find that PFV.NEG arrive INF 3SG child leave
'A woman who had a child cannot leave her child'.

In (11), a relativised noun is followed by a determinative *mìn* in the subordinative clause, while in the main clause there is a resumptive pronoun *ò*, which refers to this noun. As mentioned by Nikitina (2012), such a strategy does not fit into any of widely recognised relativisation strategies.

The second type (12) is more typologically common. It is a simple correlative strategy similar to European languages: a relativised noun in the main clause has a pronominal referent in the dependent clause.

(12)

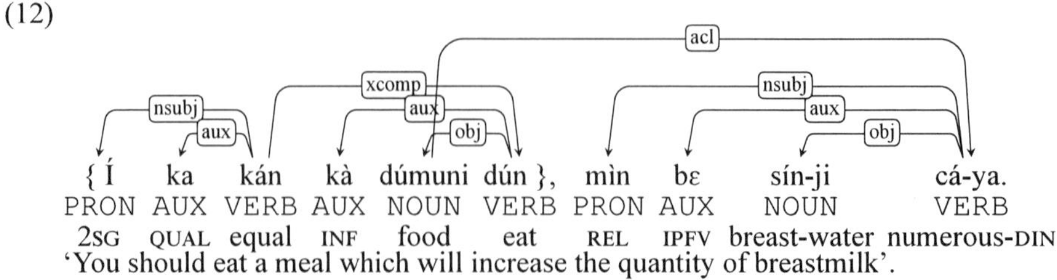

{ Í	ka	kán	kà	dúmuni	dún },	mìn	bɛ	sín-ji	cá-ya.
PRON	AUX	VERB	AUX	NOUN	VERB	PRON	AUX	NOUN	VERB
2SG	QUAL	equal	INF	food	eat	REL	IPFV	breast-water	numerous-DIN

'You should eat a meal which will increase the quantity of breastmilk'.

There are also adnominal clauses which are not relative clauses (they are not marked with a relativiser). This goes for the participle forms -/len/, -/ta/, -/bali/ and for the converb -/tɔ/ (13).

(13)

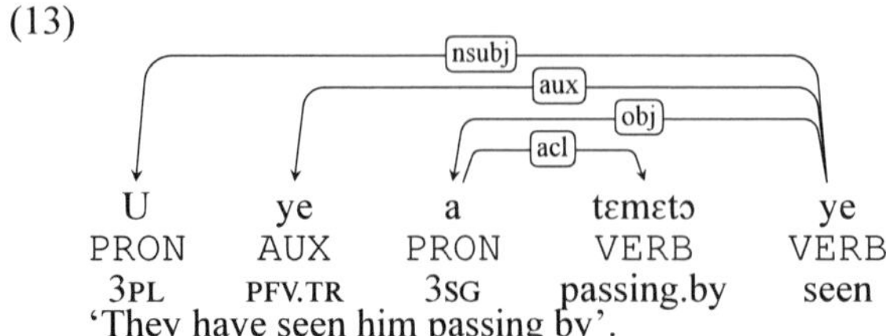

U	ye	a	tɛmɛtɔ	ye
PRON	AUX	PRON	VERB	VERB
3PL	PFV.TR	3SG	passing.by	seen

'They have seen him passing by'.

These are also annotated with the `acl` relation.

6 Future work

In terms of linguistic analysis, there are a number of avenues for future research. Bambara syntax is understudied and we would like to work on our analysis of relativisation strategies, the quotative *kó* and the various predication/copula markers.

In terms of the treebank, the immediate objective is to annotate 10,000 tokens in order to solidify the annotate scheme and produce a first version. After this, we aim to annotate up to 100,000 tokens. We are planning to compile an annotation guide available to download. The work will be continued as part of the first author's masters thesis work. Moreover, there are also corpora for other Mande languages which could be annotated under a similar scheme and we would also like to experiment with cross-lingual parsing for this language group.

7 Concluding remarks

We have presented a large part-of-speech annotated corpus converted to Universal Dependencies along with a small proof-of-concept section annotated for dependency relations. We have described how a number of constructions in Bambara can be annotated and laid out the future work for the corpus.

Acknowledgements

Many thanks to Valentin Vydrin for his help and encouragement and for permission to use the Corpus Bambara du Référence. We thank the anonymous reviewers for their extremely helpful advice and comments.

References

Maslinsky, K. (2014). Daba: a model and tools for Manding corpora. In *Proceedings of TALAf 2014 : Traitement Automatique des Langues Africaines*, pages 114–122.

Nikitina, T. (2012). Clause-internal correlatives in Southeastern Mande: A case for the propagation of typological rara. *Lingua*, 122:319–334.

Nivre, J., de Marneffe, M.-C., Ginter, F., Goldberg, Y., Hajič, J., Manning, C., McDonald, R., Petrov, S., Pyysalo, S., Silveira, N., Tsarfaty, R., and Zeman, D. (2016). Universal Dependencies v1: A Multilingual Treebank Collection. In *Proceedings of Language Resources and Evaluation Conference (LREC'16)*.

Senuma, H. and Aizawa, A. (2017). Toward universal dependencies for Ainu. In *Proceedings of the NoDaLiDa 2017 Workshop on Universal Dependencies (UDW 2017)*, pages 133–139.

Straka, M., Hajič, J., and Straková, J. (2016). UDPipe: trainable pipeline for processing CoNLL-U files performing tokenization, morphological analysis, POS tagging and parsing. In *Proceedings of the Tenth International Conference on Language Resources and Evaluation (LREC'16)*, Paris, France. European Language Resources Association (ELRA).

Streiter, O., Scannell, K., and Stuflesser, M. (2006). Implementing NLP projects for non-central languages: Instructions for funding bodies, strategies for developers. *Machine Translation*, 20(4):267–289.

Tyers, F. M., Sheyanova, M., and Washington, J. N. (2018). UD ANNOTATRIX: An annotation tool for Universal Dependencies. In *Proceedings of the 16th International Workshop on Treebanks and Linguistic Theories*, page [this volume].

Vydrin, V. (2013). Bamana reference corpus (BRC). *Procedia - Social and Behavioral Sciences*, 95:75–80.

Выдрин, В. (2017). Бамана язык. In Vydrin, V., Mazurova, Y., Kibrik, A., and Markus, E., editors, *Языки мира: Языки манде*, pages 46–143. РАН. Институт языкознания.

A Supplemental material

Table 2 gives the conversion table for part-of-speech tags from the CBR to UD annotation schemes. The conversion table for morphological features is too long to include here but may be found online.[4]

Description	CBR	UD POS	UD Feats
Adjective	adj	ADJ	
Adverb	adv	ADV	
Postpositional adverb	adv.p	ADV	
Expressive adverb	adv.ex	ADV	
Numeral	num	NUM	
Noun	n	NOUN	
Proper noun	n.prop	PROPN	
Verb	v	VERB	
Qualitative verb	vq	VERB	
Participle	ptcp	VERB	VerbForm=Part
Personal pronoun	pers	PRON	PronType=Prs
Pronoun	prn	PRON	
Modal word	pm	AUX	
Copula	cop	VERB	
Conjunction	conj	CCONJ SCONJ	
Postposition	pp	ADP	
Determiner	dtm	DET	
Particle	prt	PART	

Table 2: Conversion table for the parts of speech. Choice of conjunction type is determined lexically.

---

[4]https://github.com/KatyaAplonova/UD_Bambara

Merging the Trees
Building a Morphological Treebank for German from Two Resources

Petra Steiner
Institut für Deutsche Sprache
`steiner@ids-mannheim.de`

Abstract

This paper deals with the creation of the first morphological treebank for German by merging two pre-existing linguistic databases. The first of these is the linguistic database *CELEX* which is a standard resource for German morphology. We build on its refurbished and modernized version. The second resource is *GermaNet*, a lexical-semantic network which also provides partial markup for compounds. We describe the state of the art and the essential characteristics of both databases and our latest revisions. As the merging involves two data sources with distinct annotation schemes, the derivation of the morphological trees for the unified resource is not trivial. We discuss how we overcome problems with the data and format, in particular how we deal with overlaps and complementary scopes. The resulting database comprises about 100,000 trees whose format can be chosen according to the requirements of the application at hand. In our discussion, we show some future directions for morphological treebanks. The Perl script for the generation of the data from the sources will be made publicly available on our website.

1 Introduction

Lexical productivity is a characteristic for German word formation. This leads to bottleneck problems in different fields such as the building of terminology or Information Retrieval. Concerning the morphological analyses and structures, there are three main problems:

A. the wealth of ambiguous forms on the level of morph segmentation
B. the lack of deeper structural analyses in current approaches
C. for morphological analysis in general, the lack of frequency counts or a robust estimation for affixes.

A morphological treebank of the most common lemmas or word forms of German can serve as a starting point for addressing all of these issues. Although the demand for such a morphological treebank with hierarchical analyses was recognized some time ago (Zielinski and Simon, 2009, 230), to our knowledge, morphological treebanks for German do not exist so far, besides some mostly internally used gold standards. Deep morphological analyses can be used as

1. input for statistical approaches for full morphological parsing of German words
2. base of counts for testing of quantitative hypotheses about morphological tendencies and laws
3. gold standards and test suites for morphological analyzers
4. morphological resources for morphological analyzers
5. input for textual analyses

We derive a morphological treebank for German from two different databases: the first resource is the linguistic database *CELEX* which is a standard resource for German morphology. The second resource is the *GermaNet* database which contains partial markup for compounds.

Proceedings of the 16th International Workshop on Treebanks and Linguistic Theories (TLT16), pages 146–160,
Prague, Czech Republic, January 23–24, 2018. Distributed under a CC-BY 4.0 licence. 2017.

Keywords: morphological analysis, morphological treebank, German, GermaNet, compounding

Section 2 describes the current state of research for German deep-level morphological data. The first part of Section 3 describes the German part of the refurbished CELEX database with an emphasis on the data which are relevant for the tree extraction process as well as problems and errors in the data. It also gives a sketch of the preprocessing. The second part deals with the GermaNet (GN) database and the characteristics that are relevant for our project. Section 4 presents the procedures we use. It starts with the extraction of all relevant information from both databases, followed by the recursive construction of the morphological analyses. The derivation of the morphological trees for both sources is not trivial and we show how we overcome problems with the data and format. In Section 5, we show how we merge the two sources which have distinct annotation styles as well as overlaps and complementary scopes in their morphological classifications. We discuss the decisions used for the classification underlying our unified annotation. The results of the script are presented in Section 6. The resulting database comprises about 100,000 morphological trees whose format can be chosen according to the requirements of the applications. The conclusion in Section 7 provides some future directions for morphological treebanks. The Perl script for the generation of the data from the sources will be made publicly available on our website.

2 Related work

German is a language with complex processes of word formation, of which the most common are compounding and derivation. Segmentation and analysis of the resulting word forms are challenging as spelling conventions do not permit spaces as indicators for boundaries of constituents. Therefore, so far the main concern of morphological analysers for German is finding the correct splits on the level of the morphs. Morphological segmentation tools for German such as SMOR (Schmid et al., 2004), Gertwol (Haapalainen and Majorin, 1995), MORPH (Hanrieder, 1996), TAGH (Geyken and Hanneforth, 2006) generate dozens of analyses for relatively simple words. For instance, *Kellerassel* "common rough woodlouse" could be erroneously segmented to *♯Kelle|Rassel* "(ladle|rattle)" instead of *Keller|Assel* (basement|woodlouse) common rough woodlouse". Also, there are many sets of homonyms comprising both free and bound morphemes. For example, the form *bar* is a suffix in *machbar* mach|bar (make|able) "feasible", a free morph in *Hotelbar* (hotel|bar) "hotel bar" and a sequence without synchronically transparent meaning in *Nachbardistrikt* "neighboring district" which can be wrongly analysed to *♯nach|Bar|Distrikt* (after|bar|district) (see Figure 1).

Figure 1: Ambiguous analysis of *Nachbardistrikt*

This ambiguity problem has been tackled by using ranking scores for the different morphological analyses. For example, Cap (2014) and Koehn and Knight (2003) use the geometric mean as a weighting measure for each possible analyses of SMOR and then choose the one with the highest rank. Another possibility are methods of exploiting the sequence of letters, e.g by pattern matching with tokens (Henrich and Hinrichs, 2011, 422), lemmas (Weller-Di Marco, 2017), or normalization (Ziering and van der Plas, 2016) which is combined with ranking by the geometric mean. Ma et al. (2016) apply Conditional Random Fields modeling for letter sequences. Daiber et al. (2015) extract candidates of compound splits by string comparisons with corpus data.

More recent approaches exploit semantic information for the ranking. Riedl and Biemann (2016) take sets of constituent candidates they generate by combining a compound splitter and look-ups of similar terms inside a distributional thesaurus generated from a large corpus. Their ranking score is a modification of the geometric mean. Ziering et al. (2016) use the cosine as a measure for semantic similarity between compounds and their hypothetical constituents and combine these similarity values by computing the geometric means and other scores for each produced split. The scores are then used as factors to be multiplied by the results of former splits, which were produced by morphological segmentation tools such as SMOR. The re-ranking shows a slight improvement over the initial values, while the pure distributional similarities were inferior to the initial results from the splitter. The reason for this is mainly the rate of word ambiguity which for large corpora is mirrored within the distributional patterns.

Most tools for word analyses of German word forms provide flat sequences of morphs or morphemes but no hierarchical parses which could give important information for word sense disambiguation. Only Würzner and Hanneforth (2013) tackle the problem of full morphological parsing, restricted to adjectives, by using a probabilistic context free grammar for parsing. Steiner and Ruppenhofer (2015) developed a method for building parts of morphological structures by reducing the set of all possible low-level combinations by ranking SMOR splits with the gmean score. They derived the frequencies from different lexical and textual sources, showing some effects which hint at the importance of carefully choosing the source of frequency counts.

Ziering et al. (2016) discuss left-branching compounds consisting of three lexemes such as *Arbeitsplatz-mangel* "(Arbeit|Platz|Mangel) (work|place|lack) job scarcity". Their distributional semantic modelling fails to find the correct binary split, if the head (here *Mangel* "lack") is too ambiguous to correlate strongly with the first part (here *Arbeitsplatz* "employment"). Ziering and van der Plas (2016) develop a splitter which makes use of normalization methods and can be used recursively by re-analyzing the results of splits. Their evaluation however is based only on the binary compounds of GermaNet (Hamp and Feldweg, 1997).

All these approaches build strongly upon corpus data but none of them uses lexical data. Only Henrich and Hinrichs (2011) enrich the output of morphological segmentation with information from GermaNet to disambiguate such structures. This can yield hierarchical structures but presupposes that the entries for the components exist inside the database.

Databases of correct morphological splits and deep-level analyses could save a lot of effort, as there are almost no cases of forms with two different analyses which are really used, even if structure and splits can be analysed ambiguously. The second analysis in Figure (1) will hardly ever occur in real text. At most, it could be merely understood as a pun.

In most cases, German morphological data resources are restricted to lists of flat analyses, for instance, the test set of the 2009 workshop on statistical machine translation,[1] which was used by Cap (2014). It comprises 6,187 word tokens with binary top-level splits. Henrich and Hinrichs (2011) augmented the GermaNet database with information on noun compound splits of the top-level. DErivBase (Zeller et al., 2013) comprises derivational families (word nests) and could be used to infer derivational trees from its sets and rules, however, it is based on heuristics and therefore contains some errors.

The only publicly available source which comprises German word tree information is the German part of the CELEX database (Baayen et al., 1995). The linguistic information is combined with frequency information based on corpora (Burnage, 1995) which makes it useful for automated morphological analysis of unknown words.

That CELEX is a standard resource for research in morphology is demonstrated by Shafaei et al. (2017) who use its German data for inferring derivational families (DErivCELEX) which are more precise than DErivBase. This data is obviously drawn from the original CELEX version with its old orthographical standard.[2] Shafaei et al. (2017) claim that CELEX does not treat prefixation as a form of derivation. In general, this assertion is unjustified, though some first constituents of verbs are classified as free morphs which Shafaei et al. (2017) consider as prefixes. While the CELEX classification is justifiable from a linguistic viewpoint of consistency and difference between prefixes and particles, this proves as an error source for the algorithms of derivational families. For this reason, a second version of DErivCELEX is based on some "pragmatic changes" in categorization concerning compound verbs.

---

[1] http://www.statmt.org/wmt09/translation-task.html
[2] cf. http://www.ims.uni-stuttgart.de/forschung/ressourcen/lexika/DErivBase/DErivCelex-v1.txt

Cotterell et al. (2016) reanalyse part of the deep-level morphological analyses for English and thus generate 7,454 morphological parses which to our knowledge is the only morphological treebank for English besides the aforementioned. Dutch morphological analysis is covered by CELEX too. For other languages, the situation is even less fortunate. But if there are resources of derivational families with information on their generating rules such as in CroDeriV (Filko and Šojat, 2017) for Croatian, Démonette for French (Hathout and Namer, 2016), DeriNet for Czech (Žabokrtský et al., 2016) or DerIvaTario for Italian (Talamo et al., 2016), hierarchical trees could be derived though compounds are not considered by these lists.

The original drawbacks of the German part of the CELEX database were an outdated format and use of former orthographical conventions. However, these problems were tackled by Steiner (2016), and so the database yields a foundation for further exploitation. We decided to take it as the foundation for the morphological treebank and then augment it by other sources, the first of which is the GermaNet database.

3 Lexical resources for morphological trees

3.1 The Refurbished CELEX-German Database

The CELEX database comprises 51,728 entries of which 38,650 are derivates or compounds and 2,402 conversions. This seems to be a small set, however, the lemmas are similar to the small dictionary *Der kleine Wahrig* (Wahrig-Burfeind and Bertelsmann, 2007) which represents the core vocabulary for German. Being developed in the early Nineties, the original CELEX database coding comprised a workaround for special characters. In German, these are mainly umlauts and characters such as *ß*. Furthermore, it uses an out-dated spelling convention which makes the lexicon partially incompatible with text written after 1996. For instance, the modern spelling of the original CELEX entry *Abschluß* 'conclusion' is *Abschluss*. About 20 percent of the data is in an outdated format. Steiner (2016) refurbished the encoding and the spelling of the database completely. A version with modern encoding but old spelling was also created. Now, trees as in Figure (2) and (3) can be derived from the database.

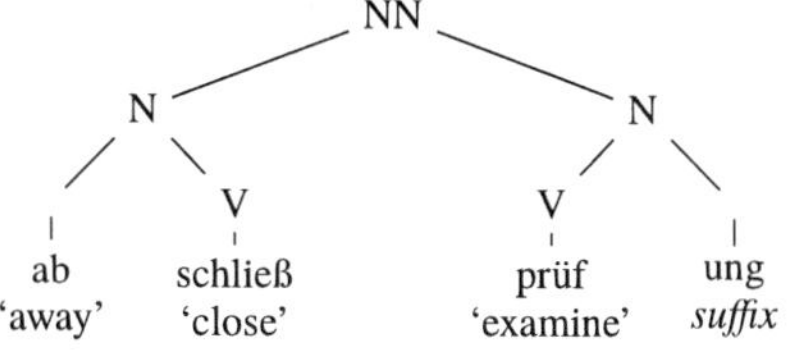

Figure 2: Morphological analysis of *Abschlussprüfung* 'final exam'

Figure 3: Morphological analysis of *Abgangszeugnis* 'leaving certificate'

However, these kinds of trees do not contain categorial information for affixes nor for the derivation process, e.g. the noun *Abschluss* 'finalization' in the derivation of (2). Morever, some derivations in the German CELEX database provide diachronic information which is correct but often unwanted for many applications, for example in *Abdrift* 'leeway' in example (1) which is diachronically derived from *treiben* 'to float'. On the other hand, some derivations such as the ablaut change between *gehen* 'to go' and *Gang* 'gait,path,aisle' in *Abgangszeugnis* 'leaving certificate' in example (2) could be of interest.[3]

(1)   97\Abdrift \ab+drift\xV\. . . \((ab)[N|.V],((treib)[V])[V])[N]

(2)   207\Abgangszeugnis\. . . \Abgang+s+Zeugnis\NxN\. . . \
        (((((ab)[V|.V],(geh)[V])[V])[N],(s)[N|N.N],((zeug)[V], (nis)[N|V.])[N])[N]

Figure 3 shows that the filler letters (interfix)[4] can be inferred from the database entry, where they are

---

[3] Please note that these examples of CELEX entries only present the essential and abridged information of the structure information and the morphological trees.

[4] Depending upon the framework, these entities are also called *Fugenmorpheme*. However, their morphological and phonological status can be discussed, and we prefer the term *filler letters* which refers to the form.

represented within the categories of the immediate constituent structure. As every complex entry has this information, this enables one to recursively collect them from the entries.

Though most of its data is free of errors, the original CELEX database contains some mistakes which were not treated by the refurbishment of Steiner (2016) which involved only changes of coding and spelling. We found missing constituents and missing part of speech information within the morphological trees and within the field of immediate constituency information as well as inconsistent morphological analyses. We augmented the script for the transformation to a modern standard by 18 additional rules, which covered 65 instances before we could use the data for extracting the morphological trees. We are aware of the fact that we could not find all mistakes.

3.2 Compound Analyses from GermaNet

Henrich and Hinrichs (2011) augmented the GermaNet database with information on compound splits. This is restricted to nouns and does not provide filler letters or deep-level structures. The data was revised since then. We are using version 11 which was most recently updated in February 2017.[5] Example (3) presents a typical entry for *Werkstück* 'work piece'. The parts of interest are marked by bold letters. As two derivational processes are possible, two modifiers *werken* 'to work' and *Werk* 'work, noun' exist for the head, leading to two splits.

(3)   <synset id="s5552" **category="nomen"** class="Artefakt"> <lexUnit id="l8355" sense="1" source="core" namedEntity="no" artificial="no" styleMarking="no"> <orthForm>Werkstück </orthForm> **<compound>** **<modifier category="Nomen">Werk</modifier>** **<modifier category="Verb">werken</modifier>** **<head>Stück</head>** **</compound>** </lexUnit> </synset>

Different to the CELEX data, the filler letters are missing in the analyses, such as in (4a). Therefore, we insert them by a heuristic method to get analyses as in (4b). Furthermore, we exclude compounds with proper names as constituents such as (5) and foreign expressions as in (6). We did not correct any mistakes of the database but automatically excluded a few deficient entries, for example those with missing part-of-speech classes, and compounds with affixoids or fossilized morphemes.

(4)   a. Abfahrtszeit 'departure time': Abfahrt|Zeit (departure|time)

          b. Abfahrtszeit 'departure time': Abfahrt|s|Zeit (departure|*filler letter*|time)

(5)   Bodenseeregion 'Lake of Constance region'

(6)   After-Show-Party

4 Procedures

4.1 Data Extraction

For extracting all relevant information from the refurbished CELEX data, we build an inverted index of all lemmas and extract all immediate constituents and their categories. Then we internally add the infinitive forms of the verbs which are included within these entries. This is necessary so that these forms can be found within the inverted index of the entries. We also refurbish the German syntactic database of CELEX to the modern standard and extract the parts of speech of the entries. As the users can choose if they like to generate not just compounds and derivatives but also conversions, we extract the relevant information for this word-formation type too but exclude 724 cases of lexicalized inflection (see Gulikers et al., 1995, 54) such as (7).

(7)   anhaltend (continuing, present perfect) 'persistent'

---

[5]see http://www.sfs.uni-tuebingen.de/GermaNet/compounds.shtml#Download for a description.

The data finally comprises an inverted list of 40,081 entries with 38,650 different word splits of complex entries (compounds and derivations) and 1,678 conversions.

From the GermaNet data, we extract all completely annotated compounds with their splits and filler letters according to the restrictions. We also infer the category of the head from the entry. This leads to a list of 64,468 entries with 67,466 different word splits; all of them are nominal compounds. (8) shows the analyses for (3). The variation in spelling of *nomen* is due to the original data.

(8)   Werkstück Werk_Nomen|Stück_nomen
               Werkstück werken_Verb|Stück_nomen

4.2 Building the Trees

For each entry of the extracted data, the procedure starts from the list of its immediate constituents and recursively collects all information. Algorithm 1 in Appendix A presents the recursive process for the CELEX data, Algorithm 2 for the GN data.

4.3 Diachronic Information

Diachronic information can be of interest, however, for many applications it is considered as unnecessary or even unhelpful. Therefore, the script permits users to choose a threshold of similarity within the range of [0:1] which is compared to a measure we devised based on the Levenshtein distance.

For accepting or rejecting two parts of words, the procedure will calculate the Levensthein distance (LD) for the strings of the smaller length of the two compared constituents $(min(c_1, c_2))$, and then compare their quotient *dis* to a threshold *t* as in (9):

$$dis = \frac{LD}{min(c_1, c_2)} \leq t \tag{9}$$

For calculating the dissimilarity quotient of the example (1), in (10) the stem of the derived form (e.g. *treib*) and its component (e.g. *driften*) are reduced to the smaller size of these forms. In this case, the smaller length is 5. After this, the quotient of *LD* and the length is compared to the threshold. (10) shows that the analysis will stop for a threshold at 0.8 or below.

$$\frac{LD}{min(c_1, c_2)} = \frac{4}{5} \tag{10}$$

Just in case, that singular variations were needed, we also added a small list of exceptions.

4.4 Formats of output

The output can be configured in many ways. The following options are available:

- Depth of analysis for compounds
- Parts of speech for the constructs and/or the smallest constituents
- Choice of the output format (parentheses or a notation with | for the splits on the same level)
- Addition of filler letters for GN
- Transfering the GN annotation scheme to CELEX scheme
- Removing compounds with proper names and/or foreign words as constituents for GN
- Analysis of conversions for CELEX
- Depth of analysis for conversions for CELEX
- Dissimilarity measure for CELEX diachronic analyses

The analyses in (11) for (3) and a complex compound containing (3) as a constituent are from the GN part in the format without any linguistic information. Due to combination of ambiguous entries, it comprises multiples trees for some forms. Example (12) shows an output for CELEX data of the same form in parenthesis notation. Here only one analysis is assigned to the word form with the verb as a result of conversion from the noun. More examples are given in the Appendix.

$$
(11) \quad
\begin{array}{lll}
\text{Werkstück} & \text{Werk|Stück} & \text{'work(noun)|piece'} \\
\text{Werkstück} & \text{werken|Stück} & \text{'to work|piece'} \\
\text{Glaswerkstück} & \text{Glas|(Werk|Stück)} & \text{'glass|work(noun)|piece'} \\
\text{Glaswerkstück} & \text{Glas|(werken|Stück)} & \text{'glass|to work|piece'}
\end{array}
$$

(12)   Werkstück   (*werken_V* (Werk_N)(en_x))(Stück_N)   '(*to work_V* (work_N)(en(suffix))(piece_N)'

5 Merging the trees

The CELEX trees comprise not only compounds but also deep-level analyses of derivatives and conversions, while the GN morphological data is restricted to compound nouns which are partially very complex. For instance, the flat analysis of *Währungsausgleichsfond* 'currency adjustment fond' (13) from the GN database can be recursively augmented to the tree in (14). Its constituent *Ausgleich* 'adjustment' is not further analyzed within the GN database, but has an entry as a complex conversion (15) in the CELEX database. Therefore, the combination of both sets and their parameters for building complex trees seems promising.

(13)   Währungsausgleich_N|s_x|Fonds_N   'currency adjustment|*filler letters*|fund'

(14)   (*Währungsausgleich_N* Währung_N|s_x|Ausgleich_N)|s_x|Fonds_N)
         '(*currency adjustment_N* currency_N|s_x|adjustment_N)|s_x|fund_N'

(15)   Ausgleich (*ausgleichen_V* aus_x|(*gleichen_V* gleich_A|en_x))
         'adjustment (*to adjust_V aus(*prefix*)_x|(*to equal_V equal_A|en(*suffix*)_x))'

Moreover, GN compounds which were formerly excluded during the procedure of data extraction because their part of speech categories are missing inside the database (see 3.2), can be assigned the category from CELEX if available.

The main problem consists in two annotation sets and their different classification schemes, especially for roots. Table (1) shows the mapping. While the main part-of-speech categories are almost perfectly mappable between the CELEX and the GN data, the classification of function words and bound morphemes is less consistent. There are cases of different interpretations with a tendency of CELEX to prefer affix analyses for cases such as (16) and (17) with *a.* presenting the GN entry and *b.* the entry of CELEX. There are differing analyses of morphological constituency. In (18) GN's compound analysis is opposed to the conversion of CELEX. The classes of roots and word groups have the same or complementary scopes, e.g. (19) and (20) have the same analysis in both sources. We decided to unify the tagset but to leave different trees such as in (11) and (12) to the choice of the users. Some more complex analyses as well as the algorithm are presented in Appendix A.

(16) a. Abwasser   (ab_P)(Wasser_N)   '(away_P)(water_N) waste water'
      b.   (ab_x)(Wasser_N)   '(away_x)(water_N) waste water'

(17) a. afroasiatisch   (afro_R)(Asiatisch_N)   '(afro_R)(Asian_N)'
      b. afroamerikanisch   (afro_x)(amerikanisch_A)   '(afro_x)(American_A)'

(18) a. Maßnahme   (Maß_N)(Nahme_N)   '(measure_n)(taking_N) measure'
      b.   maßnehmen_V   '(to measure_take_V) measure'

(19)   Kondenswasser   (kondens_R)(Wasser_N)   '(condensed_R)(water_N)'

(20)   Zwölftonmusik   (zwölf Ton_n)(Musik_N)   '(twelve tone_n)(music_N)'

Part of Speech/morph type	GN	CELEX	GermanTreebank
noun	nomen, Nomen	N	N
adjective	Adjektiv	A	A
adverb	Adverb	B	B
preposition	Präposition	P	P
verb	Verb, verben	V	V
article	Artikel	D	D
interjection	Interjektion	I	I
pronoun	Pronomen	O	O
abbreviation	Abkürzung	X	X
word group	Wortgruppe	n	n
root/confix	Konfix	R	R
filler letters, affixes	-	x	x

Table 1: Mapping of two morphological tagsets

6 Results

Table 2 provides the number of the trees for CELEX, GermaNet and their merge in GermanTreebank. The parameters for the deep-level analyses are 6 for the levels of complex words and 2 for conversions. The Levenshtein dissimilarity threshold was set to 0.5. Double entries were removed. As the combinatorial power of GN's ambiguous trees grows with the depth of the trees, the numbers have to be considered with a grain of salt. The set of trees in the GermanTreebank consists of the unification of both sources. For examples, see (21)-(23) in A.

Structures	GN entries	CELEX entries	GermanTreebank
flat	67,452	40,097	100,095
deep-level	68,163	40,097	104,424
merged with CELEX	68,171	n/a	100,986

Table 2: A German Treebank

7 Conclusions and future work

This paper decribes our recent work on merging two types of morphological trees from GermaNet and CELEX. The resulting resource contains 95,506 lemmas connected with 100,986 merged trees and is currently the biggest available data resource of its kind. In principle, the treebank is extensible and combinable with other analyses, and we intend to enlarge it. The resource can be especially useful for all kind of data-intense morphological analyses. We plan to use it especially as a source for depth-level word analyses in combination with a word splitter.

Acknowledgments

The author was supported by the German Research Foundation (DFG) under grant RU 1873/2-1.

References

Harald Baayen, Richard Piepenbrock, and Léon Gulikers. 1995. The CELEX lexical database (CD-ROM).

Gavin Burnage. 1995. CELEX: A Guide for Users. In Harald Baayen, Richard Piepenbrock, and Léon Gulikers, editors, *The CELEX Lexical Database (CD-ROM)*, Linguistic Data Consortium, Philadelphia, PA.

Fabienne Cap. 2014. *Morphological processing of compounds for statistical machine translation*. Ph.D. thesis, Universität Stuttgart. http://elib.uni-stuttgart.de/opus/volltexte/2014/9768.

Ryan Cotterell, Arun Kumar, and Hinrich Schütze. 2016. Morphological Segmentation Inside-Out Language Processing, EMNLP 2016, Austin, Texas, USA, November 1-4, 2016. In Jian Su, Xavier Carreras, and Kevin Duh, editors, *Proceedings of the 2016 Conference on Empirical Methods in Natural Language Processing, EMNLP 2016, Austin, Texas, USA, November 1-4, 2016*. The Association for Computational Linguistics, pages 2325–2330. http://aclweb.org/anthology/D/D16/D16-1256.pdf.

Joachim Daiber, Lautaro Quiroz, Roger Wechsler, and Stella Frank. 2015. Splitting compounds by semantic analogy. In *Proceedings of the 1st Deep Machine Translation Workshop*, ÚFAL MFF UK, pages 20–28. http://aclweb.org/anthology/W15-5703.

Matea Filko and Krešimir Šojat. 2017. Expansion of the derivational database for Croatian. In *First Workshop on Resources and Tools for Derivational Morphology (DeriMo)*. http://derimo2017.marginalia.it/index.php/proceedings.

Alexander Geyken and Thomas Hanneforth. 2006. TAGH: A Complete Morphology for German based on Weighted Finite State Automata. In *Finite State Methods and Natural Language Processing. 5th International Workshop, FSMNLP 2005, Helsinki, Finland, September 1-2, 2005. Revised Papers*, Springer, volume 4002, pages 55–66. https://doi.org/10.1007/11780885_7.

Léon Gulikers, Gilbert Rattink, and Richard Piepenbrock. 1995. German Linguistic Guide. In Harald Baayen, Richard Piepenbrock, and Léon Gulikers, editors, *The CELEX Lexical Database (CD-ROM)*, Linguistic Data Consortium, Philadelphia, PA.

Mariikka Haapalainen and Ari Majorin. 1995. GERTWOL und morphologische Disambiguierung für das Deutsche. In *Proceedings of the 10th Nordic Conference on Computational Linguistics, Helsinki, Finland*.

Birgit Hamp and Helmut Feldweg. 1997. GermaNet - a Lexical-Semantic Net for German. In *In Proceedings of ACL workshop Automatic Information Extraction and Building of Lexical Semantic Resources for NLP Applications*. pages 9–15. http://www.aclweb.org/anthology/W97-0802.

Gerhard Hanrieder. 1996. MORPH - Ein modulares und robustes Morphologieprogramm für das Deutsche in Common Lisp. In Roland Hauser, editor, *Linguistische Verifikation Dokumentation zur Ersten Morpholymics 1994*, Niemeyer, Tübingen, pages 53–66.

Nabil Hathout and Fiammetta Namer. 2016. Giving Lexical Resources a Second Life: Démonette, a Multi-sourced Morpho-semantic Network for French. In Nicoletta Calzolari, Khalid Choukri, Thierry Declerck, Sara Goggi, Marko Grobelnik, Bente Maegaard, Joseph Mariani, Hélène Mazo, Asunción Moreno, Jan Odijk, and Stelios Piperidis, editors, *Proceedings of the Tenth International Conference on Language Resources and Evaluation (LREC 2016)*. European Language Resources Association (ELRA), Paris, France. http://www.lrec-conf.org/proceedings/lrec2016/pdf/279_Paper.pdf.

Verena Henrich and Erhard Hinrichs. 2011. Determining Immediate Constituents of Compounds in GermaNet. In *Proceedings of the International Conference Recent Advances in Natural Language Processing 2011*. Association for Computational Linguistics, pages 420–426. http://www.aclweb.org/anthology/R11-1058.

Philipp Koehn and Kevin Knight. 2003. Empirical methods for compound splitting. In *Proceedings of the tenth conference of the European Chapter of the Association for Computational Linguistics-Volume 1*. Association for Computational Linguistics, pages 187–193. http://www.aclweb.org/anthology/E03-1076.

Jianqiang Ma, Verena Henrich, and Erhard Hinrichs. 2016. Letter Sequence Labeling for Compound Splitting. In *Proceedings of the 14th SIGMORPHON Workshop on Computational Research in Phonetics, Phonology, and Morphology*. Association for Computational Linguistics, Berlin, Germany, pages 76–81. http://anthology.aclweb.org/W16-2012.

Martin Riedl and Chris Biemann. 2016. Unsupervised Compound Splitting With Distributional Semantics Rivals Supervised Methods. In *Proceedings of the Conference of the North American Chapter of the Association for Computational Linguistics: Human Language Technologies (NAACL-HLT 2016)*. Association for Computational Linguistics, pages 617–622. https://doi.org/10.18653/v1/N16-1075.

Helmut Schmid, Arne Fitschen, and Ulrich Heid. 2004. SMOR: A German computational morphology covering derivation, composition and inflection. In *Proceedings of the Fourth International Conference on Language Resources and Evaluation (LREC'04)*. European Language Resources Association (ELRA). http://www.aclweb.org/anthology/L04-1275.

Elnaz Shafaei, Diego Frassinelli, Gabriella Lapesa, and Sebastian Padó. 2017. DErivCELEX: Development and Evaluation of a German Derivational Morphology Lexicon based on CELEX. In *Proceedings of the DeriMo workshop*. Milan, Italy. http://derimo2017.marginalia.it/index.php/proceedings.

Petra Steiner. 2016. Refurbishing a Morphological Database for German. In Nicoletta Calzolari, Khalid Choukri, Thierry Declerck, Sara Goggi, Marko Grobelnik, Bente Maegaard, Joseph Mariani, Hélène Mazo, Asunción Moreno, Jan Odijk, and Stelios Piperidis, editors, *Proceedings of the Tenth International Conference on Language Resources and Evaluation LREC 2016, Portorož, Slovenia, May 23-28, 2016*. European Language Resources Association (ELRA). http://www.lrec-conf.org/proceedings/lrec2016/summaries/761.html.

Petra Steiner and Josef Ruppenhofer. 2015. Growing trees from morphs: Towards data-driven morphological parsing. In *Proceedings of the International Conference of the German Society for Computational Linguistics and Language Technology, GSCL 2015, University of Duisburg-Essen, Germany, 30th September - 2nd October 2015*. pages 49–57. http://www.gscl.org/proceedings/2015/GSCL-201508.pdf.

Luigi Talamo, Chiara Celata, and Pier Marco Bertinetto. 2016. DerIvaTario: An annotated lexicon of Italian derivatives. *Word Structure* 9(1):72–102. https://doi.org/10.3366/word.2016.0087.

R. Wahrig-Burfeind and Gütersloh Lexikoninstitut Bertelsmann. 2007. *Der kleine Wahrig: Wörterbuch der deutschen Sprache ; [der deutsche Grundwortschatz in mehr als 25000 Stichwörtern und 120000 Anwendungsbeispielen ; mit umfassenden Informationen zur Wortbedeutung und detaillierten Angaben zu grammatischen und orthografischen Aspekten der deutschen Gegenwartssprache]*. Wissen Media Verlag.

Marion Weller-Di Marco. 2017. Simple Compound Splitting for German. In *Proceedings of the 13th Workshop on Multiword Expressions (MWE 2017)*. Association for Computational Linguistics, Valencia, Spain, pages 161–166. http://www.aclweb.org/anthology/W17-1722.

Kay-Michael Würzner and Thomas Hanneforth. 2013. Parsing morphologically complex words. In *Proceedings of the 11th International Conference on Finite State Methods and Natural Language Processing, FSMNLP 2013, St. Andrews, Scotland, UK, July 15-17, 2013*. pages 39–43. http://aclweb.org/anthology/W/W13/W13-1807.pdf.

Zdeněk Žabokrtský, Magda Sevcikova, Milan Straka, Jonáš Vidra, and Adéla Limburská. 2016. Merging Data Resources for Inflectional and Derivational Morphology in Czech. In Nicoletta Calzolari (Conference Chair), Khalid Choukri, Thierry Declerck, Sara Goggi, Marko Grobelnik, Bente Maegaard, Joseph Mariani, Helene Mazo, Asuncion Moreno, Jan Odijk, and Stelios Piperidis, editors, *Proceedings of the Tenth International Conference on Language Resources and Evaluation (LREC 2016)*. European Language Resources Association (ELRA), Paris, France. http://www.lrec-conf.org/proceedings/lrec2016/pdf/994_Paper.pdf.

Britta Zeller, Jan Šnajder, and Sebastian Padó. 2013. DErivBase: Inducing and evaluating a derivational morphology resource for German. In *Proceedings of the 51st Annual Meeting of the Association for Computational Linguistics (Volume 1: Long Papers)*. Association for Computational Linguistics, volume 1, pages 1201–1211. http://www.aclweb.org/anthology/P13-1118.

Andrea Zielinski and Christian Simon. 2009. Morphisto –An Open Source Morphological Analyzer for German. In *Proceedings of the 2009 Conference on Finite-State Methods and Natural Language Processing: Postproceedings of the 7th International Workshop FSMNLP 2008*. IOS Press, Amsterdam, The Netherlands, The Netherlands, pages 224–231. http://dl.acm.org/citation.cfm?id=1564035.1564061.

Patrick Ziering, Stefan Muller, and Lonneke van der Plas. 2016. Top a splitter: Using distributional semantics for improving compound splitting. In *Proceedings of the 12th Workshop on Multiword Expressions*. Association for Computational Linguistics, Berlin, Germany, pages 50–55. http://anthology.aclweb.org/W16-1807.

Patrick Ziering and Lonneke van der Plas. 2016. Towards Unsupervised and Language-independent Compound Splitting using Inflectional Morphological Transformations. In *Human Language Technologies, San Diego California, USA, June 12-17, 2016*, Association for Computational Linguistics, pages 644–653. http://aclweb.org/anthology/N/N16/N16-1078.pdf.

A   Appendix

Formats

The following shows the entries of *Abschlussprüfung* 'final exam', see (2), *Abdrift* 'leeway', see (1), and *Abgangszeugnis* 'leaving certificate', see (3). For all linguistic information, | notation, and a Levenshtein threshold of 0.5, the results are presented in (21), for parenthesis notation and no restrictions on diachronic conversions in (22) and for a flat representation of the immediate constituents see (23).

(21)   Abschlussprüfung

```
       Abschlussprüfung
       (*Abschluss_N*
       (*abschließen_V*
       ab_x|
       schließen_V))|
       (*Prüfung_N*
       prüfen_V|
       ung_x)

       Abdrift
       ab_x|
       (driften_V)

       Abgangszeugnis
       (*Abgang_N*
       (*abgehen_V*
       ab_x|
       gehen_V))|
       s_x|
       (*Zeugnis_N*
       zeugen_V|
       nis_x)
```

(22)   Abschlussprüfung

```
       Abschlussprüfung
       (*Abschluss_N*
       (*abschließen_V*
       (ab_x)
       (schließen_V)))
       (*Prüfung_N*
       (prüfen_V)
       (ung_x))
```

```
       Abdrift
       (ab_x)
       (*driften_V*
       treiben_V)

       Abgangszeugnis
       (*Abgang_N*
       (*abgehen_V*
       (ab_x)
       (gehen_V)))
       (s_x)
       (*Zeugnis_N*
       (zeugen_V)
       (nis_x))
```

(23)   Abschlussprüfung

```
       Abschlussprüfung
       Abschluss_N|
       Prüfung_N

       Abdrift
       ab_x|
       driften_V

       Abgangszeugnis
       Abgang_N|
       s_x|
       Zeugnis_N
```

Example of the Treebank: Augmentation of a GermaNet tree

The following shows how an entry from GermaNet (GN), *Währungsausgleichsfonds* 'currency adjustment fund' (24) can be augmented recursively from GN (25) and the CELEX database (26). The complete tree is presented in (4).

(24)   Währungsausgleich_N|s_x|Fonds_N   'currency adjustment|*filler letters*|fund'

(25)   (*Währungsausgleich_N* Währung_N|s_x|Ausgleich_N)|s_x|Fonds_N
        '(*currency adjustment_N* currency_N|s_x|adjustment_N)|s_x|fund_N'

(26)   (*Währungsausgleich_N* Währung_N|s_x|(*Ausgleich_N*
        (*ausgleichen_V* aus_x|(*gleichen_V* gleich_A|en_x))))|s_x|Fonds_N
        '(*currency adjustment_N* currency_N|s_x|(*adjustment_N*
        (*to adjust_V* aus,Prefix_x|(*to equal_V* equal_A|en_x))))|s_x|fund_N'

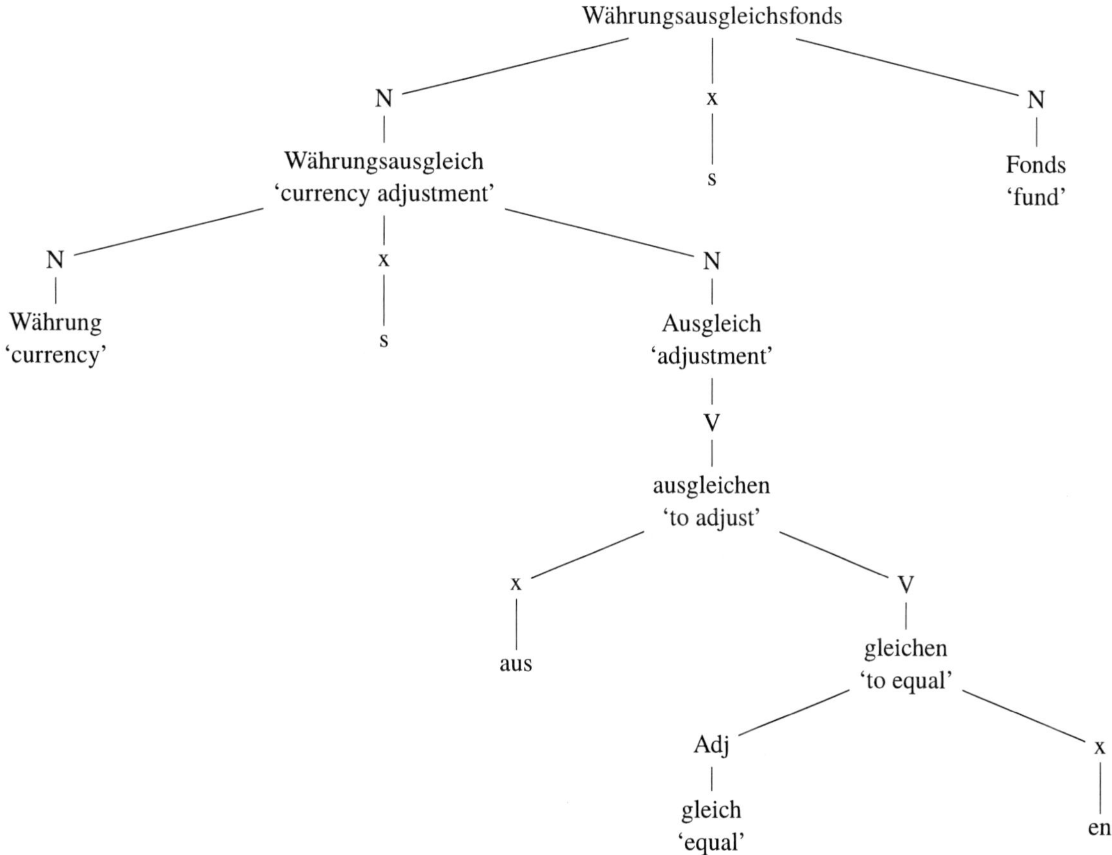

Figure 4: Merged morphological analysis of *Währungsausgleichsfonds* 'currency adjustment fund'

Algorithms

Algorithm 1: Building a morphological treebank from CELEX German data

Input: CELEX-German revised
Output: A Morphological Treebank
initialization of parameters: depths of analysis, levenshtein threshold, linguistic information, parts
  of speech, style of output;
forall *entries of CELEX* **do**
  if *entry is complex or a conversion* **then**
    foreach *constituent of entry* **do**
      if *constituent is simplex*
        or *depth of analysis reached* **then**
          retrieve linguistic information/PoS as required;
          return linguistic information and constituent
      end
      else
          foreach *part of constituent* **do**
            depth of analysis++;
            analysedeepercelex part with parameters and depth;
            return result of **analysedeepercelex**
          end
      end
    end
  end
end

  sub analysedeepercelex part (parameters and level)
  if *part is simplex*
  or *depth of analysis reached*
  then
    retrieve linguistic information/PoS as required;
    return linguistic information and part
  end
  else
    foreach *subpart of part* **do**
      analysedeepercelex subpart
      if *levenshtein threshold **and analysedeepercelex** subpart is dissimilar* **then**
        skip deeper analysis;
        return subpart
      end
      else
        return result of **analysedeepercelex** subpart
      end
    end
  end

Algorithm 2: Building a morphological treebank from GermaNet flat compounds

Input: GN flat compounds
Output: A Morphological Treebank
initialization of parameters: depth of analysis, linguistic information, parts of speech, style of
 output;
forall *entries of GN flat compounds* **do**
   if *entry is a compound*
  then
     foreach *constituent of entry* **do**
       if *constituent is simplex*
      or depth of analysis reached **then**
        retrieve linguistic information/PoS as required;
        return linguistic information and constituent
      end
      else
        foreach *part of constituent* **do**
         depth of analysis++;
         analysedeeper part with parameters and depth;
         return result of **analysedeeper**
        end
      end
     end
  end
end

sub analysedeeper part (parameters and level)
 if *part is simplex*
 or depth of analysis reached
 then
  retrieve linguistic information/PoS as required;
  return linguistic information and part
end
else
  depth of analysis++;
  foreach *subpart of part* **do**
   analysedeeper subpart
   return result of **analysedeeper** subpart
  end
end

Algorithm 3: Building a merged morphological treebank from GermaNet and CELEX

Input: CELEX-German revised, GN flat compounds
Output: A Morphological Treebank
initialization of parameters: depth of analysis, linguistic information, levenshtein threshold, parts
  of speech, style of output;
add CELEX data to the knowledge base
  forall *entries of GN flat compounds* **do**
    if *entry is a compound* **then**
      foreach *constituent of entry* **do**
        if *depth of analysis reached* **then**
          retrieve linguistic information/PoS as required;
          return linguistic information and constituent
        end
        else if *constituent not found in GN data* **then**
          depth of analysis++;
          analysedeepercelex as in Algorithm 1 part with parameters and depth;
          return result of **analysedeepercelex**
        end
        else
          foreach *part of constituent* **do**
            depth of analysis++;
            analysedeeper part with parameters and depth;
            return result of **analysedeeper**
          end
        end
      end
    end
  end
end

sub analysedeeper part (parameters and level)
  if *part is simplex*
  or *depth of analysis reached*
  then
    retrieve linguistic information/PoS as required;
    return linguistic information and part
  end
  else if *constituent not found in GN data* **then**
    depth of analysis++;
    analysedeepercelex as in Algorithm 1 part with parameters and depth;
    return result of **analysedeepercelex**
  end
  else
    depth of analysis++;
    foreach *subpart of part* **do**
      analysedeeper subpart
      return result of **analysedeeper** subpart
    end
  end

What I think when I think about treebanks

Anders Søgaard
Dpt. of Computer Science
University of Copenhagen
`soegaard@di.ku.dk`

Abstract

In this opinion piece, I present four somewhat controversial suggestions for the design of future treebanks: a) Treebanks should be based on *adversarial* samples, rather than pseudo-representative samples. b) Treebanks should include *multiple* splits of the data, rather than just a single split, as in most treebanks today. c) They should include multiple annotations of each sentence, whenever possible, instead of adjudicated annotations. d) There is no real motivation for adhering to a notion of well-formedness, since we now have parsers based on deep learning that generalize easily and perform well on any type of graphs, and treebanks therefore do not have to limit themselves to trees or directed acyclic graphs.

1 Introduction

Treebanks are some of the most ambitious and expensive resources the NLP community has produced, and over the last two decades, they have enabled us to push research horizons and develop more advanced technologies. While treebanks remain invaluable, and we owe thanks to all the people who have contributed to existing ones, I nevertheless think future treebanks will have significantly more value if they are designed slightly differently.

Treebanks are supposed to enable us to induce syntactic parsers and estimate their performance on held-out, unseen data; that is, their performance in the wild. We have treebanks for more than 50 languages, albeit some of them very small, but typically only one treebank for each language. Reported parsing results vary quite a bit from treebank to treebank, and such results are often taken as indicative of our ability to parse the relevant languages in the wild, given our current linguistic resources.

Differences in parsing results, from treebanks to treebanks, are often explained on linguistic grounds. Here is an example from the shared task description paper from the CoNLL 2007 dependency parsing shared task (Nivre et al., 2007):[1]

> ... *the languages involved in the multilingual track this year can be more easily separated into three classes with respect to top scores:*
>
> - *Low (76.31–76.94): Arabic, Basque, Greek*
>
> - *Medium (79.19–80.21): Czech, Hungarian, Turkish*
>
> - *High (84.40–89.61): Catalan, Chinese, English, Italian*
>
> *It is interesting to see that the classes are more easily definable via language characteristics than via characteristics of the data sets. [...] The most difficult languages are those that combine a relatively free word order with a high degree of inflection.*

---

[1] This shared task is a predecessor to the CoNLL 2017 dependency parsing shared task which included many more languages, but the survey paper produced by the organizers did *not* provide a similar explanation for differences in performance.

Proceedings of the 16th International Workshop on Treebanks and Linguistic Theories (TLT16), pages 161–166,
Prague, Czech Republic, January 23–24, 2018. Distributed under a CC-BY 4.0 licence. 2017.

Keywords: treebanks, design principles, generalization

While explaining parsing performance by language characteristics such as freeness of word order and morphological complexity, is quite intuitive, and pleasing for someone with a background in linguistic typology, like me; this explanation was later disputed in Søgaard and Haulrich (2010), who claimed that what they called *derivational perplexity*, i.e., (a particular way of measuring) the average complexity of the tree structures in the tree structures, explained performance differences better. Linguistic properties may of course be confounds, but tree structures are influenced heavily by linguistic theory and annotation guidelines, which also determine the complexity of the structures we use to analyze sentences. Other factors that influence performance include how homogeneous the underlying corpus is. Is the text single-authored? If multi-authored, were the texts written with different intended audiences? Do the authors span multiple demographics? Do they speak different dialects? Etc.

Nevertheless, explanations based on linguistic grounds are far more common, and we often hear claims based on treebank results that some languages are harder to parse than others. This was also the motivation behind a recent shared task in parsing morphologically rich languages.[2] You may think that linguistic differences are much more important than other factors. This is not always true, however. Foster et al. (2010), for example, evaluate a dependency parser trained on newswire (the English Penn Treebank) on hand-annotated Twitter data. On held-out newswire data, the parser has an unlabeled attachment score of 90.6%, but on Twitter data, the score is 73.6%. This 19% relative drop (17% absolute) is bigger than a lot of the drops we observe transferring models across languages. About the same time, Foster et al. (2010) ran the Twitter experiments, McDonald et al. (2011) revisited the idea of transferring the non-lexical part of parsing models across languages. Their impoverished English model scored 82.5% in unlabeled attachment score on English data. When evaluating their model on Portuguese, for example, scores dropped to 68.4%, which is a 17% relative drop (14% absolute). Changing the domain hurts model performance more than changing the language in this case. It is easy to find similar examples in the literature. These factors, by the same token, also influence how well we can generalize from validation and test set performance to *performance in the wild* or practical usefulness. This paper discusses different dimensions of this problem and proposes design principles for building treebanks in the future. My main observation is that our treebanks are being too nice on us, i.e., leading us to overestimate our performance in the wild.

2 Sampling for Treebanks

No one has to the best of my knowledge ever claimed that the sentences in the English Penn Treebank[3] were representative of the English language. All the sentences were written by Wall Street Journal journalists in the 1980s, who were trained to write in a particular way and asked to write about particular topics, of interest to the readers of the newspaper. The first version of the Slovene Dependency Treebank[4], used in the CoNLL 2006 Shared Task, was the annotation of a single novel, written by a single author. Clearly, a single piece of prose is not representative in any way of a language. The sentences in the Croatian Dependency Treebank[5] come from the newspaper Croatia Weekly. Other treebanks claim to be based on more representative language samples. The Danish Dependency Treebank[6] and the Turku Dependency Treebank,[7] for example, contain sentences from newswire, magazines, blogs, and literature.

In all the above treebanks (English, Slovene, Croatian, Danish, and Finnish), however, the training and test sentences come from the same sources, and while treebanks will never be i.i.d., there is a clear intention to sample training and test sentences in near-identical ways; I return to this in §3. Approximating i.i.d. makes sense if you can sample representative sentences at random. I argue that we can't, and that we therefore need to abandon the ideal of nearly identically sampled train and test portions in our treebanks. The argument relies on the observation that we cannot sample randomly from language.

---

[2] http://www.spmrl.org/
[3] LDC95T7
[4] http://nl.ijs.si/sdt/
[5] http://hobs.ffzg.hr/en/
[6] https://github.com/UniversalDependencies/UD_Danish
[7] http://bionlp.utu.fi/fintreebank.html

2.1 How can we sample from language?

Imagine you were to design an English treebank from scratch. You had a team of trained annotators, ready to annotate, just waiting for you to send them raw text files they can decorate with linguistic analyses. Now the question is what texts you send them.

How would you sample your sentences? Where would you go? A knee jerk reaction may be to say that you would sample them from a representative corpus, but that is putting your eggs in someone else's basket, relying on their ability to sample from English. What would you do? Would you get your sentences from the Wall Street Journal? Probably not exclusively. What else, then? Sentences from literary works? From Harry Potter? How about comics, then? How about 19th century literary works? From Facebook? Google Search queries? Speech logs? Learner data? Dialect? Expat English? Or how about the language of neurodiverse speakers of English? You probably feel you get my point, but stop for a minute and think about it. What *would* you do?

You may arrive at the conclusion that treebanks should be domain-specific. *Okay, so English comes in a lot of different flavors. Let us just build treebanks for each one of them.* This approach has three problems: a) It is not possible to enumerate the number of domains. The concept of *domains* is usually ambiguous between *topics* and *platforms/media/registers*, but it should be clear that both the list of topics covered in human history, and the list of platforms available to us, are growing and unbounded. Also, b) authors have different linguistic traits, and c) language is constantly changing.

The next conclusion – that it is simply *not possible to sample from language* – means sample bias is inevitable, inescapable, and something you have to embrace. This is, in my view, extremely important, and many things follow from this observation:

- A single test set is simply not gonna cut it.

- Your multiple test sets must be very different, with varying degrees of bias.

- Even so, you are likely to still overestimate performance on unseen data.

In other words, my first advise to designers of future treebanks is to include *multiple* test datasets and to make them as different as possible. To the best of my knowledge, no treebanks are designed that way. A few treebanks, such as OntoNotes,[8] contain meta-data that allow you to easily set up experiments with multiple test data sets, though.

3 Cutting the Cake Unfairly Again and Again

One way to achieve better data points for estimating performance in the wild with our current treebanks is by introducing multiple, more or less adversarial training-test splits. Here is a couple of ideas:

Splits based on meta-data   Some treebanks, including for example the English Penn Treebank and the Danish Dependency Treebank, contain meta-information about where each sentence is from, and when it was written or published. Such data enables us to estimate cross-domain robustness, or how performance drops over time.

Splits based on divergence   In the domain adaptation literature, divergence measures such as Jensen-Shannon divergence or $\mathcal{A}$-distance are often used to quantify the similarity of domains (Ben-David et al., 2007). Such measures can be used to construct splits of varying difficulty. The more such data points, the better we can estimate performance on future samples.

Splits based on sentence length   In the recurrent neural network literature , as well as in unsupervised dependency parsing, it is customary to evaluate the ability of a model to generalize from short to long strings (Chalup and Blair; Spitkovsky et al., 2009). This is another interesting set of splits of a treebank. What is our performance on sentences of length $> n$ when training on sentences of length $\leq n$?

---

[8]LDC2013T19

My second advise to designers of future treebanks is thus to devise *alternative splits*. Again, if a treebank contains rich meta-data, such as Ontonotes, we can easily set up such splits. However, a list of standard splits would ensure comparability across the work of different research groups.

4   Learning from Disagreements

One thing that makes parsing harder than necessary, is our insisting on perfect agreement with the human gold-standard annotation. There are often multiple possible analyses of a sentence, even when whole-heartedly adopting a particular linguistic theory, but parsers are only rewarded for picking the analysis accepted by the treebank annotators after adjudication (Plank et al., 2014b).[9]

In unsupervised dependency parsing, some researchers have proposed alternative, less conservative metrics that would not penalize linguistically acceptable deviation from the gold standard (Schwartz et al., 2011; Tsarfaty et al., 2012). An alternative, however, is to use multiple reference annotations for each sentence in the test data. This is the approach taken in machine translation, for example.

I am confident that performance across multiple reference annotations (multiply annotated test data) is more predictive for downstream performance than performance on adjudicated annotations. Moreover, we already know that dependency parsers benefit from observing disagreements between annotators at training time (Plank et al., 2014a); learning from such disagreements using cost-sensitive agreements can lead to better performance even within datasets, and to big improvements across samples and annotation projects. My third advise therefore is therefore to rather spend the adjudication time on annotating more data. In other words, future treebank designers should not adjudicate, but *include multiple, possibly inconsistent, annotations* of each sentence.

5   Crazy Trees

In addition to sampling data adversarially, introducing multiple splits, and collecting multiple, unadjudicated annotations, I also would like to question another straight-jacket in treebanking projects, namely the need for our annotations to be well-formed trees (or directed acyclic graphs for that matter). Some linguists have argued that some sentences are best described by cyclic structures, for example (Pollard and Sag, 1994). Such analyses never make it into treebanks,[10] and I think the main motivation is the idea that modern parsers require well-formed input trees.

Many parsers *are* designed to work only on trees, whether dependency trees or constituent trees, but recently several architectures have been introduced that do not hardwire this constraint into their models. Examples include sequence-to-sequence parsers (Luong et al., 2016) and so-called *tensor-LSTMs* (Schlichtkrull and Soegaard, 2017).

Sequence-to-sequence parsers encode input sentences using recurrent neural networks, recurrently applying the transition parameters of the encoder. In their simplest version, they then generate a sequence of output symbols, one symbol at a time. After encoding the input sentence, the initial state is the vector sentence representation. From this vector, the parsers predict the most likely output symbol. The next state, frmo which the next output symbol is predicted, is obtained by applying the transition parameters of the decoder to the current state.

The encoder, responsible for learning a representation of the input sentence, and the decoder, which generates the parse, only interact through the vector representation. The sequence-to-sequence parser does not guarantee well-formed tree output. On the other hand, this also means the parser is not restricted to generating trees. Sequence-to-sequence models can learn to generate sets of edges from strings and thus associate input sentences with general graphs.

---

[9]One reviewer raised the fair concern, reading this, that *in practice, most inconsistencies in annotation involve silly stuff like the proper annotation of named entities, foreign language, titles, annotating collocations as fixed expressions or compositionally, etc. All of these are not 'real' ambiguities [...], but just a matter of detailed instructions.* I agree, but for the same reason we should a) either not insist on there being a correct annotation in these cases, or b) simply not annotate these cases at all (see §5 for why it is not necessary to insist on fully connected trees).

[10]One reviewer rightly points out that some treebanks actually contain cyclic structures, because of secondary edges, but these are ignored in parsing papers. Good news is that we do not need to ignore such edges anymore.

Tensor-LSTMs run recurrent neural networks over the rows of weight matrices of input sentences. They produce weights over potential heads of possible dependent. In Schlichtkrull and Soegaard (2017), minimum spanning tree search is used to find the best output tree, but this decoding step – which is only used at test time, not during training – is easily removed, and the output matrices can be scored directly against gold-standard general graphs.

6 Is the World Ready?

You may be thinking whether the parsing community is ready for this? Even if you agree that adversarial splits and multiple annotations are great for scientific reasons or engineering purposes, you may wonder whether researchers are not too conservative to adopt treebanks that depart radically from what has been standard methodology for ages.

The answer to this question is that yes, it is unlikely that everyone in the parsing community will adopt this over night, but that designing adversarial, multiply annotated treebanks could pave the way for the researchers who *are* ready.

One reason to think that more and more researchers are ready, is the steadily growing interest in topics such as transfer learning, multi-task learning and robust generalization. This interest is evidenced by the growing number of papers at our main conferences on these topics, recent workshops fully dedicated to one or more of these topics, as well as conference tutorials giving young researchers the necessary background to engage in these topics.

One example of this was the builders-and-breakers workshop at EMNLP 2017 in Copenhagen, Denmark.[11] Here, attendants were encouraged to come up with hard examples that would fool state-of-the-art NLP models. This is exactly why I am proposing adversarial splits in treebanks with multiple, difficult test sets. In order to understand how our models generalize, we need to prevent our evaluation set-ups from rewarding overfitting.

7 Summary

This is clearly an opinion piece. While I feel I have provided some justifications for my opinions, the paper clearly does not live up the standards of a technical track paper. I nevertheless the community will gradually, over time, adopt the following principles: a) Include several test sets in your treebanks that diverge more or less from the training data, but are generally as heterogeneous as possible. b) Devise multiple training-test splits, providing researchers with more data points for estimating the performance of their parsers in the wild. c) Choose several annotations per sentence over adjudication. d) Do not necessarily restrict the citizens of treebanks to be trees. Parsers can handle more complex structures, so include them if linguistically motivated.

Acknowledgments

Thanks to the anonymous reviewers for their comments that helped improve the paper. This research is funded by the ERC Starting Grant LOWLANDS No. 313695.

References

Shai Ben-David, John Blitzer, Koby Crammer, and Fernando Pereira. 2007. Analysis of representations for domain adaptation. In *NIPS*.

Stephan Chalup and Alan Blair. ???? *Neural Networks pages = 955–972, title = Incremental training of first order recurrent neural networks to predict a context-sensitive language, volume = 16, year = 2003* .

George Foster, Cyril Goutte, and Roland Kuhn. 2010. Discriminative instance weighting for domain adaptation in statistical machine translation. In *EMNLP*.

Minh-Thang Luong, Quoc V Le, Ilya Sutskever, Oriol Vinyals, and Lukasz Kaiser. 2016. Multi-task sequence to sequence learning. In *ICLR*.

---

[11]https://generalizablenlp.weebly.com/

Ryan McDonald, Slav Petrov, and Keith Hall. 2011. Multi-source transfer of delexicalized dependency parsers. In *EMNLP*.

Joakim Nivre, Johan Hall, Sandra Kübler, Ryan McDonald, Jens Nilsson, Sebastian Riedel, and Deniz Yuret. 2007. The CoNLL 2007 Shared Task on Dependency Parsing. In *EMNLP-CoNLL*.

Barbara Plank, Dirk Hovy, and Anders Søgaard. 2014a. Learning POS taggers with inter-annotator agreement loss. In *EACL*.

Barbara Plank, Dirk Hovy, and Anders Søgaard. 2014b. Linguistically debatable or just plain wrong? In *ACL*.

Carl Pollard and Ivan Sag. 1994. *Head-driven phrase structure grammar*. The University of Chicago Press, Chicago, Illinois.

Michael Schlichtkrull and Anders Soegaard. 2017. Cross-lingual parsing with late decoding for truly low-resource languages. In *EACL*.

Roy Schwartz, and Omri Abend, Roi Reichart, and Ari Rappoport. 2011. Neutralizing linguistically problematic annotations in unsupervised dependency parsing evaluation. In *ACL*.

Anders Søgaard and Martin Haulrich. 2010. On the derivation perplexity of treebanks. In *TLT*.

Valentin Spitkovsky, Hiyan Alshawi, and Daniel Jurafsky. 2009. Baby steps: how "less is more" in unsupervised dependency parsing. In *NIPS Workshop on Grammar Induction, Representation of Language and Language Learning*.

Reut Tsarfaty, Joakim Nivre, and Evelina Andersson. 2012. Cross-framework evaluation for statistical parsing. In *EACL*.

Syntactic Semantic Correspondence in Dependency Grammar

Cătălina Mărănduc
Faculty of Computer Science,
"Al. I. Cuza" University
Iasi, Romania
Academic Institute of Linguistics
"Iorgu Iordan - Al. Rosetti",
Bucharest, Romania
catalinamaranduc@gmail.com

Cătălin Mititelu
Bucharest
Romania
catalinmititelu@yahoo.com

Victoria Bobicev
Technical University
of Moldova
Chişinău
Republic of Moldova
victoria.bobicev@ia.utm.md

Abstract

This paper describes the semantic format of the UAIC Ro-Dia Dependency Treebank, based on the previous classical syntactic annotation. The discussed format exploits all the semantic information annotated in the morphological level. The transformation of syntactic annotation into semantic one is made semi-automatically, using a tool called Treeops, which is a converter of an XML format to another XML format, in accordance with a set of rules. Non-ambiguous syntactic relations are transformed automatically, while ambiguous ones are manually corrected. The paper also contains some explanations of the generic rapport between syntactic and semantic structures. We elaborated a set of types of judgement which govern the selection of semantic roles for the syntactic tags based on the morphological ones, which are ambiguous for the semantic annotation. After the creation of the large enough semantically annotated corpus, a statistical semantic parser will be trained for the further automate annotation of ambiguous syntactic relations.

1 Introduction

Natural language theorists have diversified their studies from three perspectives: The **syntax** is the study of relationships between signs, **semantics** is the study of the relationships between the signs and their denotation, and the **pragmatics** is the study of the relations between the signs and the situation of communication.

But as the linguistic sign is a relationship between a form (a significant) and a signifier (de Saussure, 1916), the syntax that studies the relationships between signs can not ignore their signifier. So it is not possible to make a tangible separation of these linguistic layers; we will observe that morphology also contains semantic and even pragmatic data, because persons 1,2,3 refer to roles in the communication situation, as deictics, interjections and some adverbs. Punctuation also has clearly defined pragmatic and semantic functions (Druguş, 2015).

Transformational syntax also tried to separate a surface level of language, and a deep level. Although computer scientists do had not came to an agreement about this, transformation rules are still written, for example, in some question answering programs that can deduce that "the novel is written by Orwell" means "Orwell wrote the novel".

For Chomsky Chomsky (1965), the deep structure is a simple, logical, general one, and the surface one is an evolution from the first; it generally truncates relationships and eliminates redundancy. Both are syntactic structures. But while he starts from the same data Fillmore Fillmore (1968), states that the deep structure is one of semantic roles. The deep structure would thus contain the relations between the signs and the real world in which their denotations are located. The surface structure that remains to be the syntactic one is in fact more abstract than the deep one. The syntax is obtained by abstracting and generalizing the semantic relations of signs with the real world. Fillmore only considers the verb as the center of the communication, and enumerates six cases that he considers the core relationships of the predicate: Agentive, Dative, Instrumental, Factitive (Result), Objective and Locative.

The number of cases is too reduced in this theory, and all the researchers added other cases to this list. It is not clear why only the core of the sentence should have a semantic structure, as if the optional

Proceedings of the 16th International Workshop on Treebanks and Linguistic Theories (TLT16), pages 167–180,
Prague, Czech Republic, January 23–24, 2018. Distributed under a CC-BY 4.0 licence. 2017.

Keywords: dependency, format converter, Old Romanian, semantic relations, syntactic relations

dependencies were meaningless. Being less abstract than the syntactic structure, the semantic structure should have more roles than the first one.

2 Related Work

There is no universal consensus about semantic annotation, and about the number of semantic categories. Bonial et al. (2014) made the remark that previously, annotation focused on event relations expressed by verbs, but the meaning of words is not necessarily linked to their morphological value - nouns, adverbs, and interjections can also express an event. They propose to expand the PropBank annotations to nouns, adjectives, and complex predicates. This research is called Predicate Unification.

In the UAIC-FII (Faculty of Computer Science, "Al. I. Cuza" University, Iaşi, Romania) NLP (Natural Language Processing) group, Diana Trandabǎţ (2010) has imported about 1,000 sentences from the English FrameNet. She has translated in Romanian the sentences and has imported their semantic annotation. In this way, she has made a first set of semantic annotations in Romanian. Just as the English FrameNet, the NLP annotations only cover the core structure of the sentence, called Semantic Frame, the predicate arguments, called Semantic Roles; the semantic functions of other members of the structure are neglected.

Another group of semantic annotations is related to the VerbNet (Kipper et al., 2006), project based on PWN, or to a combination between the two semantic annotation systems: FrameNet and VerbNet (Shi and Mihalcea, 2005). The problem is the same; they emphasize the importance of the predicate and of the action scenarios (events), but the other words of the language make sense as well, and not all judgments describe events.

The UAIC-RoDia DepTb is annotated in Dependency Grammar, a flexible formalism founded by Tesnière (1959), and actualized as Functional Dependency Grammar by Tapanainen and Jarvinen (1998), Mel'čuk (1988). Actually, a big number of corpora in the world have adopted the same formalism. Looking at the old corpora, that have been united during the few years under at the Universal Dependencies (UD) portal, we find that many of them share the same way of development by going from syntactic to semantic annotation.

This group contains a Treebank for the Standard Contemporary Romanian, affiliated by the RACAI (Artifical Intelligence Academic Institute or Research) which imported 4,000 sentences from the UAIC Treebank (of the Al. I. Cuza University). However, not all the Natural Romanian Language is a standard one. A small percent of communication acts are in the standard language; spoken language, poetry, regional and old language, Social Media communication are not in the standard language. In all these styles of communication innovation is permitted. We have decided to annotate all kinds of nonstandard language and we have recently become affiliated with the UD as the UD-Romanian Nonstandard Treebank, which was created at the UAIC, but also has contributors from the Republic of Moldova, a country where Romanian is also spoken.

The other treebanks affiliated with the UD have the same problem; it is an enormous advantage that the annotation conventions are strictly the same, but the attention paid to morphology in the classification of the syntactic relations leads to the loss of semantic information previously annotated in the original formats of affiliated treebanks.

In 2003, the PDT authors described the three level structure of their treebank and the Tectogrammatic level (which includes semantic, logical and syntactic information) (Bohmová et al., 2003). They have for a long time been interested in semantics and its links with syntax (Sgall et al., 1986). In a previous paper (Mǎrǎnduc et al., 2017), we have shown that our semantic annotation system has affinities with the PDT Tectogrammatic layer. The authors of BulTreebank are also interested in semantics (Simov and Osenova, 2011). The PENN Treebank is also involved in semantics, or in the annotation of entities and events (Song et al., 2015).

3 Semantic Information in Annotated Data

The syntactic annotation in the classic UAIC format (originally created with the intention to serve pedagogical purposes) contains 14 types of circumstantial modifiers: c.c.conc. (concession), c.c.cond.

Judgment	nsubj	dobj	npred	other
Process	ACT	RSLT	-	-
Performance	PERFR	PERF	QLF	-
Actantial	ACT	PAT	-	BEN
Experience	EXPR	EXP	-	BEN
Comunic.	EMT	CTNT	-	RCPT
Definition	DFND	-	DFNS	CNCOP
Chang.idnt	DFND	-	DFNS	CNCOP
Characteriz	CTNT	-	QLF	CNCOP
Existence	QEXIST	-	-	LOC, TIME

Table 1: The semantic core dependencies in relation of the type of judgment.

(condition), c.c.cons. (consecutive), c.c.cumul. (cumulative), c.c.cz. (causal), c.c.exc. (exception), c.c.instr. (instrumental), c.c.l. (local), c.c.m. (modal), c.c.opoz. (opposition), c.c.rel. (relative, referential), c.c.scop. (purpose), c.c.soc. (associative), and c.c.t. (temporal). For these modifiers, we used the semantic tags: CNCS, COND, CSQ, CUMUL, CAUS, EXCP, INSTR, LOC, MOD, OPPOS, REFR, PURP, ASSOC, TEMP. The modal modifier is the the only one ambiguous among those 14 circumstantial modifiers, which can have more values, as: Comparative, Intensifier, Restrictive, Iterative, Privative, Qualifier, Quantitative, for which we used the tags: COMP, INTNS, ITER, PRV, RESTR, QLF, QNT, manually annotated for the moment. The other syntactic relations with semantic meaning are in the UAIC convention: voc. (vocative, addressee), ap. (apposition, resumption), c.ag. (agent complement), incid. (incident), neg. (negative). For these ones, we used the tags: ADDR, RSMP, ACT (the same tag for the active agent), INCID, QNEG (one of the quantifiers in our system). All these tags can be automatically replaced.

However, these values are not necessarily related to verb subordination. There may be nouns from the semantic sphere of these notions or derived from verbs and having such subordinate semantic values. From a syntactic point of view, they are hidden under ambiguous tags, such as noun modifiers. These cases are also manually annotated. Examples:

- *Bani pentru excursie* "Money for the trip" is a nominal modifier with a purpose meaning;

- *Casa de acolo* "The house there" is an adverbial modifier of a noun, with a local meaning;

- *Generaţia de mâine* "The generation of tomorrow" is an adverbial modifier of a noun having a temporal meaning.

Therefore, we can have syntactic tags containing non-ambiguous semantic information and other tags that are not related to any particular semantic information, i.e. they are semantically ambiguous. Our intention is to use a statistical parser to annotate the words with such semantically ambiguous syntactic relations, after we get a sufficiently large training corpus by means of the manual annotations.

The most ambiguous are the core elements of the clause, and for interpreting them, we propose a table of rules and the roles which each type presupposes or admits. The table can be completed with other types if necessary. Our rules are are not similar to frames, because they also take into consideration the sentences that do not describe an event, but an affirmation of the existence of some things, an identification, a description of a state, acts of speech, etc. (see Table 1 3).

Our treebank is annotated and supervised on a multilayer basis. Therefore, we can use the semantic information contained in the fine and correct morphological annotation of the Treebank. The type of the pronoun and pronominal determiners is semantically established: For the possessives, the semantic value is appurtenance (APP), for the demonstratives, the semantic value is deictic (DX), for the interrogatives the semantic value is INTROG, for the negatives, the semantic value is QNEG, and for the emphatic pronoun and pronominal determiner the semantic value is IDENT. For the indefinite pronoun and a restricted number of them, the value can be, QUNIV; "all", "whichever", are universal quantifiers, and the rest of indefinites have the semantic value UNCTN (uncertain).

Articles, which come from pronouns, have the same semantic values as these ones: DX, (deictic) for the demonstrative article, APP (appurtenance) for the possessive article, and DEF, UNDEF (defined / undefined) for the determinative articles. The reflexive pronoun can have a restricted number of values, depending on the verb which has this mark and they indicate its possible patterns: impersonal, passive, dynamic, reciprocal or continuant, with the semantic tags: IMPRS, PASS, DYN, RCPR, CTNU. Interjections also have a restricted number of semantic values, in accordance with their word form: affect, alert, imitation, imperative, with the tags: AFF, ALRT, IMIT, IMPER.

As it can be seen, we do not intend to annotate certain entities, such as the ones in information retrieval programs, but semantic categories of great generality and logical connectors or quantifiers. There are similarities with the roles-based models, but we extend this to all the components of the sentence; in addition, judgments are not necessarily seen as events. Our purpose is to make a pattern dictionary of Romanian verbs (PDRoV), taking into consideration, the syntactic relations required for or allowed by each verb. The dictionary will be linked to RoWN (the Word Net for Romanian), and it will take from this dictionary the most particular semantic values for the dependencies.

Verbal dependencies cannot be easily separated into optional and obligatory ones; for some languages, such as Romanian, the presence of the subject in the clause is optional. For some verbs, the presence of local, temporal or quantitative modifiers is mandatory. Examples:

- *to go to Prague* (we cannot say *to go* without showing the target of the movement).

- *The session lasted three hours* (or *a long time*, but not without a temporal determiner).

- *The truck weighs 4 tons*, (or *a lot*, but not without a quantitative determiner).

Of course there are several types of information we have annotated in the semantic format, some are closer to the pragmatic layer and, establishing relations between the participants to the communication act in a certain situation. Interjections, together with deictics, the pronouns of person I-II, with some adverbs and the punctuation link the semantic and the pragmatic levels.

Punctuation has different semantic values when it is at the end of sentence from the cases when it is inside it. In the last position, the dot/full stop marks only the end of the communication, while the exclamation and the question marks indicate both the end and the interrogative or exclamatory forms. The semantic tags for these values are: END, INTROG, EXCL. Inside the sentence, the comma can be the mark of coordination, being a CNCONJ, just as the coordinating conjunctions. Also, the comma can mark the introduction of an explanatory sequence or a topic different from the natural one, some constructions being dislocated. The tags are: ELAB, DISL. A big number of punctuation elements are used to isolate the incident constructions: they are non-appurtenance marks : NOAPP. Other punctuation marks, for example inverted commas, parentheses, dashes, indicate the limits of the text introduced in another text, and we have used for all of them a single semantic tag: QUOT. We have found semantic values in the time and modality of verbs. Some conjunctions or prepositions are specialized for a semantic value: *fiindcă* "because" (CAUS) *pentru* "for" (PURP), etc.

4 Logical-Semantic System

In the UAIC treebank, the relations between clauses are marked with the same labels as those of the words that fulfill the same roles. For a subordinate clause, the tag is annotated as the relation of its predicate with the predicate of the head clause, but it is a relationship of the whole subtree.

Example:

- *Persoanele atente pot învăţa.* "Mindful people can learn." *Persoanele* "People" has the syntactic relation sbj. (and the semantic relation PERFR) subordinated to the root *învăţa* "learn".

- *Cine are urechi de auzit, poate învăța.* "Whoever has ears to hear, can learn." The same tags mark the relation of *are* "has", and all the subtree above comma, also subordinated to the root *învăța* "learn".

Our trees are not clauses but long sentences, so that their construction can be likened to a logical expression consisting of full-meaning elements and operators to which clauses are connected, and the truth value of the whole sentence can be calculated according to the truth values of the component clauses.

Our system has 6 connectors, the copulative connector (which resembles the logical conjunction), the disjunctive connector (which shows that the clauses are excluded), the opposing connector (which shows that the clauses are opposed without being exclusive), the conclusive connector (which resembles the logical relation of implication), the dependence (subordinate) connector, and the copulative connector. The last usually marks a relationship of equivalence between the subject and the predicative name.

Connectors have the following semantic tags: CNCONJ, CNDISJ, CNADVS, CNCNCL, CNSBRD, CNCOP. The relational words are included among the connected elements in the UAIC syntactic system, being subordinated to the first connected element and simultaneously being the head for the second one. In the UAIC semantic system, we have subordinated them to the second element of the relationship, to emphasize the words with full meaning and especially to conform to most international annotation systems.

Connectors are operators that indicate a relation between two elements. Other operators apply to one element and we call them quantifiers. They form judgments with a general character, which apply to all the set of elements (as universal quantifiers); or they form judgments that apply to at least one element (as an existential quantifier). Other quantifiers modulate the truth value, giving a necessary, possible or impossible character (with negative polarity). Semantic tags used for quantifiers are: QUNIV, QEXIST, QNECES, QPOSIB, QNEG.

Examples:

- Logical computing with dyadic operator (connector):

  El va trece testele sau va fi eliminat din competiție. "He will pass the tests or he will be eliminated from the competition." *Sau* "or" is a connector for disjunction (CNDISJ). The expression has the truth value=1 (true) if one of the two clauses is denied. The expression obtained by the affirmation of both clauses or by negation of both, has the truth value=0 (false).

  "And" is a connector for the reunion (conjunction) and the expression formed by "and" shows that both the related clauses have the same truth value.

  He will pass the tests and he will be eliminated=0

  He will not pass the tests and he will not be eliminated=0.

- Logical computing with monadic operator (quantifier):

  Trebuie să trec acest test. "I must pass this test." *Nu este posibil să nu trec acest test.* "It is not possible for me not to pass this test."

  The quantifier necessity (QNECES) is equivalent to the negation (QNEG) of the quantifier possibility (QPOSIB) applied to the negation of the modulated sentence as necessary:

  QNECES (to pass this test) is equivalent to QNEG (QPOSIB(QNEG(to pass this test)))

  i.e. "It is necessary that I pass the test" is equivalent to "It is not possible that I do not pass the test."

5 Treeops - A Tool for Changing the UAIC-Syntactic Format in the UAIC-Semantic Format

All non-ambiguous transformations are done automatically using a tool called Treeops. It is a rule-based XML transformer. Having an XML as input and using a customized set of rules, it produces a new XML structure. This process is similar to the eXtensible Style sheet Language Transformation (XSLT) process[1]. The set of rules is a function that takes as input an XML structure and produces another XML structure. A non-ambiguous transforming rule can be formulated as an `if-then` statement:

```
if (condition) then action
```

During a transformation process the XML is traversed node by node and the Treeops rule is converted into an if-then statement:

```
if (selector matches node) then action
```

Treeops requires the selector to be an XML Path Language (XPath) expression[2]. The action must be internally defined by taking parameters, for example:

```
changeAttrValue(<new value>)
```

changes the value of the current XML attribute.

For this reason, Treeops is currently working only on the XML format, where it takes the name of the features to be changed. In future, the program could be made to have an XML as input and to display the result in the CONLLU format. Obviously, Treeops is language-independent, while the rules are formulated according to the language of the document, and the result will be in the language that is required by the rules (it may be different from the one in the input).

For example, the rule defined as:

```
//word[@deprel='superl.']/@deprel => changeAttrValue('SUPER')
```

becomes an XSLT template:

```
<xsl:template match="//word[@deprel='superl.']/@deprel">
  <xsl:call-template name="changeAttrValue">
    <xsl:with-param name="new_value" select="'SUPER'"/>
  </xsl:call-template>
</xsl:template>
```

where the `changeAttrValue` template is pre-defined as:

```
<xsl:template name="changeAttrValue">
  <xsl:param name="new_value"/>
  <xsl:attribute name="{name(.)}">
    <xsl:value-of select="$new_value"/>
  </xsl:attribute>
</xsl:template>
```

This is a rule with a single condition for transforming a UAIC syntactic tag into a semantic one. It transforms the syntactic relationship superl. into the semantic tag SUPER (Superlative). This type of rule is used to change the syntactic tag of 13 types of circumstantial complement (except c.c.m., which is semantically ambiguous) and also for the relations: vocative, comparative, subordination, agent complement, negation, and apposition.

There are other rules for transforming non-ambiguous syntactic tags into semantic tags that need to fulfill multiple conditions. Example:

```
//word[@deprel='coord.' and (@lemma='sau' or @lemma='ori'
  or @lemma='ci')]/@deprel => changeAttrValue('CNDISJ')
```

This rule changes the syntactic coordination into a logical-semantic tag for the relation of disjunction, taking into account the conjunctions *sau, ori, ci* "or".

There are also more complex rules for the tree structure transformation. The relational elements are used in the UAIC syntactic structure input as heads, and the semantic structure output has the relational elements subordinated to the meaningfull words. Example:

---

[1] https://www.w3.org/TR/xslt
[2] https://www.w3.org/TR/1999/REC-xpath-19991116/

```
//word[@deprel='narativ.' and @head=../word/@id]/@head
   => (@head <- $n/../word[@id=$n/@head]/@head)
//word[@id=../word[@deprel='narativ.']/@head]/@head
   => (@head <- $n/../word[@deprel='narativ.']/@id)
//word[@deprel='narativ.' and head=../word/@id]/@deprel
   => (@deprel <- $n/../word[@id=$n/@head]/@deprel)
```

This is a transformation rule which changes the syntactic relation "narrative." In the UAIC convention, narrative connectors are treated as textual ones, they are roots for the sentence, having no relation, and subordinating the principal verb of the sentences, which effects the narrative relationship. The above rule reverses the sense of the relationship, i.e. the head becomes subordinated and vice versa; it creates a relationship for the narrative conjunction, and deletes the relationship of its current head, which becomes the root.

What we understand by *a semantically ambiguous syntactic relation* does not mean that the sentence may have more interpretations, but the same general or morphologically defined syntactic relation (eg, nominal modifier) can be transposed into a large number of less general semantic relations. The table in the appendix contains correspondences between UD syntactic tags, UAIC syntactic tangs, and the semantic tags of the formats described here. 214 lines of the table do not mean that the system has 214 semantic tags, but that there are 214 combinations of the 45 UAIC syntactic tags, the 53 tags of Romanian specific subclassifications in the syntactic UD system, and the 96 semantic tags. Empty boxes in the table of judgment types are marked with DASH because there is no specific syntactic or semantic relation to that position in that type of judgment. For example, there is no direct object if the type of judgment requires a predicative name. Examples from the table: On row 199, column 3, we have the *sbj.* tag, which annotates the subject in the UAIC syntactic convention. On the row 199, column 2, four values correspond at it in the UD syntactic convention, those for a word subject, a clause subject, each of them active or passive: *nsubj, csubj, nsubj:pass, csubj:pass*. The tags of the 199 row, if repeated, can correspond to the 199 - 211 rows on the 4th column, i.e. there are 12 possible semantic tags, which demonstrates that the subject is a semantically ambiguous syntactic relationship. The QUOTES mark in this table the repetition of the previous row.

The Treeops program was used both to get an automatically semi-transformed variant of the semantic format (5,566 sentences are completely manually transformed in the semantic format), and, by writing another set of rules, to transform the treebank from the XML-UAIC syntactic format into XML-UD syntactic format. Another program performed the transformation from the XML-UD into CONLLU UDV2, the format required to introduce the first 1,200 phrases in the UD, under the name UD-Romanian Nonstandard. Currently, the UAIC treebank has 18,000 sentences, (except the 4,000 earlier + 1,200 now), 12,800 to be added on the upcoming releases.

6 Applications

These annotations are now applied to 5,200 sentences, most of them the four New Testament Gospels of 1648, the first published in Romanian, with Cyrillic letters, which were obtained by an Optical Character Recogniser (OCR) built at the Institute of Mathematics and Computer Science of Chisinau (Colesnicov et al., 2016). Various research could be applied to the corpus, such as those on incident texts nested in one another. Example:

Iară Iisus zise ucenicilor Săi: Adevăr zic voao: anevoe va întra bogatul întru Împărăţiia Ceriurelor. "And Jesus said unto his disciples, Verily I say unto you: the rich shall scarcely enter the Kingdom of the Heavens."

In this example, the first part, up to the first colon, has the evangelist Matthew as emitter (EMT) and the reader as receiver (RCPT). Jesus and the disciples are designated here by the third person. The second text introduced by the verbum dicendi has as emitter Jesus and as receivers, the disciples. Here Jesus is designated by the first person, and the disciples by the second person. The third text, introduced in the second one by another verbum dicendi and another colon, is the content (CTNT) of Jesus' teaching, a general judgment that does not refer either to himself or to the disciples, but to a generic character, the

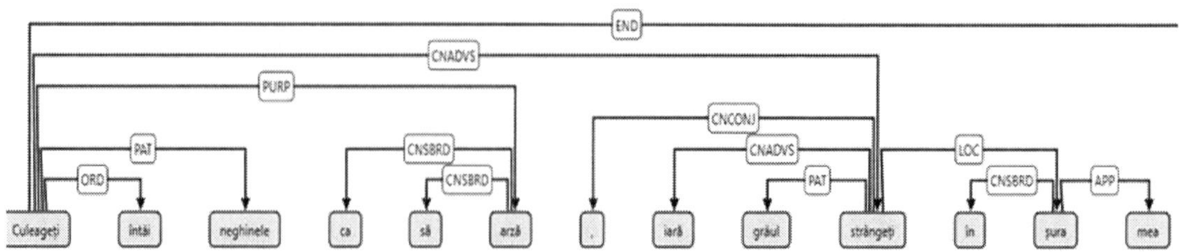

Figure 1: The parabolic original text.

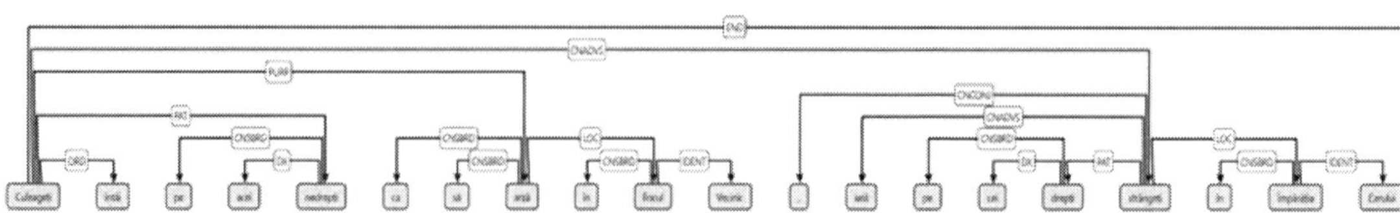

Figure 2: The text obtained by replacing the words with their parabolic key.

rich man, designated by the third person. The structure of roles in the three texts is different, as the verbal persons selection shows.

Another study can analyze the parabolic levels. This means that fully meaningful words are replaced by completely different ones and the connectors are preserved; we have two isomorphic parallel stories, a surface one, and another one containing the meaning. Example:

Omul samănă sămânţă bună în holda sa. Veni duşmanul şi sămănă între grâu neghini. La vreamea secerişului, stăpânul va porunci secerătorilor: Culegeţi întâi neghinele ca să arză, iară grâul strângeţi în şura mea. "Man sow good seed in his field. Come the enemy, and sow the tares among the wheat. At the time of the harvest, the owner will command to the reapers: First reap the tares to burn, and the wheat gather in my barn."

Key:

omul=Fiul omenesc "man=Human Son"

holda=lumea "the field=the world"

sămânţă bună=cei drepţi "good seed=the righteous"

neghinele=cei nedrepţi "the tares=the unrighteous"

duşmanul=diavolul "enemy=devil"

vremea secerişului=sfârşenia veacului "the time of the harvest=the end of the world"

secerătorii=îngerii "reapers=angels"

săarză=să arză în focul veşnic "to burn=to burn in the Eternal Fire"

şura mea=Împărăţia Ceriului "my barn=the Kingdom of the Heaven"

Replacement:

Fiul omenesc samănă pe cei drepţi în lume. Veni diavolul şi sămănă între cei drepţi pe acei nedrepţi. La sfârşenia veacului, Fiul omenesc va porunci îngerilor: Culegeţi întâi pe cei nedrepţi ca să arză în Focul veşnic, iară pe cei drepţi strângeţi în Împărăţia Cerului. "The human Son sows the righteous in the world. The devil comes and sows those unrighteous among the righteous. At the end of the world, the Human Son will command to the angels: First reap those unrighteous to burn in the Eternal Fire, and the righteous gather in the Kingdom of Heaven."

In Figures 1 and 2 it can be seen that although the semantic contents of the nodes change, the basic structure remains the same (see Figure 1 and 2).

7 Conclusion and Future Work

In this paper we discussed the transformation process of UAIC RoDia-Dep-Treebank syntactic annotation into the logical-semantic annotation. This transformation is done automatically for non-ambiguous syntactic relations, and manually for ambiguous relations. We also described the applications created for the annotation format tranformation. We show the examples of the linguistic and pragmatic research using corpora with semantic annotation.

In future, we plan to annotate morphologically and syntactically the second part of the New Testament, the Acts of Apostles, and to transform all the syntactic treebank into the new format. We plan to train a statistical parser on this corpus, in order to transform the ambiguous syntactic relations.

References

Alena Bohmová, Jan Hajič, Eva Hajičova, and Barbora Hladka. 2003. *The Prague Dependency Treebank: A Three-Level Annotation Scenario. Text, Speech and Language Technology.* Springer Publisher, Prague.

Claire Bonial, Julia Bonn, Kathryn Conger, Jena D. Hwang, and Martha Palmer. 2014. Propbank: Semantics of new predicate types. In *Proceedings of LREC.* pages 3013âĂŞ–3019.

Noam Chomsky. 1965. *Aspects of the Theory of Syntax.* MIT Press, Cambridge, UK.

Alexandru Colesnicov, Ludmila Malahov, and Tudor Bumbu. 2016. Digitization of romanian printed texts of the 17th century. In *Proceedings of the 12th International Conference Linguistic Resources and Tools for Processing the Romanian Language.* Alexandru Ioan Cuza University Press, pages 1–11.

Ferdinand de Saussure. 1916. *Cours de Linguistique generale.* Payot, Paris.

Ioachim Druguş. 2015. Metalingua: a metalanguage for the semantic annotation of natural languages. In *Proceedings of the 11th International Conference Linguistic Resources and Tools for Processing the Romanian Language.* Alexandru Ioan Cuza University Press, pages 79–94.

Charles J. Fillmore. 1968. The case for case. In *Universals in Linguistic Theory.* Holt, Rinehart, and Winston, pages 1–88.

Karin Kipper, Anna Korhonen, Neville Ryant, and Martha Palmer. 2006. Extensive classifications of english verbs. In *Proceedings of the 12th EURALEX International Congress.*

Cătălina Mărănduc, Monica Mihaela Rizea, and Dan Cristea. 2017. Mapping dependency relations onto semantic categories. In *Proceedings of the International Conference on Computational Linguistics and Intelligent Text Processing (CICLing).*

Igor Mel'čuk. 1988. *Dependency Syntax: Theory and Practice.* The SUNY Press, Albany, NY.

Petr Sgall, Eva Hajičová, and Jarmila Panevová. 1986. *The meaning of the sentence in its semantic and pragmatic aspects.* Academic Press and Reide, Prague, Dordrecht.

Lei Shi and Rada Mihalcea. 2005. Putting pieces together: Combining framenet, verbnet and wordnet for robust semantic parsing. In *Proceedings of the Sixth International Conference on Intelligent Text Processing and Computational Linguistics.* Mexico.

Kiril Simov and Petya Osenova. 2011. Towards minimal recursion semantics over bulgarian dependency parsing. In *Proceedings of the RANLP 2011 Conference.* Hissar, Bulgaria.

Zhiyi Song, Ann Bies, Stephanie Strassel, Tom Riese, Justin Mott, Joe Ellis, Jonathan Wright, Seth Kulick, Neville Ryant, and Xiaoyi Ma. 2015. From light to rich ere: Annotation of entities, relations, and events. In *Proceeding of 14th Annual Conference of the North American Chapter of the Association for Computational Linguistics.*

Pasi Tapanainen and Timo Jarvinen. 1998. Towards an implementable dependency grammar. In *CoLing-ACLâĂŹ98 workshop Processing of Dependency-based Grammars, Montreal.*

Lucien Tesnière. 1959. *Eléments de syntaxe structurale.* Klincksieck, Paris.

Diana Trandabăţ. 2010. *Natural Language Processing Using Semantic Frames - PHD Thesis.* Faculty of Computer Science, Al. I. Cuza University, Iaşi.

 Table of semantic tags, their explanation, and their correspondence whit UAIC and UD syntactic tags

Nr.crt.	UD syntactic	UAIC syntactic	UAIC semantic	Explanation
1	amod, det, nummod	a.adj.	COMP	Comparative
2	”	”	QEXIST	Quantifier:existential
3	”	”	QUNIV	Quantifier:universal
4	”	”	DX	Deictic
5	”	”	IDENT	Identifier
6	”	”	INTROG	Interrogative
7	”	”	QNEG	Quantifier:negative
8	”	”	APP	Appurtenance
9	”	”	QLF	Qualifier
10	”	”	QNT	Quantity
11	”	”	UNCTN	Uncertain
12	advmod	a.adv.	LOC	Local
13	”	”	MOD	Modal
14	”	”	PRV	Privative
15	”	”	RESTR	Restrictive
16	”	”	ITER	Iterative
17	”	”	TEMP	Temporal
18	appos	ap.	RSMP	Resumption
19	nmod	a.pron.	QUNIV	Quantifier:universal
20	”	”	QEXIST	Quantifier:existential
21	”	”	DX	Deictic
22	”	”	IDENT	Identifier
23	”	”	INTROG	Interrogative
24	”	”	QNEG	Quantifier:negative
25	”	”	APP	Appurtenance
26	”	”	UNCTN	Uncertain
27	nmod	’a.subst.	ASSOC	Associative
28	”	”	CAUS	Causative
29	”	”	CNCS	Concessive
30	”	”	COND	Conditional
31	”	”	CSQ	Consequence
32	”	”	CUMUL	Cumulative
33	”	”	DFNS	Definiens
34	”	”	EXCP	Exception
35	”	”	INSTR	Instrumental
36	”	”	LOC	Local
37	”	”	MOD	Modal
38	”	”	OPPOS	Opposite
39	”	”	PARS	Pars
40	”	”	APP	Appurtenance
41	”	”	POLIT	Politness
42	”	”	PRV	Privative
43	”	”	PURP	Purpose
44	”	”	REFR	Reference
45	”	”	TEMP	Temporal

Nr.crt.	UD syntactic	UAIC syntactic	UAIC semantic	Explanation
46	aux	aux.	ABIL	Ability
47	,,	,,	FTR	Future
48	,,	,,	OPTV	Optative
49	aux:pass	,,	PASS	Passive
50	aux	,,	PAST	Past
51	,,	,,	POTN	Potentiality
52	acl	a.vb.	ASSOC	Associative
53	,,	,,	CAUS	Causative
54	,,	,,	CNCS	Concession
55	acl	a.vb.	COND	Condition
56	,,	,,	CSQ	Consequence
57	,,	,,	CUMUL	Cumulative
58	,,	,,	DFNS	Definiens
59	,,	,,	EXCP	Exception
60	,,	,,	INSTR	Instrumental
61	,,	,,	LOC	Local
62	,,	,,	MOD	Modal
63	,,	,,	OPPOS	Opposite
64	,,	,,	PARTV	Partitive
65	,,	,,	RESTR	Restrictive
66	,,	,,	PAT	Patient
67	,,	,,	POLIT	Politness
68	,,	,,	APP	Appurtenance
69	,,	,,	PRV	Privative
70	,,	,,	PURP	Purpose
71	,,	,,	QLF	Qualifier
72	,,	,,	REFR	Reference
73	,,	,,	TEMP	Temporal
74	,,	,,	ASSOC	Associative
75	,,	,,	CAUS	Causative
76	nmod:agent	c.ag.	ACT	Actant, Agent
77	obl, advmod, advcl	c.c.conc.	CNCS	Consequence
78	,,	c.c.cond.	COND	Condition
79	,,	c.c.cons.	CSQ	Consequence
80	,,	c.c.cumul.	CUMUL	Cumulative
81	,,	c.c.cz.	CAUS	Causative
82	,,	c.c.exc.	EXCP	Exception
83	,,	c.c.instr.	INSTR	Instrumental
84	,,	c.c.l.	LOC	Condition
85	,,	c.c.m.	MOD	Modal
86	,,	,,	INTNS	Intensifier
87	,,	,,	ITER	Iterative
88	,,	,,	PRV	Privative
89	,,	,,	RESTR	Restrictive
90	,,	,,	MOD	Modal
91	,,	,,	QLF	Qualifier
92	,,	,,	QNT	Quantity
93	,,	c.c.opoz.	OPPOS	Opposite
94	,,	c.c.rel.	REFR	Reference

Nr.crt.	UD syntactic	UAIC syntactic	UAIC semantic	Explanation
95	”	c.c.scop.	PURP	Purpose
96	”	c.c.soc.	ASSOC	Associative
97	nmod:tmod, adv-mod:tmod, advcl:tcl	c.c.t.	TEMP	Temporal
98	obj, expl, ccomp	c.d.	QPOSIB	Quantifier:possibility
99	”	”	BEN	Beneficiary
100	”	”	CTNT	Content
101	”	”	EXP	Experience
102	”	”	GREET	Greeting
103	”	”	INSTR	Instrumental
104	”	”	APP	Appurtenance
105	”	”	PURP	Purpose
106	”	”	OBJ	Object
107	”	”	RSLT	Result
108	”	”	PAT	Patient
109	iobj, expl, xcomp	c.i.	PERF	Performance
110	”	”	RSLT	Result
111	”	”	BEN	Beneficiary
112	”	”	EXPR	Experiencer
113	”	”	RCPT	Receiver, Recipient
114	”	”	APP	Appurtenance
115	advmod	comp.	COMP	Comparative
116	cc, conj	coord.	CNCNCL	Connect:conclusion
117	”	”	CNDISJ	Connect:disjunction
118	orphan	-	EQVH	Ellipse, Equivalent with the head
119	”	”	EQVHP	Equivalent with the head, but positive
120	”	”	EQVHZ	Equivalent with the read, but negative
121	cc, conj	”	CNADVS	Connect:adversative
122	”	”	CNCONJ	Connect:reunion
123	cop	-	CNCOP	Connect:copulative
124	nmod:pmod	c.prep.	ASSOC	Associative
125	”	”	BLAM	Blam
126	”	”	BEN	Beneficiary
127	”	”	CAUS	Causative
125	”	”	BLAM	Blam
128	”	”	CNCS	Concession
129	”	”	COND	Condition
130	”	”	CSQ	Consequence
131	”	”	CTNT	Content
132	”	”	CUMUL	Cumulative
133	”	”	EQVL	Equivalent
134	”	”	EXCP	Exception
135	”	”	EXP	Experience

Nr.crt.	UD syntactic	UAIC syntactic	UAIC semantic	Explanation
137	,,	,,	OPPOS	Opposite
138	,,	,,	PURP	Purpose
139	,,	,,	RCPT	Recipient, Receiver
140	,,	,,	REFR	Reference
141	det	det.	UNDEF	Undefined
142	,,	,,	DEF	Defined
143	,,	,,	DX	Deictic
144	,,	,,	APP	Appurtenance
145	xcomp	el.pred.	QNT	Quantity
146	,,	,,	UNCTN	Uncertain
147	,,	,,	DFND	Definiendum
148	,,	,,	EQVL	Equivalent
149	,,	,,	EXPR	Experiencer
150	,,	,,	IDENT	Identifier
151	,,	,,	PERF	Performance
152	,,	,,	APP	Appurtenance
153	,,	,,	RESTR	Restrictive
154	,,	,,	RSLT	Result
155	,,	,,	QLF	Qualifier
156	expl	-	EXPL:APP	Expletive:appurtenance
157	,,	,,	EXPL:BEN	Expletive:beneficiary
158	,,	,,	EXPL:EXP	Expletive:experience
159	,,	,,	EXPL:EXPR	Expletive:experiencer
160	,,	,,	EXPL:OBJ	Expletive:object
161	,,	,,	EXPL:DFND	Expletive:definiendum
162	,,	,,	EXPL:PAT	Expletive:patient
163	,,	,,	EXPL:RCPT	Expletive:receiver
164	parataxis	incid.	INCID	Incident
165	discourse	interj.	AFF	Affect
166	,,	,,	ALRT	Alert
167	,,	,,	IMIT	Imitation
168	,,	,,	IMPER	Imperative
169	cc	narativ.	CNCNCL	Connect:conclusion
170	mark	,,	CNSBRD	Connect:subordination
171	cc	,,	CNDISJ	Connect:disjunction
172	,,	,,	CNADVS	Conect:adversative
173	,,	,,	CNCONJ	Connect:reunion
174	-	n.pred.	RSMP	Apposition
175	,,	,,	EMT	Emitter
176	,,	,,	DFNS	Definiens
177	,,	,,	EXP	Experience
178	,,	,,	IDENT	Identifier
179	,,	,,	APP	Appurtenance
180	,,	,,	PRV	Privative
181	,,	,,	QLF	Qualifier
182	mark	part.	GNR	Generic
183	,,	,,	GREET	Greeting
184	,,	,,	POTN	Potentiality
185	,,	,,	IMPER	Imperative
186	punct	punct. (non-final)	DISL	Dislocation

Nr.crt.	UD syntactic	UAIC syntactic	UAIC semantic	Explanation
187	"	"	QUOT	Quotation
188	"	"	NOAPP	Non-appurtenance
189	"	"	CNCONJ	Connect:reunion
190	"	"	ELAB	Elaboration
191	"	punct.(final)	END	End
192	"	"	EXCL	Exclamation
193	"	"	INTROG	Interrogative
194	expl:pv, expl:poss	refl.	CTNU	Continuant
195	"	"	DYN	Dynamic
196	"	"	RCPR	Reciprocal
197	expl:pass	"	PASS	Passive
198	expl:impers	"	IMPRS	Impersonal
199	nsubj, csubj, nsubj:pass, csubj:pass	sbj.	ACT	Actant, Agent
200	"	"	PERFR	Performer
201	"	"	PERF	Performance
202	"	"	DFND	Definiendum
203	"	"	EMT	Emitter
204	"	"	QEXIST	Quantifier:existence
205	"	"	QUNIV	Quantifier:universal
206	"	"	QUPOSIB	Quantifier>possibility
207	"	"	QUNECES	Quantifier>necessity
208	"	"	EXPR	Experiencer
209	"	"	EXP	Experience
210	"	"	PAT	Patient
211	"	"	RCPT	Receiver
212	mark	subord.	CNSBRD	Connect:subord
213	advmod	superl.	SUPER	Superlative
214	vocative	voc.	ADDR	Addressee

Multi-word annotation in syntactic treebanks

Propositions for Universal Dependencies

Sylvain Kahane
Université Paris Nanterre
Modyco (CNRS)
`sylvain@kahane.fr`

Marine Courtin, Kim Gerdes
Sorbonne Nouvelle
ILPGA, LPP (CNRS)
`marine.courtin@etud.sorbonne-`
`nouvelle.fr, kim@gerdes.fr`

Abstract

This paper discusses how to analyze syntactically irregular expressions in a syntactic treebank. We distinguish such Multi-Word Expressions (MWEs) from comparable non-compositional expressions, i.e. idioms. A solution is proposed in the framework of Universal Dependencies (UD). We further discuss the case of functional MWEs, which are particularly problematic in UD.

1   Introduction

In every linguistic annotation project, the delimitation of lower and upper boundaries of the annotation units constitutes a basic challenge. In syntactic annotation, the lower boundaries are between morphology and syntax, the upper boundaries between syntax and discourse organization. This paper discusses the lower boundaries in syntactic treebank development. We place our analysis in the Universal Dependency framework (UD), which constitutes a large community of more than 100 teams around the globe (Nivre et al. 2016).

In this paper, we want to discuss the problem caused by idioms in syntactic annotation. The literature on idioms and MWEs is immense (Fillmore et al. 1988, Mel'čuk 1998, Sag et al. 2002, etc.). Our goal is not to mark the extension of MWEs on top of the syntactic annotation (see Savary et al. 2017 for a recent proposition). Our purpose is to tackle the impact of idiomaticity on the syntactic annotation itself. Most idioms (such as *kick the bucket* or *green card*) do not cause any trouble for the syntactic annotation because their internal syntactic structure is absolutely transparent (and it is precisely because they have an internal syntax that they are idioms and not words). Some expressions, however, such as *not to mention, heaven knows who, by and large, Rio de la Plata* (in English), are problematic for a syntactic annotation, because they do not perfectly respect the syntactic rules of free expressions.

We propose two contributions:

- For a coherent annotation it is crucial to distinguish **syntactically irregular** structures from **semantically non-compositional** units. These notions are highly correlated but distinct and we propose criteria to distinguish them.

- We explore different ways of annotating these two kinds of Multi-Word Expressions and their combinations in a syntactic treebank, with a special focus on functional MWEs.

Section 2 proposes a simple typology of MWEs opposing semantic compositionality and syntactic regularity. In section 3, we lay the basis of our analysis by discussing the syntactic units of a dependency annotation and point to problems in the current UD scheme (version 2.1). In section 4, we propose to analyze MWEs with an internal syntactic structure according to their level of syntactic regularity. We show how an MWE can be introduced into the current CoNLL-U format as a unit with its own POS. In section 5, we introduce two convertible dependency schemes for functional MWEs before concluding in section 6 with an example combining the MWE as a separated unit with the new convertible scheme for functional MWEs.

Proceedings of the 16th International Workshop on Treebanks and Linguistic Theories (TLT16), pages 181–189,
Prague, Czech Republic, January 23–24, 2018. Distributed under a CC-BY 4.0 licence. 2017.

Keywords: dependency, annotation, syntax, UD, MWE, idioms

2 Idioms and syntactic irregularity

We distinguish idiomatic expressions from syntactically irregular constructions. Idiomaticity is a semantic notion and semantics has to be annotated apart from syntax.

Even if it is not our purpose to define idiomaticity here, let us give some thoughts to the matter. Following Fillmore 1988 (with his *encoding* and *decoding idioms*) or Mel'cuk 1998 (with his *phraseme* and *collocation*), we distinguish two levels of non-compositionality. We adopt the point of view of *encoding*: "Compositionality [...] is to be distinguished from analysability, which pertains instead to the extent to which speakers are cognizant [...] of the contribution that individual component structures make to the composite whole." (cf. Langacker 1987:457). An MWE is an *idiom* (i.e. *non-compositional*) if its components cannot be chosen individually by the speaker (*kick the bucket* is chosen as a whole and there is no possible commutation on its components).[1] An MWE is a *collocation* (i.e *semi-compositional*) if one of its component is chosen freely (the basis) and the other one (the collocate) is chosen according to the basis (in *wide awake*, *wide* can be suppressed and *awake* keeps the same contribution: *awake* is the basis and *wide* is a collocate expressing intensification with *awake*).

We also consider three levels of syntactic irregularity. First, natural languages contain some syntactic subsystems which do not follow the general properties of syntactic relations. For instance, most languages have particular constructions for named entities such as dates or titles. English has a regular construction N N, where the second noun is the head (*pizza boy, Victoria Lake*) but it also has a subsystem where the first noun is the head, used for named entities (*Lake Michigan, Mount Rushmore, Fort Alamo*). These subsystems are in some sense "regular irregularities", that is, productive unusual constructions. Similarly, English produces a high number of multi-word adverbs from a preposition and a bare noun as in *on top (of)* or *in case (of)*, thus forming another sub-system that does not conform to the typical syntactic system of English.

Second, languages have non-productive irregular constructions. Most of these irregular constructions are idioms, but some are compositional. This is the case of Fr. *peser lourd* 'weigh a lot/be significant', lit. weigh heavy, where *lourd* is an adjective that commutes only with NPs (*peser une tonne* 'weigh one ton').[2] Even the commutation with its antonym *léger* 'light' is impossible. Another example is Fr. *cucul la praline* 'very silly', lit. silly the praline. It is a collocation: the adjective *cucul* can be used alone and the NP *la praline* is an intensifier. The POSs of the units are clear, and the dependency structure can be reconstructed, but it is unusual to have an NP modifying an adjective.

We consider four cases of non-productive irregular constructions.

a. Structures with a clear POS and dependency structure but that function as a whole differently than their syntactic head: the coordinating conjunction headed by a verb *not to mention* (*they gave us their knowledge, not to mention their helpfulness*), the adjective *top of the range*, headed by a noun (as in *a very top of the range restaurant*), the French pronoun *Dieu sait quoi* 'heaven knows what', headed by a verb.

b. For some sequences, the POS are clear, but the dependency structure has to be reconstructed diachronically (the Fr. pronoun *n'importe quoi* 'anything', lit. no matter what)[3] or inversely, the dependency structure is clear but the POS have to be reconstructed (the adverb *by and large* – *by* being originally an adverb).

c. Other sequences have no clear internal dependency structure at all, while the POS remain clear: *each other*, Fr. *à qui mieux mieux* 'each trying to do better than the other', lit. to whom better better.

---

[1] An idiom can be semantically transparent (Svensson 2008). For example, it is quite clear that a *washing machine* is a machine that is used to wash something, but is an idiom because it is arbitrary that this denotes a machine for washing clothes and not a dishwasher or a high-pressure water cleaner. An idiom can even be semantically analyzable, cf. Gibbs 1994:278: "Idioms like *pop the question* [...], *spill the beans*, and *lay down the law* are 'decomposable', because each component obviously contributes to the overall figurative interpretation."

[2] How the relation between *peser* and *lourd* must be analyzed in UD is not quite clear. *Lourd* should probably be analyzed as an xcomp of *peser* but if we do that we lose the fact that *lourd* is in the paradigm of NPs analyzed as obj.

[3] Diachronically, *quoi* is the subject of *importe* but now it is recognized as an object due to its position.

d. Some sequences have neither clear POS nor an internal structure in the language of the corpus: the adjective *ad hoc*, the proper noun *Al Qaeda*, and the Fr. SCONJ *parce que* 'because'.[4]

	Compositional	Semi-compositional	Non-compositional
Regular construction	Typical syntax (*the dog slept*)	*[wide] awake, [heavy] smoker, rain [cats and dogs]*	*kick the bucket, green card, cats and dogs, in the light (of)*, Fr. *pomme de terre* 'potato'
Sub-system	Dates: *5th of July, tomorrow morning* Titles: *Miss Smith*	*Ludwig van Beethoven* in German (*van* is a Dutch word similar to Ger. *von*)	*on top (of), in case (of)*, Fr. *à côté (de)* 'next (to)' Meaningful dates: *September 11th, 4th of July Mount Rushmore, Fort Alamo*
Irregular construction	Fr. *peser lourd* 'weigh a lot', lit. weigh heavy	Fr. *cucul la praline* 'very silly', lit. silly the praline	a) *not to mention, a lot (ADJ-er), top of the range*, Fr. *Dieu sait quoi* 'heaven knows what' b) Fr. *n'importe quoi* 'anything', *by and large* c) *each other*, Fr. *à qui mieux mieux* 'each trying to do better than the other', lit. to whom better better d) *ad hoc, Al Qaeda*, Fr. *parce que* 'because'

Table 1. Different types of MWEs

Table 1 opposes degrees of syntactic regularity in the rows and semantic compositionality in the columns. In section 4, we will propose an annotation scheme for irregular constructions and for some non-compositional sub-systems.

3 MWE in UD

3.1 MWE and tokenisation

The tokenization of UD follows the underlying principle that tokens must be words or parts of words. A priori no token contains spaces (except well delimited cases of polysyllabic words) and therefore multi-word expressions are described syntactically and not morphologically. This is a vital choice for practical and theoretical reasons: Ambiguous sequences cannot be disambiguated on a morphological level without taking into account the whole sentence. Therefore, the alternative choice of multi-word tokens containing spaces is problematic: In the manual annotation process, creating the tokenization and the syntactic analysis at the same time is time-consuming, annotating a special link for MWE is much more user-friendly. For automatic parsing, too, a tokenization as a separate task that precedes the actual dependency annotation is redundant because both tools need a global view on the sentence – and syntactic parsers are specialized tools to do just that. Moreover, two annotations of the same sentence are harder to compare if they are based on different tokenizations and a spelling-based annotation makes that possible because it does not depend on the possibly ambiguous syntactic annotation itself.

Inversely, grouping Multi-Word Expressions together in a syntactic annotation scheme can at its most simple form always be achieved by introducing into the set of relations special ad hoc links for multi-words. UD makes use of this approach with the links `fixed`and `flat`[5] where no internal structure is annotated. In UD terms we could reformulate the purpose of the paper simply as: When must the `fixed` relation be used?

3.2 Problems with the MWE encoding in UD

This work springs from a recognition that the treatment of functional MWEs in UD is unsatisfactory for at least four reasons:

---

[4] Historically *parce* is the preposition *par* 'through' and the pronoun *ce* 'that', but this is not visible in today's orthography. The attribution of a POS to *parce* seems arbitrary and the French UD treebanks are subsequently incoherent: Fr-Original calls *parce* an ADV, Fr-Sequoia an SCONJ, and Fr-ParTUT has both versions.

[5] `flat` is a relation used for headless constructions (such as *Bill Clinton* for which is it not easy to decide which word is the head). This relation concerns productive and regular sub-systems and will not be discussed here.

1) The relation `fixed` is commonly used for MWEs with a very clear internal syntactic structure (see Figure 1).[6]

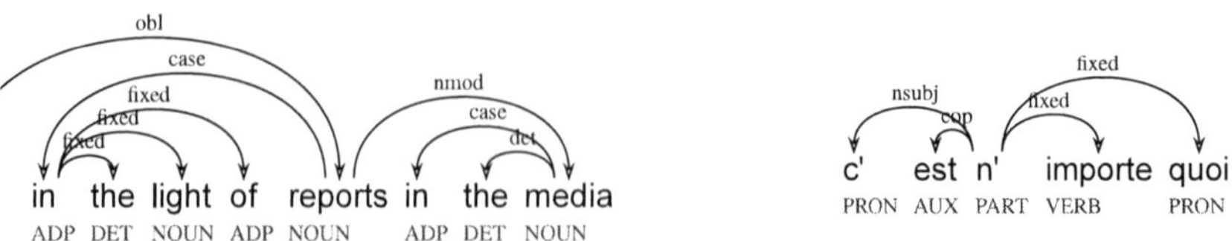

Figure 1. Analyses with `fixed` in En-PartTUT and Fr-Original

When analyzing them as `fixed` MWEs, we flatten the structure, losing precious information in the process, which will give us fewer instances of these syntactic relations on which to train our parser (cf. Gerdes & Kahane 2016's principles as well as the principles given on the UD introduction page). Moreover, the analysis is somewhat contradictory: If we recognize the POSs of the components (such as the verbal nature of *importe* in Fr. *n'importe quoi* 'anything', lit. no matter what), then we could also recognize the dependency relations that the tokens entertain.

2) Currently, the criteria to decide which constructions enter the realm of MWEs are insufficient and we observe a lot of discrepancies between different treebanks and even inside a single treebank.

For instance *along with* appears with three analyses. In En-ParTUT *along* is considered as the `case` marker of the noun phrase and *with* as *along*'s `fixed` dependent. On the other hand, En-Original mainly favors a compositional analysis with both *along* and *with* as `case` markers, but there is also one occurrence where *along* is a `cc` dependent of the noun phrase and *with along*'s `fixed` dependent.

Tables 2 and 3 give an overview of the usage of the MWE-relations in the English and French UD treebanks. When comparing the highlighted lines in the English and the French tables, we observe that the usage that annotators make from the three MWE relations `compound`, `fixed`, and `flat` go beyond what can be expected as language and genre differences and rather seems to indicate that the annotators understood the relations differently. This is corroborated by the high inter-corpus variation, for French, too. The two French treebanks Fr-FTB and Fr-Sequoia, for example, do not use `compound` at all. The significant number of observed incoherences in these two languages suffices to show that the UD annotation guide for MWE relations clearly deserves an overhaul in order to achieve a higher inter-language, inter-corpus, and inter-annotator annotation.

3) The POS of an MWE as a whole does not appear explicitly.

The assumption made is that the MWE will have the same POS as its syntactic head but many examples show that this is not the case. For example *not to mention* is a coordinating conjunction, a useful information for a syntactic parser that cannot be retrieved from the POS of its units.

---

[6] UD's definition of `fixed` refers to Sag et al. (2002) who say: "Fixed expressions are fully lexicalized and undergo neither morphosyntactic variation (cf. **in shorter*) nor internal modification (cf. **in very short*). As such, a simple words-with-spaces representation is sufficient. If we were to adopt a compositional account of fixed expressions, we would have to introduce a lexical entry for "words" such as *hoc*, resulting in overgeneration and the idiomaticity problem (see above)." Let us remark that, first, limits on modification do not imply weird lexical entries, as the example *in short* shows itself – the two words being in the lexicon anyhow. Second, and most importantly, an MWE can have constraints on modification for a specific meaning while still remaining transparent for the speaker, not only diachronically: *in short*, for example, is identifiable as a prepositional phrase, even if *short* is originally an adjective. This leads to multiple but syntactically constrained internal modifications of MWEs, not only in puns and journalistic style, but more generally also in ordinary coordinations and elisions as we will see below. Note also that the current 2.0 En-Original corpus consistently annotates *in short* (3 occurrences) and *for short* (1 occurrence) as a compositional prepositional phrase (`case-nmod`), contrarily to Sag's paper referenced in the annotation guide.

English	compound	fixed	flat
En-Original	4,38 %	0,24 %	0,73 %
En-Lines	2,63 %	0,49 %	0,72 %
En-ParTUT	0,40 %	0,56 %	1,24 %
total number of MWE	9194	966	1882
max freq variation between corpora	1107%	43%	59%
total nb links	11993	1091	2625
total frequency of links	3,58 %	0,33 %	0,66 %
total nb MWE types	7067	122	1215
average nb of occurrences per type of MWE	1,3	7,9	1,5
non-contiguous types	292	4	0

Table 2. Measures for MWE of the English UD v2

French	compound	fixed	flat
Fr-Original	0,21 %	1,04 %	1,79 %
Fr-FTB	0,00 %	8,75 %	0,70 %
Fr-ParTUT	0,23 %	1,04 %	0,44 %
Fr-Sequoia	0,00 %	2,56 %	1,25 %
total number of MWE	786	33190	9444
max freq variation between corpora	N/A	843%	411%
total nb links	877	55975	11858
total frequency of links	0,08 %	5,36 %	1,14 %
total nb MWE types	660	8544	7329
average nb of occurrences per type of MWE	1,2	3,9	1,3
non-contiguous types	24	58	0

Table 3. Measures for MWE of the French UD v2

4) The span of MWEs in the current UD scheme is questionable in some cases, especially concerning governed prepositions, which are not separated from the MWE itself (cf. *of* in Figure 2, below).[7]

4   Propositions for the encoding of MWEs in UD

All regular constructions from Table 1, including idioms, should be analyzed internally because:

1. Such a tree is syntactically more informative than any type of flattened structure where readily available syntactic relations have been removed.

2. We can expect a higher inter-annotator agreement on the syntactic relations if the annotation of MWE is kept independent from syntax, because of the difficulty of defining and recognizing MWEs

3. Equally, we can expect better parsing results because we have more instances of every relation and unknown idioms can obtain a correct parse, too.

The same holds for all compositional and semi-compositional constructions. We even go as far as proposing to analyze non-productive irregular constructions in case a) and b) by regular syntactic relations, but for some MWEs, we need means of encoding the POS of the whole expression because its POS is not identical to its head's POS. We propose to use `fixed` only for parts of c) and d) where the regular syntax does not provide appropriate syntactic relations.

In some MWE of c) and d), some relations remain transparent and we could annotate partial structures whenever they are available. For example *à qui mieux mieux* contains a clear *à* <case- *qui* relation independent of the analysis of the rest of the expression.

---

[7] The preposition can be repeated (*According to the President and **to** the Secretary of State* – the repetition can disambiguate the scope of the shared element in the coordination) which seems incompatible with the `fixed` analysis favored in the English treebanks. In other languages, such as French, the repetition is quite systematic. In English, governed prepositions are particularly cohesive with their governor, giving us what is called *preposition stranding* in extraction (*the girl I talk to*). But even in this case, nobody denies that the verb *talk* subcategorizes a preposition phrase and that the preposition *to* is not part of the verb form. The fact that the preposition is not a part of the idiom becomes even clearer with expressions such as *in front of X*, where the subcategorized phrase can be suppressed (*she stopped in front*) or pronominalized (*in its front*). Note that the alternative classical dependency analysis where prepositional phrases are governed by prepositions results in a more coherent analysis because the governor (the verb or the expression) always forms a subtree with the sub-categorized preposition, independently of the extension given to the MWE.

For those remaining `fixed` relations, dependency distance measures would give more reliable result if the standard bouquet annotation (all words depending on the first token) would be replaced by a series of left-to-right relations connecting one word to its neighbor, because the absence of any recognizable syntactic relation rather implies some relation of simple juxtaposition than a structure headed by the first word.

The CoNLL-U format can easily be extended to allow for a fully expressive annotation of MWEs. One solution is to devote one specific column holding the idiomatic information (or equally, put this information into a specific attribute in the feature column of CoNNL-U). This choice does not allow embedding MWEs in one another. A better choice is to extend the current multi-word token format by adding a line for each MWE. This additional line could also include the POS of the whole expression.[8] It constitutes an additional unit that can constitute a node of a semantic graph. This could be combined with a specific MWE column or simply a specific feature in the additional line's FEATS column that distinguishes different types of non-compositionality, following the Parseme project: for instance idioms, light-verb constructions, and named entities.

In the following example, the governor of the MWE *top of the range* is *shoe*. But the head/root of the MWE is *top*.

1	a	a	DET	_	_	7	det
2	very	very	ADV	_	_	3-6	**advmod**
3-6	top of the range	_	ADJ	_	_	7	amod
3	top	top	NOUN	_	_	3-6	*root*
4	of	of	ADP	_	_	6	case
5	the	the	DET	_	_	6	det
6	range	range	NOUN	_	_	3	nmod
7	shoe	shoe	NOUN	_	_	0	root

Figure 2. UD analysis of the adjective *top of the range* (case a)Functional MWEs in UD

UD presents a particular problem with functional MWEs, because UD favors dependencies between content words (determiners and prepositions are dependents of the noun following them). It appears that the choice made by UD to have the prepositions as dependent of their complement is the source of some "catastrophes" (in the mathematical sense of the term) as soon as "prepositional" MWEs are in-volved (Gerdes & Kahane 2016). The goal of this section is to present the problem and to propose a solution to smooth it.

Let us consider the following examples illustrating what is often called a complex determiner (1a) and a complex preposition (1b):

1.   (a) She asked me **a lot of** questions.
       (b) She lives **in front of** my house.

We can compare these sentences with (2a) and (2b):

2.   (a) She asked me **many** questions.
       (b) She lives **near** my house.

According to the choices made by UD, we have dependencies between *asked* and *questions* in (2a) and between *lives* and *house* in (2b) (Figure 3)

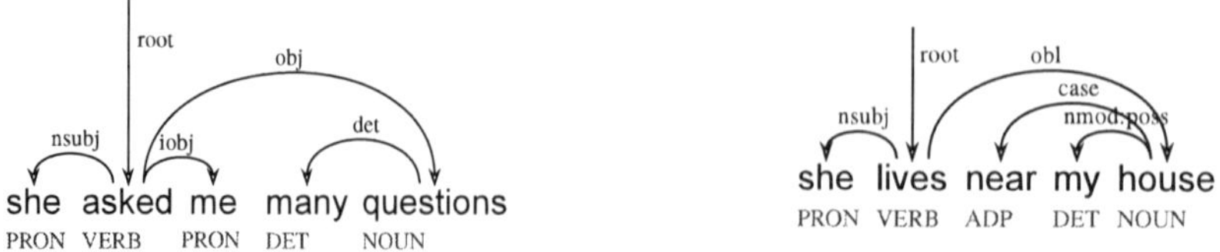

Figure 3. UD analysis of 2a and 2b

---

[8] Currently the format is only used for contiguous items. The format can be extended to non-contiguous expressions, e.g. we could have "3-5,7-8" as an index.

It is tempting to preserve these dependencies and to treat *a lot of* and *in front of* respectively as a complex determiner and a complex preposition. Let us first remark that *of* in these expressions is not part of the MWE, but is part of the sub-categorization of the MWE, by parallelism with verbal sub-categorization (cf. footnote 7, although the coherence of these expressions is higher and the preposition cannot always be repeated alone). In other words, the MWEs in question are *a lot* and *in front*. Theses MWEs are syntactically transparent and we do not want to analyze them with `fixed`. Two analyses are possible.

Analysis A respects the surface syntax and *of N* is treated as the complement (`nmod`) of the MWE. This is the most common analysis in the current English UD treebanks.[9]

Figure 4. Analysis A for *a lot (of)* and *in front (of)*

Analysis B favors the relation between content words, as in the analyses of Figure 3. In this analysis, we propose to introduce special relations `det:complex` and `case:complex` when the dependents of `det` and `case` are MWEs.

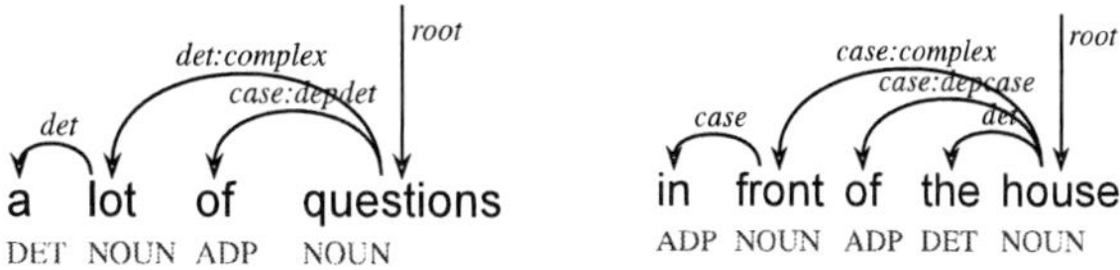

Figure 5. Analysis B for *a lot (of)* and *in front (of)*

The sub-categorized preposition *of* is governed by the complement noun. We introduce a feature on the case relation to indicate that this preposition is subcategorized by a dependent of the noun. We need to distinguish `case:depdet` and `case:depcase` because both can be present: *in front of a lot of houses*, where *front*, *lot* and the two *of* will depend on *houses*.

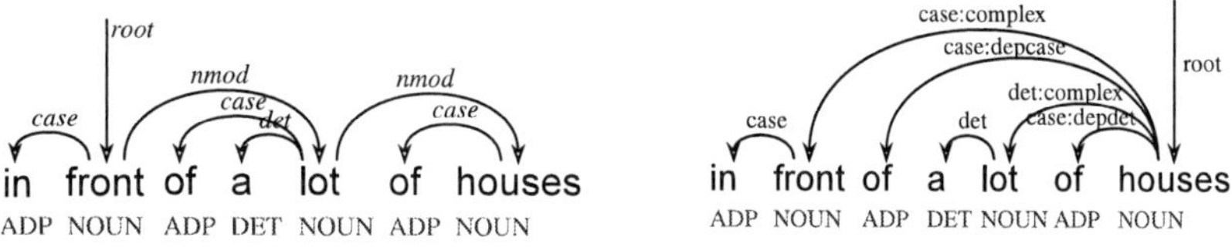

Figure 6. Analyses A and B for *in front of a lot of houses*

Both analyses A and B are interesting. It is possible not to choose and to allow the conversion from one analysis to the other. For that we need to enrich analysis A, by adding the subtype `:antidet` and `:anticase` to the standard `nmod` relations which go the other way in the B analysis (and are labeled `det:complex` and `case:complex`).

Figure 7. Enhanced analysis B for *a lot (of)* and *in front (of)*

---

[9] Since *quite a lot (of questions)* is possible, *a lot* has actually become an adverb (just like in *a lot better* – or other comparative adjectives) and the relation between *a lot* and the noun complement *of questions* should be of type `obl` and not `nmod` as it is in the current English UD treebanks. This irregular behavior of *a lot* can be captured by the introduction of an MWE unit as in Section 4.

Our rules of conversion are:

Similar rules could be used to get a surface syntax-based representation from UD:[10]

5 Conclusion

We have shown that irregular structures need to be introduced as units because we have to associate a POS to them. In cases a) and b) the internal structure is transparent but the POS of the complete unit is not predictable. In cases c) and d), where we use `fixed` relations, it is all the more necessary to indicate the POS of the MWE. For regular idioms, too, we can add the MWE as a unit.

For regular functional MWEs, we propose to add sub-types to the relation to capture the relations between content words, as well as the syntactic dominance relations. A tree does not allow expressing both types of relations at the same time, but the proposed sub-types relations can be converted from one to another.[11]

The two proposals are orthogonal and can be combined. For example, if we want to treat *a lot* as an adverb, we can have the analysis of Figure 8:

Figure 8. Analysis A and B for *quite a lot of questions*

The proposed schemes and distinctions clarify some underspecifications in the current UD scheme that lead to incoherent analyses. The usage of subtypes fits in unintrusively into the current scheme and could be used for upcoming versions. More generally, it allows back and forth conversions of UD and more classical subcategorization-based dependency annotation schemes.

Acknowledgments

We thank our three reviewers for valuable remarks and corrections. This work is supported by the French National Research Agency (ANR) with the project NaijaSynCor.

---

[10] The conversion of chains of auxiliaries (*would have been done*) to a surface syntax-based representation (would −anti−aux> have −antiaux> been −antiaux> done) is presently problematic in UD 2 because all auxiliaries depend on the lexical verb. This suggests enriching the UD annotation either in the same way as proposed here in analysis A (with a `casedep` feature for a second `case` introduced by a first `case`) or by replacing the current bouquet style annotation with a chain of auxiliaries, an auxiliary depending on the auxiliary it subcategorizes.

[11] In this paper, we started from the UD annotation scheme and we have used UD's relation names. The names `case` and `anticase` could suggest that `case` has a sort of primacy on `anticase`. But `anticase` is simply the `obj` relation between a preposition and its direct complement.

References

Timothy Baldwin, C. Bannard, T. Tanaka, and D. Widdows. 2003. An empirical model of multiword expression decomposability. In *Proceedings of the ACL workshop on Multiword Expressions: analysis, acquisition and treatment,* Association for Computational Linguistics.

Charles Fillmore, Paul Kay, and Michael O'Connor. 1988. Regularity and Idiomaticity in Grammatical Constructions: The case of "Let Alone". *Language,* 64:501-538.

Kim Gerdes and Sylvain Kahane. 2016. Dependency Annotation Choices: Assessing Theoretical and Practical Issues of Universal Dependencies. In *Proceedings of LAW X.*

Raymond W. Gibbs. 1994. *The poetics of mind: Figurative thought, language, and understanding.* Cambridge University Press, New-York.

Martin Jönsson. 2008. *On compositionality. Doubts about the Structural Path to Meaning.* PhD thesis, Lund University.

Ronald W. Langacker. 1987. *Foundations of cognitive grammar, Volume 1: Theoretical Preresquistes.* Stanford University Press, Stanford.

Igor Mel'čuk. 1998. Collocations and lexical functions. In Anthony P. Cowie (ed.) *Phraseology. Theory, analysis, and applications,* 23-53.

Joakim Nivre, Marie-Catherine de Marneffe, Filip Ginter, Yoav Goldberg, Jan Hajič, Christopher D. Manning, Ryan McDonald, Slav Petrov, Sampo Pyysalo, Natalia Silveira, Reut Tsarfaty, Daniel Zeman. 2016. Universal Dependencies v1: A Multilingual Treebank Collection. In *Proceedings of LREC.*

Geoffrey Nunberg, Ivan A. Sag, and Thomas Wasow. 1994. Idioms. *Language,* 70:491-538.

V. Rosén, G. Losnegaard, K. De Smedt, E. Bejcek, A. Savary, A. Przepiórkowski, M. Sailer, and V. Mitetelu. 2015. A survey of multiword expressions in treebanks. In *Proceedings of the Treebanks and Linguistic Theories conference* (*TLT*), Warsaw, Poland.

Ivan A. Sag, T. Baldwin, F. Bond, A. Copestake, and D. Flickinger. 2002. Multiword expressions: A pain in the neck for NLP. *Computational Linguistics and Intelligent Text Processing,* 189-206.

Agata Savary, C. Ramisch, S. Ricardo Cordeiro, F. Sangati, V. Vincze, B. QuasemiZadeh, M. Candito, F. Cap, V. Giouli, I. Stoyanova, and A. Doucet, A. 2017. The PARSEME Shared Task on Automatic Identication of Verbal Multiword Expressions. In *Proceedings of the 13th Workshop on Multiword Expressions* (*MWE 2017*).

Maria Helena Svensson. 2008. A very complex criterion of fixedness : Non-compositionality. In Sylviane Granger and Magali Paquot (eds.). *Phraseology: An interdisciplinary perspective,* 81-93. John Benjamins, Amsterdam / Philadelphia.

A Universal Dependencies Treebank for Marathi

Vinit Ravishankar

Institute of Formal and Applied Linguistics
Faculty of Mathematics and Physics
Charles University in Prague
vinit.ravishankar@gmail.com

Abstract

This paper describes the creation of a free and open-source dependency treebank for Marathi, the first open-source treebank for Marathi following the Universal Dependencies (UD) syntactic annotation scheme. In the paper, we describe some of the syntactic and morphological phenomena in the language that required special analysis, and how they fit into the UD guidelines. We also evaluate the parsing results for three popular dependency parsers on our treebank.

1 Introduction

The Universal Dependencies (UD) project (Nivre et al., 2016) is a recent effort to attempt to arrive at 'universal' annotation standards for dependency treebanks. These annotation standards also cover POS tags and morphology, in addition to the expected dependency relations. In recent years, the UD project has been growing more popular; the CoNLL 2017 shared task on dependency parsing (Zeman et al., 2017) resulted in the development and release of a number of dependency parsing pipelines that parse raw text to UD annotated trees.

UD's treebanks cover a number of languages; however, there are, as with most language resources, several gaps in treebank availability for certain languages or families. In this paper, we describe the creation of a treebank for Marathi, an Indic language spoken primarily in the state of Maharashtra in western India.

In Section 2 of our paper, we briefly describe the grammar and political status of Marathi. Section 3 describes some prior work on Marathi NLP, including work relevant to our treebank. Section 4 describes the creation and size of our corpus. Section 5 describes some of the more interesting linguistic phenomena in Marathi and how they fit into UD guidelines. Section 6 describes our evaluation methodology and our results. We conclude with Section 7, where we discuss future avenues for expansion.

2 Marathi

Marathi is an Indic language spoken by approximately 71 million speakers, most of these in the western Indian state of Maharashtra. It is one of the 22 scheduled languages of the Indian government.[1] Due to Maharashtra's position as the state with the longest border with Dravidian language-speaking states, Marathi has adopted several features typical to the Dravidian language family, beyond those present in the south Asian sprachbund: these include clusivity, reduced relative clause construction, and a range of negative auxiliaries (Junghare, 2009). Marathi is written in the Devanagari script, with a few minor modifications and extra characters. Throughout this paper, we transliterate all examples using the International Alphabet of Sanskrit Transliteration (IAST).

Whilst not the first Indic language with a Universal Dependencies treebank, the existing Hindi and Urdu treebanks are conversions of another annotation schema (Tandon et al., 2016), that can be lossy when converting to UD. The treebank we describe is, therefore, the first (to our knowledge) manually

---

[1]A 'scheduled' language in this context refers to a language in which Indian public service candidates are entitled to be examined, amongst other obligations on part of the government.

Proceedings of the 16th International Workshop on Treebanks and Linguistic Theories (TLT16), pages 190–200,
Prague, Czech Republic, January 23–24, 2018. Distributed under a CC-BY 4.0 licence. 2017.

Keywords: dependency, UD, universal, Indic, Indo-Aryan, Marathi, annotation

annotated Universal Dependencies treebank release in an Indic language. Our motivation for choosing the UD formalism is twofold: first, we believe that the growing popularity of the framework and related conferences and shared tasks could be beneficial to work on Marathi computational linguistics. Second, the 'universal' nature of the Universal Dependencies project can only be tested by the addition of more language treebanks: the creation of a Marathi treebank, therefore, the creation of this treebank is mutually advantageous to both the project and to the state of Marathi computational linguistics.

Marathi is, compared to other Indic languages, fairly morphologically complex. Nouns tend to adopt the *three-layer* morphology described in Masica (1993): nouns first form an oblique case (often through non-transparent modifications), then take a direct case suffix, then, optionally, a postpositional suffix. Unlike in many other Indic languages, these layers are often orthographically joint in Marathi. Verbs show a wide variety of infinitives and participle forms, which are described in a later section.

Syntactically, Marathi tends to follow SOV alignment, although word order is relatively free. Marathi also shows split ergativity: the perfective aspect induces the ergative—absolutive alignment.

3 Prior work

The AnnCorra project describes a dependency annotation schema for Indian languages, based on a 'Paninian grammatical model' (Bharati et al., 2002). A Marathi treebank annotated under this schema appears to be a work in progress; this was described by Tandon and Sharma (2017), who also describe parsing strategies for Marathi and other underresourced Indian languages, based on this schema.

Whilst Marathi grammars do exist, our primary resource was Masica's pan-Indic descriptive grammar (Masica, 1993). In addition to this, Dhongade and Wali (2009) provide a fairly comprehensive grammar of Marathi; however, there is some disagreement between their grammar and Masica's. Finally, we also used a grammar by Navalkar (1868); despite being considerably dated, the grammar is quite succinct and well-written.

Several tools for Marathi exist, ranging from POS taggers (Singh et al., 2013) to morphological analysers. These tools are sometimes released under non-free licenses, or are otherwise opaque; we used a free and open-source morphological analyser (Ravishankar and Tyers, 2017) written in the Apertium formalism (Forcada et al., 2011), deeming this to be sufficient for POS tagging. All morphological disambiguation was performed manually; if incorrect, they were fixed manually.

4 Corpus

Our corpus primarily consists of stories from Wikisource. The collection of stories available is fairly large; we chose those that resembled modern spoken or written Marathi the most, as there is a significant difference between formal written Marathi, especially in the past, and written forms available today. This is reflected primarily in the use of certain morphological forms that have fallen out of use in modern spoken Marathi,[2] something that we tried to avoid for an initial treebank release. The text in our corpus, therefore, would be considered fairly standard in Pune, if a bit old-fashioned in places.

Whilst we would have liked to include news in our corpus, this was complicated: our attempts to scrape a news corpus stopped rather abruptly on the discovery that the most widely distributed Marathi newspapers were all published online as images or GIFs. A future goal is to convert these newspapers, assuming licenses permit, to text using OCR utilities.

Our final parsed corpus consisted of 3,506 tokens and 486 sentences.

4.1 Preprocessing

We ran our corpus through the Apertium morphological analyser cited above, forcing the output to be in the VISL format (Bick and Didriksen, 2015) rather than Apertium's default format. The main reason for this was that we judged it easier, ergonomically, to annotate in this format: morphological disambiguation simply involved deleting lines with inappropriate analyses, and dependency relations were added to the end of every line (representing a token). These were later converted to the required CoNLL-U format with

---

[2]Our dialect of reference is urban Marathi spoken primarily in the city of Pune; Marathi is fairly diverse in terms of dialects, which vary by region, caste and social class.

a script; another script converted the POS tags to UD POS tags, and the morphology to UD morphology. This conversion required some minor additional manual editing in areas where UD morphology required more specificity than our Apertium analyser provided. Appendix A has an example of a sentence in the VISL format, and the CoNLL-U equivalent. Around the final quarter of our treebank, we switched to using UD-Annotatrix (Tyers et al., 2018) for annotation, with positive results.

4.2   Word segmentation

An important issue we had to address during our creation of the treebank was that of word segmentation, also referred to here as tokenisation. A major issue we faced was the very fuzzy line between cases and postpositions in Marathi. Whilst it was clear that we would not split nouns and their cases into two tokens (despite being agglutinative and clearly separable in nature), we had problems deciding precisely what suffixes could be classed as case suffixes, and what suffixes would be classed as postpositions. There are several tests for distinguishing between the two: one is, for instance, the ability of the genitive oblique to intervene between nouns and true postpositions, whilst another is the relative morphological freedom of postpositions and their ability to form attributive adjectives. None of these tests, however, is perfect, though we eventually arrived at a closed set of cases, partially by relying on tradition and partially by consulting grammars of other Indic languages to attempt to arrive at some standardisation. Our final closed set of cases included the nominative, accusative, dative, ergative, instrumental, comitative/sociative, locative, ablative, vocative and oblique, with the oblique case being the case to which postpositions attach. We do not attach genitives to their heads: this is for consistency with Hindi, and also to avoid the verbose [psor] morphology that UD uses to mark possessives.

5   Annotation

Our annotation of the treebank followed the UD version 2.0 guidelines. Our justification for choosing the UD standards was the *universal* nature of the treebank collection. The inclusion of a UD Marathi treebank would benefit both UD - by adding yet another language that would test the validity of the universality of UD's annotation standards - and Marathi, by not requiring us to come up with our annotation standards and documentation.

In the following subsections, we describe some of the more interesting morphological and syntactic constructions in Marathi, and how we chose to annotate them.

5.1   Subject case

Like many other Indic languages, Marathi displays some variation in the possible cases the semantic agent of a construction can take. Part of this is due to split ergativity; ergative-absolutive alignment is triggered by the perfective aspect, whilst the imperfective follows nominative-accusative alignment.

We decided to consider all semantic agents, irrespective of case, to be the syntactic subject of the construction. This results in three standard subject cases: the nominative, for unmarked subjects in the imperfective aspect, the ergative, for subjects marked with the ergative suffix *-ne*, and the dative, for experiencer predicates.

Whilst justifying the existence of dative subjects in Marathi by UD standards is far from obvious, our decision to do so stems from the ability of the dative subject to fulfill several subjecthood tests, such as adjunct subject control. It should be noted, however, that the dative subject in Marathi does fail *other* subjecthood tests, such as verbal agreement. An example of the dative subject is the simple sentence *rātrabhar tilā jhop ālī nāhī* 'she couldn't sleep at night', glossed in Figure 1a. Note the aux relation with the negation 'particle', which is actually a verb: it agrees with the subject.

We decided to use the language specific relation nsubj:own to denote certain specific ownership constructs that had no clear parallel in other languages we examined; in these constructs, indicating ownership, a postposition (*-kaḍe*) would combine with the oblique case of the owner. This is similar to the use of the locative (*-DA*) in Turkish, or the adessive (*-llA*) in Finnish. We do not subtype cop as this is the standard existential use of the copula. Whilst this relation appears to be suitable for now, we are considering modifying it to nmod:own in a future release.

Figure 1b is a simple (truncated) sentence from the treebank that demonstrates this construction well.

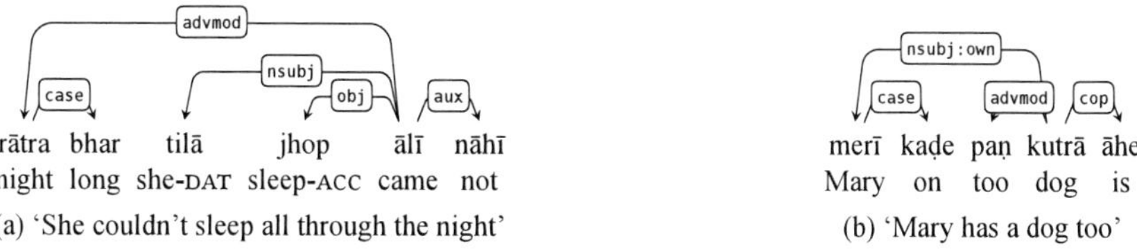

(a) 'She couldn't sleep all through the night'   (b) 'Mary has a dog too'

Figure 1: Various non-nominative subject cases

5.2   Object case

Objects in Marathi also tend to adopt a number of cases. Our treebank has objects in four cases - the accusative, dative, genitive[3] and the sociative. Distinguishing between accusative objects and dative objects was interesting, as Marathi displays differential object marking: 'accusative' objects in Marathi can be glossed with an 'accusative' null suffix, or with the dative suffix *-lā* for the same verb argument structure, with the latter implying definiteness.

(1) a. *mī   pakṣī   baghto*
         I-NOM bird-PL.ACC watch-IMPF.1MSG

         'I watch birds'

     b. *mī   pakṣīmnā   baghto*
         I-NOM bird-PL.DAT watch-IMPF.1MSG

         'I watch (some specific) birds'

Example 1a glosses the object as an accusative due to its non-definiteness, with a null morpheme, whilst Example 1b glosses it as a dative. UD's guidelines specify that a construction with only two verbal arguments should *not* use the indirect object (iobj) relation. Taking these things into account, we could do one of two things: either we gloss every noun corresponding to the subcategorisation frame of the governing verb and treat the accusative and dative suffixes as alternative morphological realisations of the same case, or we gloss every noun based on its morphology, thus allowing dative direct objects. We chose the latter.

The inclusion of the sociative (referred to as 'comitative' in UD) case as a direct object was another contentious issue: these objects occurred with verbs that were typically intransitive. The line between treating these arguments as core arguments of a transitive variant of the verb (that warranted the obj relation) and between treating them as non-core dependents of the intransitive (warranting an obl relation) was a thin one, and we preferred the former analysis in some instances, such as in the (slightly modified) sentence from the treebank in Figure 2: *lok kutryāṃśī bolat hote* 'people were talking to dogs'.

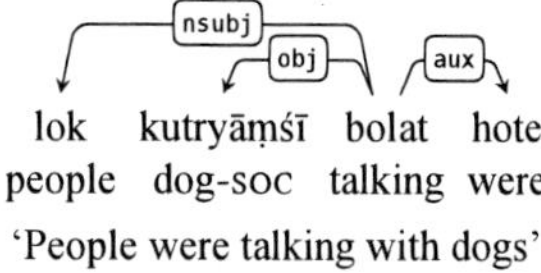

Figure 2: Sociative/comitative objects

We did not encounter examples of indirect objects in any case other than the dative.

---

[3]Technically the oblique as we split genitives.

5.3 Light verbs

Similar to many other Indic languages and several Indo-Iranian and Turkic languages, Marathi frequently makes use of light verb constructions (LVCs). These are a form of complex verbal predicates, *typically* noun + verb combinations that function as a semantic verb. Most of these constructions involve the verb *karṇe* 'to do/make' as the verbal head of the construction; we used the language specific relation compound:lvc to attach dependent nouns. A simple example of light verb constructions from our treebank is the (truncated) sentence in Figure 3: literally 'the frog was hitting a jump', with 'jump' being the nominal part and 'to hit' being the verbal part of the light verb construction. Despite being non-finite, we chose our verb to be the head of the construction for consistency with other treebanks, particularly the Persian treebank, where LVCs are frequent (Seraji et al., 2016).

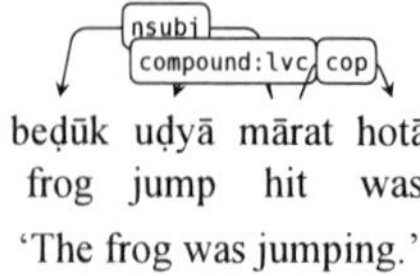

Figure 3: Light verb constructions

LVC's display varying degrees of lexicalisation. The LVC *uḍyā mārṇe* 'to hit a jump' is fairly unlexicalised: it can be both qualified with an adjective (*moṭhyā uḍyā mārṇe* 'to hit a large jump'), or modified with an adverb (*jorāt uḍyā mārṇe* 'to forcefully hit a jump'). Other constructs, like *kāḷjī gheṇe* 'to worry' cannot be qualified; it functions as a fully lexicalised verb. We do not take the degree of lexicalisation into account when assigning this relation.

5.4 Compound verbs

Perhaps one of the more interesting linguistic phenomena that we model in our treebank is the existence of what we refer to as 'compound verbs'. Deoskar (2006) provides an excellent description of compound verbs in Marathi; note, however, that they refer to the phenomenon as 'light verbs', as do other works on the subject (Butt, 2010; Seiss et al., 2009). The reason we use the term 'compound verb' is to prevent confusion with light verbs as described in section 5.3, which are a very distinct syntactic construct. The term 'compound verb' is also not unused in Marathi literature (Pardeshi, 2001).

Compound verbs are, essentially, a combination of two verbs, a *main* verb, very often a converb in Marathi (but a participle or an infinitive in some constructs), and a *secondary* verb, that has no real semantic value, but acts solely to modify the Aktionsart or some minor semantic meaning of the main verb (often, there is no semantic change). The set of secondary verbs is a closed set, and verbs from outside this set function as full, semantically valid verbs.

(2) a. *mī   goṣṭa   vāchlī*
        I-NOM story.F.SG read-PERF.3FSG

        'I read (the) story'

    b. *mī   goṣṭa   vāchūn   ṭāklī*
        I-NOM story.F.SG read-CONV.PERF put-PERF.3FSG

        'I finished off reading (the) story'

Whilst Example 2b has the same fundamental meaning as the simpler Example 2a, the addition of the vector verb results in a minor semantic shift, indicating finality, or suddenness in completion of the action denoted by the main verb. Whilst it appears that the aux relation would be appropriate here, Deoskar (2006) shows that the two classes (vector verbs and auxiliaries) are not the same. We, therefore, subtype another relation and use compound:svc to mark this relation, as in the figures 4a[4] and 4b. Despite 'serial

---

[4]Interestingly, dropping the compound construct would change absolutely nothing about this sentence.

verbs' being a distinct syntactic construct that have very little to do with these sorts of compound verbs, the absence of a dependency relation that better suits this phenomenon compelled us to use `compound:svc` for now.

(a) 'His eyes filled (with tears)'

(b) 'He cried (a lot, without stopping)'

Figure 4: Compound verbs

5.5 Passive voice

Whilst the use of the passive voice is not extremely frequent in Marathi, we did come across several examples in our treebank, which led to the creation of two subtypes that are fairly common in UD: `nsubj:pass` and `aux:pass`. Marathi uses the verb *jāṇe* 'to go' as an auxiliary in the formation of certain passive constructions. The main verb is in the perfective aspect and agrees with the passive subject. An exapmle sentence from our treebank is *rājvāḍā śṛngārlā gelā* 'the palace was decorated', as in Figure 5a.

Another verbal construction common to written Marathi occured quite frequently in our treebank. This is a form of 'formal' passivisation, and uses the the auxiliary verb *yeṇe* 'to come' instead of 'to go'. The main verb, interestingly, is as infinitive in the locative case. The above sentence could be re-written as *rājvāḍā śṛngārnyāt āle* (Figure 5b) without any major change in meaning.

(a) 'The palace was decorated'

(b) 'The palace came to be decorated'

Figure 5: Two forms of passivisation

5.6 Dislocation

Dislocated pronouns to emphasise nominals or nominal clauses are fairly common in Marathi. These constructions use a demonstrative pronoun along with the clause, similar to dislocation in French. We use the `dislocated` relation to mark these, as in Figure 6.

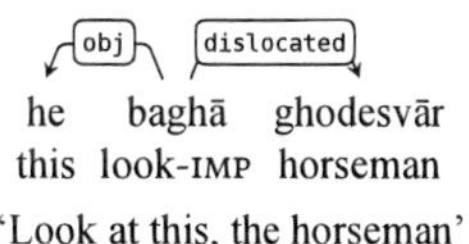

Figure 6: Dislocation

It is important to note that 'this' in the example does not determine 'horseman', but is a standalone pronoun - fairly visibly, it does not even agree with 'horseman' in gender and number.

6 Evaluation

The pipeline that we primarily use for tokenisation and tagging is the popular UDPipe (Straka and Straková, 2017); it is a trainable pipeline consisting of a tagger, a tokeniser (MorphoDiTa) (Straková et al., 2014) and a parser (Parsito) (Straka et al., 2015). Having tagged and tokenised our text using UDPipe, we evaluate three parsers.

The first of these parsers is Parsito, included in UDPipe itself. It (like many modern parsers) uses a neural network to learn transitions for parsing dependencies. We evaluate UDPipe twice - once using the

	Precision	Recall	F_1 score
Multiwords	99.09	45.31	61.88
Words	94.90	90.18	92.48
Sentences	92.24	92.72	92.44

Table 1: Tokeniser results on raw text.

	UPOS	Feats	All tags	Lemma
Gold standard	78.82	65.99	62.67	74.40
Tokenised	74.11	64.73	61.87	75.37

Table 2: Tagger F_1 scores evaluated with both gold standard and automatic tokenisation.

default settings, and again using external word embeddings trained on the Marathi wiki. We used pre-trained fastText embeddings of dimension 300 (Bojanowski et al., 2016); we believed that these would perform better than embeddings generated by other tools, as fastText also takes into account subword units to build word embeddings, which can have better results for more morphologically complex languages.

The second is the newer BIST parser (Kiperwasser and Goldberg, 2016). Similar to UDPipe, it uses neural networks for parsing: sentences are processed using bidirectional LSTMs. Unlike UDPipe, however, it also offers an implementation that uses a graph-based parsing strategy. Whilst BIST also allows us to use custom word embeddings, we did not do so for infrastructural reasons: using custom embeddings results in exponential model size blowup. We intend to rectify these issues and evaluate BIST with embeddings in the future.

Finally, our third parser is the much older MaltParser (Nivre et al., 2007). Unlike the others, MaltParser does not use a neural network for learning transitions. Given that our treebank is still fairly small, we were interested in comparing the performance of the two approaches: neural networks famously require substantial amounts of data, and despite neural parsers showing clearly better results averaged across all treebanks in competetive evaluations, we wanted to compare their performance on our treebank.

Whilst our primary evaluation is on end-to-end parsing, we also perform a secondary evaluation given gold-standard tokenisation and POS tags. We evaluated both labelled (LAS) and unlabelled (UAS) attachment scores; we also evaluated the *weighted* LAS, which underweights the contribution of correctly labelling certain relations (like case and punct) to the final score. Evaluation was carried out using the same script that was officially used for the CoNLL 2017 shared task. Each evaluation involved training 10 models for use in 10-fold cross-validation.

BIST parser required some held-out data to be used as a dev set; we used 45 (fixed) sentences for this data, and ran 10-fold CV on the remainder. We ran all parsers with the default parameters, except for BIST parser, where we raised the number of training epochs to 50.

6.1 Results

	Raw text			Gold standard		
	UAS	LAS	(w)LAS	UAS	LAS	(w)LAS
UDPipe	63.00	51.79	46.14	77.74	68.88	64.61
BIST	**67.60**	**54.18**	**47.25**	68.70	55.05	47.99
MaltParser	62.02	49.45	44.01	**80.75**	70.35	65.16
UDPipe[+emb]	59.77	48.20	42.63	79.48	**71.94**	**68.47**

Table 3: Unlabelled, labelled and weighted labelled attachment scores for our parsers, evaluated on a raw text pipeline and on gold-standard tokenisation and POS tags.

Table 1 refers to our tokeniser's results. The poor performance of the tokeniser on multiword tokens stands out; the relatively high frequency of multiword tokens due to orthographically joined postpositions is likely one of the reasons. Table 2 is the performance of two taggers: one on gold-standard tokenised data, and the other on data tokenised by UDPipe in the previous step.

Finally, we present our dependency parsing results in Table 3.

6.2   Discussion

As expected, our results for gold standard tokenisation and POS tags are significantly better than our results for parsing raw text. What we expected a lot less is the drastic differences in the performance of different parsers, and the performance of different parsers in different situations.

Whilst BIST has the best scores for parsing raw text, this advantage quickly vanishes as it does not improve much in performance on gold standard text at all, and drops to being the worst parser amongst the lot. Interestingly, the results bore out our intuition that MaltParser would be competitive despite its age: whilst not the *best* parser based on the more important LAS anywhere, it does have the best UAS for gold standard tokenisation and POS tags, and is fairly close to the best LAS scores.

Another interesting result worth noting is UDPipe's performance on raw text with word embeddings included; whilst these embeddings intuitively ought to improve (or at least not worsen) results, they do result in a noticeable parsing performance drop on raw text. Gold standard text parses much better, giving us our best LAS scores. We propose that this might occur due to word embeddings trained on external corpora being unable to deal with poorly segmented multiwords: the small size of the treebank does not explain the significant difference between raw text and gold standard POS-tagged text.

7   Future work

Obviously, our most important short-term goal is to increase the size of our treebank, aiming for a release of 10,000 manually parsed tokens. This was the treebank size expected from a surprise language in the CoNLL-2017 shared task. Another short-term goal is to generate data sets for easier evaluation of Marathi word embeddings (Abdou et al., 2018). Apart from this, we have several medium-term goals.

UD have some rudimentary support for language-family specific documentation. As Marathi is the only Indic treebank (that we know of) directly annotated according to UD specifications, we intend to use it as a starting point for writing documentation for Indic languages, contrasting with Marathi wherever possible, and expanding where not. A manual conversion of UD Hindi to fit these standards would be a place to start.

Finally, we also intend to add *enhanced* dependency relations: this has been done for some languages already (Schuster and Manning, 2016), and would be an interesting addition.

Acknowledgements

Work on this paper was partially funded through the stipend provided by the Erasmus Mundus Language and Communication Technologies program. We thank Dan Zeman, Francis M. Tyers and Memduh Gökırmak for their valuable insight on annotation standards. We also thank our anonymous reviewers for their comments.

References

Mostafa Abdou, Artur Kulmizev, and Vinit Ravishankar. 2018. MGAD: Multilingual Generation of Analogy Datasets. In *Proceedings of Language Resources and Evaluation Conference (LREC'18) [to appear]*.

Akshar Bharati, Rajeev Sangal, Vineet Chaitanya, Amba Kulkarni, Dipti Misra Sharma, and KV Ramakrishnamacharyulu. 2002. Anncorra: building tree-banks in Indian languages. In *Proceedings of the 3rd workshop on Asian language resources and international standardization-Volume 12*. Association for Computational Linguistics, pages 1–8.

Eckhard Bick and Tino Didriksen. 2015. Cg-3 – beyond classical constraint grammar. In *Proceedings of the 20th Nordic Conference of Computational Linguistics, NODALIDA*. Linköping University Electronic Press, Linköpings universitet, pages 31–39.

Piotr Bojanowski, Edouard Grave, Armand Joulin, and Tomas Mikolov. 2016. Enriching word vectors with sub-word information. *arXiv preprint arXiv:1607.04606* .

Miriam Butt. 2010. The light verb jungle: still hacking away .

Tejaswini Deoskar. 2006. Marathi light verbs. In *Proceedings from the Annual Meeting of the Chicago Linguistic Society*. Chicago Linguistic Society, volume 42, pages 183–198. http://www.ingentaconnect.com/content/cls/pcls/2006/00000042/00000002/art00012.

R. Dhongade and K. Wali. 2009. *Marathi*. London Oriental and African language library. John Benjamins Publishing Company. https://books.google.co.in/books?id=zVVOvi5C8uIC.

M. L. Forcada, M. Ginestí-Rosell, J. Nordfalk, J. O'Regan, S. Ortiz-Rojas, J. A. Pérez-Ortiz, F. Sánchez-Martínez, G. Ramírez-Sánchez, and F. M. Tyers. 2011. Apertium: a free/open-source platform for rule-based machine translation. *Machine Translation* 25(2):127–144.

Indira-Y Junghare. 2009. Syntactic convergence: Marathi and Dravidian. *von Kopp, B.: Texts and the Art of Translation. The Contribution of Comparative* 2:163.

Eliyahu Kiperwasser and Yoav Goldberg. 2016. Simple and Accurate Dependency Parsing using Bidirectional LSTM Feature Representations. *TACL* 4:313–327. https://transacl.org/ojs/index.php/tacl/article/view/885.

C.P. Masica. 1993. *The Indo-Aryan Languages*. Cambridge Language Surveys. Cambridge University Press. https://books.google.cz/books?id=Itp2twGR6tsC.

G.R. Navalkar. 1868. *The Student's Manual of Marathi Grammar, Etc. [By Gan(a) Pat(i) Ráv(a) Raghunath(a).].*. https://books.google.cz/books?id=VJYhMwEACAAJ.

Joakim Nivre, Marie-Catherine de Marneffe, Filip Ginter, Yoav Goldberg, Jan Hajič, Chris Manning, Ryan McDonald, Slav Petrov, Sampo Pyysalo, Natalia Silveira, Reut Tsarfaty, and Dan Zeman. 2016. Universal Dependencies v1: A Multilingual Treebank Collection. In *Proceedings of Language Resources and Evaluation Conference (LREC'16)*.

Joakim Nivre, Johan Hall, Jens Nilsson, Atanas Chanev, Gülşen Eryigit, Sandra Kübler, Svetoslav Marinov, and Erwin Marsi. 2007. Maltparser: A language-independent system for data-driven dependency parsing. *Natural Language Engineering* 13(2):95–135.

Prashant Pardeshi. 2001. The Explicator Compound Verb in Marathi: Definitional. *Linguistics* 38:68–85. http://www.lib.kobe-u.ac.jp/repository/80010010.pdf.

Vinit Ravishankar and Francis M Tyers. 2017. Finite-State Morphological Analysis for Marathi. In *Proceedings of the 13th International Conference on Finite State Methods and Natural Language Processing (FSMNLP 2017)*. pages 50–55.

Sebastian Schuster and Christopher D Manning. 2016. Enhanced English Universal Dependencies: An improved representation for natural language understanding tasks .

Melanie Seiss, Miriam Butt, and Tracy Holloway King. 2009. On the difference between auxiliaries, serial verbs and light verbs. In *Proceedings of the LFG09 Conference*. CSLI Publications, pages 501–519. http://web.stanford.edu/group/cslipublications/cslipublicationsLFG/14/papers/lfg09seiss.pdf.

Mojgan Seraji, Filip Ginter, and Joakim Nivre. 2016. Universal Dependencies for Persian. In *Tenth International Conference on Language Resources and Evaluation (LREC 2016)*.

Jyoti Singh, Nisheeth Joshi, and Iti Mathur. 2013. Development of Marathi Part of Speech Tagger using Statistical Approach. *CoRR* abs/1310.0575. http://arxiv.org/abs/1310.0575.

Milan Straka, Jan Hajič, Jana Straková, and Jan Hajič jr. 2015. Parsing Universal Dependency Treebanks using neural networks and search-based oracle. In *Proceedings of Fourteenth International Workshop on Treebanks and Linguistic Theories (TLT 14)*.

Milan Straka and Jana Straková. 2017. Tokenizing, POS Tagging, Lemmatizing and Parsing UD 2.0 with UDpipe. In *Proceedings of the CoNLL 2017 Shared Task: Multilingual Parsing from Raw Text to Universal Dependencies*. Association for Computational Linguistics, Vancouver, Canada, pages 88–99. http://www.aclweb.org/anthology/K/K17/K17-3009.pdf.

Jana Straková, Milan Straka, and Jan Hajič. 2014. Open-Source Tools for Morphology, Lemmatization, POS Tagging and Named Entity Recognition. In *Proceedings of 52nd Annual Meeting of the Association for Computational Linguistics: System Demonstrations*. Association for Computational Linguistics, Baltimore, Maryland, pages 13–18. http://www.aclweb.org/anthology/P/P14/P14-5003.pdf.

Juhi Tandon, Himani Chaudhary, Riyaz Ahmad Bhat, and Dipti Misra Sharma. 2016. Conversion from pāṇinian kārakas to universal dependencies for hindi dependency treebank. *LAW X* page 141.

Juhi Tandon and Dipti Misra Sharma. 2017. Unity in diversity: A unified parsing strategy for major Indian languages. In *Proceedings of the Fourth International Conference on Dependency Linguistics (Depling 2017)*. pages 255–265.

Francis M. Tyers, Mariya Shejanova, and Jonathan North Washington. 2018. UD Annotatrix: An annotation tool for universal dependencies. In *Proceedings of the 16th International Workshop on Treebanks and Linguistic Theories*. page *this volume*.

Daniel Zeman, Martin Popel, Milan Straka, Jan Hajic, Joakim Nivre, Filip Ginter, Juhani Luotolahti, Sampo Pyysalo, Slav Petrov, Martin Potthast, Francis Tyers, Elena Badmaeva, Memduh Gokirmak, Anna Nedoluzhko, Silvie Cinkova, Jan Hajic jr., Jaroslava Hlavacova, Václava Kettnerová, Zdenka Uresova, Jenna Kanerva, Stina Ojala, Anna Missilä, Christopher D. Manning, Sebastian Schuster, Siva Reddy, Dima Taji, Nizar Habash, Herman Leung, Marie-Catherine de Marneffe, Manuela Sanguinetti, Maria Simi, Hiroshi Kanayama, Valeria dePaiva, Kira Droganova, Héctor Martínez Alonso, Çağrı Çöltekin, Umut Sulubacak, Hans Uszkoreit, Vivien Macketanz, Aljoscha Burchardt, Kim Harris, Katrin Marheinecke, Georg Rehm, Tolga Kayadelen, Mohammed Attia, Ali Elkahky, Zhuoran Yu, Emily Pitler, Saran Lertpradit, Michael Mandl, Jesse Kirchner, Hector Fernandez Alcalde, Jana Strnadová, Esha Banerjee, Ruli Manurung, Antonio Stella, Atsuko Shimada, Sookyoung Kwak, Gustavo Mendonca, Tatiana Lando, Rattima Nitisaroj, and Josie Li. 2017. Conll 2017 Shared Task: Multilingual Parsing from Raw Text to Universal Dependencies. In *Proceedings of the CoNLL 2017 Shared Task: Multilingual Parsing from Raw Text to Universal Dependencies*. Association for Computational Linguistics, pages 1–19. https://doi.org/10.18653/v1/K17-3001.

A Formats

```
"<">"
        """ qt @punct #1->5
"<माझी>"
        "मी" prn p1 mf sg @nmod:poss #2->4
              "चा" gen f sg @case #3->2
"<जमीन>"
        "जमीन" n f sg nom @obj #4->5
"<विकणार>"
        "विकणे" vblex pros mfn sp @root #5->0
"<नाही>"
        "नाही" vaux neg p1 sg @aux #6->5
"<.>"
        "." sent @punct #7->5
"<">"
        """ qt @punct #8->5
```

Figure 7: An example of the VISL format. The sentence is *mājhī jamīn vikṇār nāhī* 'I will not sell my land'.

```
# sent_id = 355
# text = "माझी जमीन विकणार नाही."
1    "    "    PUNCT    _    _    5    punct    _    SpaceAfter=No
2-3  माझी    _    _    _    _    _    _    _    _
2    _    मी    PRON    _    Number=Sing|Person=1    4    nmod:poss    _    SpaceAfter=No
3    _    चा    ADP    _    Gender=Fem|Number=Sing    2    case    _    _
4    जमीन जमीन    NOUN    _    Case=Acc|Gender=Fem|Number=Sing    5    obj    _    _
5    विकणार विकणे    VERB    _    Aspect=Prosp|VerbForm=Fin    0    root    _    _
6    नाही नाही    AUX    _    Number=Sing|Person=1|Polarity=Neg|VerbForm=Fin    5    aux    _    SpaceAfter=No
7    .    .    PUNCT    _    _    5    punct    _    SpaceAfter=No
8    "    "    PUNCT    _    _    5    punct    _    _
```

Figure 8: The same sentence in the CoNLL-U format.

Dangerous Relations in Dependency Treebanks

Chiara Alzetta[+], Felice Dell'Orletta[*], Simonetta Montemagni[*], Giulia Venturi[*]
[+] Università degli Studi di Genova
[*] Istituto di Linguistica Computazionale "A. Zampolli" (ILC–CNR), ItaliaNLP Lab
`chiara.alzetta@edu.unige.it,`
`{felice.dellorletta,simonetta.montemagni,giulia.venturi}@ilc.cnr.it`

Abstract

The paper illustrates an effective and innovative method for detecting erroneously annotated arcs in gold dependency treebanks based on an algorithm originally developed to measure the reliability of automatically produced dependency relations. The method permits to significantly restrict the error search space and, more importantly, to reliably identify patterns of systematic recurrent errors which represent dangerous evidence to a parser which tendentially will replicate them. Achieved results demonstrate effectiveness and reliability of the method.

1 Introduction

Dependency-based syntactic representations are playing more and more a key role in applications such as machine translation and information extraction (Kübler et al., 2009). If on the one hand current state-of-the-art approaches to dependency parsing require large training corpora, on the other hand dependency treebanks are very expensive to build in terms of both time and human effort.

The process of developing a treebank can be carried out in different ways, i.e. through: fully manual annotation; semi-automatic annotation, obtained via human editing of the automatic output of relevant NLP tools (e.g. POS taggers, dependency parsers); (semi-)automatic conversion from pre-existing resources. If fully manual annotation is time-consuming, costly and prone to inconsistencies even from a single annotator (Fort et al., 2012), semi-automatic annotation is faster, less prone to inconsistencies deriving from arbitrary decisions of the single annotator, but is subject to so-called "anchoring" effects according to which human decisions are affected by pre-existing values, which include parser errors (Berzak et al., 2016). More recently, available resources are more and more the result of a conversion process exploiting already existing annotated corpora: depending on whether conversion is carried out within the same syntactic representation paradigm, approaches can be *constituency-to-dependency* (Magerman, 1994; Yamada and Matsumoto, 2003; Nivre et al., 2006; Johansson and Nugues, 2007) or operate against dependency-based representations. Conversion can also be combined with merging and harmonization of different resources (Bosco et al., 2012): Nivre and Megyesi (2007) refers to this case as "cross-corpus harmonization". The conversion approach is particularly significant for less-resourced languages with limited annotated corpora or in the case of multi-lingual resources. The latter case is exemplified by the Universal Dependencies (UD) initiative (Nivre, 2015),[1] a recent community-driven effort to create cross-linguistically consistent dependency annotated corpora, where 70% of the released treebanks originate from a conversion process and only 29% of them has been manually revised after automatic conversion.

Whatever strategy is adopted for treebank construction, the resulting annotated corpus unavoidably contains errors. For this reason, the treebank annotation phase is usually followed by another step aimed at detecting and correcting errors. But treebank validation is as time-consuming as the annotation process: from this, the need follows for methods and techniques to support treebank validation by making the overall task fast and its result consistent and reliable. In principle, treebank validation is concerned

---

[1] http://universaldependencies.org

201

Proceedings of the 16th International Workshop on Treebanks and Linguistic Theories (TLT16), pages 201–210,
Prague, Czech Republic, January 23–24, 2018. Distributed under a CC-BY 4.0 licence. 2017.

Keywords: error detection, Universal Dependency Treebanks, quality control of treebanks

with different types of errors. Following Agrawal et al. (2013), we distinguish: random errors, which are inherently unpredictable being typically due to annotators' distraction; errors connected with the annotation guidelines, due either to misinterpretation of the guidelines by the annotator, or to constructions not explicitly or comprehensively covered in the annotation guidelines and even errors in the provided guidelines, which are always evolving as long as annotation continues. To these, conversion errors should be added, i.e. errors due to either erroneous automatic mapping of an original annotation scheme to a new scheme or grey areas in the annotation of specific linguistic constructions. Whereas random errors are caused by unpredictable decisions by annotators, all other errors types can be classified as systematic and recurrent errors, that are not just determined by chance but are introduced by inaccuracies inherent to the procedure which generated them (automatic pre-annotation or conversion) or gaps in the annotation guidelines. In this paper, we will mainly focus on systematic and recurrent errors, which we qualify as "dangerous" for the fact of providing potentially "misleading" evidence to a parser during training, i.e. evidence leading to the replication of errors in the parser output.

In the literature, both pattern-based and statistical approaches have been adopted for carrying out error detection and correction in a rapid and reliable way. Relying on the intuition that "variation in annotation can indicate annotation errors", Dickinson and Meurers (2003, 2005) and Boyd et al. (2008) proposed a *variation n-gram* detection method where the source of variation is the so-called *variation nucleus*, i.e. "a word which has different taggings despite occurring in the same context, in this case surrounded by identical words". This methodology has been recently reimplemented and extended by de Marneffe et al. (2017) to detect inconsistencies in the UD treebanks. The idea that the cases where two "parsers predict dependencies different from the gold standard" are "the most likely candidates when looking for errors" was experimented by Volokh and Neumann (2011), who trained two parsers based on completely different parsing algorithms to reproduce the training data (i.e. the Penn Treebank). A similar pattern-based approach has been also proposed by Ambati et al. (2011) who complemented their method with a statistical module that, based on contextual features extracted from the Hindi treebank, was in charge of pruning previously identified candidate erroneous dependencies.

If all the aforementioned methods exploit corpus-internal evidence to detect inconsistencies within a given treebank, van Noord (2004) and de Kok et al. (2009) use external resources, i.e. they rely on the analysis of large automatically parsed corpora *external* to the treebank under validation. The underlying idea of these error mining techniques is that sentences with a low *parsability* score, i.e. sentences which have not received a successful analysis by the parser, very likely contain a parsing error.

This paper aims at testing the potential of algorithms developed to measure the reliability of automatically produced dependency relations for detecting erroneously annotated arcs in gold treebanks. In the literature, the result of this type of algorithms varies from a binary classification (correct vs. wrong) as in Che et al. (2014), to the ranking of dependencies on the basis of a quality score reflecting the reliability and plausibily of the automatic analysis (Dell'Orletta et al., 2013). Although these algorithms typically work on corpora automatically annotated (Dickinson, 2010), they have also been tested against corpora with manually revised (i.e. "gold") annotation: in this case, the typical aim is the identification of errors or simply inconsistencies in the annotation (Dickinson, 2015). In this work, we used an algorithm ranking dependencies by reliability, LISCA (Dell'Orletta et al., 2013), that was applied to a gold treebank to limit the search space for bootstrapping error patterns, i.e. systematic recurring errors (as opposed to random errors). Identified error patterns were then projected against the whole corpus. Like Ambati et al. (2011), here error detection is driven by statistical evidence which, in our approach, is acquired from an external automatically annotated large reference corpus.

2 Error Detection Methodology

The methodology devised to detect candidate errors in dependency treebanks is based on the parse quality assessment algorithm named LISCA (LInguiStically–driven Selection of Correct Arcs) (Dell'Orletta et al., 2013). As illustrated in details in Section 2.1, the algorithm exploits statistics about a wide range of linguistic features (covering different description levels, going from raw text to morpho-syntax and dependency syntax) extracted from a large reference corpus of automatically parsed sentences and uses

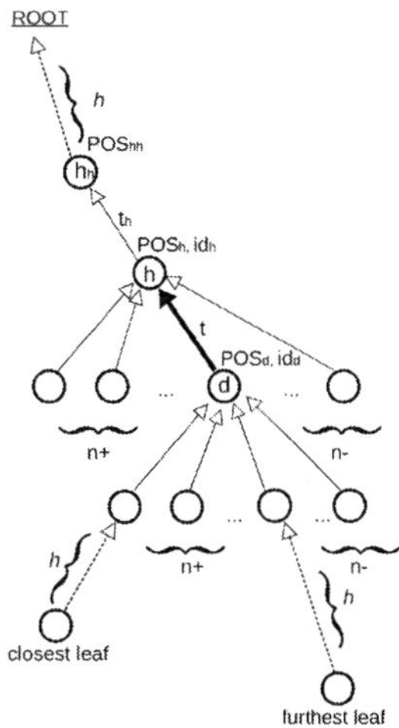

Figure 1: Features used by LISCA to measure $\mathrm{arc}(d, h, t)$ plausibility.

them to assign a *quality* score to each dependency arc contained in a target corpus belonging to the same variety of use (e.g. textual genre) of the automatically parsed corpus, thus producing a decreasing ranking of arcs from correct to anomalous ones, potentially including incorrect ones. The underlying assumption is that syntactic structures that are more frequently generated by a parser are more likely to be correct than less frequently generated structures.

2.1 The LISCA Algorithm

LISCA takes as input a set of parsed sentences and it assigns a plausibility score to each dependency, which is defined as a triple (d, h, t) where d is the dependent, h is the head, and t is the type of dependency connecting d to h. The algorithm operates in two steps: 1) it collects statistics about a set of linguistically motivated features extracted from a dependency annotated corpus obtained through automatic dependency parsing, and 2) it combines the feature statistics extracted from the corpus used during the previous step. The final plausibility score associated with a given dependency arc results from the combination of the weights associated with these features: the score is computed as a simple product of the individual feature weights.[2]

Figure 1 summarizes the features taken into account by LISCA for measuring the plausibility of a given syntactic dependency (d, h, t). For the purposes of the present study, LISCA has been used in its de–lexicalized version in order to abstract away from variation resulting from lexical effects. In particular, two different types of features are considered: *local* features, corresponding to the characteristics of the syntactic arc considered (e.g. the distance in terms of tokens between d and h, or the associative strength linking the grammatical categories, i.e. POS_d and POS_h, involved in the relation, or the POS of the head governor and the type of syntactic dependency connecting it to h); *global* features, aimed at locating the arc being considered within the overall syntactic structure of the sentence, with respect to both its hierarchical structure and the linear ordering of words (for example, the distance of d from the root of the tree, or from the closest or most distant leaf node, or the number of "siblings" and "children" nodes of d, recurring respectively to its right or left in the linear order of the sentence).

LISCA was successfully used against both the output of dependency parsers and gold treebanks. While in the first case the plausibility score was meant to identify unreliable automatically produced dependency relations, in the second case it was used to detect shades of syntactic markedness of syntactic constructions in manually annotated corpora. The latter is the case of Tusa et al. (2016), where the LISCA ranking was used to investigate the linguistic notion of "markedness" (Haspelmath, 2016): a given linguistic construction is considered "marked" when it deviates from the "linguistic norm", i.e. it

---

[2]For a detailed description of the features and the metrics used by LISCA see Dell'Orletta et al. (2013).

is "abnormal". Accordingly, unmarked constructions are expected to be characterized by higher LISCA scores and – conversely – constructions characterized by increasing degrees of markedness are associated with lower scores. In the analysis of their linguistic results, Tusa et al. (2016) noticed that low scored relations also included annotation errors. This observation prompted our hypothesis of research, i.e. that the identification of problematic areas of human annotation can be carried out by measuring the *distance* of the linguistic context characterizing the arcs in a gold treebank from the "linguistic norm" computed by LISCA with respect to a large reference corpus.

2.2 Chasing errors with LISCA

According to these premises, errors in gold treebanks were searched for with LISCA assuming that a higher number of *variations* of the linguistic context for an arc in the manual annotation with respect to the automatically generated arcs corresponds to a greater chance for the observed variation to be an error. In this respect, arc *variation* is observed whenever the linguistic context of an arc in the treebank differs with respect to the corresponding one captured in the large reference corpus used to compute the LISCA score. Similarly to Ambati et al. (2011), we exploited the contextual features of an arc to identify erroneous annotations but differently from them we looked for these features *outside* the treebank under analysis, thus overcoming the widely ackowledged data sparsity problem. By doing so, the error search space is restricted to relations with lower LISCA scores.

The proposed error detection method is articulated into the following steps:

1. LISCA is run against the gold treebank and arcs are ordered by decreasing LISCA scores;

2. the resulting ranking of arcs is partitioned it into 10 groups, henceforth "bins", each corresponding to 10% of the total (plus an 11th bin for the remaining ones);

3. the analysis was limited to the last three bins containing relations associated with the lowest LISCA scores: these bins were expected to gather a higher occurrence of "abnormal" annotations, be they errors or less frequent constructions;

4. the selected bins were manually inspected to identify errors, both random errors and systematic errors (i.e. "dangerous relations");

5. recurring systematic errors which emerged from this manual inspection were formalized as error patterns which were then projected onto the whole treebank;

6. potentially erroneous identified arcs in all bins were manually validated and - whenever needed - corrected.

Let us exemplify how the decreasing LISCA scores assigned to different instances of the same relation occurring within different linguistic contexts can be used to guide error detection.

	B1	B2	B3	B4	B5	B6	B7	B8	B9	B10
Total occurrences	785	543	449	353	333	168	132	97	106	114
Errors (occurrences)	0	0	0	1	6	5	12	7	9	4
Errors (percentages)	0	0	0	0.28	1.80	2.97	9.09	7.21	8.49	3.51

Table 1: Occurrences of *mark* relation in the IUDT newspaper section and erroneously annotated instances across the LISCA bins.

Table 1 reports the distribution of the UD *mark* relation (linking the function word introducing a subordinated clause to the verbal head of the clause) across the LISCA bins in the newspaper section of the Italian Universal Dependency Treebank (the gold treebank we used to test our methodology, as described in Section 3). Although the relation occurs in all bins, the frequency of occurrence decreases proportionally to the decreasing of the scores assigned by LISCA. The higher frequency of the *mark* relation in the top LISCA bins can be explained by the generally fixed or slightly variable structure underlying it: these occurrences correspond to canonical linguistic contexts which are closer to the "linguistic norm" as computed by LISCA with respect to the large reference corpus. By contrast, anomalous *mark* structures ended up in the last bins, in particular in the 7th-9th bins, for which a higher percentage of errors is reported (ranging between 7% and 9%).

3   Corpora

The proposed error detection methodology was tested against the Italian Universal Dependency Treebank (henceforth IUDT) (Bosco et al., 2013), which contains 13,815 sentences corresponding to 325,816 tokens. As de Marneffe et al. (2017) pointed out, UD treebanks represent a good testing bed for error detection techniques: most part of them originate from a conversion process, often combined with merging and cross-corpus harmonization. In particular, IUDT results from the harmonization and merging of smaller dependency–based resources adopting incompatible annotation schemes into the Universal Dependencies annotation formalism, with the final aim of constructing a standard-compliant and bigger resource for the Italian language: the Turin University Treebank (TUT, Bosco et al. (2000)) and ISST–TANL (originating from the ISST corpus, (Montemagni et al., 2003)).

For the specific concerns of this study, we focused on the section of IUDT containing newspaper articles, composed by 10,891 sentences, for a total of 154,784 tokens. This choice was aimed at avoiding possible interferences in detecting anomalies due to textual genre variation: in this case, "abnormal" relations do not only include possible errors but also constructions peculiar to a specific genre.

The corpus used to collect the statistics to build the LISCA model is represented by the *La Repubblica* corpus, a collection of newspaper articles part of the CLIC-ILC Corpus (Marinelli et al., 2003) for a total of 1,104,237 sentences (22,830,739 tokens). The corpus was morpho-syntactically annotated and parsed by the UDPipe pipeline (Straka et al., 2016) trained on IUDT, version 2.0 (Nivre et al., 2017).

4   Results

LISCA was used to rank the journalistic section of IUDT: the ranked relations were partitioned into 10 bins of about 14,600 arcs each, with an 11th bin with the remaining 8723 arcs. The manual revision focused on the last three bins (from 9th to 11th), covering 24.5% of the total number of arcs.

At the end of the error detection and correction process, 789 arcs were modified, corresponding to 0.51% of the number of arcs in IUDT news, distributed into 567 sentences (i.e. 5.21% of the number of sentences in IUDT news). Of those 789 arcs, 286 arcs (36.01%) are random errors: interestingly, 185 of them (i.e. 65% of random errors) are located in the 11th LISCA bin. The remaining detected errors, i.e. 503 (63.99%), represent systematic errors which have been identified on the basis of error patterns manually identified in the last bins and which have then been projected back onto the whole IUDT news section. These error patterns turned out to represent real errors in 85.63% of the cases, involving 483 sentences: this demonstrates the effectiveness of identified potential error patters.

4.1   Typology of Dangerous Relations

In what follows, we will illustrate the main systematic errors, corresponding to so–called "dangerous relations", which emerged from the analysis of relations in the last three bins and which were formalized as the following six error patterns.[3]

Auxiliary verbs (*aux_head*): it refers to cases where an auxiliary verb (i.e. *essere* 'to be', *avere* 'to have', modals, periphrastic or copular verbs) was erroneously treated as the head of a dependency relation, as in the following example where the personal pronoun *noi* 'us' was erroneously governed by the auxiliary verb *è* rather than by *sufficiente*, which represents the nonverbal predicate and root of the sentence:

---

[3]In the following examples the original wrong sentence is marked with O (*Original*), and the corrected one is marked with C (*Correct*)

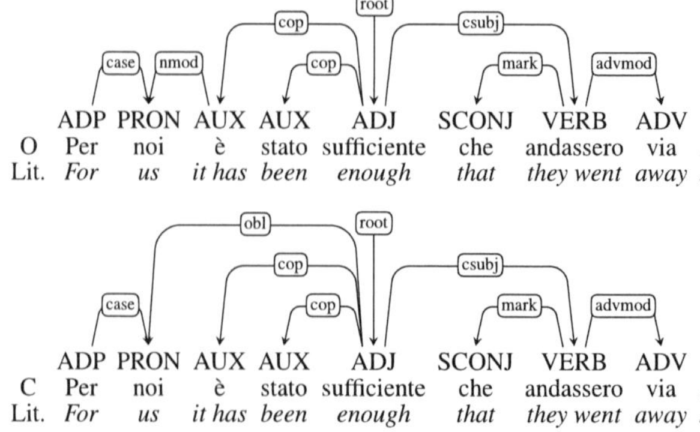

Clausal modifier of a noun (*acl4amod*): it refers to cases where bare past participles functioning as adjectival modifiers of nouns were erroneously annotated as clausal modifiers (i.e. *acl*). In these cases, the lemma, the part of speech and the type of dependency were modified, as in the following example where the past participle *gettonati* 'selected' was erroneously *i)* associated with the lemma *gettonare* 'to select' instead of the lemma *gettonato* 'selected', *ii)* morpho-syntactically tagged as VERB rather than ADJ, and *iii)* linked to the head word *nomi* 'names' with the relation *acl* rather than *amod*:

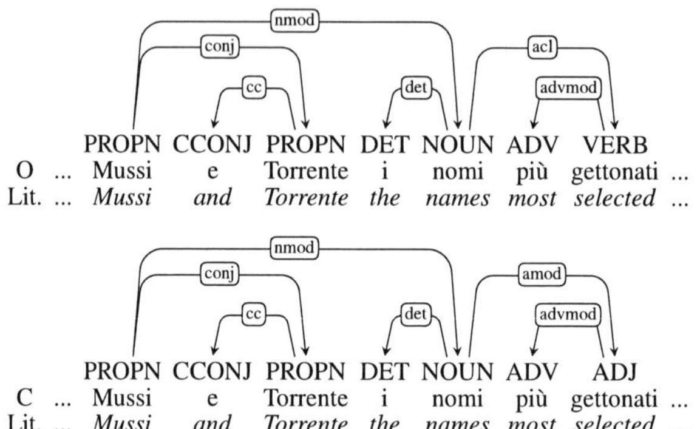

Adjectival modifiers (*amod4xcomp*): it refers to cases where adjectives functioning as secondary predicates of a verb were erroneously annotated as *amod* rather than *xcomp*, as in the following example where the syntactic function of adjectival modifier (*amod*) holding between the adjective *vivo* 'alive' and the head verb *sepolto* 'buried' was erroneously identified:

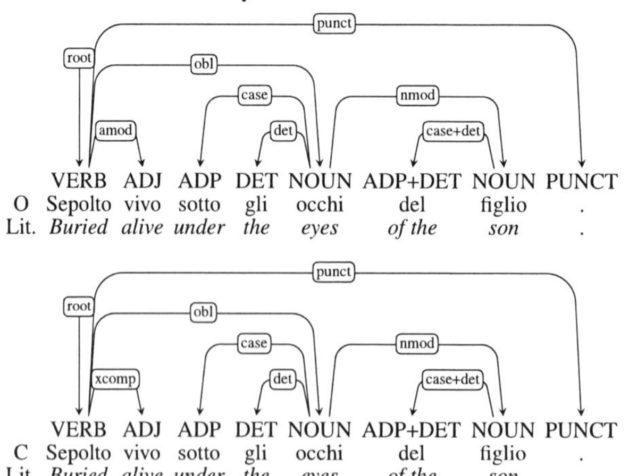

Coordinating conjunctions (*conj_head*): it refers to cases where a coordinating conjunction was erroneously headed by the first conjunct (coordination head), as in the following example where the conjunction *e* 'and' was headed by *notte* 'night' rather than by *giorno* 'day':

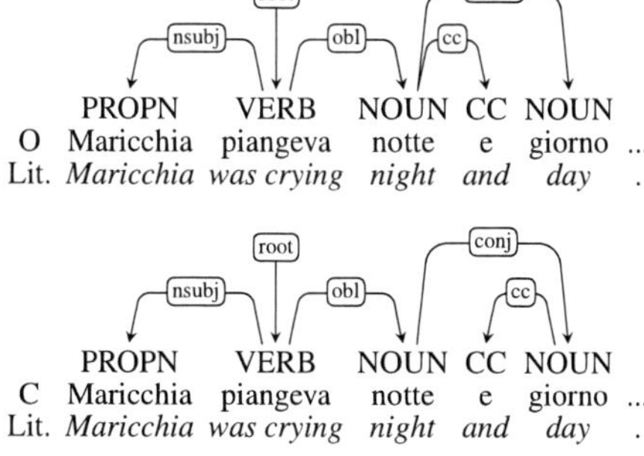

Nominal modifiers (*nmod4obl*): it refers to cases where an oblique argument was erroneously annotated as nominal modifier (*nmod*) rather than as oblique nominal (*obl*) when occurring in multiword expressions which were not correctly identified, as in the following example where the noun *tabella* 'chart' was erroneously headed by the preposition *di* 'of' rather than by the verb *andando* 'going', and linked by the dependency relation *nmod* rather than *obl*:

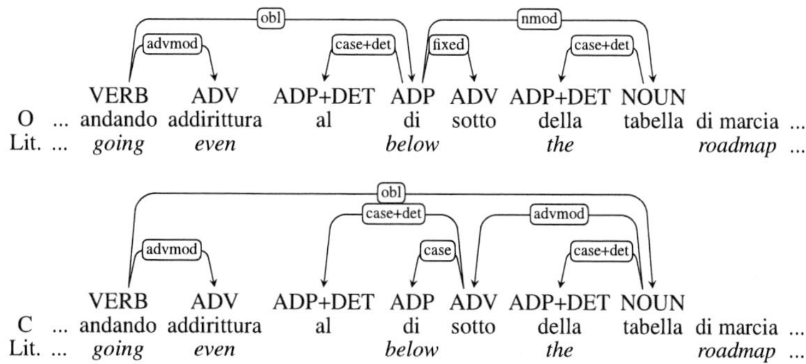

Nonfinite verbs (*obl4advcl|acl*): it refers to cases where nonfinite verbal constructions functioning as nominals were erroneously annotated as oblique nominals (*obl*) rather than adverbial or adjectival clauses (*advcl* or *acl*), as in the following example represented by the verb *pubblicare* 'publish':

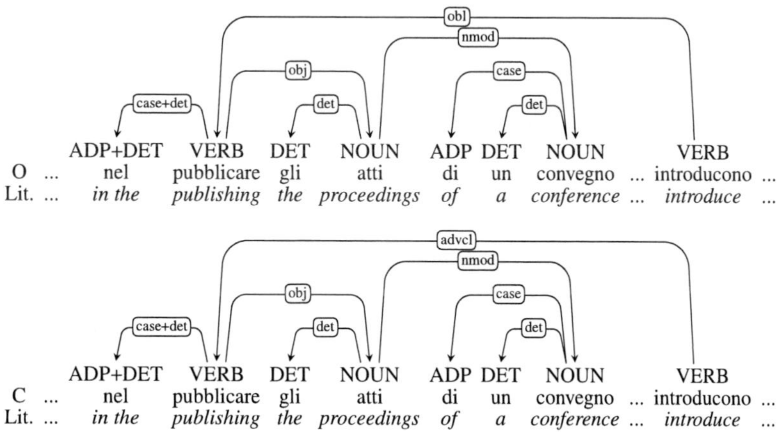

4.2 Discussion

The patterns illustrated above can be classified under three main categories: 1) head identification errors (*aux_head*, *conj_head*), 2) labeling errors (*acl4amod*, *amod4xcomp*, *obl4advcl|acl*), and 3) combined head identification and labeling errors (*nmod4obl*). Table 2 shows the detail of the modified arcs for each pattern, while Figure 2 visualizes their distribution across the LISCA bins. The chart confirms the hypothesis we started from, i.e. that most part of systematic errors are concentrated in the last bins and that, on the other hand, the first LISCA bins tendentially do not contain errors, or very few of them.

Note that the 11th bin is not included in the chart since it turned out to only contain random errors (as opposed to systematic ones). If we try to track the origin of the identified and corrected recurrent errors, it is worth noting that the most frequent error type recorded in Table 2 – *acl4amod* – corresponds to a quite problematic annotation area for all treebanks, i.e. the distinction between participial and adjectival usages. More interestingly, this corresponds to an area for which the original resources which were combined in IUDT (i.e. TUT and ISST–TANL) followed different guidelines: for TUT, the verbal reading was preferred, which naturally led to the interpretation of (reduced) relative clause, whereas ISST–TANL resorted in these cases to a general modifier relation. The second and third most frequent errors (namely, *conj_head* and *aux_head*) are connected with substantial changes from version 1.4 to 2.0 of Universal Dependencies annotation guidelines. Last but not least, the error types *amod4xcomp* and *nmod4obl* seem rather to be connected to annotation inconsistencies internal to the treebank.

Error pattern	Frequency
Auxiliary verbs (aux_head)	13.32 (67)
Clausal modifiers of noun (acl4amod)	36.98 (186)
Adjectival modifiers (amod4xcomp)	12.52 (63)
Coordinating conjunctions (conj_head)	24.65 (124)
Nominal modifiers (nmod4obl)	6.76 (34)
Nonfinite verbs (obl4advcl|acl)	5.77 (29)
Total number of errors:	**503**

Table 2: Distribution (percentage and absolute values) of error types in IUDT.

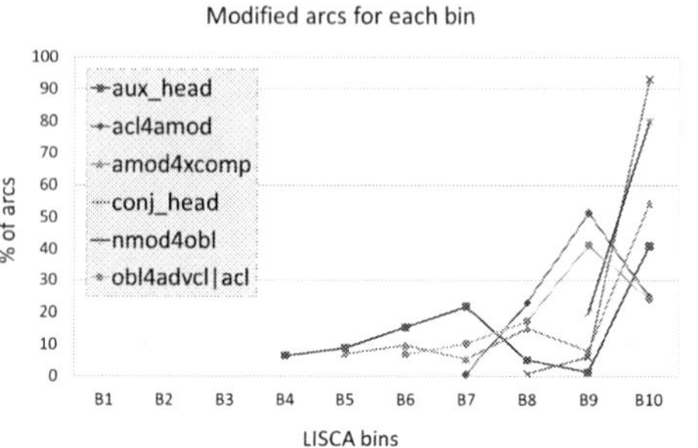

Figure 2: Distribution of modified arcs for each error pattern across the LISCA bins.

5 Conclusion and Current Directions of Research

We proposed an effective and innovative method for detecting erroneously annotated arcs in gold treebanks based on an algorithm originally developed to measure the reliability of automatically produced dependency relations, LISCA. This method permits to significantly restrict the error search space and, more importantly, to reliably identify patterns of systematic recurrent errors which represent dangerous and misleading evidence to a parser. Achieved results demonstrate the effectiveness of the method. Within the whole amount of corrected errors (both random and systematic), 64% corresponds to systematic errors, typically originating from semi-automatic annotation or conversion. The effectiveness of identified patterns is demonstrated by the fact that in the whole IUDT news section 85.67% of the sentences instantiating at least one error pattern contains real errors. In principle, this method, operating within the dependency-based representation framework, is independent from language and annotation scheme. As a preliminary experiment in this direction, we checked the presence of some detected error patterns (i.e. those due to problematic annotation areas and guidelines changes between different treebank versions) in other UD treebanks.[4] We looked for sentences instantiating the constructions corresponding to our error patterns in different UD treebanks: patterns turned out to appear both in languages typologically close to Italian (e.g. French, Spanish and Portuguese) and typologically distant (e.g. English, Arabic, Czech, Finnish, Turkish and Chinese). For most of those languages, the total number of sentences containing the patterns is in line with the number of sentences we found for Italian (between 3-7% over the total number of sentences in the treebank), with the exception of Turkish and Chinese where the number is much higher (around 15%). This holds true also for the distribution of patters: like for Italian, the most frequent pattern observed in all UD treebanks taken into account is *acl4amod*. This very preliminary evidence extracted from different UD treebanks needs however to be validated through a collaboration between different UD national teams, to assess whether identified anomalous patterns represent real errors. Current developments also include the assessment of impact and role of detected and corrected errors in the performance of dependency parsers.

---

[4]For this purpose we used the Dep_search tool developed by the Turku NLP Group.

Acknowledgments

The work reported in the paper was partially supported by the 2–year project (2016-2018) *Smart News, Social sensing for breaking news*, funded by Regione Toscana (BANDO FAR-FAS 2014). Thanks are also due to the University of Pisa who funded a post-graduate fellowship with a Google gift.

References

B. Agrawal, R. Agarwal, S. Husain, and D.M. Sharma. 2013. *An Automatic Approach to Treebank Error Detection Using a Dependency Parser*, Springer Berlin Heidelberg, Berlin, Heidelberg, pages 294–303.

B. R. Ambati, R. Agarwal, M. Gupta, S. Husain, and D. M. Sharma. 2011. Error Detection for Treebank Validation. In *Proceedings of 9th International Workshop on Asian Language Resources (ALR)*.

Y. Berzak, Y. Huang, A. Barbu, A. Korhonen, and B. Katz. 2016. Anchoring and Agreement in Syntactic Annotations. In *Proceedings of the 2016 Conference on Empirical Methods in Natural Language Processing*. Association for Computational Linguistics, Austin, Texas, pages 2215–2224.

C. Bosco, V. Lombardo, L. Lesmo, and D. Vassallo. 2000. Building a Treebank for Italian: a Data-driven Annotation Schema. In *Proceedings of the 2nd Language Resources and Evaluation Conference (LREC'00)*. Athens, Greece, pages 99–105.

C. Bosco, S. Montemagni, and M. Simi. 2012. Harmonization and Merging of two Italian Dependency Treebanks. In *Proceedings of the LREC 2012 Workshop on Language Resource Merging*. Istanbul, Turkey.

C. Bosco, S. Montemagni, and M. Simi. 2013. Converting Italian Treebanks: Towards an Italian Stanford Dependency Treebank. In *Proceedings of the ACL Linguistic Annotation Workshop & Interoperability with Discourse*. Sofia, Bulgaria.

A. Boyd, M. Dickinson, and W. D. Meurers. 2008. On Detecting Errors in Dependency Treebanks. *Research on Language & Computation* 6(2):113–137.

W. Che, J.Guo, and T.Liu. 2014. Reliable Dependency Arc Recognition. *Expert Systems with Applications* 41(4):1716–1722.

D. de Kok, J. Ma, and G. van Noord. 2009. A Generalized Method for Iterative Error Mining in Parsing Results. In *Proceedings Workshop on Grammar Engineering Across Frameworks (GEAF 2009)*.

M.C. de Marneffe, M. Grioni, J. Kanerva, and F. Ginter. 2017. Assessing the Annotation Consistency of the Universal Dependencies Corpora. In *Proceedings of the 4th International Conference on Dependency Linguistics (Depling 2007)*. Pisa, Italy, pages 108–115.

F. Dell'Orletta, G. Venturi G., and S. Montemagni. 2013. Linguistically-driven Selection of Correct Arcs for Dependency Parsing. *Computaciòn y Sistemas* 2:125–136.

M. Dickinson. 2010. Detecting Errors in Automatically-Parsed Dependency Relations. In *Proceedings of the 48th Annual Meeting of the Association for Computational Linguistics*. Uppsala, Sweden, pages 729–738.

M. Dickinson. 2015. Detection of Annotation Errors in Corpora. *Language and Linguistics Compass* 9(3):119–138.

M. Dickinson and W. D. Meurers. 2003. Detecting Inconsistencies in Treebank. In *Proceedings of the Second Workshop on Treebanks and Linguistic Theories (TLT 2003)*.

M. Dickinson and W. D. Meurers. 2005. Detecting Errors in Discontinuous Structural Annotation. In *Proceedings of the 43rd Annual Meeting of the ACL*. pages 322–329.

K. Fort, A. Nazarenko, and S. Rosset. 2012. Modeling the Complexity of Manual Annotation Tasks: a Grid of Analysis. In *Proceedings of COLING 2012*. pages 895–910.

M. Haspelmath. 2016. Against Markedness (and what to Replace it with). *Journal of Linguistics* 42:25–70.

R. Johansson and P. Nugues. 2007. Statistical Dependency Analysis with Support Vector Machines. In *Proceedings of NODALIDA 2007*.

S. Kübler, R. McDonald, and J. Nivre. 2009. *Dependency Parsing. Synthesis Lectures on Human Language Technologies*. Morgan & Claypool Publishers.

D. M. Magerman. 1994. *Natural Language Parsing as Statistical Pattern Recognition*. Ph.D. thesis, Stanford University.

R. Marinelli, L. Biagini, R. Bindi, S. Goggi, M. Monachini, P. Orsolini, E. Picchi, S. Rossi, N. Calzolari, and A. Zampolli. 2003. The Italian PAROLE Corpus: an Overview. *Linguistica Computazionale* XVIXVII:401–421.

S. Montemagni, F. Barsotti, M. Battista, N. Calzolari, A. Lenci, O. Corazzari, A. Zampolli, F. Fanciulli, M. Massetani, R. Basili, R. Raffaelli, M.T. Pazienza, D. Saracino, F. Zanzotto, F. Pianesi, N. Mana, and R. Delmonte. 2003. Building the Italian Syntactic-Semantic Treebank. In Anne Abeillé, editor, *Treebanks. Building and Using Parsed Corpora*, Springer Science Business Media, LLCs, pages 189–210.

J. Nivre. 2015. Towards a Universal Grammar for Natural Language Processing. In *Computational Linguistics and Intelligent Text Processing - Proceedings of the 16th International Conference, CICLing 2015, Part I*. Cairo, Egypt, pages 3–16.

J. Nivre, J. Hall, and J. Nilsson. 2006. Maltparser: A Data-driven Parser Generator for Dependency Parsing. In *Proceedings of LREC2006*.

J. Nivre and B. Megyesi. 2007. Bootstrapping a Swedish Treebank Using Cross-Corpus Harmonization and Annotation Projection. In *Proceedings of the 6th International Workshop on Treebanks and Linguistic Theories (TLT)*. pages 97–102.

J. Nivre, A. Željko, and A. Lars et al. 2017. Universal Dependencies 2.0. LINDAT/CLARIN digital library at the Institute of Formal and Applied Linguistics, Charles University.

M. Straka, J. Hajic, and J. Strakova. 2016. UD-Pipe: Trainable Pipeline for Processing CoNLL-U Files Performing Tokenization, Morphological Analysis, POS Tagging and Parsing. In *Proceedings of the Tenth International Conference on Language Resources and Evaluation (LREC)*.

E. Tusa, F. Dell'Orletta, S. Montemagni, and G. Venturi. 2016. Dieci sfumature di marcatezza sintattica: verso una nozione computazionale di complessitá. In *Proceedings of the Third Italian Conference on Computational Linguistics (CLiC-it)*. Napoli, Italy, pages 3–16.

G. van Noord. 2004. Error Mining for Widecoverage Grammar Engineering. In *Proceedings of the 42nd Annual Meeting of the Association for Computational Linguistics*.

A. Volokh and G. Neumann. 2011. Automatic Detection and Correction of Errors in Dependency Treebanks. In *Proceedings of ACL-HLT (2011)*.

H. Yamada and Y. Matsumoto. 2003. Statistical Dependency Analysis with Support Vector Machines. In *Proceedings of 8th International Workshop on Parsing Technologies*.

Keyword Index